This collection foregrounds the institutional fault lines, ideas and ideologies that make today's EU a uniquely "segmented" political order. Its thought-provoking contributions help us see that different aspects of European governance are simultaneously moving in several different directions – and that this has major consequences for how we understand its whole system.

— *Craig Parsons, University of Oregon, USA*

TOWARDS A SEGMENTED EUROPEAN POLITICAL ORDER

This book makes a distinctive contribution to the crucial debate on the European Union (EU)'s present and future development.

It systematically examines how the range of crises and challenges over the last decade have transformed the EU and relates those findings to the discussion of an increasingly differentiated EU. It argues that the post-crises EU shows clear signs of becoming a segmented political order with in-built biases and constraints. The book spells out the key features of such an order in ideational and structural terms and shows how it more concretely manifests itself in the EU's institutional and constitutional make-up and in how member states constrain and condition EU action. Different states impose different types of constraints, as is underlined through paying explicit attention to the Visegrád countries.

This book will be of key interest to scholars and students of EU politics/ studies, European integration and politics, East European politics and foreign policy.

Jozef Bátora is Professor at the Department of Political Science, Faculty of Arts, Comenius University in Bratislava, Slovakia, and at the International Relations Department, Webster Vienna Private University, Austria.

John Erik Fossum is Professor at the ARENA Centre for European Studies, University of Oslo, Norway.

ROUTLEDGE STUDIES ON DEMOCRATISING EUROPE

This series focuses on the prospects for a citizens' Europe by analysing the kind of order that is emerging in Europe. The books in the series take stock of the EU as an entity that has progressed beyond intergovernmentalism and consider how to account for this process and what makes it democratic. The emphasis is on citizenship, constitution-making, public sphere, enlargement, common foreign and security policy, and Europe society.

Series editors: *Erik Oddvar Eriksen and John Erik Fossum, ARENA, University of Oslo, Norway.*

The New Politics of European Civil Society
Edited by Ulrike Liebert and Hans-Jörg Trenz

Rethinking Democracy and the European Union
Edited by Erik Oddvar Eriksen and John Erik Fossum

The Politicization of Europe
Contesting the constitution in the mass media
Paul Statham and Hans-Jörg Trenz

Democratic Decision-making in the EU
Technocracy in disguise?
Anne Elizabeth Stie

States of Democracy
Gender and politics in the European Union
Edited by Yvonne Galligan

The European Union's Non-Members
Independence under hegemony?
Edited by Erik Oddvar Eriksen and John Erik Fossum

TOWARDS A SEGMENTED EUROPEAN POLITICAL ORDER

The European Union's
Post-Crises Conundrum

Edited by Jozef Bátora and John Erik Fossum

Routledge
Taylor & Francis Group

LONDON AND NEW YORK

First published 2020
by Routledge
2 Park Square, Milton Park, Abingdon, Oxon OX14 4RN

and by Routledge
52 Vanderbilt Avenue, New York, NY 10017

Routledge is an imprint of the Taylor & Francis Group, an informa business

British Library Cataloguing in Publication Data
A catalogue record for this book is available from the British Library

Library of Congress Cataloging in Publication Data
A catalog record has been requested for this book

ISBN: 978-1-138-49532-6 (hbk)
ISBN: 978-1-138-49533-3 (pbk)
ISBN: 978-1-351-02434-1 (ebk)

Typeset in Bembo
by Deanta Global Publishing Services, Chennai, India

CONTENTS

FIGURES

TABLES

CONTRIBUTORS

Jozef Bátora is Professor at the Department of Political Science, Comenius University in Bratislava, and at the International Relations Department, Webster Vienna Private University. His previous posts include positions at ARENA Centre for European Studies, University of Oslo, Norway, and the Austrian Academy of Sciences; and visiting fellowships at Stanford University. His main research interests include processes of institutional change in international institutions, such as diplomacy and war, organisation theory, the development of the EU's political order and processes of identity formation in international relations. His work has been published in a number of peer-reviewed journals including *Journal of European Public Policy*, *Journal of Common Market Studies*, *West European Politics*, *Cambridge Review of International Affairs* and *Journal of International Relations and Development*. His most recent book is *The European External Action Service: European Diplomacy Post-Westphalia*, co-edited with David Spence, (Palgrave, 2015). Previously, he has served as lead editor of *Journal of International Relations and Development*. His most recent article is "EU-supported Reforms in the EU Neighbourhood as Organized Anarchies: The Case of post-Maidan Ukraine," *Journal of European Integration*, (2018) 40 (4): 461–478, with Pernille Rieker.

John Erik Fossum is Professor at ARENA Centre for European Studies, University of Oslo, Norway. He has worked and published widely on issues of identity, democracy and constitutionalism in the EU and Canada. He is project co-ordinator for the H2020-project EU3D – Differentiation, Dominance, Democracy (2019–2023), and was substitute co-ordinator for the 5-year EU FP6-funded RECON (Reconstituting Democracy in the European Union, 2007–2011) project and co-director of the NORCONE project, which focused on the Europeanisation of Norway. Fossum has written extensively on questions of identity and belonging and on the challenges currently facing Europe, including Brexit. His most recent books are: *Squaring the Circle on Brexit – Could the Norway Model Work?* (2018), with Hans Petter Graver; and *Diversity and Contestations over Nationalism in Europe and Canada*, (2018), co-edited with Riva Kastoryano and Birte Siim. His most recent articles are "Federal Challenges and Challenges to Federalism: Insights from the EU and Federal States," *Journal of European Public Policy*, (2017) 24 (4): 467–485, with Markus Jachtenfuchs; and "European Federalism: Pitfalls and Possibilities," *European Law Journal*, (2017) 23 (5): 361–379.

John A. Gould is Lloyd E. Worner Distinguished Service Professor of Political Science at Colorado College. He has held a Robert Schuman Fellowship at the European University Institute in Florence, Italy; a post-doctoral fellowship at the Korbel School of International Studies, Denver University; and a Fulbright Fellowship at Comenius University in Slovakia. He has (co-)published refereed journal articles in *Comparative European Politics, Europe-Asia Studies, Business and Politics, Global Goverance, Problems of Postcommunism, Research in Social Movements, Conflict and Change* and *Review of International Political Economy*. His book *The Politics of Privitization: Wealth and Power in Postcommunist Europe* was published by Lynne Rienner Publishers in April 2011. He has won several awards for his teaching and research. He lives in Manitou Springs, Colorado, with his wife and two sons.

Cathrine Holst is Professor in the Department of Sociology and Human Geography and Research Professor at ARENA Centre for European Studies, both at the University of Oslo, Norway. Among her research interests are democratic theory, political epistemology and sociology, the role of expertise in policy-making, and European integration. She is currently co-coordinator of the research pro-ject Expertization of public inquiry commissions in a Europeanised administrative order (EUREX). In 2020–2021, she will be co-coordinator of a research group at the Centre for Advanced Studies (CAS) in Oslo, Norway, with the project entitled *What Is a Good Policy? Political Morality, Feasibility and Democracy* (GOODPOL). Among Holst's recent publications are "Epistemic Democracy and the Role of Experts," *Contemporary Political Theory*, (2019), forthcoming, with Anders Molander; "Asymmetry, Disagreement and Biases: Epistemic Worries about Expertise," *Social Epistemology*, (2018) 32 (6): 358–371, with Anders Molander; "The Socio-political Ties of Expert Bodies. How to Reconcile the Independence Requirement of Reliable Expertise and the Responsiveness Requirement of Democratic Governance," *European Politics and Society*, (2019) 20 (1): 117–131, with Eva Krick; and "Advisory Commissions, Academic Expertise and Democratic Legitimacy: The Case of Norway," *Science and Public Policy*, (2017) 44 (6): 821–833, with Johan Christensen. *Expertisation and Democracy in Europe*, co-edited with Magdalena Góra and Marta Warat, came out in 2018.

Christopher Lord is Professor at ARENA Centre for European Studies, University of Oslo, Norway. He has written extensively on problems of legitimacy, democracy and the European Union. He is currently co-ordinator of the Marie Sklodowska/

Curie-funded PLATO project of 15 PhD researchers who are investigating legitimacy crises in the EU. He is also principal investigator on the Benchmark project, funded by the Norwegian Research Council, on the legitimacy of different models of "non-membership" of the European Union. His most recent articles include "The European Parliament. A Parliament without a Public?" *Journal of Legislative Studies*, (2018) 24 (1): 34–50; "No Epistocracy without Representation. The Case of the European Central Bank," *European Politics and Society*, (2019) 20 (1): 1–15; "An Indirect Legitimacy Argument for a Directly Elected European Parliament," *European Journal of Political Research*, (2017) 56 (3): 512–528; "How can Parliaments Contribute to the Legitimacy of the European Semester?" *Parliamentary Affairs*, 70 (4): 673–690; and "Utopia or Dystopia? Towards a Normative Analysis of Differentiated Integration," *Journal of European Public Policy*, (2015) 22 (6): 783–789.

Darina Malová is Professor in the Department of Political Science, Comenius University in Bratislava. Her current research interests include democratisation, Europeanisation, nationalism, gender, and minority issues. Her work has been published in a number of edited volumes and academic journals, including *West European Politics*, *European Journal of Political Research*, *Problems of Post-Communism*, and *Political Psychology*. She has served as a past or current member of the editorial board of the journals *Austrian Journal of Political Science*, *West European Politics*, *Acta Politologica*, *Studia Politica Slovaca*, and *East Central Europe-L'Europe du Centre-Est*.

Asimina Michailidou is a senior researcher at ARENA Centre for European Studies, University of Oslo, Norway. She works on the digital public sphere, political communication and EU legitimacy. Her current research under the projects Benchmark, GLOBUS and REFLEX analyses the role of digital news and social media in filtering and shaping public perceptions about the EU but also in facilitating democratic accountability and citizen mobilisation, particularly in times of crisis. Her work has been published in a number of peer-reviewed journals, including *Information, Communication & Society*, *Internationa Political Science Review*, *National Identities*, *European Journal of Political Research*, *Journal of European Public Policy*, *Journalism Practice*, *European Journal of Communication Research*, and *Journal of Contemporary European Research*. Her most recent book is *Social Media and European Politics*, co-edited with Mauro Barisione, (2017). Her most recent article is "Understanding a Digital Movement of Opinion: The Case of #RefugeesWelcome," *Information, Communication & Society*, doi.org/10.1080/1369118X.2017.1410204, with Maro Barisione and Massimo Airoldi.

Anders Molander is Professor at the Centre for the Study of Professions, Oslo Metropolitan University, Norway. His fields of interest are moral, political and social theory, and his current research is on welfare state issues and on democracy and expertise. Among his recent publications are "Getting People into Work: What (if Anything) Can Justify Mandatory Activation of Welfare Recipients?" *Journal of Applied Philosophy*, (2015) 32 (4): 373–392, with Gaute Torsvik; *Discretion in the*

Welfare State. Social Rights and Professional Judgment, (2016); "Welfare Reform and Public Justification," *Policy Studies,* (2019) forthcoming, doi.org/10.1080/0144287 2.2018.1538487, with Andreas Eriksen; and "Epistemic Democracy and the Role of Experts," *Contemporary Political Theory* (2019), forthcoming, doi.org/10.1057/ s41296-018-00299-4, with Cathrine Holst.

Espen D.H. Olsen is Senior Researcher at ARENA Centre for European Studies, University of Oslo, Norway. He holds a PhD in political science from the European University Institute, Florence. His main research interests are in the areas of citizenship theory, European citizenship, EU democracy and constitution-making, European crises, migration policies, citizen deliberation, theories of deliberative democracy, and political theory. He is currently part of the ARENA-led EU3D project on democracy and differentiation in the EU and has previously taken part in, among others, the RECON project, which focused on empirical and theoretical issues regarding democratic polity models for the European Union; and in Europolis, a research project that dealt with citizen deliberation in a transnational setting. His main publications include *Transnational Citizenship in the European Union: Past, Present, and Future* (2012); and *Challenging European Citizenship: Ideas and Realities in Contrast* (2019), co-authored with Agustín José Menéndez. He has also written a range of articles in journals such as *Political Science, Journal of European Public Policy, Perspectives on European Politics and Society,* and *Critical Review of International Social and Political Philosophy.* He has also published several book chapters on a range of topics, from Norwegian citizenship under Europeanisation and expertise in the refugee crisis to European citizenship between re-nationalisation and cosmopolitan Europe.

Michal Onderco is Assistant Professor of International Relations at Erasmus University Rotterdam. He was previously Junior Faculty Fellow at the Center for International Security and Cooperation at Stanford, Max Weber Fellow at the European University Institute, and researcher at the Peace Research Institute Prague. His main research interests include informal governance in international institutions, nuclear non-proliferation, and foreign policy analysis. He is the author of *Iran's Nuclear Program and the Global South: The Foreign Policy of India, Brazil, and South Africa* (2015), and his work has appeared, among others, in *International Studies Quarterly, European Journal of Political Research,* and *Cooperation and Conflict.*

Rafał Riedel is Professor at Opole University, Poland, and Guest lecturer at Sankt Gallen University, Switzerland. He holds a PhD in Political Science, obtained his habiliation degree (in EU Studies) at the University of Wroclaw, and graduated from the Silesian University and Economic University in Katowice; he was also guest researcher at ARENA Centre for European Studies, University of Oslo, Norway, Gastdozent at TUC, Germany, and Wissenschaftliche Mitarbeiter at ETH Zürich, Switzerland. He has performed research as a scholar, co-organiser or fellow at the European University Institute, Open Society Institute, Deutscher Akademischer

Austauschdients, Marie Curie Fellowship Programme, Max Plank Institute, European Values Network, and Fundacji Rozwoju Systemu Edukacji – EEA/ Norway Grants. His research interest are European integration process, institutions and policies, Europeanisation, democratisation, democratic deficit, transitology, considology (transition and consolidation studies) and other *problématiques* in the field of political science, European Studies and the economy.

Herman Mark Schwartz is Professor of Politics and Public Policy at Inland Norway University of Applied Sciences. He is currently researching the relationship between changes in corporate strategy and structure and secular stagnation in the rich OEDC economies. His most recent books are *Subprime Nation: American Power, Global Finance, and the Housing Bubble*, (2009); and *States versus Markets*, 4th edition (2018). His most recent articles are "Thinking about Thinking about Comparative Political Economy: From Macro to Micro and Back," *Politics & Society*, (2019) 47 (1): 23–54, with Bent Sofus Tranøy; and "No Exit: Social Reproduction in an Era of Rising Income Inequality," *Politics & Society*, (2017) 45 (4): 471–503, with Lindsay Flynn.

Max Steuer holds a PhD in political science from the Department of Political Science, Comenius University in Bratislava. His research interests include political institutions, in particular constitutional courts in Central Europe; freedom of speech; and democracy and legitimacy in the EU. He has been involved in several research projects, including JUDICON – Judicial Constraints on Legislation in Central Europe – and in academic service, such as editor-in-chief of *Politikon: The IAPSS Journal of Political Science*. His recent publications include "The Slovak Constitutional Court: The Third Legislator?" in Kálmán Pócza (ed), *Constitutional Politics and the Judiciary: Decision-making in Central and Eastern Europe*, (2019), pp. 184–212, with Erik Láštic; "Constitutional Pluralism and the Slovak Constitutional Court: The Challenge of European Law," *The Lawyer Quarterly*, (2018) 8 (2): 108–128; and "The Non-Political Taboo: Why Democracies Ban Holocaust Denial," *The Slovak Sociological Review*, (2017) 49 (6): 673–693, as well as entries on "Democratic Security" and "Militant Democracy" in the *Palgrave Encyclopedia of Global Security Studies* (forthcoming).

Bent Sofus Tranøy is Professor of Political Science at Inland Norway University of Applied Sciences and a guest researcher at ARENA Centre for European Studies, University of Oslo, Norway. Most of his publications are within the field of Comparative Political Economy but he has also published on Public Policy, Organizational Theory, Qualitative methods and the Sociology and History of Science. His most recent publications are: "Thinking about Thinking about Comparative Political Economy: From Macro to Micro and Back". *Politics & Society*, 47(1), 23–54. (with Herman Schwartz), "Equality as a driver of inequality? Universalistic welfare, generalised creditworthiness and financialised housing markets". West European Politics, 1–22 (with Mary Ann Stamsø and Ingrid

Hjertaker); "The Norwegian Petroleum Fund as institutionalised self-restraint", in *Great Policy Successes: How Governments Get It Right in a Big Way at Least Some of the Time*. (Mallory Compton and Paul 't Hart eds.) Oxford, OUP 2019 (with Camilla B. Øvald and Ketil Raknes; "Failing forward in financial stability regulation", (with Eirik Stenstad), in Riddervold, Trondal and Newsome (eds) *Handbook on EU Crisis London*: Palgrave Macmillan 2020; "The ECB – Unchecked transgressions and formal extensions", (with Ingrid Hjertaker), in Riddervold, Trondal and Newsome (eds) *Handbook on EU Crisis* London: Palgrave Macmillan 2020.

Hans-Jörg Trenz is a professor in the Department of Media, Cognition and Communication at the University of Copenhagen, and adjunct professor at ARENA, Centre for European Studies, University of Oslo, Norway. His main research interests are in the areas of media, communications and the public sphere, civil society, European civilisation and identity, political sociology and democracy. His most recent publications include *Narrating European Society: Toward a Sociology of European Integration* (2016); *The Internet and European Integration: Pro- and Anti-EU Debates in Online News Media* (2014), with Asimina Michailidou and Pieter de Wilde; *Rethinking the Public Sphere through Transnationalizing Processes: Europe and Beyond* (2013), edited with Armando Salvatore and Oliver Schmidtke; and *The Politicization of Europe: Contesting the Constitution in the Mass Media* (Routledge, 2012), with Paul Statham.

PREFACE AND ACKNOWLEDGEMENTS

This book has been long in coming. Intellectually speaking, it has roots in the *EuroDiv: Integration and Division: Towards a Segmented Europe?* research project that was devised by Erik Oddvar Eriksen and John Erik Fossum. That project did not have a strong Central and Eastern European presence. The opportunity to include this important dimension emerged through the EEA-funded project *Democratic Governance and Differentiation in Europe* (SK06-IV-02-010, 2015–2016), the main contributions of which this book presents. Work on this volume was also supported by the EURECOR project, funded by the Slovak Research and Development Agency, as well as by the EUNPACK project funded by the European Union's Horizon 2020 research and innovation programme under grant agreement no. 693337.
The book took considerably longer to complete than was initially envisaged. At the outset, we sought to structure the book around three EU developmental trajectories – segmentation, core consolidation, and fragmentation – but, once we had the contributions, we decided that this would dilute the important challenge of establishing a proper diagnosis of the type of entity the post-crises EU was becoming. We therefore decided that we needed to come up with a more narrow and specific focus for the book. We became more convinced of this when it became clear to us that the notion of differentiation did not adequately capture what was going on. Hence, it was important to develop a different term, and we settled on the notion of *segmented political order. Segment* is a household term in social science, but it is generally discussed at the meso-level, as a kind of sector-specific phenomenon. The notion of a segmented political order has roots in pre-modern political systems and refers to macro-level or core-defining features of the polity. It follows that we needed to develop a more thorough delineation of the relevant criteria for such an order if we were to be able to apply it to the present-day EU. To this end, the topical breadth and geographical spread of the contributions to the book turned out

to be very beneficial. We are grateful for the support which we have received from the institutions and colleagues at ARENA Centre for European Studies, University of Oslo; the Department of Political Science at Comenius University in Bratislava; and the IR Department at Webster Vienna Private University. A special thanks is due to Chris Engert in Florence for his excellent language editing, formatting and proof-reading of the entire manuscript. We would also like to extend our gratitude to our Routledge editors for both their support and their patience. Finally, last, but by no means least, our families were very tolerant of our long working hours, and kept on reminding us that *Life*, to quote Milan Kundera, really *is Elsewhere*, and not always in our offices. Our heartfelt thanks go out to them.

Jozef Bátora and John Erik Fossum
Bratislava/Vienna and Oslo, April 2019

ABBREVIATIONS

AFSJ	Area of Freedom, Security and Justice
BREXIT	The Exit of the United Kingdom from the EU
CEAS	Common European Asylum System
CEE	Central and Eastern Europe
CEEC	Central and Eastern European Countries
CFSP	Common Foreign and Security Policy
CJEU	Court of Justice of the European Union
CSDP	Common Security and Defence Policy
DAC	Development Aid Committee
DG	Directorate-General
DNA	Deoxyribonucleic Acid
EBA	European Banking Authority
EBCG	European Border and Coast Guard
EC	European Communities
ECB	European Central Bank
ECJ	European Court of Justice
ECSC	European Coal and Steel Community (1951)
EEAS	European External Action Service
EFSF	European Financial Stability Fund
EFSM	European Financial Stability Mechanism
EMU	European Monetary Union
EP	European Parliament
EPP	European People's Party
ERM	Exchange Rate Mechanism
ESM	European Stability Mechanism
ESMAT	Administrative Tribunal of the ESM

EU NAVFOR MED	European Union Naval Force Mediterranean (also known as Operation *Sophia*)
EU	European Union
EU-27	Austria, Belgium, Bulgaria, Croatia, Cyprus, the Czech Republic, Denmark, Estonia, Finland, France, Germany, Greece, Hungary, Ireland, Italy, Latvia, Lithuania, Luxembourg, Malta, The Netherlands, Poland, Portugal, Romania, Slovakia, Slovenia, Spain, and Sweden
EU-28	Austria, Belgium, Bulgaria, Croatia, Cyprus, the Czech Republic, Denmark, Estonia, Finland, France, Germany, Greece, Hungary, Ireland, Italy, Latvia, Lithuania, Luxembourg, Malta, The Netherlands, Poland, Portugal, Romania, Slovakia, Slovenia, Spain, Sweden, and the United Kingdom
EUAFR	European Union Agency for Fundamental Rights
EUROGROUP	Informal meetings of the finance ministers of the Eurozone
EUROJUST	EU agency for judicial co-operation, based in The Hague
EUROSUR	European Border Surveillance System
EUROZONE	The Member States that have adopted the euro: Austria, Belgium, Cyprus, Estonia, Finland, France, Germany, Greece, Ireland, Italy, Latvia, Lithuania, Luxembourg, Malta, The Netherlands, Portugal, Slovakia, Slovenia, and Spain.
FDI	Foreign Direct Investment
FRONTEX	*Frontières extérieures* - EU Border and Coast Guard Agency
FSC	Frontex Situation Centre
G30	Group of Thirty, Consultative Group on International Economic and Monetary Affairs, Inc.
GDP	Gross Domestic Product
IFI	International Financial Institutions
IMF	International Monetary Fund
INTO	Interstitial Organisation
IR	International Relations
L'S-HZDS	*Ľudová strana – Hnutie za demokratické Slovensko* (Movement for a Democratic Slovakia) SK
L'SNS	*Ľudová strana – Naše Slovensko* (People's Party-Our Slovakia) SK
MS-DOS	Microsoft Disk Operating System
NATO	North Atlantic Treaty Organization
OECD	Organisation for Economic Co-operation and Development

OPPD	Office for the Promotion of Parliamentary Democracy (EU)
PES	Party of European Socialists and Democrats (EU)
PIS	*Prawo i Sprawiedliwość* (Law and Justice Party) PL
PO	*Platforma Obywatelska* (Civic Platform) (Christian Democratic Political Party) PL
PPP	Purchasing Power Parity
RABIT	Rapid Border Intervention Teams
RBC	Real Business Cycle
SAS	*Sloboda a Solidarita* (Freedom and Solidarity Party) SK
SDKÚ-DS	*Slovenská demokratická a kresťanská únia – Demokratická strana* (Slovak Democratic and Christian Union) SK
SMER-SD	*Smer – sociálna demokracia* (Direction - Social Democracy) SK
SNS	*Slovenská národná strana* (Slovak National Party) SK
TEU	Treaty on European Union (Treaty of Maastricht 1992)
TFEU	Treaty on the Functioning of the European Union (Treaty of Lisbon 2007)
THE *TROIKA*	The European Central Bank, the European Commission, and the International Monetary Fund
TSCEG	Treaty on Stability, Coordination and Economic Governance
TTS	Transatlantic Trends Survey
UK	United Kingdom
UKIP	United Kingdom Independence Party
UN	United Nations
US	United States of America
V4	Visegrád Four/Group (Czech Republic, Hungary, Poland, and Slovakia)
VAT	Value Added Tax
WWII	Second World War

1

INTRODUCTION

Jozef Bátora and John Erik Fossum

I Introduction

A widely held governance assumption is that a unified structure yields both unified and coherent policies, whereas a differentiated and fragmented political system yields diverse and incoherent policies. *Diverse*, in this connection, refers to a political system that is composed of a (wide) range of different legal and political arrangements, organisational models, policy styles and policy instruments. The growing body of literature on European Union (EU) differentiation argues that the EU has become more diverse, as part of a transition from time-bound or temporary to more permanent differences in EU integration (along functional, territorial and structural lines).[1] In arguing this, analysts do not make clear distinctions between different types of diversity, which therefore also include ideas, ideologies and values.

From this perspective, the EU post-crises leaves us with something of a puzzle: it is clear that the EU has become more differentiated, and yet the policies that the EU instituted to deal with the Eurozone crisis were not only coherent, they were also quite ideological. Since there is consensus that the EU post-crises has become more structurally (in terms of rules, norms and institutions) differentiated, we could say that increased openness to structural and legal diversity actually combined with a form of cognitive and ideological *closure*.

How can this be? Is it a temporary feature associated with the EU's handling of the crises? It is well known that circumstances of crisis give scope for power concentration and centralisation, which would then account for closure. When the crisis is over, the expectation is that there is a return to normalcy. This, however, was hardly the case in the EU, given that today the main elements of the puzzle remain in place.

The question is whether differentiated integration provides us with suitable conceptual and analytical tools for capturing adequately what is presently unfolding. One response in the EU literature has been for analysts to argue that we need to shift our focus from differentiated integration to *differentiation*. Differentiation is a more general term that is not tied to any particular direction of development; it encompasses both differentiated integration *and* differentiated disintegration.[2] Prior to the crises, the general assumption was that, whereas Member States would integrate at different speeds (differentiated integration), they would all more or less end up at the same destination. Post-crises, it has become apparent that the EU is less capable of pulling together towards an "ever closer union"; its future development is far more open-ended than before. There is therefore a greater acceptance that Member States may not end up at the same place, but could rather come to occupy different statuses (permanently): some may be full members (participate in all forms of integration); some may stay out of the Eurozone; some will not be included in Schengen, *etc.* There appears to be a shift from a multi-speed Europe to a multi-status or structurally *differentiated* EU. The EU debate post-crises also encompasses the possibility of EU disintegration (be it unified or differentiated).[3]

Differentiation is not only a more encompassing term than differentiated integration; differentiation also operates at a higher level of generality. Differentiation reminds us that *all* modern political systems are differentiated (along functional and territorial lines). In this connection, the important point to underline is that the multi-level entity that makes up the EU is *distinctly differentiated*. The specific patterns of differentiation that we find in the EU diverge from those which we find in all other political systems. There are two main reasons for this: the distinct configuration that has emerged at EU level, coupled with very extensive diversity across the EU's Member States.

Thus, when we talk about differentiation in the multi-level EU context, we cannot solely focus on the EU level, but must also pay explicit attention to the fact that the EU's Member States are highly diverse. Institutionally speaking, the internal structures of the EU Member States and the manner in which they organise their functions along territorial lines differ along a wide range of dimensions.[4]

The scope and magnitude of Europe's structural-institutional, cultural, social, economic, ethnic and linguistic diversity is profoundly shaping and conditioning the integration process. Increased EU integration entails increased EU involvement and engagement with Europe's diversity. The more the diverse states are tied together, the more their diversity (both internal and across states) will be drawn into the EU integration process. In response, states will be seeking (and obtaining) opt-outs or opt-ins, exemptions, derogations, *etc.* Further, certain governing and managing ideas, policy styles, organisational principles and institutional arrangements will be "lifted" or "uploaded" or "grafted onto" the EU level. These can vary considerably from one policy-field to the next. In this context, it is readily apparent that increased integration will increase structural openness, in the sense that the multi-level EU structure may contain a wider repertoire of ideas, instruments and institutional arrangements.

The obvious assumption from increased differentiation is that the EU will become more unwieldy and more difficult to steer and govern as a consequence of this. Member States have different socio-economic systems and governing philosophies. That implies that the greater the number and range of member state inputs, the more difficult will it be for the EU to reconcile these. Increased differentiation, then, would entail increased contestation over which socio-economic model to prioritise, at what level(s) governing should be concentrated, how governing should proceed (including the nature and range of the policy instruments) and upon what governing should concentrate. We would thus expect that EU policy-making would be difficult to control and align with the central goals and priorities in an EU that would be highly sensitised to local concerns and rationalities.

Even if there were some uncertainty and hesitation at various stages of the EU's crises responses, the overall picture of the EU's response to the Eurozone crisis does *not* fit with these expectations. What we should expect from increased differentiation cannot easily be squared with the form of *cognitive and policy-based closure* that marks the EU's handling of the crises. As several of the contributors to this book underline, the EU appears to have locked itself into a certain approach to handling crises that *forecloses* the search for other options, and it has been pursuing this for a long time. There was a clear underlying thrust to the EU's response to the externally generated financial crisis, a stubborn insistence on deficit reduction and the need for all actors to comply with the provisions in the stability treaty. Rather than an open contestation over which socio-economic model to embrace, the EU's response exhibits a dogged determination to hold on to an economic-crisis handling approach that, in many respects, has proven to be counter-productive (Blyth, 2015). This argument has been frequently brought up in relation to the EU's role in the Greek rescue packages. It has also been applied to the Eurozone as a whole, which many claim is not a zone of convergence but a zero-sum game in which some countries' gains (notably Germany's) are other countries' losses (notably, the debtor nations) (Offe, 2016; Tranøy and Schwarz, Chapter 3 in this volume).

Indeed, the story of the EU post-crises is one of a paradoxical *mixture of openness and closure*, a type of mixture that sits uneasily with what we associate with differentiation. We need a different terminology that helps us to make sense of the factors that produced this mixture, one which must make explicit reference to the role of ideas and ideologies, the role of (professional) knowledge and cognition and the role of structural and institutional factors. Accordingly, the account must *combine* attention to ideas, actors and structures, and how they combine and interact must provide us with vital clues to what transpired, and to the type of political entity that emerged out of the poly-crises.

II What is this book about?

The basic question that this book addresses is: How to understand and type-cast the EU which has emerged from the crises? The thesis that we seek to substantiate is that the EU – post-crises – is in the process of becoming a *segmented political order*.[5] A segmented political order is not a state; it lacks the magnitude and scope of territorial control across a broad range of functional spheres that we associate with the modern state. Furthermore, functionally and institutionally speaking, a segmented political order is much more imbalanced than a state.

An important research challenge is to spell out in further detail what the distinctive features of a segmented political order are. In this introductory chapter, we provide a rough outline of the core features of such an order, which the successive chapters of the book both develop and illuminate in considerable detail. A segmented political order can have supranational traits, but since segments can vary in centralisation and density, such a system can combine supranational and intergovernmental structural traits. The defining feature is that each segment – with a segment tied to a specific policy-field – is imbued with a specific repertoire of ideas, types of expertise and ideological pre-dispositions that uphold the given segment's cognitive closure.

The main purpose of the book is to explain what such a segmented political order would look like, and to discuss to what extent the EU qualifies as such. Furthermore, we will provide some possible explanations as to *why* this has been taking place. This is, at most, a partial account, in which the main focus is on recent developments, not their deeper historical roots. Particular attention is paid to the EU's crises-driven mutations. In the concluding chapter, we sum up the key findings and discuss the implications in relation to two other possible EU developmental trajectories. The point is that a proper diagnosis of the EU is, at present, necessary in order to say something meaningful about the likelihood of other developmental trajectories.

The book adds to existing scholarship in several respects. First, the book provides a novel, empirically grounded take on the EU as a political order. We seek to substantiate the claim that, in order to understand and typecast the EU that has emerged from the poly-crises, we need to develop the notion of the EU as a segmented political order. Second, the book brings our thinking about differentiation forward, in that it not only incorporates the role of ideas, expertise and ideology, but also considers how ideas and ideologies are structurally conditioned and, at the same time, condition structures and institutional arrangements. A key contribution of the book is to understand how the dynamic interaction of ideas and ideologies, on the one hand, and structural-institutional factors, on the other, shape the very nature and operations of a complex political system such as the EU. Third, the book takes explicit account of Europe's diversity and the different conceptions of Europe that exist by focusing on developments not only at EU level, but also within the Member States. This includes paying explicit attention to those states that are critical of, actively contest and refuse to implement EU measures. To this end, the book includes a number of contributions on the Visegrád countries.

II.1 Crises and structural mutations

The book's point of departure – and what motivates our claim to the effect that the EU is developing into a segmented political order – pertains to the manner in which the EU has been transformed through the many crises which it has faced and the manner in which it has responded to them. We ascribe to these developments an EU structural mutation (Menéndez 2013). This is associated with the entrenchment of certain ideas, policy styles and institutional arrangements that are best understood from the perspective of segments and segmentation. The EU, after an initial massive fiscal stimulus both during and after the crises, has converged on a policy of fiscal restraint. Furthermore, with regard to both the refugee crisis and other external threats, coupled with a certain convergence about concerns with borders, border controls and terrorist threats, there was a re-assertion of state sovereignty as part of the concern with securitisation.[6] Fiscal restraint and securitisation have emerged as powerful frames that are guiding activities in the two main problem areas currently facing the EU: socio-economic governance; and security and border controls, broadly speaking (internal as well as external).

The developments have many sources and manifestations, of which the book tries to make sense. The EU's response to the Eurozone crisis by means of "growth through austerity" is a reflection of the particular conflation of problem and solution that has marked the EU's approach to the most serious crises and challenges with which it has been faced. A particular economic philosophy – ordoliberalism having morphed into neoliberalism – became something of a default solution when the Euro crisis struck (see Tranøy and Schwartz, Chapter 3 in this volume).

Even if a crisis response is driven by a set of hegemonic ideas that does not necessarily mean that the actors explicitly state or express that these are the ideas that motivate their actions, it may take time to discern the logics of the underlying action in the midst of the crisis responses, and different local responses may mask or conceal the deeper driving forces. Decisions made during the Euro crisis in 2010 and 2011 on setting up arrangements such as the European Financial Stability Fund (EFSF) and later the European Stability Mechanism (ESM) were made with a lack of proper information, often with severe delays due to clashing political calendars, and without clear reference points as to whether, and, if so, how, they would work (Bini Smaghi, 2011). The critical point that drove such apparently disparate actions in a certain direction was the presence of a set of dominant ideas, the prevailing presence of which has become much more apparent in the aftermath of the crisis.

The particular problem for the EU when it enters crisis mode is that it is not just an unsettled order; it also lacks an agreed-upon polity template.[7] This makes it hard for observers to establish what constitutes normality and what constitutes *a deviation from* normality. This factor contributes to the difficulties in discerning clear patterns of action. Another important and closely associated development is what we may refer to as "the rise of informality", which entails side-stepping legally entrenched arrangements and embedded procedures as well as transferring tasks to bodies less encumbered by rules (notably, the European Council, whose crisis-handling role became far more pronounced; see Wessels, 2016). Other factors relate to the rise of technocracy, not least to the key crisis-handling role of the European Central Bank (ECB) and EU agencies.

This development corresponds with, is fed by and helps to feed a populist upsurge across Europe, through the rise of both right-wing and left-wing populist parties. In effect, these developments are by now so comprehensive that we may talk about a partisan re-alignment. Of particular interest for our purposes is the fact that the rise of Eurosceptic – or Europhobe – versions of right-wing populism introduces added constraints on EU integration. Populists introduce or play upon a strong élite–populace divide, in which the EU and its officials are presented as an élite largely bereft of social roots and out-of-synch with popular views (which populist entrepreneurs actively seek to shape with a distinctive populist style and rhetoric). Populists are prone to define situations as crises (Moffitt, 2016), and, as part of this, seek to condition EU action, including through the strong *onus* on securitisation and the need for border controls, which threatens the Schengen system of open internal EU borders.

Populists and parts of the EU have a mutual interest in maintaining a permanent form of crisis. Right-wing populists strongly underline security, border controls and regulation of the flow of people across borders. Brexit is a further element in this picture through the *onus* which the Brexiteers place on "taking back control" and re-asserting UK sovereign rule.

The same emphasis on re-asserting national sovereignty and control can be found in such states as Hungary and Poland, which are actively involved in "democratic backsliding."

The weakened commitment to internal EU law and order is closely associated with an increasingly authoritarian Russia and a Trump-led United States (US) that are also bent on undermining multilateralism and international law.

The challenge is to work out what these developments imply for our understanding of the EU as a distinct political order. In the following sections, we develop an analytical framework to this end. What is of theoretical importance for this endeavour is that, even if segmentation is a well-known and -commented-on phenomenon in states (often depicted as "iron triangles" – see Allison and Zelikow, 1999), the phenomenon has generally been observed and analysed at meso-level and as a phenomenon that is confined to certain issue-areas. The question which we raise is what such traits imply for a political system that falls well short of being a state. In such a context, the structural implications of segmentation processes are likely to be different. Democratic states may have segmental traits, but they would normally not be considered segmented political systems. An important reason for this is that they have institutional arrangements that de-limit or "rein in" the exclusive and fissiparous effects of segments.

With regard to the EU, it is not a state, and it has a different overall institutional composition that is far more imbalanced. Our claim is that, in the EU context, such traits have gained in prominence and have become semi-permanent solutions to the EU's perceived or real policy failures, and, with this, we find that segmental features have taken a jump from the meso- to the macro-level of the EU as a political order. It is this development that we attribute to the EU's structural mutation, and which has compelled us to theorise the EU as a fledgling segmented political order. The guiding assumption is that it makes sense to talk about political systems as segmented political orders.

III What is meant by a *segmented political order*?

A *segmented political order* consists of three core elements. The first is what we may term *segmental logic* and refers to a cognitive *bias* that gives rise to cognitive closure and informs policy-making and (gives a particular twist to) policy co-ordination. Such a bias manifests itself in a distinct manner of framing problems, which shapes the actors' approach to how they seek to handle problems and what the actors see as the realm of relevant solutions. The cognitive bias that we find in a segment manifests itself in the lack of broad-based search, and its replacement by a *systematic selection* of certain problem conceptions, action frames and types of expertise. The closure which we find in a segment is ensured by the second element: a set of organisational or procedural arrangements that sustains the segmental logic(s). The third element is that the overall institutional system is imbalanced: those institutional arrangements that both give rise to and sustain segments are *systematically stronger* than the de-segmenting institutional arrangements, or, in other words, those parts of the political system that pry open networks and challenge entrenched ideologies, action-logics and perceptions of how things ought to be done.

There is an extensive body of literature on segments and segmentation, but this literature generally associates segments with policy sectors. A standard definition of the term *segment* would refer to a pattern of linking participants who share common conceptions of problems, solutions and choice opportunities in policy-making (Christensen and Egeberg, 1979). In public policy-making, it is about linking the organised interests of the participants, such as private-sector organisations, non-governmental organisations (NGOs) and civil society, with various governmental agencies. The mechanisms through which segments are maintained include committees and "remiss" systems whereby public administrations consult and co-shape legislative proposals with various stakeholders. These processes gradually stabilise, and what emerges are segments defined as, more or less, stable patterns of how participants, problems, solutions and opportunities of choice are linked. As Christensen and Egeberg (1979: 253–254) argue,

> segments may be found within a particular economic issue area (agriculture, fisheries, industry, etc.), or around such functions as health care, communications, education, and defence. The participants may come from various institutions. One segment may include representatives of interest organizations, ministries, parliamentarians, representatives of research

institutions, the mass media, etc. There will not necessarily be complete agreement within each segment, but the participants are assumed to share certain basic values and perceptions, such that their models of the world coincide more with one another than with those of the representatives of other segments, or of those who are not part of any segment. Public policy as such, then, may be a by-product of the events which take place within each segment.

The distinctive feature of the post-crises EU is that we are compelled to think about segments not simply in sectoral terms at meso-level, but also in macroscopic terms and as core attributes of the multi-level EU's political order. As already noted, a segmented political order requires us to think about segments – and the logic of segmentation – as manifest features of the overall political order, in other words, as defining features of the polity.

We thus expect that there are certain distinctive features of the polity that warrant the label of *segmented political order*, with segmentation being systemic in terms of permeating the very structure and functioning not just of some sectors but also of the political system in its entirety. Such a system will encompass distinct functional domains that cut across institutional bounds and levels of governing, and, as such, make it very difficult for the overarching system both to co-ordinate and to steer clear of significant decision biases. Only those problems that "fit" with the way in which problems are framed within the relevant segments will receive attention and be handled in accordance with the distinctive "segmental logic" that marks each segment. Such an order is challenging for the governmental administrations of the Member States, as various ministries and agencies participate and co-constitute various segments and thereby operate according to different norm-sets and rule-sets. This generates specific co-ordination challenges for EU Member States' governments as well as for EU institutions (Olsen, 2003, 2010; Trondal and Bauer, 2017).

III.1 A segmented political order is a distinctly differentiated political order

As noted above, the EU post-crises exhibits increased structural differentiation in combination with a highly focused and ideologically driven crisis response (cognitive closure). Neither the label *supranational political order* nor the label *intergovernmental organisation* is well suited for capturing the defining features of such a system, because segments typically vary in their degree of centralisation and concentration.[8] A supranational political system is organised along various levels, each of which co-ordinates the functions that are performed at that level. Policy-making bears a distinct supranational imprint because the main dividing line is vertical, pitting the central level against the sub-units. In some contrast, an intergovernmental organisation is composed of, serves and responds to the Member States as the constituent units. Such a system typically struggles to develop unified action, since decision-making hinges on the consent of the Member States. What a supranational political system has in common with an intergovernmental organisation is that, in both cases, the main dividing line is *vertical*.

In contrast, a segmented political order is distinct in the manner in which it *combines* vertical and horizontal dimensions. In contrast to a supranational system, the segments cut across institutions and form around specific functional areas; they therefore cut across levels of governance. Further, a segmented political order, first and foremost, may not take its cues from the central level but could be directed by a prominent Member State that manages to impose its views on the central institutions and across the Member States. This is probably easier for a Member State to get away with in a segmented political order than in a fully fledged supranational political order because, in the former case, it is a matter of setting the terms of action within one or several policy areas, but *not* doing so system-wide. In addition, each segment may contain *different drivers* or driving forces, and, hence, each segment may vary in its degree of centralisation.

A segment will typically encompass all the system's Member States so that each segment will represent a relatively narrow functional specialism that extends system-wide. A segmented political order may therefore be more capable than an intergovernmental organisation in fostering unified political action, albeit mainly within each segment – in other words, within the functional realm that the relevant segment covers. A segmented political order will probably be more capable of fostering unified political action across levels of governing than a supranational system will, but, again, it will do so mainly within the relatively narrow functional confines of each segment. A segmented political order can accommodate different organisational principles: some segments may be more fully anchored in supranational institutions, while other segments may be more fully anchored in intergovernmental institutions. The EU is then also marked by a mixture of supranational and intergovernmental traits.[9]

As John Erik Fossum's chapter shows, the ways in which such combinations are configured in the EU setting are important for understanding how a segmented political order can be simultaneously marked by the increased structural differentiation and cognitive closure that we have referred to here. The EU's hybridity and distinct form of differentiation are important features that qualify it as a fledgling segmented political order.

III.2 A segmented political order: Analytical framework

In this section, we will outline the core components and assumptions that need to be taken into consideration when seeking to establish how and the extent to which the post-crises EU qualifies as a segmented political order. First, a segmented political order is institutionally distinct. Then, governing capacity is aligned along segmental lines, and the system's ability to co-ordinate policies across segments is limited. A segmented political order is therefore imbued with constraints and/or vulnerabilities. These may be built-in, or they may be externally imposed. Segments are established and sustained by factors and forces *within* each segment, as well as by factors and forces *outside* each segment.

The analytical framework that animates this book associates a segmented political order with specific traits along the following six lines: a) ideas and cognitions, b) policy instruments, c) institutions and procedures, d) resources, e) patterns of dependence and vulnerability, and f) a specific form of institutional bias, to wit, weak de-segmenting bodies/arrangements. Some of these are directly constitutive of segments, while others play an auxiliary role in that they support and/or sustain segments, even if we would not necessarily associate them with what is going on within a segment. A segmented political order is imbalanced, in that it is marked by particularly underdeveloped de-segmenting factors and forces.

We spell out assumptions under each of these six dimensions, which the various contributions to the book will systematically examine.

With regard to a) [ideas and cognitions], there is a "segmental logic," in other words, a cognitive *bias* that manifests itself in a distinct way of framing problems, a distinct way in which actors approach problems and distinctive ways in which actors specify what they see as the relevant solutions. A segmental logic represents a form of "closing of the mind" to segment-external ideas and influences. As we know from the literature on segments, there are many possible sources of segmentation. The literature underlines the role of professional expertise and professional networks, as well as, possibly, ideologies and other ideas- and knowledge-based modes of grasping and framing the world around us. Cognitive bias stems from "trained incapacity,"[10] which means that professions search for solutions that are close to their competence and where there is a build-up or concentration of certain forms of expertise and active exclusion of other forms, in which the bounded rationality that marks the individual expert is aggregated up to group/network size. This is one manifestation of how a given segmental logic engenders forms of closure. Technocracy (for an assessment of this challenge in the EU context, see Habermas, 2015) is a mode of governing that is highly conducive to segmentation, either when technocrats develop networks that shut out alternative forms of expertise, or when they shut out all other types of actors and their experience (for such closing processes, see, e.g., March and Simon, 1958; Cyert and March, 1963). Several of the chapters in the book focus on the types of segmental logics that have emerged in connection with the Eurozone crisis and the refugee crisis, the two main recent segmenting thrusts facing the EU (see, in particular, the chapters by Tranøy and Schwarz, Holst and Molander, Olsen, and Gould and Malová, Chapters 3, 4, 5 and 6 respectively).

It may also be useful to clarify how segment and segmentation relate to the notion of institutional logic. Institutional logics could be defined as the

> supra-organizational patterns of activity by which individuals and organizations produce and reproduce their material subsistence and organize

time and space. They are also symbolic systems, ways of ordering reality, thereby rendering experience of time and space meaningful.

(Friedland and Alford, 1991: 243)

As such, institutional logics are maintained by practices. As Thornton and Ocasio (2008) point out, institutional logics are

> socially constructed, historical patterns of material practices, assumptions, values, beliefs, and rules by which individuals produce and reproduce their material subsistence, organize time and space, and provide meaning to their social reality.

Such institutional logics can be confined to specific policy-sectors with explicit exclusion mechanisms; under such circumstances, we can see the patterns and processes of segmentation. As the various contributions to this book bring out, the most important institutional logics that have narrowed to foster segmentation in the post-crises EU are those of marketisation and sovereignty-cum-securitisation.

With regard to b) [policy instruments], a process of segmentation contains distinct policy attitudes/orientations and is furthered by a specific range of policy instruments. We do not assume that a given set of policy instruments can be directly attributed to segments and segmentation, as such. From a systemic perspective, it matters to decision-making and to questions of systematic biases what range and overall composition of policy instruments the system has available. For one, we can assume that a segment's framing of problems and solutions will be affected by the *repertoire* of policy instruments that it has at its disposal, and will, in turn, have a bearing on the *types* of policy instruments that are available. A *narrow range* of policy instruments injects its own specific bias on policy-making. An *imbalanced range* of policy instruments is similarly problematical, when, for instance, a system has well-developed regulatory instruments but lacks (re-) distributive instruments. In such circumstances, regulatory interventions that affect values and patterns of distribution can spur conflict, dissatisfaction and claims to illegitimacy if there is no mechanism to compensate for the distributive effects. A limited policy repertoire can foster segmental closure; the same applies if there is a distinct underlying logic underpinning a mode of intervention whose built-in bias remains uncorrected by other measures. Thus, whereas there is no one-on-one relationship between segmentation and a given (bundle of) policy instrument(s), certain combinations are conducive to segmentation.

With regard to c) [institutions and procedures], the assumption is that there are certain institutions that can help to entrench segmental logics. Typical candidates that can foster cognitive bias are expert and administrative bodies that hold distinct forms of knowledge and competence and have privileged decision-making access. They would probably, in turn, be closely linked to like-minded executives (with or without explicit ideological orientations), research institutions and others sharing the same outlook within and without the political system. Within a segmented political order, such institutions are closed and/or in-transparent, not least because a segmented political order is lopsided, in that those institutions, such as parliaments, that pry open networks, question and challenge expertise and ideological bias and include popular participation (parliaments, ombudsman arrangements and other transparency-enforcers) are weakly developed or side-lined.

The implication is that a segmented political order is lopsided and imbalanced in contrast to a fully fledged democratic system with executive, judicial, administrative and legislative institutions that produce expertise and ideology but ensure open contestation and thus an ongoing balancing of different world views, types of expertise, values and ideologies. A segmented political order will typically contain a much more prominent component of those institutions that foster segmentation than those institutions that deter segmentation, such as, for instance, a technocratic system with a strong reliance on experts.

A further important institutional trait of a segmented political order is some form of *lock-in* or lack of exit options for the participating states. If there were none, there would be no segmental closure. We therefore need to look for mechanisms that *compel* states to co-operate or participate. In the EU, as Fossum's chapter shows, the high level of fusion of levels implicates the Member States. This, combined with the manner in which mutual recognition is handled, leads to distinctive forms of segmental lock-ins of all the EU's Member States. The lock-in of Member States that we find in the issue-area of the internal market is distinctive to that segment; the other "securitisation" segment that we find in the area of border control – in particular with regard to migrants – is quite differently structured and institutionally sustained.

With regard to d) [resources broadly speaking], a segmented political order is typically one in which there are built-in *constraints* on the resources that the system has available. The implication of limited resources is that the system is compelled to operate based upon a given or prescribed – and therefore limited – set of policy instruments. We may operate with two core categories of resources: material and immaterial ones. The former has to do with the availability of a wide range of material resources (pecuniary, technical, intellectual, institutional), so that the system is able to summon resources that are commensurate to the problems that it is facing. For instance, some solutions will have a much higher price-tag than other ones; a system that lacks access to resources or that is strapped for resources will have limited ability to choose among different policy options or possible solutions. Resource constraints de-limit a polity's scope of action and/or foreclose options that are available to polities with more available policy options and material resources; consider the EU's *versus* Canada's responses to the financial crisis (Fossum, 2018).

The latter aspect of resources pertains to the system's support. High levels of trust, support and legitimacy are vital resources which provide a political system with slack (scope for reversing policies and adopting alternative courses of action). Conversely, the less trust there is, the more the system's support hinges on its performance, and the less overall slack it has.[11] Hostility – such as, for instance, a high instance of Europhobia among societal actors – will serve to constrain access to resources (taxing ability) as well as generate a propensity for experts and professionals to "hide" and to find ways of working out problems with as little publicity as possible, thus indirectly helping to foster forms of segmental closure.

In structural terms, the combination of c) [institutions and procedures] and d) [resources] suggests that segments may vary considerably in terms of the institutional arrangements and structures, as well as the resources – material and immaterial – supporting them. Some segments can consist of tightly coupled institutional arrangements, while others consist of loosely coupled institutional arrangements. The latter is evident in the EU's increased reliance on *interstitial organisations* – organisations that emerge in the interstices between established institutional fields, tapping into the personnel, financial, legal and legitimacy resources of organisations belonging to different institutional fields, and re-combining these to form new patterns of action and new organisational types (Bátora, 2013, 2017; Korff et al., 2015).[12] Interstitial organisations emerge in situations in which there is a need for problem-solving under strong institutional, legal, political and resource constraints, and interstitial organisations were a frequently resorted-to EU crisis-handling measure (see Bátora's chapter).

Interstitial organisations or bodies are not a necessary manifestation of a segmented political order, but the relationship has thus far not been specified. In situations in which established institutional forms either fail to generate action capacity or are hindered from doing so, interstitial organisations provide action capacity through organising across traditional institutional boundaries. This happens via creative re-combination and transposition of norms, rules and procedures from across different institutional domains, which enable co-ordinated action and the generation of various kinds of ambiguities and uncertainties. The critical issue for segmentation pertains to whether interstitial organisations generate or sustain forms of cognitive and/or decisional bias. Interstitial organisations are good illustrations of the sometimes very complex manner in which cognitive factors – ideas and ideologies – are institutionally entrenched.

With regard to e) [patterns of dependence and vulnerability], a segmented political system, precisely because it has weak access to own resources, is likely to be quite *externally dependent*, and that form of dependence will increase the more ambitious the polity is in terms of intervention and policy-making. The EU's monetary union revealed – both during and after the crises – how dependent the EU was on the financial markets. This form of dependence served to reinforce the bias because the EU needed to present itself and act in a manner that was palatable to the financial markets.

Another aspect of EU vulnerability stems from the EU's dependence on the Member States for effectuating EU policies. Such dependence, be it in the form of delays in implementation or in outright opposition or rejection of EU policy, represents a further constraint on action and highlights the system's vulnerability.

Sixth and finally, with regard to f) [a specific form of institutional bias], a segmented political system is imbued with a distinct form of institutional imbalance due to the relative weakness or even absence of institutions and arrangements that typically prevent political systems from developing into a segmental political order. Core institutions associated with *de-segmentation* are democratic institutions. We may include all types of institutions that ensure openness and transparency and are open to challenging entrenched ways of seeing and behaving and all the arrangements that hold officials and institutions to account. Weakening of democratic institutions and legal procedural arrangements enabling representative bodies, publics and media to understand, question and challenge what is going on, are – indirectly or directly – fostering segmentation. That is what we have seen in the EU post-crises.

For instance, "democratic backsliding" in Poland and Hungary will contribute to further segmentation because their democratic rejection can have system-wide implications by weakening the de-segmenting bodies with broader legitimacy implications due to contagion effects and an overall loss of EU legitimacy and credibility. Democratic backsliding in Poland, for instance, is therefore not a direct manifestation of a segmented political order, but it can contribute to entrenching further segmentation because of its weakening or undermining of the de-segmenting bodies (see Riedel's chapter).

A segmented political order is more prone to fragmentation than is a fully fledged political system. It is questionable whether a segmented political order is stable or resilient. It may be a temporary resting point, thus suggesting that a mere policy of muddling through will have devastating long-term effects.

IV The contents of the book

In the following, we provide a brief overview of the contents of the book. In this our introductory chapter, we have presented the book's basic thematic, the core research questions and the analytical framework that animates the subsequent chapters.

In Chapter 2, "The Institutional Make-up of Europe's Segmented Political Order," John Erik Fossum discusses the assertion that the EU post-crises is a fledgling segmented order. The chapter re-visits the criteria set out in the introductory chapter, but with particular emphasis on the EU's institutional and structural composition. Further, since segmentation not only overlaps with, but also is a special form of, differentiation, the chapter discusses the logic underpinning segmentation against the logic underpinning differentiation in order to show not only where they differ, but also points of convergence.

Chapter 3, "Illusions of Convergence: The Persistent Simplification of a Wicked Crisis," co-authored by Bent Sofus Tranøy and Herman Mark Schwartz, complements the institutional analysis in Chapter 2 with a focus on cognitive factors and shows how these were structurally embedded, thus giving added credence to the segmentation thesis. The authors show how the epistemic community that centred around the ECB shared an important cognitive bias which made it systematically ignore crisis-inducing divergence whilst doggedly pursuing solutions to the Eurozone crisis based upon austerity and "one-size-fits-all" policies that conformed to their previous beliefs about appropriate economic policy.

In Chapter 4, "Epistemic Worries about Economic Expertise," co-authored by Cathrine Holst and Anders Molander, the authors take a broader look at the epistemic worries about the expertisation of politics, and situate the discussion in debates on the role of economic expertise in EU governance in the light of the post-crisis reform discourse and the idea of a segmented political order. The chapter presents and assesses ten epistemic worries, some of an epistemological nature, others related to failures and biases. In discussing how these can be addressed, the chapter devotes explicit attention to possible de-segmenting strategies.

In Chapter 5, "What Kind of Crisis and How to Deal with It? The Segmented Border Logic in the European Migration Crisis," Espen Olsen discusses the European migration crisis as an example of the EU's *segmented political order*. The chapter reflects on the refugee crisis to establish what kind of crisis it is and whose crisis it is. As part of this, it shows that a segmental logic closely associated with securitisation served to re-define what was initially referred to as a *humanitarian* crisis, emphasising the precarious situation for refugees, to a shift in attention and emphasis towards issues of state security, border control and the challenges facing political institutions and the receiving states.

Chapter 6, "Toxic Ordoliberalism on the EU's Periphery: Slovakia, the Euro and the Migrant Crisis," co-authored by John Gould and Darina Malová, examines the emergence of "a segmental logic" in the EU's post-crises financial order with a specific focus on Slovak domestic politics. Slovakia's politicians have almost universally embraced the ordoliberal norm of fiscal restraint, which has shut out all and any policy alternatives of benefit to "Slovakia's internal periphery," in other words, those areas that benefit least from the Eurozone's ordoliberal policies and which have shown a propensity to vote for populist and/or racist or xenophobic actors.

Chapter 7, "European Solidarity in Times of Crisis: Towards Differentiated Integration," co-authored by Asimina Michailidou and Hans-Jörg Trenz, focuses on how the principle of European solidarity initially conceived of as a main driver of social cohesion has become replaced with a new politics of differentiated solidarity associated with the pursuit of flexible arrangements among EU members, discretionary re-distributive mechanisms and hegemony. The authors show that this notion of differentiated solidarity is quite compatible with a segmented political order.

Chapter 8, "Interstitial Organisations and Segmentation in EU Governance," by Jozef Bátora, focuses on the EU's crises-induced efforts to establish governing capacity, notably through interstitial organisations (INTOs). INTOs re-combine resources, rules, organisational norms and structures across various policy-fields and institutional spheres in order to address newly emerging and cross-cutting policy issues. The formation of INTOs, such as the European External Action Service (EEAS), the European Stability Mechanism (ESM) and the European Border and Coast Guard (EBCG), are established to gain action capacity and improve co-ordination under conditions of political, legal and institutional constraints. The resort to INTOs shows how the development of the EU's political order unfolds as a kind of segmented integration, in a manner not wholly compatible with intergovernmental or supranational modes of integration.

Chapter 9, "Undermining the Standards of Liberal Democracy within the European Union: The Polish Case and the Limits of Post-enlargement Democratic Conditionality," by Rafał Riedel, examines de-democratisation and de-Europeanisation tendencies in Poland. The illiberal tendencies in the EU's (semi-)peripheries contribute to EU segmentation. Illiberal nation states, which question and challenge the norms of the constitutional democratic order, strongly committed to traditionally understood sovereignty and sceptical towards most of the EU policies, substantially contribute to the segmentation process of the whole EU system, both by undermining the Union's democratic credentials and by constraining it.

Chapter 10, "A Different Union Being Created? Newspaper Portrayal of the EU in Crises in the Czech Republic, Slovakia and Hungary," by Max Steuer, draws on newspaper portrayals in order to understand how the EU was framed in six quality newspapers in three Visegrád countries (the Czech Republic, Slovakia and Hungary). The chapter shows that quality newspapers reproduced some common patterns of perception of the EU in the period from 2008 to June 2016, especially the contrast between the "domestic" scene and "the EU in Brussels," including the "European élite." These contrasts underpin forms of cognitive segmentation that may contribute to EU segmentation or even fragmentation.

Chapter 11, "European Crises and Foreign Policy Attitudes in Europe," by Michal Onderco, focuses on European citizens' attitudes towards the EU, the US and Russia during the crises, and, as such, queries to what extent we find shifts in allegiances and threat perceptions. Perceptions of identity threat are associated with decreased support for the EU but have no impact on attitudes towards the US and Russia in Western Europe. In Central and Eastern Europe, perceptions of identity threat are associated with more negative views of the US and more positive views of Russia. The chapter shows that the economic crisis in Europe had a wider impact on foreign policy preferences among Europeans than was previously thought and opens new avenues for the study of the knock-on effects of the economic crisis in Europe.

Chapter 12, "Integration through Differentiation and Segmentation: The Case of One Member State from 1950 to Brexit (and Beyond)," by Christopher Lord, focuses on the role of the United Kingdom (UK) in the EU, with particular emphasis on its contribution to EU segmentation. Throughout its EU membership, the UK has pushed for differentiation through special arrangements. Nevertheless, that is only part of the story, in that the UK was the single most enthusiastic supporter of the creation of the single market. Hence, the UK reconciled itself to EU membership by a mixture of differentiation and integration that was highly conducive to segmentation in cognitive and ideological terms. UK governments, as Lord notes, "were prepared to accept ambitious and supranational forms of European integration where that promoted their other ideological priorities."

Chapter 13 is the Conclusion. Here, the editors sum up the main findings of the book. The focus is on the six defining traits of a segmented political order that have been spelt out here. The summary shows how chapters that address very different themes nevertheless converge on the notion of the EU as a segmented political order. In the final part of the chapter, we briefly discuss the notion of the EU as a segmented political order against two other possible EU trajectories: core consolidation and fragmentation. What is important to stress is that the debate on EU reforms must take as its point of departure where the EU is now. This book has sought to provide such a vantage point.

Notes

1 A selection of works would include Adler-Nissen (2014); Andersen and Sitter (2006); Bickerton, Hoodson and Puetter (2015); Dyson and Sepos (2010); Fabbrini (2015); Eriksen (2018, 2019); Eriksen and Fossum (2015); Fossum (2014); Genschel and Jachtenfuchs (2014; 2016); Kölliker (2006); Leruth and Lord (2015); Leuffen, Rittberger and Schimmelfennig (2013); Lord (2017); Piris (2012); Schimmelfennig (2014); Schimmelfennig and Winzen (2014); Stubb (1996); Warleigh-Lack (2015).
2 The current debate thus encompasses four different trajectories: a) uniform integration; b) differentiated integration; c) uniform dis-integration; and d) differentiated dis-integration. For an overview and discussion, see, for instance, Fossum (2015); Schimmelfennig (2018).
3 For assessments focusing on the question of EU disintegration, see, for instance, Jones (2018); Vollaard (2014); (2018). Webber (2014), (2018); Zielonka (2014).
4 There are: (a) huge discrepancies in the size of the Member States; (b) significantly different states and political regimes – the EU is composed of federal and quasi-federal and unitary states and the EU's regions vary greatly; (c) different systems of representation and accountability; (d) different ways of connecting the citizens to the political system (electoral and party systems); and (e) different ways for parliaments/representative assemblies to relate to and hold executives accountable (with mandating and document-based scrutiny – the two main models. See Buzogany (2013).
5 This was a key concern of the Eurodiv project. Some publications that discuss this notion have already come out. See Eriksen (2018), (2019); Eriksen and Fossum (2018).
6 There is a large body of literature on securitization (see, e.g., Buzan (1991), (1997), Buzan, Wæver and de Wilde (1998).
7 For incisive assessments of emergency politics in the EU setting, see White (2015a, 2015b).
8 Børzel (2005) and Leuffen et al. (2013) underline this as a core dimension in EU differentiation.
9 Bickerton et al. (2015) underline this in their work on "the new intergovernmentalism." See, also, Fabbrini (2013; 2015) and Fossum (2017).
10 There has been a discussion as to whether this term really was coined by Thorstein Veblen. Wais (2005) notes that Veblen uses it in his 1914 book.
11 In the EU, this is often referred to as a change from "permissive consensus" to "dismissive dissensus" (Hooghe and Marks, 2009).

12 Examples of interstitial organizations include the European External Action Service, European Border and Coast Guard or the European Stability Mechanism – see Jozef Bátora's chapter in this volume.

References

Adler-Nissen, Rebecca (2014), *Opting Out of the European Union: Diplomacy, Sovereignty and European Integration*, Cambridge: Cambridge University Press.

Allison, Graham T., and Philip Zelikow (1999), *Essence of Decision: Explaining the Cuban Missile Crisis*, 2nd edn., New York: Pearson Longman.

Andersen, Svein S., and Nick Sitter (2006), "Differentiated Integration: What Is It and How Much Can the EU Accommodate?", *Journal of European Integration*, 28 (4): 313–330.

Bátora, Jozef (2013), "The 'Mitrailleuse Effect': The EEAS as an Interstitial Organization and the Dynamics of Innovation in Diplomacy", *Journal of Common Market Studies*, 51 (4): 598–613.

Bátora, Jozef (2017), "Turbulence and War: Private Military Corporations and the Reinstitutionalization of War-Making", in Ansell, C. et al. (eds.): *Governance in Turbulent Times*, Oxford: Oxford University Press, pp. 181–201.

Bickerton, Christopher J., Dermot Hodson, and Uwe Puetter (2015), *The New Intergovernmentalism: States and Supranational Actors in the Post-Maastricht Era*, Oxford: Oxford University Press.

Bini Smaghi, Lorenzo (2011), "European Democracies and Decision-making In Times of Crisis", Speech by Mr Lorenzo Bini Smaghi, Member of the Executive Board of the European Central Bank, at the Hellenic Foundation for European and Foreign Policy, 8th European Seminar, Adjusting to the Crisis Policy Choices and Politics in Europe, Poros, 8 July 2011 (available at www.bis.org/review/r110712c.pdf, last accessed on 1 April 2019).

Blyth, Mark (2015), *Austerity: The History of a Dangerous Idea*, Oxford: Oxford University Press.

Börzel, Tanja A. (2005), "Mind the Gap! European Integration between Level and Scope", *Journal of European Public Policy*, 12 (2): 217–236.

Buzan, Barry (1991), "New Patterns of Global Security in the Twenty-first Century", *International Affairs*, 67 (3): 431–451.

Buzan, Barry (1997), "Rethinking Security after the Cold War", *Cooperation and Conflict*, 32 (1): 5–28.

Buzan, Barry, Ole Wæver, and Jaap de Wilde (1998), *Security: A New Framework for Analysis*, Denver, CO: Lynne Rienner Publishers.

Buzogany, Aron (2013), "Learning from the Best? Interparliamentary Networks and the Parliamentary Scrutiny of EU Decision-Making", in: Ben Crum and John Erik Fossum (eds), *Practices of Interparliamentary Coordination in International Politics: The European Union and Beyond*, Colchester: ECPR Press, pp. 17–32.

Christensen, Tom, and Morten Egeberg (1979), "Organized Group-Government Relations in Norway: On the Structured Selection of Participants, Problems, Solutions, and Choice Opportunities", *Scandinavian Political Studies*, 2 (3): 239–260.

Cyert, Richard M., and James G. March (1963), *A Behavioral Theory of the Firm*, New York: Wiley-Blackwell.

Dyson, Kenneth, and Angelos Sepos (eds) (2010), *Which Europe? The Politics of Differentiated Integration*, Basingstoke: Palgrave Macmillan.

Eriksen, Erik Oddvar (2018), "Political Differentiation and the Problem of Dominance: Segmentation and Hegemony", *European Journal of Political Research*, 57 (4): 989–1008.

Eriksen, Erik Oddvar (2019), *Contesting Political Differentiation: European Division and the Problem of Dominance*, London: Palgrave.

Eriksen, Erik Oddvar, and John Erik Fossum (eds) (2015), *The European Union's Non-members: Independence Under Hegemony?*, London: Routledge, 2015.

Eriksen, Erik Oddvar, and John Erik Fossum (2018), "Deliberation Constrained: An Increasingly Segmented European Union", in: André Bächtiger, John S. Dryzek, Jane Mansbridge and Mark E. Warren (eds), *The Oxford Handbook of Deliberative Democracy*, Oxford: Oxford University Press, pp. 842–855.

Fabbrini, Sergio (2013), "Intergovernmentalism and Its Limits: Assessing the European Union's Answer to the Euro Crisis", *Comparative Political Studies*, XX (X): 1–27.

Fabbrini, Sergio (2015), *Which European Union?*, Cambridge: Cambridge University Press.

Fossum, John Erik (2014), "The Structure of EU Representation and the Crisis", in: Sandra Kröger (ed), *Political Representation in the European Union: Still Democratic in Times of Crisis?*, London: Routledge, pp. 52–68.

Fossum, John Erik (2015), "Democracy and Differentiation in Europe", *Journal of European Public Policy*, 22 (6): 799–815.

Fossum, John Erik (2017), "European Federalism: Pitfalls and Possibilities", *European Law Journal*, 23 (5): 361–379.

Fossum, John Erik (2018), "Looking Across the Atlantic – The European Union and Canada Compared", in: Christopher Dunn (ed), *The Handbook of Canadian Public Administration*, Oxford: Oxford University Press, pp. 501–513.

Friedland, Roger, and Robert Alford (1991), "Bringing Society Back In: Symbols, Practices and Institutional Contradictions", in: Walter W. Powell and Paul DiMaggio (eds), *The New Institutionalism in Organizational Analysis*, Chicago, IL: Chicago University Press, pp. 232–263.

Genschel, Philipp, and Markus Jachtenfuchs (2014), *Beyond the Regulatory Polity? The European Integration of Core State Powers*, Oxford: Oxford University Press.

Genschel, Philipp, and Markus Jachtenfuchs (2016), "More Integration, Less Federation: The European Integration of Core State Powers", *Journal of European Public Policy*, 23 (1): 42–59.

Habermas, Jürgen (2015), *The Lure of Technocracy*, Cambridge: Polity Press.

Hooghe, Liesbet, and Gary Marks (2009), "A Postfunctionalist Theory of European Integration: From Permissive Consensus to Constraining Dissensus', *British Journal of Political Science*, 39 (1): 1–23.

Jones, Erik (2018), "Towards a Theory of Disintegration", *Journal of European Public Policy*, 25 (3): 440–451.

Korff, Valeska, Oberg, Achim, and Walter. W. Powell (2015), "Interstitial Organizations as Conversational Bridges", *Bulletin of the Association for Information Science and Technology*, April 2015, pp. 34–38. doi:10.1002/bult.2015.1720410210

Kölliker, Alkuin (2006), *Flexibility and European Unification: The Logic of Differentiated Integration*, Lanham MD: Rowman and Littlefield.

Leruth, Benjamin, and Christopher Lord (2015), "Differentiated Integration in the European Union: A Concept, a Process, a System or a Theory?", *Journal of European Public Policy*, 22 (6): 754–763.

Leuffen, Dirk, Berthold Rittberger, and Frank Schimmelfennig (2013), *Differentiated Integration: Explaining Variation in* the European Union, Basingstoke: Palgrave Macmillan.

Lord, Christopher (2017), "Segmentation, Differentiation and the Aims of European Integration", in: Andreas Grimmel (ed), *The Crisis of the European Union: Challenges, Analyses, Solutions*, London: Routledge, pp. 185–198.

March, James G., and Herbert A. Simon (1958), *Organizations*, New York: John Wiley & Sons, Inc.

Menéndez, Agustín José (2013), "The Existential Crisis of the European Union", *German Law Journal*, 14 (5): 453–525.

Moffitt, Benjamin (2016), *The Global Rise of Populism: Performance, Political Style and Representation*, Stanford, CA: Stanford University Press.

Offe, Claus (2016), *Europe Entrapped*, London: Polity Press.

Olsen, Johan P. (2003), "Towards a European Administrative Space?" *Journal of European Public Policy*, 10 (4): 506–531.

Olsen, Johan P. (2010), *Governing through Institution Building: Institutional Theory and Recent European Experiments in Democratic Organization*, Oxford: Oxford University Press.

Piris, Jean-Claise (2012), *The Future of Europe: Towards a Two-Speed EU?* Cambridge: Cambridge University Press.

Schimmelfennig, Frank (2014), "European Integration in the Euro Crisis: The Limits of Postfunctionalism", *Journal of European Integration*, 36 (3): 321–337.

Schimmelfennig, Frank (2018), "Brexit: Differentiated Disintegration in the European Union", *Journal of European Public Policy*, 25 (8): 1154–1173.

Schimmelfennig, Frank, and Thomas Winzen (2014), "Instrumental and Constitutional Differentiation in the European Union", *Journal of Common Market Studies*, 52 (2): 354–370.

Stubb, Alexander C. G. (1996), "A Categorization of Differentiated Integration", *Journal of Common Market Studies*, 34 (2): 283–295.

Thornton, Patricia, and William Ocasio (2008), "Institutional Logics", in: Royston Greenwood, Christine Oliver, Roy Suddaby and Kerstin Sahlin (eds), *The SAGE Handbook of Organizational Institutionalism*, Thousand Oaks, CA: SAGE Publications, pp. 99–128.

Trondal, Jarle, and Michael W. Bauer (2017), "Conceptualizing the European Multilevel Administrative Order: Capturing Variation in the European Administrative System", *European Political Science Review*, 9 (1): 73–94.

Veblen, Thorstein (1914), *The Instinct of Workmanship and the Industrial Arts*, New York: B.H. Huebsch.

Vollaard, Hans (2014), "Explaining European Disintegration", *Journal of Common Market Studies*, 52 (5): 1142–1159.

Vollaard, Hans (2018), *European Disintegration: A Search for Explanations*, London: Palgrave.

Wais, Erin (2005), "Trained Incapacity: Thorstein Veblen and Kenneth Burke", *The Journal of the Kenneth Burke Society*, 2 (1), available at: www.kbjournal.org/wais.

Warleigh-Lack, Alex (2015), "Differentiated Integration in the European Union: Towards a Comparative Regionalism Perspective", *Journal of European Public Policy*, 22 (6): 871–887.

Webber, Douglas (2014), "How Likely Is It That the European Union will Disintegrate? A Critical Analysis of Competing Theoretical Perspectives", *European Journal of International Relations*, 20 (2): 341–365.

Webber, Douglas (2018), *European Disintegration? The Politics of Crisis in* the European Union, London: Palgrave.

Wessels, Wolfgang (2016), *The European Council*, London: Palgrave.

White, Jonathan (2015a), "Authority after Emergency Rule", *Modern Law Review*, 78 (4): 585–610.

White, Jonathan (2015b), "Emergency Europe", *Political Studies*, 63 (2): 300–318.

Zielonka, Jan (2014), *Is the EU Doomed?*, Cambridge: Polity Press.

2

THE INSTITUTIONAL MAKE-UP OF EUROPE'S SEGMENTED POLITICAL ORDER

John Erik Fossum

I Introduction

The European Union (hereinafter EU) has gone through a very tumultuous decade. The financial crisis struck in 2008 and morphed into a major fiscal crisis that sent tremors through the Eurozone. These tremors were amplified by the refugee issue and the political instability on Europe's frontiers, the uncertainties raised by Brexit, a more aggressive and assertive Russia and Donald Trump's hostile and erratic behaviour, associated with a pan-European "new" nationalist or ethnic nationalist reaction powered by the scepticism of supranational and transnational political and economic arrangements.

The apparent accumulation of crises and challenges seemed to be taking the EU close to breaking point. Today, given that the most ominous projections have not materialised, attention has shifted to the EU's long-term sustainability. The EU has raised the issue of its future development and resilience to the top of the political agenda. In connection with the 60th anniversary of the Treaty of Rome, the European Commission, on 1 March 2017, issued a "White Paper on the Future of Europe." The White Paper presented and assessed the main challenges facing the EU, explicitly recognising that "Europe's challenges show no sign of abating." This is despite the many measures that both the EU and the Member States have instituted thus far to address the said challenges. The White Paper outlined five different scenarios for how the EU-27 would look by 2025.[1]

The scenarios include options involving both less and more integration. Several of the scenarios envisage an increasingly differentiated EU, but one mainly achieved through the Member States integrating at different speeds (eventually reaching the same destination). How suitable these options are for the present-day EU is, however, difficult to establish from the White Paper. The White Paper focuses on functions, but it does not discuss the structural arrangements that the various scenarios pre-suppose. Further, since the White Paper does not specify the nature of the present-day EU – in structural and institutional terms – it does not provide us with a benchmark for establishing how the present-day EU can arrive at any one of these scenarios.

The EU literature has come to recognise that it is no longer sufficient to discuss the situation in the present-day EU with reference to different *speeds* of coming together.[2] Given that some states seek lasting exemptions, that some states seek to reverse or to roll back integration, and that the United Kingdom (UK) is on its way to relinquishing its EU membership, the EU debate has widened and now focuses more on *differentiation*, a term that is open to developments in both directions, to wit, integration *and* disintegration.

As we note in Chapter 1, the question is whether increased differentiation aptly captures the core features of the EU that have emerged from the polycrises. We noted that the EU post-crises presents us with a paradox: we tend to think of increased differentiation as increased structural pluralism, a structural pluralism that comes with a greater plurality of values and world views. The EU's reaction to the US-originated financial crisis was marked by cognitive closure and a dogged determination to adhere to a neoliberal austerity policy that forecloses the pursuit of any and all other values, policies and socio-economic arrangements (Blyth, 2015). We therefore need a conceptual apparatus that is capable of capturing both of these trends: increased structural pluralism (including opt-outs and opt-ins, exemptions, derogations, *etc.*), and cognitive closure. The term that we have settled for is *segmented political order*. The purpose of this chapter is to discuss the assertion that the EU post-crises is a fledgling segmented order. The chapter does so with explicit reference to the EU's institutional and structural composition.

In the following, I briefly re-visit what we mean by a segmented political order, and thereafter hold the EU up against the criteria that we presented in Chapter 1. In the subsequent sections, I discuss the logic underpinning segmentation against the logic underpinning differentiation in order to show not only where they differ, but also where they converge. The final section concludes.

II What does a segmented political order look like?

In Chapter 1, we listed six sets of traits that help us to spell out the distinctive features of a segmented political order. First is an entrenched set of ideas and ideologies that limits the search for alternatives and fosters cognitive closure. A second trait pertains to a particular (limited, narrow or strongly biased) configuration of policy instruments that contributes to lock-in forms of cognitive closure. Such a configuration typically makes up a distinct policy style (for this term, see Richardson, 1982). Third is an institutional configuration with a significant built-in bias, in the sense of locking-in certain ways of framing issues, and approaches for handling issues and conflicts. It systematically "organises in" certain ideas and ideologies and systematically "organises out" alternatives.

Fourth are significant built-in constraints that limit the scope for action and serve to entrench biases. Fifth are patterns of external dependence and vulnerability. Sixth, and finally, is that the system is biased, in that it has far weaker de-segmenting arrangements than a democratic state would have. A core trait of a segmented political order is that it is *highly imbalanced*: it is a system wherein those bodies and arrangements that we associate with segmentation are systematically more pronounced than the types of bodies and arrangements that we associate with de-segmentation.

Segment is a term that is familiar to a range of academic disciplines (sociology, economics and political science).[3] The type of *systematic selection bias* that we associate with a segment is a form of closure: it means, on the one hand, that actors confine their search for solutions to a very narrow range of familiar options, and, on the other, that the search is limited to options that the participants in the segment will readily endorse (anticipated action). Hence, in line with **Trait 1** identified here, the actors within a segment systematically exclude alternative ways of understanding problems, and shut out alternative types of expertise, alternative policy instruments and alternative solutions. When confronting problems, they are prone to close their minds to alternative institutional arrangements.

A segment consists of like-minded or similar-thinking people within a given functional sphere. As such, we think of segments as meso-level phenomena, not as a macro-level or political-system-defining feature. In Norway, for instance, it was common to talk about an agricultural segment;[4] in other systems, such as the United States (US), there was much talk about "iron triangles."[5] If we then shift to the macro-political level, we would assume that a fullyfledged segmented political order would not simply be composed of one, but of a range of different segments. Why would that be? Because our political imagination is shaped by our experience with the modern sovereign state, which, at least in principle, is based upon the notion of functional-territorial contiguity – the presumption that the state is in charge of *all* functional spheres within its territory. Such a broad and encompassing scope of state presence, it is important to underline, is a modern phenomenon. As Charles Tilly (1993) reminds us, pre-modern political systems were all somewhat segmented, albeit to different degrees, and some could consist of a single segment only.[6] A segmented political order that is not a state may therefore consist of one or several segments; the number depends on its functional reach and complexity.

The fact that, to date, we have tended to discuss segments as meso-level features within particular sectors of states, not as defining features of the political system or polity, as such, is therefore very much a modern phenomenon and is associated with the development of the modern democratic nation-state. Modern democratic states cannot be labelled as segmented political orders, because their segmental features are not sufficiently pronounced, and because they are equipped with strong de-segmenting arrangements and bodies. Thus, a *segmented political order* must naturally diverge from – be less institutionally and constitutionally developed than – a modern democratic state. It would be structurally biased, in the sense that it would contain particularly weak de-segmenting features.

A segment is functionally de-limited and embedded in a distinct set of material practices and symbolic constructions, which suggests that there may be some affinity between *segment* and *institutional logic*. The latter is a term that we can trace back to Friedland and Alford (1991). In the most comprehensive elaboration of the term to date, it is noted that

> (i)nstitutional logics represent frames of reference that condition actors' choices for sensemaking, the vocabulary they use to motivate action, and their sense of self and identity. The principles, practices, and symbols of each institutional order differentially shape how reasoning takes place and how rationality is perceived and experienced.
>
> *(Thornton et al., 2012: 2)*

Institutional logics are associated with such broad institutional orders as capitalism, the state, the family, religion and professions. Segments represent narrow renditions of such frames of reference, devices for sensemaking and cues to directing thought and action. Segments are network based, self-limiting and fragile. It is only under particular institutional circumstances that we can talk about a segmented political order.

A segment is never confined to any one single institution; it typically cuts across institutions, including various *types* of institutional arrangements (such as government ministries, government agencies, interest organisations and research institutes) and is occupied by like-minded people in the relevant functional sphere that defines the segment. Segments are very fragile – unless they are sustained by favourable institutional and structural arrangements and policy instruments.

With regard to **Trait 2**, that of policy instruments, as we note in Chapter 1, it is not possible to single out a specific type of policy instrument and claim that it somehow reflects or helps to sustain a given segment. Nevertheless, it is quite clear that certain policy styles or standard operating procedures and modes of legitimation are more conducive to segmentation than others. In this connection, it matters whether political systems can draw upon a wide range of policy instruments, or whether they only have access to a narrow range of them. Even if they have a wide range, it is important to know whether it is easy or not to switch between them, and to use one policy instrument to compensate for the negative effects of another. For instance, a polity that relies only on regulation and has no recourse to financial means and incentives has a limited ability to recompense for the distributive effects of the regulations; hence, it is likely to suffer from legitimacy shortfalls.

Trait 3 pertains to a set of organisational and procedural arrangements that sustains the segmental logic(s). This, in turn, raises two questions: whether a segment is associated with a distinct type of organisation/institution, or to put it more precisely, a) that there are certain types of institutions that will ensure segmental closure and others that will not; and b) whether a segment makes up a particular configuration of institutions. On the first question, the answer is yes, in so far as the segment includes those types of institutions that sustain a systematic selection bias. Institutions that are systematically open to various ways of framing issues, types of expertise, *etc.*, do *not* serve segmentation. Parliaments, for instance, are institutions that can pry open networks or closed communities. On the second question, a segment is typically made up of a range of organisations which are linked together and which *jointly* help to sustain a systematic selection bias. A segment is thus composed of a collection of organisations, all of which are imbued with a significant and well-entrenched cognitive bias so that this system of organisations will systematically *organise in* certain ways of understanding issues and systematically *organise out* alternatives.

A process of segmentation unfolds as a process of increasing segmental closure: the segmental logic becomes more pronounced, and the arrangements that sustain it become solidified or more entrenched. This may happen either because the political system is less developed than a state and/or there is a relative weakening of those institutional arrangements that serve as countervailing forces or that keep structures open to various frames, situational depictions and approaches to the handling of issues.

These observations have bearings on **Trait 4**, namely, that a segmented political order is fundamentally *constrained*. As Charles Tilly (1993) has underlined, pre-modern segmented political orders lack the magnitude, breadth of scope and type(s) of access to resources that mark modern democratic states. In addition, they lack the depth of citizens' support and allegiance that mark modern nation-states. Thus, when we talk about segmented political orders being constrained, we refer to both material and immaterial types and forms of constraints.

Further, as noted in Chapter 1, a segmented political order does not need to be similar or similarly institutionally anchored across the different segments; segments may vary in terms of the nature and scope of their material and immaterial constraints. Segments cut across levels of governing and, as such, a segmented political order is neither consistent with intergovernmental nor with supranational principles and arrangements. As we will see in the EU context, a segmented political order is more likely to *combine* supranational and intergovernmental principles and arrangements, with the different segments embodying different mixes.[7]

Trait 5 of a segmented political order we have labelled *external dependence*. This again relates back to the fact that a segmented political order is not a state; it lacks the size, scope and access to resources that are available to the modern state, and is therefore more dependent on factors and forces in the external world, such as other states and (global) markets.

Trait 6 is that a segmented political order is *biased*. As noted here, there are two main reasons for why such a bias emerges. One is that the political system is less developed or integrated than that of a modern democratic state; the other is that it has side-lined, weakened or undermined de-segmenting arrangements.

Turning back to the question of whether there are certain types of institutions that are particularly conducive to segmentation, we can reverse this and ask whether there are certain types of institutions that are particularly conducive to de-segmentation or which might prevent segmentation from occurring in the first place. The most obvious candidates are parliaments (and, to some extent, catch-all parties), ombudsman arrangements and other rules and procedures to ensure transparency and due process, as well as courts and legal-constitutional arrangements, insofar as they are specifically tailored to protect citizens from undue (autonomy-weakening/undermining) influences, as well as empowering citizens to hold the governing institutions accountable.

With regard to de-segmenting institutional arrangements, the relevant yardstick is a) whether they prevent or undo systematic selection bias in terms of frames, expertise, realms of possible solutions and policy and institutional arrangements through espousing a plurality of political views and values; and b) whether they are capable of prodding open institutions and networks through requirements for openness, transparency and participation. Finally, there is the question of whether they are properly attuned to accountability (providing accounts) and justification.

To sum up thus far, from a governing perspective, a segmented political order is imbued with a range of pathologies. Pathologies stem from cognitive bias, as a reinforced and entrenched form of trained incapacity, from the distinctive forms of opening and closure that mark each segment and from the fact that a segmented system generates distinct learning and decision pathologies. Each participating organisation in a segment will open itself up to *and systematically favour* certain networked relations, which privilege certain participants, certain forms of professional expertise, certain world views and ideologies and certain situational depictions. Each segment is closed; it defines away or excludes alternative world views, forms of expertise, situational depictions or frames and ideas and participants. Pathologies pertain to lack of co-ordination, systematic biases in problem conceptions that produce sub-optimal outcomes, and various legitimacy fallouts pertaining to exclusion and alienation.

III The EU – a fledgling segmented political order?

In what sense is it meaningful to discuss the EU as a segmented political order? What aspects of the EU should we refer to when discussing the EU under the heading of segmentation? The thesis that I will propound here is that the EU's response to the poly-crises facing it has further served to entrench two segments, found respectively in the EU's internal market and especially in the Eurozone, as well as in the area of border protection and control of immigration. As noted above, segmented political orders may come about through original design – with a built-in bias from the outset – or they may experience increased segmentation due to crises, ruptures or upsets. The story of the EU contains a mixture of both of these elements. The EU was explicitly barred from becoming a state through clear constraints on integration in "core state powers" such as military defence, police and taxation.[8] Further, the main drivers of integration were executives and experts, and democratisation was a matter of "catching up" with these (Crum and Fossum, 2013). Nevertheless, the EU had, over time, developed important de-segmenting arrangements. However, the poly-crises of the last decade or so have led to an EU mutation that has, on the one hand, reinforced built-in biases in a segmenting direction, and, on the other, weakened and/or side-lined the de-segmenting bodies/arrangements. In the following, I will spell out what this entails with explicit reference to the six traits of segmented political order that I have outlined. This chapter's main emphasis is on the institutional dimension. Hence, I pay particular attention to Traits 3–6.

Trait 1: Ideas and ideologies

The first type of cognitive bias and ideological component pertains to the EU's strong market orientation. Marija Bartl refers to this as "internal market rationality" and presents it as

> a specific pattern of political action in the field of internal market, which has emerged gradually due to the confluence of three main factors: first, the EU's functional institutional design; second, the processes of post-national juridification; and third, a more contingent influence of ideas. In the interplay of those three factors, the interpretation of internal market has become overdetermined, restricting thereby the space of (democratic) politics in its regulation.
>
> *(Bartl, 2015: 572)*

Clearly, Bartl combines cognitive and institutional factors in this definition. The EU's strong market-rational imprint is clearly something that emerged well before the crises. Agustín José Menéndez (2013) traces this back to at least the late 1970s, and Dieter Grimm (2015) notes that the EU's present state of over-constitutionalisation can be traced all the way back to the European Court of Justice's (CJEU) watershed *Van Gend & Loos* [1963] and *Costa* v. *ENEL* [1964] rulings. In a similar manner, Turkuler Isiksel (2016) underlines the deep roots of Europe's distinct functional constitution, a mode of constitutionalism that highlights economic integration and technocratic governance.

Market rationality is clearly a form of bias, but its defining feature in the EU context has been its *expansive dynamic*: more and more functional realms have been subsumed under the market logic. It is therefore difficult to associate market rationality with segmentation *per se*. Market rationality has clear traits of a distinct institutional logic, which, as has been pointed out here, is a far broader and more encompassing notion of bias than segmentation, which brings up the question of what precisely is the segmental logic that has emerged in the EU's internal market realm.

In order to obtain a clearer understanding of the segmental logic, we need to focus on the EU's orientation to the Eurozone crisis, which was motivated by particular economic doctrines that systematically selected in certain crisis action handling repertoires, notably of a neoliberal bent and that simultaneously systematically excluded (after the initial fiscal stimulus) Keynesian-type action repertoires. Cathrine Holst and Anders Molander (Chapter 4 in this volume), in their survey of the literature, point to a range of competing accounts stressing

> particular epistemic communities of economists, powerful stakeholders and politicians relying dogmatically on these models, or on dogmatically sound models that are however applied selectively or mechanically, without a proper understanding of the models' assumptions and conditions.
>
> *(Holst and Molander, Chapter 4 in this volume, p. 78)*

More specifically, with reference to what they refer to as the illusion of convergence in the Eurozone, Tranøy and Swartz (2019) take as their point of departure the epistemic community centred on the European Central Bank (ECB) and

> expand the austerity argument by looking at the complementarities and interaction between the dominant economic ideology of the ECB and the German ordoliberal tradition. We connect it to the second, optimal currency area argument by showing how illusions of convergence animated both pre- and post-crisis causal processes: convergence between economic theories favouring a system of rules applicable under all conditions to all societies, and an imagined convergence in the actual operation of the EU's various national and regional economies. Put simply, intellectual convergence around a flawed set of economic ideas continuously blinded EU policymakers to dangerous divergences in the real economy. A system of uniform rules and rule-based policies could not be applied effectively to a variegated continental economy, either in the boom-phase from 2001 to 2008, or after the financial and fiscal crises had set in and created even more divergence.
>
> *(Tranøy and Schwartz, Chapter 3 in this volume, p. 47–48)*

There are thus grounds for claiming that, in its approach to the crises, the EU has exacerbated and brought together certain intellectual ideas and frames that were not only already present but furthermore quite well entrenched in various parts of the EU.

The second type of bias and ideological component has its roots in state sovereignty, which is *the* constitutive principle of statehood, the modern state system and international society (Jackson, 2000; 2007). Robert Jackson underlines that there is a "common code of conduct which statespeople are called on to observe … because of reason of state" (2000: 24). We may think of this as a set of guidelines for appropriate action in the interstate realm,[9] combined with an explicit commitment to the promotion of the national interest and national security.

On the face of it, and given that the EU is not a state, it might seem strange to list this as an important cognitive bias in the EU context. The reasons have to do with the strong Member State presence in the EU and the manner in which states have imposed important constraints on supranational integration, as well as with the manner in which the EU pools and shares, rather than transcends, state sovereignty (Keohane, 2002). What Robert Jackson (2000) terms the "ethics of statecraft" is therefore well entrenched in the EU and shapes, conditions and constrains much of what is going on in the multilevel configuration that makes up the EU. As will be further developed here, the Member States have a strong direct presence in many of the EU's institutional arrangements, in particular, in the intergovernmental arrangements. This matters because these institutional arrangements are explicitly populated by "statespeople." The Council configuration is a case in point. As Frank Häge (2013) underlines, the Council's composition is one in which "bureaucrats are lawmakers," in the sense that its working groups are made up of diplomats and bureaucrats.

Statespeople share certain frames of reference, which, in turn, shape and condition how they understand the world, how they depict the world and how they understand themselves as state officials (the role expectations that they and others hold). From this, we cannot infer that they will all behave in the same manner, but there may be certain special circumstances when some aspect of this logic is triggered that will consolidate action in certain distinct directions.

This highly contingent action-generating effect reflects the fact that state sovereignty and the norms of appropriate behaviour for statespeople refer to the institutional logic of the state, and it is a much broader, more encompassing logic than the logic that informs a segment, as such. However, as was the case with market rationality, we can single out a more explicit segmental logic, which, in the EU post-crises context, could be termed *securitisation*, or a propensity to think of issues and concerns as matters of security first and foremost. An important aspect of the exercise of state sovereignty has to do with border maintenance and border controls. A securitisation logic invests in this a specific element of fear and uncertainty. As Jef Huysmans has noted, "security practices … turn an issue like migration into a security problem by mobilizing specific institutions and practices." (2000: 757) He goes on to note how securitisation has affected the migration field:

> (i)t affects the way in which migration is rendered problematic when the police and the related departments in the Ministry of Home Affairs take a prominent role in the regulation of migration. For the police it is part of their profession to produce security knowledge. They have a professional disposition to represent and categorize a policy concern in a security discourse and to propose security measures to deal with it.
>
> *(Ibid., 757)*

When all the professions involved in matters related to border controls and aspects related to migration come to share the same situational depiction, namely, that migrants are a security risk, there is a mutually reinforcing pattern and process of securitisation.

Such a sovereignty-cum-security logic has become far more pronounced in connection with the so-called refugee crisis and the constraints facing the EU in seeking to handle it. The refugee crisis was re-defined from an initial focus on the humanitarian aspects of refugee suffering and the need for solidarity to the concerns of states with borders and terrorist threats (Lazaridis and Wadia, 2015). When the main concerns of statespeople revolve around perceptions of immigrants as potential threats and the emphasis is on surveillance, border checks and controls; when these become the dominant concerns that crowd out other ones, such as human rights and solidarity; when there is a proliferation of specific security officials and professions; and when all of these factors come together to form a sustained decision bias that is supported by a range of networked organisations, we are talking about a process of segmentation. An "emergency mentality" (White, 2015a; 2015b) serves as a further impetus for segmentation in the sense that it facilitates the links between notions of crises as systemic threats with concerns for security.

Trait 2: Policy instruments and policy style

As a complex multilevel political system, the EU contains a wide range of policy approaches and policy styles, which differ considerably from one Member State to the next. There are, however, grounds for arguing that the EU *has* nonetheless developed a distinct policy style at EU level. Analysts have long underlined that the EU's core realm of action lies in the field of regulation,[10] especially in the field of internal market, which is the EU's core realm of action. The EU has very limited fiscal capacity, not least since the EU's own share of total spending is so limited, less than 1 per cent of the gross national income of the EU's Member States.[11] The EU's policy style is therefore strongly lopsided, where the emphasis is on regulation, not on re-distribution. Further, the EU's policy style relies heavily upon the mobilisation and activation of expertise, as is readily apparent in the system of Comitology. The EU has also developed tight bonds to a broad range of interest-groups as a vital element of legitimation. Reflecting on the democratic implications, Jeremy Richardson has recently noted that

> the close integration of interest groups into Commission deliberations might have had the perverse effect of distancing the Commission from broader public opinion.
>
> *(Richardson, 2018: 122)*

The crises of the last decade or so have had implications for the EU's policy style, which has

> to some degree gradually shifted from a consensus based process of policy formation (that is a process of consensus formation within the European

> elite) towards a more coercive, top–down policy style. EU policy formu-
> lation is characterised by bargaining and consensus, but there is often a
> mailed fist within that velvet glove subsequently to enforce that consensus.
>
> *(Ibid.: 124)*

The nature, range and built-in biases in the EU's policy measures give credence to the segmentation thesis. This has to do with the fact that policy-making and the distinct features of a political system's policy style have clear bearings on that system's institutional structure; in other words, we should expect biases in policy-making to have bearings on structural arrangements.[12] This works the other way as well: the institutional structure has profound bearings on the process and substance of policy-making.

Trait 3: Institutional and structural arrangements

The issue which we need to consider with regard to whether the EU's institutional make-up helps to constitute the EU as a segmented political order is not only whether a market bias mixed up with a neoliberal austerity mindset and a sovereignty-cum-securitisation bias are entrenched in institutions that systematically favour these modes of thinking and expel alternative logics, but also whether segmentation is a defining feature of the EU as a political order. We have already seen that, well before the crises struck in 2008, within the supranational Community, the EU institutions embodied a strong focus on market-making/entrenchment (this is also, in some sense, an extension of Fritz Scharpf's [2010] line of reasoning) which serves as a unifying strait-jacket and organises in those aspects of the world that fit with these pre-dispositions and *organises out* or excludes all others as dissonant voices.[13] In a similar manner, securitisation was present well before the crises struck, but was clearly amplified by the crises, especially by the refugee crisis.

An important reason why it makes sense to talk about the EU as a segmented political order stems from the fact that the two segmental logics correspond roughly to the two tracks of the EU's institutional structure. We find one track in the *supranational Community component*, which we may, broadly speaking, refer to as supranational (expert-based) regulation. The other is in the *intergovernmental component* (mainly associated with the Council and the European Council), and relies on intergovernmental interaction and bargaining.[14] These are institutionally and functionally divided. The argument then is that, along each of these tracks, we find a process of segmental closure.

The first and main track is associated with the so-called Community Method, which is based upon an independent European Commission with the exclusive right to present legislative and policy proposals; these are adopted by the European Parliament (EP) and the Council, and the European Court of Justice (CJEU) maintains the institutional balance (Majone, 2005: 44). It is situated in a unipolar federal structure (with some semblance to the German federal system) that issues authoritative commands. The system rests on the core principle that underpins the Community architecture, namely, that action addressed to common problems entails the adoption of action norms that have been decided in common upon the basis of legislative input from the Commission, and these are to be uniformly applied to all the Member States. The doctrines of supremacy and direct effect are meant to ensure that these are encoded or transformed into the legal arrangements of the Member States.

Over time, another track has emerged that is imbricated in the Community structure but operates according to a distinct decision-making procedure, which we may term the *Union Method*. We may think of this track as being composed of arrangements that foster "binding interstate co-operation without supranational submission." In this way, Member States, notably through the European Council (established in 1974), seek to co-ordinate action in particularly sensitive issue areas (such as, for instance, common foreign, security and defence policy and fiscal policy) but without transferring final decision-making authority to the institutions at the EU level (through the Community Method).

The European Council has its roots in intergovernmental summitry, and is a French idea with Gaullist roots which go back to Michel Debré's 1953 plan for political union based in a Conference of Heads of Government (Werts, 2008: 199). The European Council is made up of the heads of state and government of the EU and is charged with the responsibility of charting the Union's future direction (Wessels, 2016). The Treaty of Lisbon strengthens the European Council as an EU executive body through a full-time and more permanent European Council President and an accompanying support structure. Proponents of the so-called New Intergovernmentalism argue that the EU post-Maastricht has experienced an integration paradox, in the sense that the EU's realm of action has expanded, but that this has taken place in the absence of a commensurate transfer of powers and competences to the EU's supranational institutions (Bickerton et al., 2015). This is an important observation, although it underestimates the EU's two-track nature, and, in particular, the important fusion of levels – EU and Member State – which marks the EU.

In order to understand the situation as one of increased segmental closure, we need to look more closely at the process of integration and those features of the EU's institutional structure that would engender systematic selection biases. One set of factors stems from the nature and dynamics of the process of EU integration. A case in point is the manner in which the principle of mutual recognition has, over time, been transformed to a form of horizontally (functionally) unbounded marketisation. A critical turning-point was when "a ban on any product that was legally sold in any other Member State of the communities would, *prima facie*, constitute a disproportionate infringement on the constitutional principle of free movement of goods" (Menéndez, 2013: 479). Raising this principle to a standard of European constitutional law – which happened long before the crises struck – unleashed a significant process of integration, largely driven by private-sector actors and the interplay between private market actors and courts, notably the CJEU. This altered the equation for states, which needed to get exemptions from the EU rather than simply erecting national borders to the outside world. We thus see how one configuration of actors in the EU, within the Community system but which nonetheless cuts across the public–private divide, has been instrumental in fostering horizontal market harmonisation. Parliaments were typically on the side-lines of this dynamic process.

Supranational institutions and market actors were key drivers in this process of marketisation. What is remarkable is that this took place despite the fact that the EU is marked by an inordinately strong direct Member-State presence in the EU-level institutions.[15] This latter fact is even helping to produce a strong *fusion* of levels; in other words, the EU institutions are quite strongly embedded in the Member States, rather than making up a level of governance that is separate from the Member States.[16] The EU, however, is not a state, and the Member States have not transferred their sovereignty to the EU, but pool and share it in a set of EU-level institutions, which they fill with state executives, experts and administrators. This leads to a strong interweaving of levels, which includes the administrations of the Member States. The effect is that

> (t)he formerly closed national systems of public administration are broken up, divested of their operational independence, and fused into a transnational administrative conglomerate that provides an(imperfect) functional substitute to a centralized EU administration.
>
> *(Genschel and Jachtenfuchs, 2014: 253)[17]*

The EU's strong *onus* on regulation lends itself to such a process, as is underlined by Eva Heidbreder (2014), who refers to this as "regulation for national capacity building."

Institutionally speaking, we thus see that the EU combines *horizontal separation* (*of functional spheres*: the supranational Community *versus* the intergovernmental realm), with *vertical fusion* (*of levels*). This combination represents a unique form of differentiation, in the sense that functional spheres are horizontally separated and operated by different institutional arrangements, one with a strong supranational tenor, the other with a strong intergovernmental tenor (the two arrangements also somewhat overlap). This is combined with a strong vertical fusion of levels; in other words, the EU institutions are tightly interwoven with the Member States. This is why we underline that a segmented political order cuts across levels of governance rather than adhering to supranational or intergovernmental principles.[18]

How does this distinctive institutional configuration foster segmentation? It does this, on the one hand, by preventing or constraining horizontal co-ordination, market correction and fiscal stabilisation at EU level, because, as Fritz Scharpf (2010) has underlined, the EU decision procedures in the institutions bent on market-making are majoritarian, whereas the Member States can exercise a veto in those institutions bent on market correction and fiscal and tax harmonisation. On the other hand, the structure fosters segmentation by implicating national officials in EU-level decision-making and fusing levels of governing and administration. The combination of the specific institutional separation of tasks combined with the bringing together of executive and administrative officials across levels of governing are structural features of the EU that are conducive to segmentation, not least because these processes are removed from proper parliamentary oversight and control.

The institutionalisation of the Eurozone is a further instigator of EU segmentation. The Eurozone occupies a distinct space inside the two structural features of horizontal separation and vertical fusion, and it is very difficult for parliaments to control. Broadly speaking, monetary policy, which is an exclusive EU competence, is situated in the one supranational track, whereas fiscal policy is situated in the intergovernmental track. The supranational Monetary Union is thus backed up by a system of fiscal co-ordination that is organised along intergovernmental lines. The underlying idea is to locate de-politicised monetary policy in the supranational component, and politicised fiscal policy in the hands of the Member States. Conflicts and contentious issues are, so to speak, organised out of the supranational organisational realm and instead dealt with in the intergovernmental realm, where governments hammer out bargains on thorny and controversial issues. Monetary policy is based upon the notion that decisions are based upon expertise and therefore de-politicised (a highly problematical presumption, as the various contributions to this book underline). The fact of increasing fusion of levels reduces the scope for decisional exit and limits the possibilities for governments to come up with alternatives to the prevailing view on monetary policy and the prevailing ordo-cum-neo-liberal socio-economic model from which this emanates. In a context of fusion, all governments are co-responsible for decisions. This serves to reinforce such lock-ins.

The structure fosters segmentation in the sense that it is highly conducive to *organising in* or including certain forms of knowledge, expertise and policy solutions, and *organising out* and excluding others. Through horizontal separation, these are sheltered from political interference because monetary policy is institutionally sheltered. At the same time, through fusion, governments are reined in and made complicit in the policies that are pursued and in the decisions that are reached.

We thus see that the EU's structural make-up contains traits that are conducive to segmentation through the particular biases that they contain. The important point is that the Eurozone *crisis* has clearly reinforced segmentation. The crisis has reinforced the ties among the components that make up the distinct socio-economic policy stance that mark the Eurozone. Fiscal policy is increasingly co-ordinated across levels (and as such reflects an ever-greater pattern of fusion).[19]

In this situation, the scope for governments to pursue other policies is limited. Further, in dealing with its many crises and challenges, the EU has often resorted to intergovernmental means, with the European Council playing a central role through measures such as intergovernmental treaties (see the Treaty on Stability, Co-ordination and Governance in the Economic and Monetary Union) and informal intergovernmental bargains (notably between Germany and France). It should be noted that this does not necessarily entail the supranational institutions being side-lined or robbed of tasks. Aspects of the EU's supranational components have been strengthened, notably in the areas of macroeconomic policy and banking regulation, in which the roles of the European Commission and the ECB have been considerably enhanced (Dehousse, 2015). Nevertheless, in overall terms, what appears more likely is that the more informal (less legally regulated and constrained) intergovernmental approach that we witnessed in the crisis handling may re-programme the supranational structure and make it more attentive to the interests and views of certain core governments, especially Germany and its conception of how to deal with the crisis through a tough fiscal austerity policy with a neoliberal/ordoliberal orientation. This supports the notion of crisis-reinforced segmentation.

Trait 4: Constraints and limits on capacity

The fourth trait that we associate with a segmented political order pertains to constraints. This is an auxiliary factor; the fact that an entity is constrained does not – in itself – make it into a segmented political order. Only certain types of constraints and certain types of circumstances will foster segmentation.

The argument here is that both factors (types of constraints and specific circumstances) are relevant for the EU. As has been underlined here, the EU's institutional development has been marked by important constraints. The EU was, from the very outset, prevented from becoming a state by the strong built-in constraints on core state powers (military, policy, tax and fiscal). This, over time, has produced a curious paradox, wherein the EU has seen very little of the capacity-build-up that we find in all states. The EU is nevertheless a vital force in Europeanising the Member (and affiliated) States.[20] The EU's development is therefore a powerful story of circumventing such constraints, but with strong built-in biases: the strong reliance on a regulatory policy style and political and administrative fusion, both of which leave the Member States with a central role in effectuating EU action. This is most pronounced in the first track or the realm of the community system (which sees very little differentiation), and less so in the second track or the intergovernmental system where there is limited supranational integration, a lot of differentiation and weak democratic-constitutional controls, and where statespeople play a predominant role. The second segment, sovereignty-cum-securitisation, which is institutionally situated in the intergovernmental track, is therefore quite differently constituted and constrained from the first single-market based segment.

The EU is constrained in a material sense; it is also constrained in an ideational sense, in two respects. The first is that the Member States, as the EU's constituent units, have never agreed on a common normative script for the EU;

in other words, they have never agreed on what type of entity it *really is* and what type of entity it *should be*. This would have been unproblematic if the EU had been an ordinary international organisation, but it amounts to a normative deficit when the Member States have conferred so many tasks on the EU. The second constraint is that the EU is institutionally barred from playing a significant socialising role. In this respect, the EU is very different from all nation-states, federal or not.

These material and ideational constraints leave the EU highly vulnerable to criticism, which right-wing Europhobes are exploiting to the full. This is made very explicit in Rafał Riedel's chapter on Poland, which, together with Hungary in particular, has embarked on a major onslaught on constitutional democracy, with significant ramifications for the EU in general.

Trait 5: Dependence on external factors and patterns of external vulnerability

The fifth trait that we may associate with a segmented political order refers to vulnerability and dependence on external factors. As was the case with Trait 4, this is not a defining feature as such, but will, under certain circumstances, foster segmentation. With regard to the first segment, the financial crisis showed that the EU's socio-economic structure and built-in imbalance – monetary union without an attendant fiscal union – rendered it highly dependent on volatile international markets. This dependence on external factors was evident in the crisis responses, especially in the EU's reliance on the International Monetary Fund (IMF) in the bailout of the EU's Member States. The central crisis handling role of the *Troika* (the European Commission, the European Central Bank and the IMF) is a case in point. This type of dependence ensures that market-based imperatives play a central role in the considerations of EU decision-makers, and, as such, helps to entrench the market-based segment, especially in so far as the criteria and conditions are, broadly speaking, aligned with a neoliberal austerity policy.

The EU has also faced a significant external vulnerability and subsequent dependence in the other segment. The EU's high level of vulnerability stems from the fact that it borders on such a large number of states, not least states that are weak or dysfunctional or deeply oppressive. The EU's contrast with the US, which has only two neighbours, and friendly ones to boot, is quite instructive.

In the area of immigration and border controls, the EU's vulnerability has been turned into structural dependence on Turkey for regulating the inflow of migrants to Europe. The EU–Turkey agreement has been widely criticised and fosters segmentation in the sense that the EU has not only taken active measures to exclude migrants, but is also excluding them from European law (Spijkerboer, 2017). Whether intended or not, the effect is for the securitisation logic to crowd out humanitarian considerations across a broad range of institutions.

Trait 6: Weak de-segmentating arrangements

The final trait of a segmented political order refers to its imbalanced nature, in the sense that the institutions and arrangements that foster and sustain segmentation are systematically more developed than those institutions and arrangements that can ensure de-segmentation. In this regard, the EU has built-in constraints, in the sense that its de-segmenting features have consistently fallen short of those we find in democratic states. With regard to the EP, for instance, the EU's two-tracked structure generates a discrepancy between the EP's realm of effective legislative and controlling action, and the realm of tasks that are actually undertaken at EU level by EU institutions. This is, if anything, amplified by the fusion of levels, which greatly complicates accountability relations. Further, the EP is structurally constrained. Emerging from very modest beginnings, the EP has constantly sought to balance the need for expanding its realm of action (which depends on good relations with the executive) with holding the executive accountable (which requires putting its collective foot down and curtailing the executive). This is a very difficult balancing act.

With the crises, we see a clear weakening of democratic systems of monitoring and control at all three key levels: EU, Member State and regional. Thus, those institutions that could open up and foster de-segmentation are weakened. National parliaments have seen their fiscal sovereignty severely constrained, and the EP has not been given powers to fill the gap (Fasone, 2014a; 2014b). The EP, side-lined, at least in part, in the crisis response, has been one of the main losers, and the crisis response has reinforced technocracy, in the sense that experts have obtained a freer role and are less encumbered by legal and democratic controls. An important hallmark of this system has been summed up in *the new informality*: far more is now settled in bargains among leaders and officials; less is subjected to proper, transparent procedures.

It is also well recognised that the crises have spurred de-constitutionalisation (Menéndez, 2013), amidst profound concerns about a general weakening of the legal basis for integration (Joerges, 2014), both of which spur segmentation because the formal mechanisms for prompting de-segmentation are weakened and because of weakened "polity accountability." When the system of normative standards is in flux and this is coupled with secrecy and informality, efforts to break out of segments are more difficult to fashion because critics will be less likely to agree on the appropriate normative standards and courses of action.

To sum up thus far, the EU post-crises has clear traits of a segmented political order. The two prevailing segmental logics are a marketisation logic infused with a neoliberal/ordoliberal twist, and a sovereignty-cum-securitisation logic. The segmental logics are embedded in institutional arrangements that reinforce and sustain these cognitive and decision biases through the EU's distinct institutional configuration, which combines a two-tracked institutional structure (horizontal differentiation) combined with a lopsided process of the fusion of levels of governing (which occurs under both tracks, albeit differently).

IV The different logics of differentiation and segmentation

In the EU context, the distinction between differentiation and segmentation becomes more apparent if we try to understand some of the mechanisms that drive each of them. The account thus far suggests that segmentation occurs as a consequence of a broad range of mechanisms, including bargaining and rule-following. In this last section, I will try to tease out the differences between differentiation and segmentation by focusing on the different approaches to learning, adaptation and change that underpin each of them. For this, it is useful to draw on the important distinction that March and Olsen (1995; March, 1991) made between exploration and exploitation. *Exploration* refers to risk-taking, experimentation, flexibility, discovery and innovation. It is important to underline that exploration is not the same as experiential learning; we do not need to presume that pleas for exceptions, insistences on the need for the EU to develop and apply its rules flexibly and pleas for experimentation are necessarily powered by a rational problem orientation. *Exploitation* refers to "refinement, choice, production, efficiency, selection, implementation, execution." (March, 1991: 71; see, also, March and Olsen, 1995, Chap. 6). Exploitation is a type of search for solutions that operate very close to known alternatives. It seeks to apply solutions that are known and tried out. If the experience with established practice is favourable, then actors will be induced to repeat the performance because of efficiency considerations.

The EU literature generally situates differentiated integration under the rubric of exploration, because it focuses on variation (in terms of deviations from the established rules, regulations, institutional arrangements and policy orientations).[21] In the EU context, measures associated with differentiated integration are often introduced to alleviate political conflicts or to untie some sort of knot. They are, more often than not, responses to contingencies.

Segmentation is much more directly linked to what March and Olsen have labelled as "exploitation," but with clear pathological features. Such pathological features must be related to how integration has unfolded over time. The development of the EU towards a segmented political order has accelerated through the crises but has roots in the manner in which the EU has been integrating over time. The underlying structural bias is a *learner lock-in* and an over-propensity to exploit known alternatives (in the EU's case, market-making as one such key trait), rather than to explore new ones (market correcting or how market-making can be harmonised with market-correcting devices). The lock-in reinforces this over time so that the organisation or system falls out of step with a changing environment. The Euro crisis has exposed how the EU process of integration pre-crisis had become increasingly stuck in what March and Olsen (1995) refer to as a "competency trap" or *learner lock-in*, which

> is the consequence of mutual local positive feedback between experience and competence. Having competence with an activity leads to success,

which leads to more experience with the activity, which leads to greater competence. A learner becomes better and better at one technology while doing it more and more and being continually successful. This positive local feedback quickly pushes the learner into a competency lock-in, where efficiency in using one alternative ... makes trying other alternatives unlikely. This in turn makes it unlikely that the learner will accumulate the experience necessary with other alternatives to realize their potential.

(March and Olsen, 1995: 216)[22]

The lock-in reinforces this over time so that the organisation or system falls out of step with the changing environment, thus rendering it particularly exposed to crises as shocks or sudden ruptures. In the case of the EU, the clearest manifestation of this was the great gap between monetary and fiscal union. The competency trap had helped to generate significant progress and competence in market-making, whilst, at the same time, engendering very limited success in market-regulation.

This biased process of self-referential learning helps to account, on the one hand, for the EU's rapid and dynamic process of integration, and, on the other, for how the EU had, over time, accumulated a number of serious structural flaws that were exposed and exacerbated through the crisis. The institutional features that were outlined above help to account for the lock-in, not least the process of the fusion of levels of governing, which prevents exit. This fusion of levels reinforces the tendency to saddle the EU with a broad range of tasks, but the horizontal separation effectively deprives the EU of the proper means to deliver on these tasks. This becomes problematical precisely because the system's ability to handle shocks and conflicts is limited. The EU's distinct regulatory policy style and the capacity constraints help to reinforce the type of path-dependent learning that marks a competency trap.

Another reading of the EU's crises responses is the "failing forward" argument that was set forth by Eric Jones et al., who note that

Intergovernmental bargaining leads to incompleteness because it forces states with diverse preferences to settle on lowest common denominator solutions. Incompleteness then unleashes forces that lead to crisis. Member states respond by again agreeing to lowest common denominator solutions, which address the crisis and lead to deeper integration. To date, this sequential cycle of piecemeal reform, followed by policy failure, followed by further reform, has managed to sustain both the European project and the common currency. However, this approach entails clear risks. Economically, the policy failures engendered by this incremental approach to the construction of EMU have been catastrophic for the citizens of many crisis-plagued member states. Politically, the perception that the EU is constantly in crisis and in need of reforms to salvage the union is undermining popular support for European integration.

(Jones et al., 2016: 1010)

The competency trap and the failing forward argument both refer to different actor constellations: the former highlights the developments within the Community system, the latter the developments and dynamics in the intergovernmental realm. The two processes are driven by different logics – biased learning *versus* bargaining – but they complement each other by adding up to increased segmentation.

A segmented system is less susceptible to legal rule and predictable patterns of interaction among states and other actors, and more sensitive to relations of power. As segmentation proceeds the weakening of central co-ordination shifts political dynamics from the political centre to the Member States, with individual Member States and/or groups of Member States seeking to re-organise their relations to the EU institutions and among themselves.

The result is likely to be a far more unwieldy EU, with significant issues of co-ordination and coherence. Questions of whether the centre will hold will continue to arise. Key challenges pertain to ensuring adequate governing and co-ordination capabilities, on the one hand, and democratic legitimacy through popular authorisation and accountability, on the other.

V Conclusion

The purpose of this chapter was to assess whether the EU post-crises shows traits that warrant the label of "segmented political order," with reference to the six defining features or traits of segmented political order that we presented in Chapter 1. The emphasis in this chapter has been on the institutional and structural traits, even though the chapter discusses all six features. *Segment* is a term that is familiar across a broad range of social-science disciplines but has, within the context of the modern democratic state, been discussed as a trait of a specific policy area or functional realm, not as a core constitutive feature of the political order. In today's globalised world, where states and societies are tightly interwoven, states undergo important changes; the EU is the most important new form of political co-operation that has thus far emerged to date. Segmented political orders as political systems that fall short of statehood and embody significant imbalances (in comparison to democratic states) may result from the unwillingness of the Member States to commit themselves fully to a supranational union or from crises-induced mutations. The post-crises European Union, as this chapter has shown, results from both.

The assessment of the EU against the six traits has shown that we could discern two segmental logics. In particular, the first of these was sustained by the EU's distinct policy style, which draws on regulation in lieu of state-type capacity-building, and, as such, renders the EU highly dependent on the Member States for effectuating its laws and regulations. Institutionally speaking, the EU is a two-tracked construct, with different built-in constraints on each track. This means that the EU exhibits a distinct combination of horizontal and vertical features, which serves to embed or entrench the two logics of segmentation.

The first supranational track favours the market-making and decision procedures that sustain this. The two-track structure constrains the scope for market correction and fiscal stabilisation at EU level. At the same time, national officials are directly involved in EU-level decision-making, as part of the manner in which the EU fuses the levels of governing and administration. The combination of the specific institutional separation of tasks combined with the bringing together of executive and administrative officials across levels of governing are structural features of the EU which are conducive to segmentation, not least because these processes are removed from proper parliamentary oversight and control. Thus, a core feature of segmented political orders is that they have elements of stateness, but they deviate in important respects from modern democratic states in that segmented political orders are highly imbalanced.

This chapter confirms the general argument of the book, to the effect that a segmented political order is a differentiated political order, albeit with certain distinctive traits. The chapter also shows that some of the mechanisms that propel segmentation are distinct from those that propel differentiation.

These observations have bearings on the debate on the EU's future. They suggest that an EU that continues to "muddle through" will continue down the path of segmentation. Many analysts and officials are concerned with embarking on major reforms. The implicit assumption is that, in today's volatile situation, this may mean slipping from a competency to an incompetency trap, which "is produced by a cycle in which failure leads to search, which leads to failure, which leads to more search" (March and Olsen, 1995: 215). The obvious fear is that a large-scale process of treaty change may end up in a high-stakes and ultimately destructive incompetency trap. At the same time, there is no assurance that muddling through might not also end up there.

The EU has shown resilience and is not without resources for reform. Resources can, however, most effectively be deployed when there is a precise diagnosis, and this has been the main aim of this book.

Notes

1 These scenarios were termed "carrying on; nothing but the single market; those who want to do more; doing less more efficiently; and doing much more together." (European Commission, 2017)

2 We have referred to this literature in Chapter 1. The most comprehensive account of differentiated integration to date remains Leuffen et al., (2013).

3 See, for instance, Olsen (1988); Picot (2012).

4 This was one of the important findings in the first Norwegian power survey. See Olsen (1978); NOU, 1982:3.

5 See, for instance, the discussion in Jordan (1981).

6 Tilly (1993) uses *segment* more loosely than we do in this book, but the basic idea of sectorally confined, de-limited and in comparison to modern states, confined entities is shared in common.

7 This combination is on the one hand a reflection of a distinctive European experience, where supranational integration was deemed necessary to prevent future wars

across the European continent, and on the other how in today's globalised context states and societies are tightly interwoven.

8　For the notion of core state powers in the EU context, see Genschel and Jachtenfuchs (2014).

9　For the logic of appropriateness, see March and Olsen (1989; 1995).

10　See, in particular, the works of Giandomenico Majone (1994) who sees clear parallels between the EU and a narrowly based regulatory state.

11　"National governments in the EU spend more than 50 times what the EU does through its budget", available at: https://ec.europa.eu/info/about-european-commission/eu-budget/how-it-works/fact-check_en.

12　This has at least since Theodore Lowi's seminal work been an important insight. A recent important reminder is found in Orren and Skowronek (2017).

13　This can also generate biased or incomplete copying of institutional arrangements from one setting to another. The EMU was an incomplete copy of the German *Bundesbank* model. "In economic terms … the macroeconomic steerings functions of the model had performed in Germany were not merely nullified but perverted at the European level." (Scharpf, 2016: 33)

14　For similar assessments of a two-tracked EU, see Fabbrini (2013; 2015). Note that the term "intergovernmental" is used descriptively here to refer to an institutional feature of the EU. This is how comparative federalism would understand it, and is different from how intergovernmentalism is conceptualised by IR, which considers it as a theory of (dis-) integration. See Fossum and Jachtenfuchs (2017).

15　That applies directly to the intergovernmental bodies such as the European Council and the Council formations; Member State imprint is also clearly visible on the Commission and the Court of Justice.

16　Fusion refers to a process of "merging public resources at several state levels, leading to increasing complexities, a lack of transparency and difficulties in reversing the development." (Wessels, 1997: 267)

17　For the manner in which EU Member States and closely associated non-members such as Norway have developed two-hatted national administrations, see Egeberg and Trondal (2015).

18　It is most likely a feature that is closely related to the manner in which political systems are closely interlinked in today's globalised world, especially in economic terms.

19　That is reflected in the emergence of what Mark Dawson has labelled the *Coordinative Method*: "EU economic decision-making is coordinative in that it is formed as a policy cycle based on a constant 'back and forth' between the EU and national levels … decision-making never crystallises into a 'once and for all' agreement but is ongoing and revisable with the possibility of norms being adapted to changed factual circumstances." (Dawson, 2015a: 53; see, also, 2015b).

20　Genschel and Jachtenfuchs (2014: 252) note that "(t)he most prominent difference between the EU and federal states concerns the instruments of integration. In the US and elsewhere, federal state-making proceeded mostly by capacity building, *i.e.*, by the creation of a federal army, a federal budget, federal taxes, and a federal administration (Skowronek, 1982). Except for a common currency, the EU lacks all these capacities. The European integration of core state powers proceeds mostly by regulation. EU capacity building is limited in size and functionality. It primarily serves to mobilize national core state powers for European purposes rather than to establish genuine European core state powers."

21　Differentiation is more encompassing than differentiated integration (Fossum, 2015). It covers both exploration and exploitation – copying/emulating established patterns of differentiation that we find in modern states and innovating by developing new forms or configuring existing ones in new ways.

22　For a brief application of this notion to the EU, see Fossum (2012).

References

Bartl, Marija (2015), "Internal Market Rationality, Private Law and the Direction of the Union: Resuscitating the Market as the Object of the Political", *European Law Journal*, 21 (5): 572–598.

Bickerton, Christopher J., Dermot Hodson, and Uwe Puetter (eds) (2015), *The New Intergovernmentalism: States and Supranational Actors in the Post-Maastricht Era*, Oxford: Oxford University Press.

Blyth, Mark (2015), *Austerity: The History of a Dangerous Idea*, Oxford: Oxford University Press.

Crum, Ben, and John Erik Fossum (eds) (2013), *Practices of Interparliamentary Coordination in International Politics: The European Union and Beyond*, Colchester: ECPR Press.

Dawson, Mark (2015a), "The Euro Crisis and Its Transformation of EU Law and Politics", in: Hertie School of Governance (eds), The Governance Report *2015*, Oxford: Oxford University Press, 2015, pp. 41–68.

Dawson, Mark (2015b), "The Legal and Political Accountability Structure of 'Post-Crisis' EU Economic Governance", *Journal of Common Market Studies*, 53 (5): 976–993.

Dehousse, Renaud (2015), "The New Supranationalism", Paper Prepared for Presentation at the ECPR General Conference, Montreal, 26–29 August 2015.

Egeberg, Morten, and Jarle Trondal (2015), "National Administrative Sovereignty: Under Pressure", in: Erik Oddvar Eriksen and John Erik Fossum (eds), *The European Union's Non-members: Independence Under Hegemony?*, London: Routledge, pp. 173–188.

European Commission (2017), "White Paper on the Future of Europe – Reflections and Scenarios for the EU27 by 2025", COM(2017)2025.

European Parliament (2016), "The European Council and Crisis Management – In-Depth Analysis", European Parliamentary Research Service, PE 573.283 February 2016.

Fabbrini, Sergio (2013), "Intergovernmentalism and Its Limits: Assessing the European Union's Answer to the Euro Crisis", *Comparative Political Studies*, XX (X): 1–27.

Fabbrini, Sergio (2015), *Which European Union? Europe after the Euro Crisis*, Cambridge: Cambridge University Press.

Fasone, Cristina (2014a), "Eurozone, Non-Eurozone and 'Troubled Asymmetries' among National Parliaments in the EU. Why and to What Extent This Is of Concern", *Perspectives on Federalism*, 6 (3): 1–41.

Fasone, Cristina (2014b), "European Economic Governance and Parliamentary Representation. What Place for the European Parliament?", *European Law Journal*, 20 (2): 164–185.

Fossum, John Erik (2012), "Reflections on Experimentalist Governance", *Regulation and Governance*, 6 (3): 394–400.

Fossum, John Erik (2015), "Democracy and Differentiation in Europe", *Journal of European Public Policy*, 22 (6): 799–815.

Fossum, John Erik, and Markus Jachtenfuchs (2017), "Federal Challenges and Challenges to Federalism. Insights from the EU and Federal States", *Journal of European Public Policy*, 24 (4): 467–485.

Friedland, Roger, and Robert Alford (1991), "Bringing Society Back In: Symbols, Practices and Institutional Contradictions", in: Walter W. Powell and Paul DiMaggio (eds), *The New Institutionalism in Organizational Analysis*, Chicago, IL: Chicago University Press, pp. 232–263.

Genschel, Philipp, and Markus Jachtenfuchs (2014), *Beyond the Regulatory Polity? The European Integration of Core State Powers*, Oxford: Oxford University Press.

Grimm, Dieter (2015), "The Democratic Costs of Constitutionalisation: The European Case", *European Law Journal*, 21 (4): 460–473.

Häge, Frank M. (2013), *Bureaucrats as Law-Makers: Committee Decision-making in the EU Council of Ministers*, London: Routledge.

Heidbreder, Eva (2014), "Regulating Capacity Building by Stealth: Pattern and Extent of EU Involvement in Public Administration", in: Philipp Genschel and Markus Jachtenfuchs, *Beyond the Regulatory Polity? The European Integration of Core State Powers*, Oxford: Oxford University Press, pp. 145–165.

Holst, Cathrine, and Anders Molander (2019), "Expert Accountability and EU Economic Reform Discourse", in: Jozef Bátora and John Erik Fossum (eds), *The EU Post-Crises: The Rise of a Segmented Political Order?*, Chapter 4 in this volume.

Huysmans, Jef (2000), "The European Union and the Securitization of Migration", *Journal of Common Market Studies*, 38 (5): 751–777.

Isiksel, Turkuler (2016), *Europe's Functional Constitution: A Theory of Constitutionalism beyond the State*, Oxford: Oxford University Press.

Jackson, Robert (2000), *The Global Covenant: Human Conduct in a World of States*, Oxford: Oxford University Press.

Jackson, Robert (2007), *Sovereignty*, Cambridge: Polity Press.

Jones, Erik, R. Daniel Kelemen, and Sophie Meunier (2016), "Failing Forward? The Euro Crisis and the Incomplete Nature of European Integration", *Comparative Political Studies*, 49 (7): 1010–1034, special issue on the Euro crisis.

Joerges, Christian (2014), "Law and Politics in Europe's Crisis: On the History of the Impact of an Unfortunate Configuration", *Constellations*, 21 (2): 249–261.

Jordan, A. Grant (1981), "Iron Triangles, Woolly Corporatism and Elastic Nets: Images of the Policy Process", *Journal of Public Policy*, 1 (1): 95–123.

Keohane, Robert O. (2002), "Ironies of Sovereignty: The European Union and the United States", *Journal of Common Market Studies*, 40 (4): 743–765.

Lazaridis, Gabriella, and Wadi Khursheed (eds) (2015), *The Securitisation of Migration in the EU: Debates since 9/11*, Basingstoke: Palgrave Macmillan.

Leuffen, Dirk, Berthold Rittberger, and Frank Schimmelfennig, (2013), *Differentiated Integration: Explaining Variation in* the European Union, Palgrave Macmillan.

Majone, Giandomenico (1994), "The Rise of the Regulatory State in Europe", *West European Politics*, 17 (3): 77–101.

Majone, Giandomenico (2005), *Dilemmas of European Integration*, Oxford: Oxford University Press.

March, James G. (1991), "Exploration and Exploitation in Organizational Learning", *Organization Science*, 2 (1): 71–87.

March, James G., and Johan P. Olsen (1989), *Rediscovering Institutions: The Organizational Basis of Politics*, New York: The Free Press.

March, James G., and Johan P. Olsen (1995), *Democratic Governance*, New York: Free Press.

Menéndez, Agustín José (2013), "The Existential Crisis of the European Union", *German Law Journal*, 14 (5): 453–525.

NOU (1982), *Maktutredningen. Sluttrapport*, Bergen: Oslo, Tromsø: Universitetsforlaget.

Olsen, Johan P. (ed) (1978), *Politisk Organisering*, Bergen: Oslo, Tromsø: Universitetsforlaget.

Olsen, Johan P. (1988), *Statsstyre og institusjonsutforming* [*State Governance and Institutional Design*], Oslo: Universitetsforlaget.

Orren, Karen, and Stephen Skowronek (2017), *The Policy State: An American Predicament*, Harvard, MA: Harvard University Press.

Picot, Georg (2012), *Politics of Segmentation: Party Competition and Social Protection in Europe*, London: Routledge.

Richardson, Jeremy (1982) (ed), *The Concept of Policy Style*, London: Routledge.

Richardson, Jeremy (2018), "Brexit: The EU Policy-Making State Hits the Populist Buffers", *Political Quarterly*, 89 (1): 18–126.

Scharpf, Fritz W. (2010), "The Asymmetry of European Integration, or Why the EU Cannot Be a 'Social Market Economy'", *Socio-Economic Review*, 8 (2): 211–250.

Scharpf, Fritz W. (2016), "The Costs of Non-disintegration: The Case of the European Monetary Union", in: Damian Chalmers, Markus Jachtenfuchs and Christian Joerges (eds), *The End of the Eurocrats' Dream: Adjusting to European Diversity*, Cambridge: Cambridge University Press, pp. 29–49.

Skowronek, Stephen (1982), *Building a New American State: The Expansion of National Administrative Capacities, 1877–1920*, Cambridge: Cambridge University Press.

Spijkerboer, Thomas (2017), "Bifurcation of People, Bifurcation of Law: Externalization of Migration Policy before the EU Court of Justice", *Journal of Refugee Studies*, 31 (2): 216–239.

Thornton, Patricia H., William Ocasio, and Michael Lounsbury (2012), *The Institutional Logics Perspective: A New Approach to Culture, Structure and Process*, Oxford: Oxford University Press.

Tilly, Charles (1993), *European Revolutions, 1492–1992*, Oxford: Wiley-Blackwell.

Tranøy, Bent-Sofus, and Herman Mark Schwartz (2019), "Illusions of Convergence: The Persistent Simplification of a Wicked Crisis", Chapter 3 in this volume.

Werts, Jan (2008), *The European Council*, London: John Harper Publishing.

Wessels, Wolfgang (1997), "An Ever Closer Fusion? A Dynamic Macropolitical View on Integration Processes", *Journal of Common Market Studies*, 35 (2): 267–299.

Wessels, Wolfgang (2016), *The European Council*, London: Palgrave.

White, Jonathan (2015a), "Emergency Europe", *Political Studies*, 63 (2): 300–318.

White, Jonathan (2015b), "Authority after Emergency Rule", *Modern Law Review*, 78 (4): 585–610.

3

ILLUSIONS OF CONVERGENCE

The persistent simplification of a wicked crisis

Bent Sofus Tranøy and Herman Mark Schwartz

I Introduction

What variables should we be looking at when measuring economic convergence, how is this choice related to economic theory, and what are the consequences of getting it wrong? European Monetary Union (EMU) was expected to spur economic growth and reverse "eurosclerosis" through three major convergences in pricing, production, and financing. But even when the political authorities in Europe confronted reasonably clear evidence that what they had perceived as stability-inducing convergence was actually crisis-inducing divergence, those authorities doggedly continued to pursue solutions to the Eurozone crisis based upon austerity and "one size fits all" policies. In this chapter, we try to explain why this is so, highlighting how an increasingly segmented epistocracy had an understanding of convergence that first allowed it to ignore the massive build-up of debt that made the Euro crisis possible, and then produced rigidity instead of resilience. This rigidity stemmed from cognitive biases that were structurally encoded into institutions of economic surveillance and governance that were unconstrained by other institutions with a broader perspective.

Many analyses blame the epistemic community centred on the European Central Bank (ECB) for an orthodoxy emphasising austerity, or locate policy failures in the lack of the conditions that might have constituted an optimal currency area in most of the European Union (EU) (Matthijs and Blyth 2015). We expand the austerity argument by looking at the complementarities and inter-action between the dominant economic ideology of the ECB and the German ordoliberal tradition. We connect it to the second, optimal currency area argument by showing how illusions of convergence animated both pre- and post-crisis causal processes: convergence between economic theories favouring a system of rules applicable under all conditions to all societies, and an imagined convergence in the actual operation of the EU's various national and regional economies. Put simply, intellectual convergence around a flawed set of economic ideas continuously blinded EU policy-makers to dangerous divergences in the real economy. A system of uniform rules and rule-based policies could not be applied effectively to a variegated continental economy, either in the boom-phase from 2001 to 2008, or after the financial and fiscal crises had set in and created even more divergence.

The supposed benefits of convergence served to justify integration, but, as with all such justifications, these benefits had some basis in prior economic theory. In particular, neo-classical economics in its real business cycle (RBC) or the New Macro version emphasised that economies naturally came to a state of equilibrium, and that any disturbances were the result of exogenous political or technological factors. In this world view, the job description for governments is to establish clear rules that anchor (rational) expectations and otherwise leave everything to private actors. Central bankers and economists wedded to RBC populated the committee authoring the Delors Report (Delors, 1989; Verdun, 1999). Perfecting markets in the EU via financial and product market integration would thus lead to a convergence in performance. But New Macro and a rules-based system of political economy contained a de-socialised view of the economy. This could have come into conflict with the dominant economic governance ideology in Germany, namely, ordoliberalism, which has a more socially embedded view. But both RBC and ordoliberalism share a reliance on rules, rather than discretion. In effect, a more de-socialised hybrid version of the two liberalisms has carried the day, upholding the ordoliberal principle of constancy in economic policy, but disregarding ordoliberalism's equally fundamental principles of liability and, arguably, legitimacy.

Meanwhile, in the real economy, open financial markets facilitated a huge transfer of capital from northern savers to southern borrowers. This created the illusion of convergence, confirming the prior beliefs of the epistemic élites in the EU's financial bureaucracy. Interest-rate differentials with Germany essentially collapsed after 1999. Growth rates in the south exploded, suggesting that income levels might converge with the north. Labour market reforms raised southern (and Irish) female labour market participation at a much more rapid rate than the rest of the EU, even though the absolute level remained relatively low. But these re-assuring measures of convergence were dependent variables that masked equally important and measurable divergence in the underlying causes for convergence. In particular, current account imbalances increased markedly, with northern countries in surplus and southern in deficit; large increases in southern private debt were the counterpart to this imbalance. While facilitating superficial convergence along nominal indicators, financial flows created deeper divergences in economic developments, and the risk of a financial crisis.

When the crisis erupted, German politicians, the epistocrats in the ECB and the other *Troika* members doubled down on a rules-based response for states while bending over backwards to save banks. Although the intellectual prism of the German social market economy might have suggested leniency and subordinating market forces to social aims, the entrenched northern disdain for southern polities – particularly Greece – put the southern economies beyond the boundaries of normal society. While the super-abstractions of New Macro travelled frictionlessly upwards and across governance levels, the more grounded ideas of ordoliberalism did not. Thus, epistocrats applied a de-socialised view of what constituted proper policy to those countries, with disastrous results. The New Macro/rules-based approach prescribed austerity in the short run in order to restore confidence and structural adjustment in the medium run as the only path back towards long-term growth. By contrast, ordoliberalism as a theoretical construct was not frictionless. It could only work in the context of specific conditions – namely, Wilhelm Röpke's "mature economic discernment" in the quotation here – and, if those conditions were not present, then all that was left to discipline bad actors was strict external application of the rules. This strict application accelerated economic divergence among Eurozone members while increasing control by the functionally distinct segment of actors that span key EU financial institutions. These institutions, linking the German politicians, the epistocrats in the ECB, and the other *Troika* members, shared institutionalised forms of knowledge, situational understandings and definitions, values, and problem definitions.

The chapter thus has four sections largely centred on these shared institutionalised forms of knowledge. Section I lays out the basis for a rules-based system of economic governance and, in particular, monetary policy, and then compares that to German ordoliberalism with respect to its belief in convergence. Section II discusses how EU bureaucrats selectively perceived the convergence which they demanded (by way of fiscal policy and structural reform) and expected (in observable nominal indicators) after EMU began. Section III discusses the unmasking of convergence and the application of rules-based austerity by EU bureaucrats, central bankers, and their allies in the *Troika*. The final section (IV) concludes by considering the contrast between a Keynesian approach and a rules-based approach to economic governance.

II Economic theory, divergence and convergence

In this section, we will lay out the basic tenets of Keynesianism, neo-classical/RBC economics, and ordoliberalism, with an emphasis on their respective implications as to what degree and what kind of convergence they lead us to expect.

The problem of the fallacy of composition is *a* – if not *the* – central premise of Keynesian thought. In fact, the insight that what constitutes a rational line of action for an individual actor in an economic system might lead to disastrous results for the system as a whole was the key argument for inventing and establishing macro-economics as a discipline in the early 1930s (Tranøy, 2011: 187). John Maynard Keynes and like-minded economists of his generation departed from the prevailing neo-classical school and its practical manifestation in the

"Treasury view" in two ways. First, they started from the assumption that markets are inherently unstable, and thus that state intervention in the market was not only justifiable, but also necessary. Second, they rejected the contemporaneous (and still current) dominant logic conflating what constitutes proper management of the state's finances with what holds for a single household. This meant that, if the state remained fiscally passive while all other actors (firms, banks, and households) did the appropriate thing and saved in a downturn, aggregate demand would fall, leading to a further fall in output and employment. As Irving Fisher (1933) argued, this would create a vicious downward spiral in which efforts to save (or de-leverage) out of a smaller income would further reduce demand, investment, and thus income. Thus, what Keynes termed the "paradox of thrift" led to the policy recommendation of public deficit spending in a downturn.

The fallacy of composition holds equally for the relationship between states. At both the Versailles (1919) and Bretton Woods (1944) conferences, Keynes focussed keenly on the symbiosis between surplus and deficit states, and warned against the detrimental effects of sustained imbalances between trading partners. Keynes' remedy would have addressed persistent imbalances using some form of controlled exchange-rate flexibility, co-ordinated economic policies between surplus and deficit countries, limited capital mobility, and some sort of mechanism forcing surplus countries to increase their domestic demand and thus their imports.

Applied to the Eurozone, a Keynesian perspective would direct our attention to the fact that, while northern European Eurozone members tended to be export-oriented surplus countries with an institutional capacity for wage restraint in pursuit of competitiveness, southern European countries have none of these traits. Furthermore, a Keynesian prediction would be more or less exactly what played out over the first nine years of the Euro. Increasing differences in competitiveness – unmediated by exchange-rate policies and financed through a fully integrated market for capital – led to a build-up of imbalances and eventually a crash.

While Keynesianism took its point of departure in the fallacy of composition, RBC and New Macro simply ignore this problem, assuming that the economy is inherently stable and preferring, instead, to start their modelling with "representative agents" blessed with rational expectations and full information. The assumption about representative agents makes it impossible to have (or to see) a fallacy of composition. In New Macro and RBC, private actors are fully rational agents who always optimise inter-temporally and know the future probability distributions of all important economic returns and variables. When you combine the beliefs about stability with the absence of any fallacy of composition, all that is left on the agenda for macroeconomic policy is to establish clear rules on inflation, spending, and borrowing, *i.e.*, create something like the ECB plus the Stability and Growth Pact. The justification is that nothing desirable can come from positive, discretionary government action; the government can only make mistakes. The chief mistakes are policy interventions that produce higher-than-needed inflation without any corresponding gains in employment and growth, because the representative agent naturally anticipates the inflationary effects or unemployment that are above the "natural" level of both.

Two of the founding fathers of RBC were very clear about this, in particular as to the argument that central banks should be independent. Kydland and Prescott (1977: 473) argued that

> Even if there is an agreed-upon, fixed social objective function and policymakers know the timing and magnitude of the effects of their actions, discretionary policy…does not result in the social objective function being maximized. The reason for this apparent paradox is that economic planning is not a game against nature but rather a game against rational economic agents. We conclude that there is *no* way [active monetary or fiscal policy] can be made applicable to economic planning when expectations are rational.

Thus, the policy agenda of the New Macro movement was fairly restricted, concentrating on issues such as rules, and on topics that naturally flowed from a focus on rules, such as how to design institutions able to make credible commitments. Independent central banks were the chief example of this, but so were rigid fiscal rules and the privatisation of as much state activity as possible.

The corollary to this abnegation of active fiscal and monetary policy is that room for economic improvement exists if market actors are given a stable framework and good incentives. RBC and orthodox economics have thus placed a heavy emphasis on structural reform and liberalisation over the last 30 years or so. The efficient-market hypothesis – the idea that asset prices in financial markets always reflect all the available information and that, in financial markets, information flows freely and abundantly – served to reinforce this impetus with respect to policy for financial markets. The most significant conclusion flowing from this view is that, left to their own devices (and in the absence of the rare events that count as "real shocks" stemming from genuinely new information), financial markets tend to be stable and self-correcting. In RBC's view of the world, banks and capital markets do not create any endogenous instability that might have real economy effects. RBC thus habitually omitted banks, the financial system, and debt from its macroeconomic models until very recently.

The international version of this argument bears the name of the "Lawson doctrine," espoused by Margaret Thatcher's long-serving Chancellor of the Exchequer, Nigel Lawson. He argued that current-account deficits stemming from private-sector behaviour were nothing to worry about, because, when the deficit is created by the rational saving and investment decisions of private firms and individuals, there is no reason why the government should know any better than they do about the likely future path of the economy. Indeed, private actors presumably have a better idea about their ability to service their debts consequent to prolonged current account deficits. However, there will always be some actors that misjudge their capacity to service debt. But actors who misjudge their debt-service capacity just go bankrupt, without significant macroeconomic effects. The proper policy here is simply to make sure that the level of public debt is sustainable. And indeed, in the late 1980s and early 1990s, many states with large public debts and prolonged current account deficits successfully transformed public debt into private debt (Schwartz, 1994). This transformation assumed that markets would always perceive public debt as a unified whole, making any default a huge, uncontainable shock, while simultaneously always perceiving private debt in granular terms, making any default a unique event pertaining to a specific firm, and thus easily contained.

The gap between a Keynesian fallacy of composition view on prolonged, large deficits or unmanageable debt and that of orthodox economics should now be evident: in Keynes' world, one actor's misjudgement about debt-service capacity can affect other actors' capacity to service debt, because any drop in aggregate demand can reduce cash flow to illiquid debtors, transforming them into insolvent debtors and thereby damaging liquid debtors enough to transform them into illiquid debtors, triggering Fisher's (1933) debt deflation cycle. Private-sector defaults are not necessarily discrete, containable events. Indeed, Fisher's debt-deflation dynamic happened at an international level in the 1982 Latin American debt crises, when default by insolvent Mexico pushed illiquid Brazil into insolvency and liquid Korea into illiquidity; and it happened in the 1997 Asian financial crisis, when insolvent Thailand pushed illiquid Korea into insolvency and liquid Malaysia into illiquidity. The Euro crisis also follows this pattern domestically and internationally. Insolvent Greece triggered bank runs that rendered illiquid Spain essentially insolvent and liquid, if economically torpid, Italy illiquid. Domestically, just as *Lehman's* failure drove the illiquid *Fannie Mae* and *Freddie Mac* into insolvency, the failure of a handful of banks in Greece and, in particular, Ireland, triggered runs that eventually bankrupted a multitude of European banks while pushing most others to the brink of insolvency.[1]

Yet a peculiar fusion of RBC and the German variant of economic liberalism, most often referred to as *ordoliberalism*, dominated EU-policy both before and after the Euro crisis, rather than a fusion of German social market thinking with Keynes. Ordoliberalism starts from two premises distinguishing it from other varieties of liberalism, including the kind of Chicago-school liberalism that produced RBC. Schnyder and Siems (2012: 3) note the difference clearly, arguing that ordoliberalism contains "a prominent and positive role for the state in upholding the liberal economic order and the importance of the 'social question' due to the need to embed economic activity in a sound society."

Ordoliberalism thus does not believe that a market order characterised by functioning competition appears spontaneously. Rather, consistent with more general institutionalist traditions such as that of John Commons (1936), it starts from the premise that market power is distributed unevenly, and that private interest can therefore undermine competition. Free markets require strong states to contain bad actors. Thus, a strong state is not, as Ronald Reagan would have it, the problem, but rather the solution to the real problem of dysfunctional or monopolised markets. Ordoliberalism thus argues that the rules of the game should not favour the powerful and wealthy. While a narrow conception of ordoliberalism concentrates on competition policy and on the importance of having an economic constitution that secures stability, predictability, and property rights for economic actors in a competitive market, it is also socially aware, as is reflected in the associated term the "social market economy."

This partly stems from a deeper sociological orientation that would come across as very foreign in Chicago. For instance, one of the founding fathers of ordoliberalism, Walter Eucken (Eucken, 1932, quoted in Schnyder and Siems, 2012: 4), used the concept of "interdependence of orders," making the point that the economic order is interdependent with "all other governmental, societal and cultural orders in a society." Thus, ordoliberalism is intellectually and ethically highly compatible with a status (or "order") which preserves the welfare state and the basic tenets of "Rhenish" capitalism (Albert, 1993). Because ordoliberalism saw markets as socially embedded, it necessarily also believed that its fundamental principles could "manifest themselves differently given individual national historic contexts, reflecting societal norms that have acquired legitimacy over time" (Hadeed, 2017).

While ordoliberals see capitalism without clear rules as disorderly, this instability is not the same as Keynes' instability. Keynes was concerned with economic instability, as such, and thus was, in many ways, consistent with the de-socialised view of the economy prevalent in orthodox economics. While Keynes (re-) introduced human psychology – animal spirits – into economic models, and while he was concerned about production, efficiency, and growth, not so much for their own sake as for the sake of enabling humans to live a better life, he did not have a fully prescriptive vision of what that life should look like. By contrast, ordoliberalism has a positive view of society, and argues that the economy should be embedded in, and the servant of, a specific, largely Catholic, social order (van Kersbergen, 2003; van Kersbergen and Manow, 2009). But as a positive vision, Catholic social thought also strictly delineates who is in and who is out of society when it comes to *caritas*, and contains a strict status hierarchy.

Ordoliberalism has a similar "insider-outsider" perspective. Like economic orthodoxy and RBC, ordoliberalism sees the market as inherently stable if bad actors can be controlled, or, put more gently, if everyone follows the rules. *Ordnungspolitik* is the concept used to describe the kind of regulation that the ordoliberal vision of stability and predictability requires. Wilhelm Röpke (1982: 188), a founding father of post-war ordoliberalism, was clear about this regulation:

> [Our programme] consists of measures and institutions which impart to competition the framework, rules, and machinery of impartial supervision which a competitive system needs as much as any game or match if it is

not to degenerate into a vulgar brawl. A genuine, equitable, and smoothly functioning competitive system cannot in fact survive without a judicious moral and legal framework and without the regular supervision of the conditions under which competition can take place pursuant to real efficiency principles. This presupposes mature economic discernment on the part of all responsible bodies and individuals and a strong impartial state.

The principle of liability is of fundamental importance to the ordoliberal vision of the competitive system and its ability to induce "mature economic discernment." In Eucken's (1952/90) words:

Investments are made more cautiously in proportion to the amount of liability borne by the investor. In this way, liability has a prophylactic effect against the dissipation of capital …

Because private actors are capable of bad behaviour, Röpke raises the possibility of making demands for surveying and regulating private economic activity – for instance, in the credit market – to a degree that the rational expectations school would never find permissible. Yet the emphasis on rules simultaneously made it possible for an intellectual alliance between these main German theoretical strands and economic orthodoxy. This was particularly true with respect to policy recommendations favouring rules such as the Maastricht criteria in the run-up to the crisis, and such as the European semester, the Treaty on Stability, Co-ordination and Governance, and the Six-Pack and Two-Pack legislation after the crisis. Equally so, these largely normative beliefs coloured interpretations of the data around convergence and crisis. Convergence towards German levels of debt, inflation, and employment "obviously" showed how rules enabled good actors pursuing good economic outcomes to constrain bad actors; crisis and divergence "obviously" demonstrated both that bad actors had sabotaged economic progress and that an even stricter application of rules and discipline was needed to constrain bad actors.

The combination of New Macro/RBC wedded to ordoliberalism expected that a single integrated market for goods and services would reduce rent-seeking and production inefficiencies by causing production to re-locate in search of economies of scale and a more efficient mix of inputs. A single currency would reduce transaction costs for continental-scale production and transport, while making prices transparent and comparable. In short, a more competitive market would emerge. Free movement of capital complemented these changes by shifting investment towards higher return activities, while a single – and credible – monetary policy would bring the price of capital down in countries previously burdened by high-risk *premia*. The integrated market and EMU was expected to bring convergence in production costs, prices, interest rates, and risk-adjusted returns. These four changes would unleash balanced growth in the EU, propelling it ahead of the United States (US). At the same time, rules such as the Maastricht criteria would constrain governments – the only plausible bad actors – from interfering in this process. This vision can be seen clearly in the Delors Report, which we briefly survey in the next section.

III Convergence predicted and assumed: The Delors Report, new rules, and visions of convergence

Academic, political, and central banking actors all shared a common desire for, and belief in, the importance and necessity of rules to produce convergence inside EMU. The Delors EMU Report expected that free factor mobility under EMU would produce convergence. But it also sought rules to govern the conduct of Member States in order to produce this convergence. Towards the end of the report, the committee (1989: 19–20) channelled both ordoliberalism and a rules-based public policy by arguing that

> An economic and monetary union could only operate on the basis of mutually consistent and sound behaviour by governments and other economic agents in all member countries. In particular, uncoordinated and divergent national budgetary policies would undermine monetary stability and generate imbalances in the real and financial sectors of the Community.

Yet while the report nodded in the direction of ordoliberalism's worries about private actors, it singled out fiscal misconduct as the real worry for a post-EMU Europe. The Delors Report was not alone in this orientation. In public speeches, Jacques Santer (1998), president of the Commission from 1995 to 1999, noted that convergence around common rules was essential to the success of EMU:

> The euro calls for a high degree of convergence of economic thinking in the common currency area. And when I say economic policy, I include the policy line taken by the social partners on wages. Any deviation from convergence will bring a penalty in the shape of high political and economic adjustment costs. That is precisely why mutual understanding is so vital.

This world view shaped how key European policy-makers filtered and interpreted the data flowing across their desks. Expecting convergence, they read convergence and causality into the outcomes post-dating the Single Integrated Market and the adoption of the euro. From the late 1990s until around 2008, various indicators of economic ill-health improved in Europe, especially in southern Europe. However, the selection and assessment of these variables very much depended on the point of view of the observer. In the run-up to EMU, many economic variables did improve, particularly the interest rate and inflation variables that were most susceptible to the influence of financial flows. But this convergence was never as dramatic as theory and expectation might have hoped. Moreover, as the saying goes, "the data don't speak (unambiguously) for themselves." While the data indicated convergence, this said nothing about why convergence was occurring. Proponents of compliance with Maastricht criteria, monetary rules, fiscal balance, flexible labour markets, and minimal government intervention read convergence as structural changes in southern economies that had unleashed their productive power.

The European Central Bank's annual report (2008: 10) provides the best indication of the epistocracy's reading of the data just before the US housing finance crash and consequent Eurozone crisis:

> With annual inflation averaging only slightly above 2% in the euro area, we have witnessed a decade of relatively stable prices, in line with the ECB's mandate to deliver price stability. Likewise, longer-term inflation expectations have remained broadly anchored at levels in line with price stability during this time, reflecting the high degree of credibility enjoyed by the ECB's monetary policy. This success is also tangible proof of the institutional robustness, coherence and unity of the Euro system – of its capacity to act in a truly European spirit on the basis of shared values, high standards and common principles.

Why did they see convergence and improvement? Because there was, in fact, some convergence and improvement in six crucial variables: government debt and deficits, inflation rates, long-term interest rates, female labour force participation, unemployment and the employment-to-population ratio, and GDP growth. The first two mattered for the all-important convergence to, and maintenance of, the Maastricht criteria for participation in the EMU. The third had three effects: the budgetary burden of government debt, the ability of private actors to finance investment, and outside observers' assessments of inflation going forward. The fourth measured the degree to which societies were converging on a northern European norm of high labour participation; the fifth measured whether the labour market was well functioning in general; and the last measured the economic growth that open markets were supposed to unleash. In the paragraphs and charts here, with one exception, we norm these indicators against the German level, as convergence implicitly meant convergence towards German and/or northern European norms, with a red line to indicate the onset of the crisis. The information contained in each variable could support a different story. In particular, a more Keynesian-oriented analysis, particularly with respect to (un-)employment levels, could read convergence as a more or less predictable consequence of the aggregate demand associated with housing bubbles in the south (and their absence in Germany, if not all of the north), rather than the outcome of successful European rules-based integration (Becker and Schwartz, 2005).

With respect to gross government debt, convergence trends were well underway before 1999, as southern states struggled to meet the Maastricht criteria. The difference between columns 2 and 3 in Table 3.1 displays gross government

TABLE 3.1 Average Gross Public Debt or Net Lending* as a Percentage Of GDP, Net of the German Level of Debt, Select Countries, 1995–2015

Average gross public debt (stock)

	1995–1999	2000–2008	2009–2015
EZ17**	-13.6	-5.0	-7.9
Greece	-41.1	-42.2	-93.8
Spain	-4.9	16.9	8.8
France	-1.4	-0.7	-6.9
Italy	-55.4	-39.4	-38.2
Portugal	3.0	0.8	-33.1

Average net government lending (flow)

	1995–1999	2000–2008	2009–2015
EZ17**	0.6	0.2	-3.5
Greece	-3.2	-4.7	-9.2
Spain	-0.1	2.0	-8.6
France	0.7	-0.6	-4.1
Italy	-0.4	-0.9	-2.5
Portugal	-0.2	-2.2	-6.4

* Positive numbers mean debt or deficit levels lower than the corresponding German level.

** for reference.

Source: Authors' construction from Eurostat data.

debt and deficits net of the German level. The closer the number is to zero, the greater the degree of convergence; positive numbers indicate a lower gross debt than Germany. Table 3.1 shows that Spain actually attained lower levels of gross debt than Germany during the 2000s. Table 3.2 shows the absolute level of government net lending. Consistent with the EMU planners' desires, both Spain and Italy made significant progress in lowering gross debt levels, while the others largely kept pace with Germany. In the eight years after the introduction of the euro, debt and deficit levels improved markedly everywhere but Greece. Indeed, an especially buoyant economy meant that Spain outperformed Germany with respect to debt and deficits. With respect to deficits, Table 3.1 shows relative

TABLE 3.2 Average Net Government Lending as a Percentage of GDP, Absolute Level (negative numbers indicate deficits)

	1995–1999	*2000–2008*	*2009–2015*
Germany	-4.0	-2.1	-1.1
Greece	-7.2	-6.8	-9.9
Spain	-4.1	-0.1	-8.3
France	-3.3	-2.7	-5.1
Italy	-4.4	-3.0	-3.5
EZ-17*	*-3.7*	*-2.0*	*-4.0*

* for reference.

Source: Authors' construction from Eurostat data.

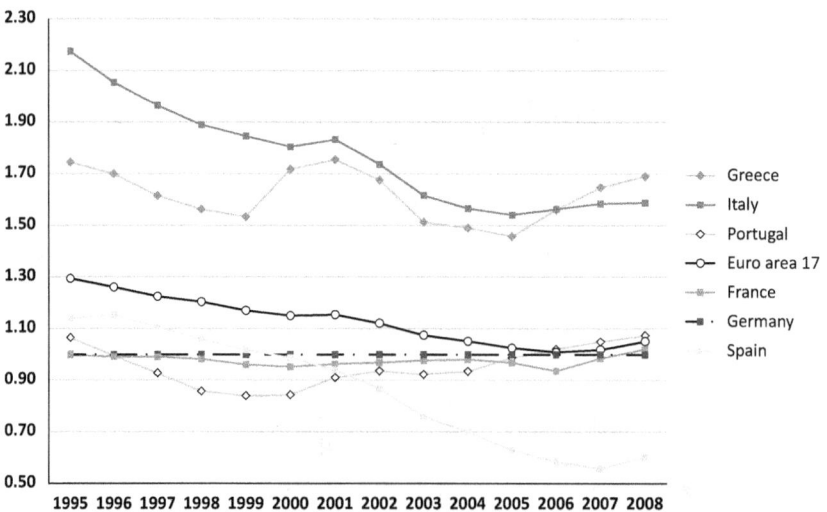

FIGURE 3.1 Government debt to GDP relative to German debt to GDP ratio.

change, but, given that Germany's deficit fell absolutely by 2.1 per cent of GDP from their average 1995–1999 level to their average 2000–2008 level, convergence towards or a position around German levels seemed to indicate rather good performance. Thus, even though, for example, France fell behind Germany in budget consolidation, it was still moving in the right direction. Greece also seemed to be moving towards balance, albeit more slowly, and with the help of creative bookkeeping and Goldman Sachs' *legerdemain*.

The single biggest help in lowering debt, aside from robust US import demand, was falling interest rates, which lowered the budget cost of government debt and also stimulated all European economies. Here, too, the hopeful could find confirmation of their views if they wanted. As Table 3.3 shows, Greece more than halved the relative gap with Germany in public interest payments as a percentage of GDP, as did Italy. The rest actually pushed their interest expenses below the German level, offsetting their slightly worse gross debt positions.

Falling interest rates reflected both falling inflation and the removal of currency risk for lending in the Eurozone. Consumer inflation and, even more so, long-term interest rates converged on German levels, as Table 3.4 shows. Here those wary of Greece's continuing deficit troubles could find solace in rapidly falling inflation and a dramatic convergence of long-term rates. But outside of Greece, there was strong convergence towards German inflation and interest rate levels.

Observers construed a supply-side response behind these improving fiscal and monetary numbers. Thus, for example, ECB president Jean-Claude Trichet (2008) credited the EMU for these positive outcomes:

> The euro area has been a source of stability. [...] Over these ten years, we have observed greater price stability, greater macroeconomic stability, as well as increasing economic and financial integration.

TABLE 3.3 Average Interest Payments on Public Debt as a Percentage of GDP, Net of the German Level of Payments*

	1995–1999	2000–2008	2009–2015
EZ-17**	-1.5	-0.3	-0.5
Greece	-5.6	-2.4	-4.8
Spain	-1.1	0.7	0.0
France	0.0	0.1	-0.1
Italy	-5.9	-2.3	-2.2
Portugal	-0.7	0.0	-1.8

* Positive numbers mean interest payments lower than the corresponding German level.

** for reference.

Source: Authors' construction from Eurostat data.

TABLE 3.4 Average Consumer Price Inflation and Long-Term Interest Rates Relative to the Corresponding German Rate (positive number means higher inflation or interest rate)

	Consumer price inflation (%)			Long-term interest rate (%)		
	1996–1999	2000–2008	2009–2015	1995–1999	2000–2008	2009–2015
EZ-17*	0.5	0.5	0.4	0.7	0.1	1.2
Greece	4.0	1.6	-1.1	5.7	0.4	9.4
Spain	1.4	1.5	0.3	1.6	0.2	2.2
France	0.2	0.3	0.1	0.2	0.1	0.6
Italy	1.4	0.7	1.2	2.1	0.3	2.1
Portugal	1.3	1.2	0.7	1.7	0.2	4.2

* for reference.

Source: Authors' construction from Eurostat data.

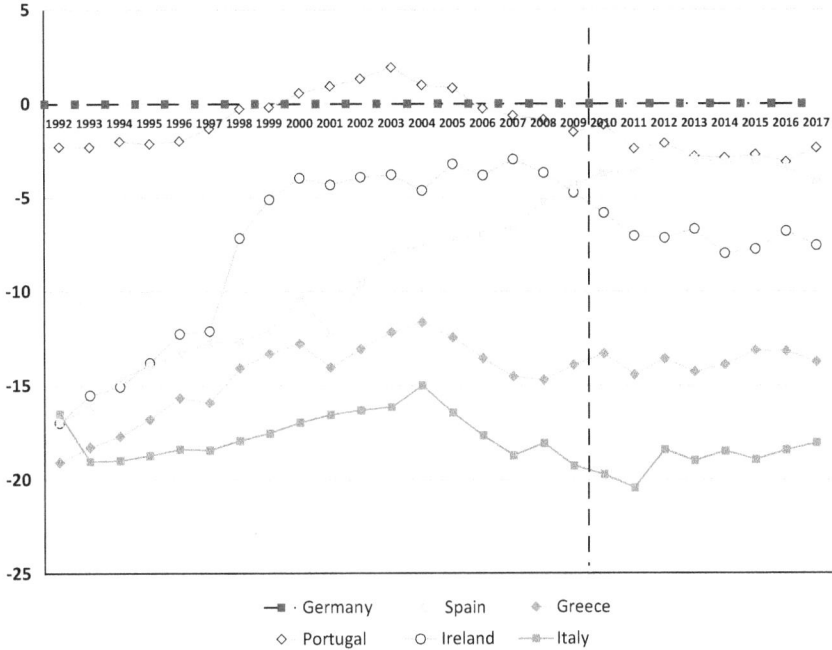

FIGURE 3.2 Female labour force participation (% of 16-64-year-olds) relative to the German level.

EU Commissioner for Economic and Monetary Policy Joaquín Almunia (2008) similarly credited the EMU:

> I am happy to say the euro has proved its critics wrong. EMU underpins prosperity in euro area countries, it drives economic integration and it has enlarged and is set to enlarge further in the next years.

In the real economy, female labour force participation and the employment-to-population ratio also seemed to be improving. Figure 3.2 presents the trends, once again normed against German levels. As the figure shows, Spain made considerable progress in pushing female labour force participation up to German levels (the "Y" axis). This progress persisted well into the crisis. Equally so, female labour force participation rose in Ireland, Portugal, and Greece. Figure 3.3 shows the same trends for the entire labour force, with even stronger convergence by Spain and Ireland.

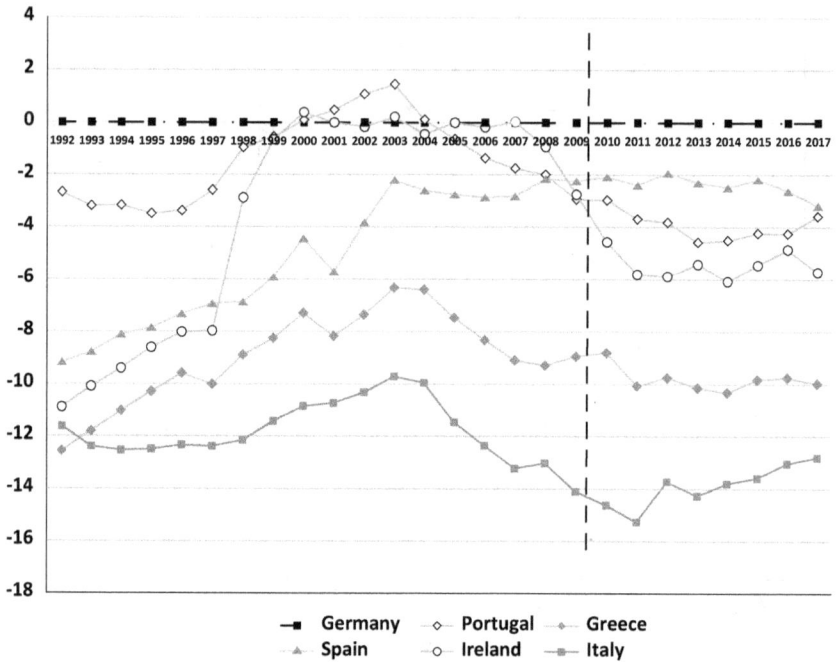

FIGURE 3.3 Total (M+F) labour force participation (% of 16-64-year-olds) relative to the German level.

IV Convergence unmasked

Beneath and behind the apparent convergence of the epistocracy's favoured indicators, a second set of indicators was rapidly diverging. As the next figures show, current account imbalances were growing both absolutely and as a percentage of GDP. Household debt in the deficit, mostly southern, countries was rapidly rising, and housing prices were rising well above trend levels. In turn, higher housing prices were inducing a shift of resources into the non-traded sector, imperilling the ability of households and countries to service debt in the absence of a massive increase in northern consumption of southern traded goods.

These trends should have worried the Commission and the ECB, yet they did not. Those trends concerned private debt and current account deficits, which were diverging rapidly. But the RBC-derived theoretical framework prevailing in Brussels and Frankfurt meant that these numbers had no relevance. Surely, private actors knew what they were doing when northern banks abetted an astounding increase in credit to southern private borrowers, thus driving southern current account deficits to historic highs! Surely, this was not the main causal driver of prosperity as compared to better rules and the unleashing of the private sector! And, in any case, the single currency had removed the risk of devaluation by debtors, or, put differently, from the epistocracy's point of view, the fact that debtors earned in Euro meant that the mass of debtors could easily pay back in Euro, even if a few debtors went bankrupt.

Figure 3.4 (which is not normed against Germany) shows the sharp divergence in external positions after the introduction of the euro. Conventional wisdom identifies a sustainable current account deficit in two different ways. First, most commonly, a rule-of-thumb 3 per cent of GDP threshold is a cause for worry. Likewise, so is a debt-to-GDP ratio over 30 or 40 per cent. Both reflect the more formal and general definition that says current account deficits as a percentage of GDP should not exceed nominal GDP growth if debt levels are to be stable in relation to GDP (and thus, presumably, sustainable). But Figure 3.4 shows that – at peak – Spain, Greece, and Portugal were running deficits exceeding 10 per cent of GDP, while Ireland was running a deficit of over 5 per cent of its harder-to-measure GDP.[2] There is and was no plausible scenario in which any of those countries might attain annual GDP growth rates over 10 per cent.

Beneath the aggregate measure of current account balances was a sharp divergence in private household debt levels, which exploded in the southern countries and Ireland (Figure 3.5). Those households dramatically increased their borrowing as interest rates, and thus what looked like the future stream of debt-service payments, fell. Data for the pre-crisis era are only available for Italy, Spain, Greece, and Germany, and those for Greece are so extreme that Figure 3.5 below omits them for clarity. The increase was especially pronounced in Greece (217%), Ireland (101%), Spain (75.2%), and Portugal (49%). By contrast, household debt levels in Germany were falling slightly, and the EU average increase was only

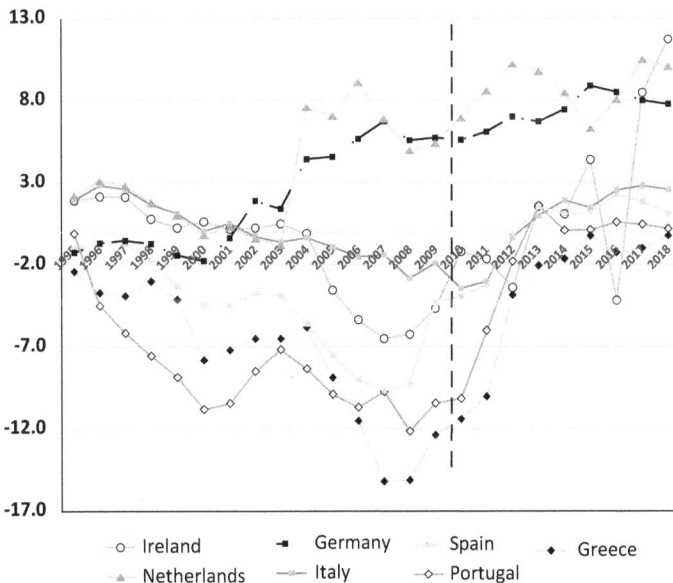

FIGURE 3.4 Current account balance, % of GDP.

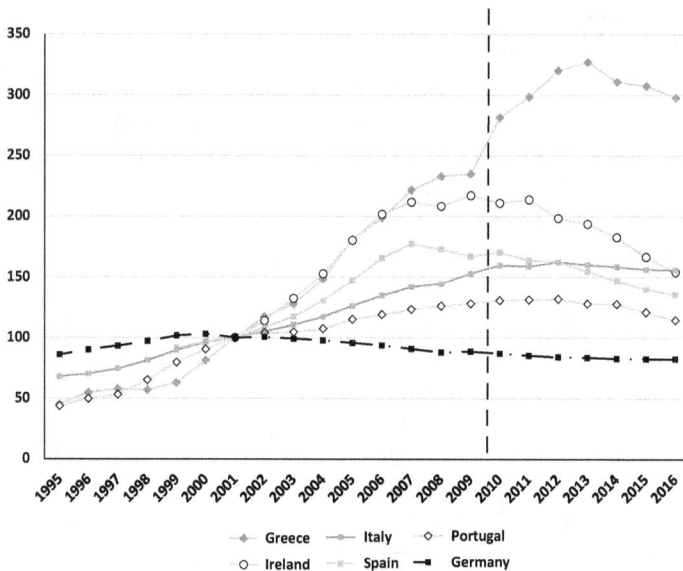

FIGURE 3.5   Household debt, index, 1995 = 100.

27 per cent. That said, in other northern European countries, rising household debt also accompanied rising housing prices, and the Dutch and Scandinavians carried household debt relative to income generally higher than southern Europeans as of 2006. Nonetheless, the general pattern here is that the south was not converging on the relevant part of the north, namely, Germany.

Finally, behind private debt was a rapid divergence in house prices, with enormous increases in Ireland and Spain *versus* stagnation in Germany. Most of the increase in household debt, unsurprisingly, was home mortgages. The ratio of mortgage debt to GDP increased in Greece, from 9 per cent in 2000 to 36 per cent in 2010; in Spain, from 30 per cent to 63 per cent; in Italy, from 10 per cent to 22 per cent. In Germany, by contrast, mortgage debt as a percentage of GDP fell from 53 per cent to 45 per cent (EMF, 2007; 2016).

All of this is easily accommodated in the usual analyses of the Euro crisis as a consequence of Europe not being an optimum currency area (Matthijs and Blyth, 2015). But beyond this were more subtle divergences around the absence of a common identity in Europe, and therefore a common sense of shared responsibility. As the crisis unfolded, Germans put the blame on the Greeks (and *vice versa*), reflecting the complete sense that this was a "national" crisis within a Europe of nations. By contrast, most people in the US did not frame the corresponding crisis as stemming from the behaviour of people in a particular state (racial and ethnic, rather than geographical lines mattered). By 2015, 68 per cent of Germans thought the Greeks were to blame for the crisis and resisted a bail-out, reflecting a framing of the crisis that contrasted hard

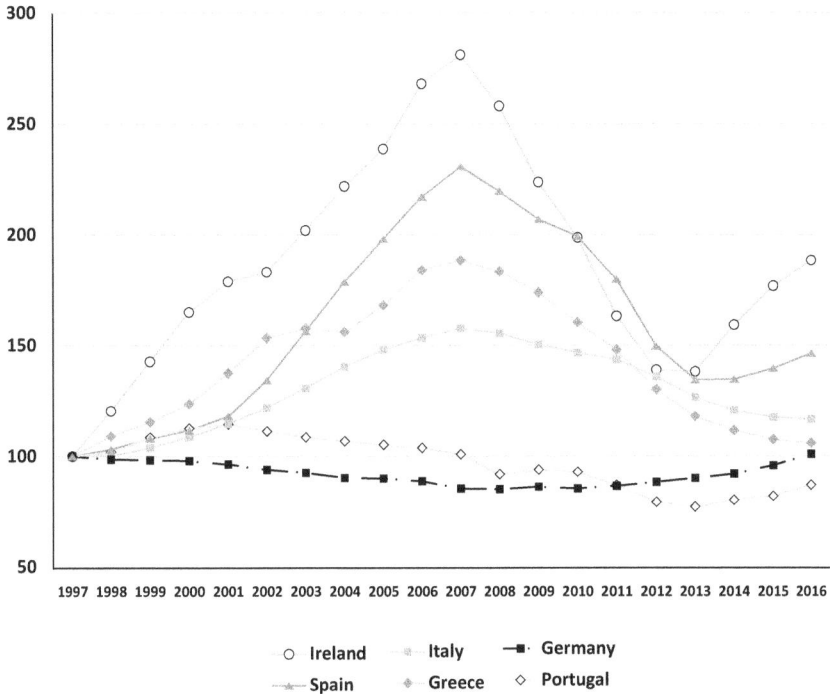

FIGURE 3.6 Housing price index, $2000 = 100$.

working and austere Germans with lazy, profligate Greeks.[3] This framing was consistent with an attitude that rule or law-breakers should be punished for their deviant behaviour, for their lack of "mature economic discernment." In the epistemic world created by the convergence of RBC and ordoliberalism, strict rules were needed to tame bad behaviour in the south. (Unsurprisingly, this distrust spread to all European institutions. By 2013, 63 per cent of Europeans surveyed by the Eurobarometer blamed the post-crisis austerity on the EU ([Anderson, 2015: 216].)

So while the indicators favoured by RBC, the ECB, and the Commission were converging, other important variables were diverging in ways that should have signalled danger ahead. RBC, the ECB, and the Commission shared a common belief in the dangers of state economic fine-tuning and expanded state spending; to this, the Germans added a fear of the lack of "*Ordnung*" in everything southern. Thus indicators relating to the state mattered: public debt, the public interest burden, and inflation rates. Similarly, RBC and the ordoliberals could converge on the need for more competition in labour markets and be re-assured by rising participation rates. But since RBC and the ECB considered private actors to have more and better information about the economy than state planners, indicators relating to the private sector were irrelevant.

Household debt, over-leveraged banks, and regional housing bubbles were not matters of concern for the state.[4]

Not all members of the ECB's leadership, however, remained as singularly focused on the role of government. In a speech to the G30 in May 2010, Lorenzo Bini Smaghi (2010) spoke of "misplaced assumptions," revealing both the earlier world view of the ECB and a change of the cognitive frame among at least some of its members:

> The first [assumption] was that markets would exert strong pressure on euro area fiscal policies. The second assumption was that if the first assumption were insufficient to discipline public finances, then the Stability and Growth Pact, based on monitoring, peer pressure and sanctions, would do the job. The third assumption, reinforcing the previous ones, is that if a member of the euro area were unable to implement sound fiscal policies, it would be left to its own devices. The final assumption was that national economic policies would be geared to ensure convergence among euro area economies, within a strengthened single market.

In the same speech, Bini Smaghi went on to explain that financial markets had overshot in an "abrupt procyclical way," producing unsustainably low interest rates in the peripheral economies) before the crisis and unsustainably high ones afterwards. He goes on – like Trichet – to speak of the difficulties that the EU had in implementing surveillance of macroeconomic policy, while underlining that simply leaving Member States "to their own devices" in moments of crisis was impossible given the probability that financial markets would produce contagion. He then ends that section of his speech with reference to the build-up of imbalances.

But at the top, things remained the same, with Bini Smaghi leaving the Executive Board in late 2011. Pronouncements from the core of the European financial epistocracy reveal no sense of the fallacy of composition, or of unstable financial markets, or that, in the Eurozone crisis, both creditors and debtors shared some blame. In a set of speeches after 2009, ECB president Jean-Claude Trichet opined that the real problem lay in labour markets and the lack of clear fiscal rules. In terms of ECB policy, of course, Trichet engineered an increase in interest rates in April and July of 2011, just as the southern European countries were diving more deeply into recession, and simultaneously talked of drawing a line in the sand on Greece.

At the onset of the crisis, Trichet (2009a) called attention to labour markets and fiscal deficits:

> The persistent inflation and labour cost differential with the average of the euro area during the expansion has hampered competitiveness which will have to be regained. The present situation suggests a need for labour market reform and wage moderation in particular by discontinuing wage indexation. Appropriate structural reforms will support a sustainable economic

upswing and also the consolidation of public finances, which will be crucial not only in Spain but in the entire euro area, for confidence to be restored.

One year later, Trichet (2010), virtually a personification of encoded cognitive bias, was still blaming the crisis on fiscal problems rather than on private over-lending. After reference to imbalances and the need to improve risk management in the financial sector, he claimed that

> It is very important to understand – and it has perhaps not yet been suffi-ciently understood – that the developments we are currently witnessing in Europe's economy have to do with the 'Economic' functions of Economic and Monetary Union. They have essentially three origins: unsound fis-cal policies in a number of Member States; inappropriate macroeconomic policies in a number of Member States; and overall an inadequate system of surveillance by all Member States.

And not only Trichet; Vítor Constâncio (2011; see also Constâncio, 2013), vice-president of the ECB, stated that "rule-based frameworks must act a [*sic*] substi-tute for centralised authority" when it came to preventing the emergence of large imbalances of public and private sector debt. The idea that Keynesian demand-stimulus might help was notably absent from most speeches after the crisis, even though this produced even more divergence in EU fiscal balances, as southern GDP shrank faster than government spending (Table 3.2).

V Implications

Conventional wisdom lays the blame for the Eurozone crisis on the absence of an optimum currency area in the EU economy. More recent revisionist argu-ments have stressed the absence of a common sense of shared social purpose (Matthijs and Blyth, 2015). Here, we have tried to expand on that relatively broad notion by narrowing our focus down to what a segmented set of decision-makers believed. The Euro project was built on a variety of false assumptions about the best form of economic governance. Intellectual convergence around a flawed set of economic ideas continuously blinded EU policy-makers to dangerous diver-gences in the real economy. A system of uniform rules and rule-based policies could not be applied effectively to a variegated continental economy, either in the boom-phase from 2001 to 2008, or after the financial and fiscal crises had set in. A functionally distinct segment of actors spanning key EU financial institu-tions, and including German politicians, the epistocrats in the ECB, and the other *Troika* members, shared institutionalised values, forms of knowledge, situational understandings, and definitions of what constituted an economic problem.

This intellectual convergence occurred between the real business-cycle fla-vour of macroeconomic theorising that was present in the ECB and other national central banks with the German governance philosophy called ordoliberalism.

Convergence occurred because of a shared belief in the importance of rules limiting forms of bad behaviour. This convergence need not have happened. Though this is necessarily crude, we can posit three different philosophies of economic governance with a plausible chance of making their way into policy circles, and we can characterise these three along two different dimensions.[5] The first is whether or not a given philosophy believes the market can exist independently of some larger social structure. The second is whether or not a given philosophy believes that the fallacy of composition exists. Put far too simply, Keynesian perspectives are more or less consistent with neo-classical economics in denying or minimising the existence of social embeddedness, but diverge from neo-classical views in emphasising the fallacy of composition. Real business-cycle theory, of course, denies both social embeddedness and the fallacy of composition. And ordoliberalism recognises social embeddedness, indeed elevates it into a commanding principle, but denies fallacy of composition.

Viewed this way, it is plausible that actors with an ordoliberal outlook could have coalesced with Keynesians along some second order principles, in which ordoliberals recognised that a massive economic slowdown would undermine the social structures that contained bad behaviour in the market, and in which Keynesians accepted, probably more happily, that the economy did have *some* moral aspects. But the alliance between ordoliberalism and real business-cycle theory along the primary line of agreement over the need for rules was always more likely, even if it produced complaisance before the crisis and counter-productive policy afterwards. The general disparagement of Keynesian views by the economics profession also probably impeded a joining up of Keynesian and ordoliberal views.

But 10 years after the crisis, and 20 years after introduction of the Euro, it is clear that the Kydland and Prescott view of the world is simply wrong. Rules alone will not prevent disequilibria from emerging, because the fallacy of composition does operate, and because private actors are not in any fundamental way wiser or more honest than public actors. Private actors face collective-action problems around excessive credit creation that only the state can (try to) solve (Minsky, 1992). As Keynes argued, private actors are likely to be subject to herd-like behaviour that exacerbates a crisis, and to individually rational, but collectively irrational, refusals to invest in the aftermath of a crisis.

Evaluating the contribution of the ordoliberal school to the policies that have given us the present crisis demands a more nuanced analysis. This is because the marriage of ordoliberalism to the RBC/Chicago school of economics has left the EU with an incomplete version of the school's main structure. Governance of the Eurozone is performed mostly by autonomous technocrats (tick), characterised by clear rules (tick), and meant to produce restrictive fiscal policies and sound money (tick). But on the creditor side of the ledger, bureaucrats systematically violated the principles of liability and legitimacy. In reality, the only actors who have faced real consequences for not showing sufficiently mature economic discernment are governments that have either borrowed irresponsibly (Greece) or have had domestic banks doing the same (Spain and Ireland).

Either way, the real liability and cost has been transferred to, and borne by, largely innocent citizens and taxpayers in austerity deals forced upon democratically elected governments by the *Troika* of the Commission, the ECB, and the IMF. The *Troika's* technocratic powers reflect Germany's political power and intellectual norms. Thus, we have seen a perversion of the logic and ideals of *Ordnungspolitik*. Anti-debtor normative content led to self-destructive policies. Not only did it code some societies as being outside the social bounds, and thus as deserving the "pariah treatment," but it also aggravated the fallacy of composition around stimulating the economy in the face of deflation, default, and diminishing employment.

Keynes, by contrast, emerges as the only theorist with mature economic discernment. Attaining and maintaining full employment requires active and often discretionary government intervention to maintain investment levels. Moreover, intervention often has the salutary effect of preventing the formation of bubbles by decreasing the room that private actors have to create credit simply for the purpose of credit creation and financial speculation. This behaviour ultimately was the source of the housing-finance bubble that triggered the Eurozone crisis (Schwartz, 2016). It was Europe's private actors, not its states, perhaps with the exception of Greece, that burst southern Europe's and Ireland's housing bubbles. It was the puncturing of these bubbles that produced a financial crisis that required a massive increase in public debt to bail-out banks – precisely the moral hazard that ordoliberalism decries and the kind of discretionary policy real business-cycle that theorists decry. Europe's financial epistocracy needs to converge back towards what Keynes pointed out almost a century ago. The economy is not a morality play.

Keynes' comment on neo-classical economics applies with equal force to its RBC progeny. Because RBC

> reached conclusions quite different from what the ordinary uninstructed person would expect, added, I suppose, to its intellectual prestige. That its teaching, translated into practice, was austere and often unpalatable, lent it virtue. That it was adapted to carry a vast and consistent logical superstructure, gave it beauty. That it could explain much social injustice and apparent cruelty as an inevitable incident in the scheme of progress, and the attempt to change such things as likely on the whole to do more harm than good, commanded it to authority. That it afforded a measure of justification to the free activities of the individual capitalist, attracted to it the support of the dominant social force behind authority.
>
> *(Keynes, 1936)*

Notes

1 Moreover, it is often forgotten that the non-Euro economies of Eastern Europe had their own housing bubble and subsequent banking crises, which started in January 2009, more than a year earlier than the official Euro crisis, and that bank failures started in the north, and not the south, beginning with bank failures in Ireland and Britain and by the multinational ABN-Amro.

2 Irish GDP is about 20 per cent larger than GNP because multinational firms park profits in Ireland using transfer pricing. This artificially increases Irish GDP.
3 *Financial Times*, "German Public Resists Debt Cut for Greece", 23 January 2015, available at: https://www.ft.com/content/3a9de4de-a191-11e4-b176-00144feab7de.
4 In this respect, the ECB, in particular, paralleled the attitude of the US FED under Alan Greenspan, who famously said in 2005 that it was impossible to know when a bubble existed, and who also downplayed the dangers of non-traditional mortgage products.
5 A 2 × 2 framework, of course, gives rise to a fourth type, but as this type is associated with Marxism and with schools of economic thought that have not been taught since the 1920s (e.g., the institutional economics of John Commons or Thorstein Veblen), this fourth type never had any chance of traction in policy-making circles.

References

Albert, Michel (1993), *Capitalism against Capitalism*, New York: John Wiley & Sons Incorporated.
Almunia, Joaquín (2008), "Future Challenges Facing the Euro", *Speech*, European Commission, 15 April 2008, available at: http://europa.eu/rapid/press-release_SPEECH-08-194_en.htm.
Anderson, Karen (2015), *Social Policy in the European Union*, Basingstoke: Palgrave Macmillan.
Becker, Uwe, and Herman Mark Schwartz (eds) (2005), *Employment Miracles: A Critical Comparison of the Dutch, Scandinavian, Swiss, Australian and Irish Cases versus Germany and the US*, Amsterdam: Amsterdam University Press.
Commons, John R. (1936), "Institutional Economics", *The American Economic Review*, 26 (1): 237–249.
Constâncio, Vítor (Vice-President of the ECB) (2011), "The Macroeconomic and Financial Landscape in the Aftermath of the 2007 Crisis: New Challenges and Perspectives", *Speech*, 7 June 2011, available at: www.ecb.europa.eu/press/key/date/2011/html/sp110607.en.html.
Constâncio, Vítor (Vice-President of the ECB) (2013), "The European Crisis and the Role of the Financial System at the Bank of Greece Conference on 'The Crisis in the Euro Area'", *Speech*, Athens, 23 May 2013.
Delors Report (Commission of the European Communities, Committee for the Study of Economic and Monetary Union) (1989), "1. Report on Economic and Monetary Union in the European Community 2. Collection of Papers Submitted to the Committee for the Study of Economic and Monetary Union", Luxembourg: Office for Official Publications of the European Communities.
Eucken, Walter (1932), "Staatliche Strukturwandlungen und die Krisis des Kapitalismus", *Weltwirtschaftliches Archiv*, 36 (1): 297–323.
Eucken, Walter ([1952] 1990), *Grundsätze der Wirtschaftspolitik*, Tubingen: Mohr.
ECB (2008), *Annual Report*, Frankfurt: European Central Bank.
European Mortgage Federation (EMF) (2007), *Hypostat: A Review of Europe's Mortgage and Housing Markets*, Brussels: European Mortgage Federation.
European Mortgage Federation (EMF) (2016), *Hypostat: A Review of Europe's Mortgage and Housing Markets*, Brussels: European Mortgage Federation.
Fisher, Irving (1933), "The Debt-deflation Theory of Great Depressions", *Econometrica: Journal of the Econometric Society*, 1 (4): 337–357.

Hadeed, Marcel (2017), "The Ordoliberal Ghost," *Social Europe*, 2 August 2017, available at: www.socialeurope.eu/the-ordoliberal-ghost.

van Kersbergen, Kees (2003), *Social Capitalism: A Study of Christian Democracy and the Welfare State*, London: Routledge.

van Kersbergen, Kees, and Philip Manow (2009), *Religion, Class Coalitions, and Welfare States*, Cambridge: Cambridge University Press.

Keynes, John Maynard (1936), *General Theory of Employment, Interest, and Money*, New York: Harcourt, Brace.

Kydland, Finn E., and Edward C. Prescott (1977), "Rules Rather Than Discretion: The Inconsistency of Optimal Plans", *Journal of Political Economy*, 85 (3): 473–491.

Matthijs, Matthias, and Mark Blyth (eds) (2015), *The Future of the Euro*, New York: Oxford University Press.

Minsky, Hyman (1992), "The Financial Instability Hypothesis", Levy Institute Working paper #74.

Röpke, Wilhelm (1982), "The Guiding Principles of the Liberal Programme", in: Horst Friedrich Wünche (ed), *Standard Texts on the Social Market Economy*, New York: Gustav Fischer Verlag, pp. 187–192.

Santer, Jacques (1998), "Shaping Europe's Future", *Speech*, International Bertelsmann Forum, Berlin, available at: http://europa.eu/rapid/press-release_SPEECH-98-151_en.htm.

Schnyder, Gerhard, and Mathias M. Siems (2012), "The Ordo-liberal Variety of Neoliberalism", in: Suzanne Konzelmann and Marc Fovargue-Davies (eds), *Banking Systems in the Crisis: The Faces of Liberal Capitalism*, Abingdon: Routledge, pp. 250–268, available at: https://ssrn.com/abstract=2142529.

Schwartz, Herman Mark (1994), "Small States in Big Trouble: State Reorganization in Australia, Denmark, New Zealand, and Sweden in the 1980s", *World Politics*, 46 (4): 527–555.

Schwartz, Herman Mark (2016), "The Euro as a House of Straw: Why Europe's Crisis is (still) Linked to American Housing", in: Bruno Dallego, Gert Geri and John McGowan (eds), *A Global Perspective on the European Economic Crisis*, Abingdon: Routledge, pp. 224–240.

Tranøy, Bent Sofus (2011), "Poor Governance in a Very Rich and Advanced (Micro) State: Reflections from Political Science", *European Political Studies*, 10 (3): 277–291.

Trichet, Jean-Claude (2008), "The Current State of the Euro Area and its Future", *Speech*, 10 July 2008, at conference entitled: "The Euro's 10th anniversary: History and Presence of the Euro", held in Munich, available at: www.ecb.europa.eu/press/key/date/2008/html/sp080710.en.html.

Trichet, Jean-Claude (2009), "Supporting the Financial System and the Economy: Key ECB Policy Actions in the Crisis", *Speech*, 22 June 2009, available at: www.ecb.europa.eu/press/key/date/2009/html/sp090622.en.html.

Trichet, Jean-Claude (2010), "Lessons from the Crisis", Speech, 3 December 2010, available at: www.ecb.europa.eu/press/key/date/2010/html/sp101203.en.html.

Verdun, Amy (1999), "The Role of the Delors Committee in the Creation of EMU: An Epistemic Community?", *Journal of European Public Policy*, 6 (2): 308–328.

4

EPISTEMIC WORRIES ABOUT ECONOMIC EXPERTISE[1]

Cathrine Holst and Anders Molander

I Introduction

Economists play a pivotal role in economic governance, and their influence has arguably increased – and not decreased, as predicted by some[2] – after the economic crisis of 2008. The rising power of economists in contemporary policy-making is connected to what Frank Vibert (2007) refers to as "the rise of the unelected": the increasing role of central banks, agencies and other expert bodies inhabited by academics – including a large share of economists – with substantive discretionary powers. Another sign of economists' rising power is the ascent of economics professors to high bureaucratic and political positions (Markoff and Montecinos, 1993; Fourcade, 2006). We can add to this the high and arguably increasing significance of economics-derived arguments in parliamentary processes and the public sphere, as civil society organizations and political parties exceedingly feel the need to support their proposals with references to economic research and reasoning (Earle, Moran and Ward-Perkins, 2017; see, also, Porter 1996). Expressions of this can also be found when governments seek policy advice from "experts" and "expert groups" to make policies more "knowledge based," "science based" or "evidence based" (Douglas, 2009; Cairney, 2016; Grundmann, 2017; Gornitzka and Krick, 2018), and often, and in some settings increasingly (Christensen and Hesstvedt, 2018; Christensen 2018), consult economists.

Unsurprisingly, these developments have come under criticism. Extra political power to the most knowledgeable, what has been called "epistocracy"[3] – or, in the case of economists, "econocracy" (Earle, Moran and Ward-Perkins, 2017) – raises obvious democratic concerns. How can it be "a rule by the people" if public policies are left in the hands of professional economists and other experts? Critics see severe participatory and representative deficits developing, and a contemporary democracy that is becoming increasingly "disfigured" (Urbinati, 2014).

However, concerns are also raised from an epistemic perspective. The involvement of economists in policy-making is justified with reference to outcome improvements: economic and other expertise is supposed to be the "filter" that ensures the "truth-sensitivity" of policies and legislation (Christiano, 2012). Yet, critics worry that the increasing role of economists in policy-making does not contribute to enlightenment and problem solving. The involvement of economic experts, they claim, may even make decisions and policies come out worse.

The focus of the chapter will be on this epistemic worry. On the one hand, epistemic concerns are often underplayed, if they are considered at all, by those who defend the increasing role of economic expertise in policy-making (see, for example, Pincione and Tesón, 2006; Caplan, 2007; Brennan, 2016; Sunstein, 2018). Scholars in this camp typically fear "irrationality," "deliberative failures," "economic illiteracy" and disregard for "evidence" when decision-making is left to politicians, while paying less attention to disagreements, biases and mistakes among economists and other experts. On the other hand, when epistemic critique of the role of economic expertise in policy-making is raised explicitly, it tends, first, to be embedded in a rather sweeping critical discourse that does not distinguish between the different concerns involved. Second, it is often assumed – we will argue, misleadingly – that the epistemic problems connected to the use of economic expertise in governance and that policy-making cannot be addressed effectively through institutional measures. The implication seems to be that we have either to make public policies without economic expertise or live with its supposed dysfunctional effects on policy and decision quality, hoping that the epistemic benefits of our reliance on the decisions and advice of economists will outweigh the costs.

In what follows, we show that the substantive involvement of economic experts in policy-making raises some real epistemic concerns. However, we move beyond the uneasiness that many critics articulate, and present a list of ten discrete claims: (1) that we cannot know who the "real" or "best" economic experts are; (2) that all political decisions, including those on economic policy, have moral dimensions and that there is no moral expertise; (3) that proper economic expertise is only possible under conditions of "normal science" and political "well orderedness"; (4) that economists, like laypeople, make cognitive errors; (5) that economists, representing a particular disciplinary perspective and epistemic cultures, are one-eyed, overstretch their competence and fail to see their own perspective as one of many relevant perspectives; (6) that economists may be influenced by self-interest, or (7) have ideological commitments that bias their judgements; (8) that we cannot be sure that economic experts speak truth to power; (9) that economists often lack the competence (or willingness) to translate their expert knowledge to make it understandable for policy-makers and concerned citizens; and, finally, (10) that economic experts do not understand the logic of politics and lack good political judgement.

The list gives more flesh to the ideas of "cognitive and ideological closure" and "segmentation logics" outlined in the introductory chapter to this volume. It also makes visible the considerable complexity of the epistemic challenge that arises from the use and reliance on economic expertise in policy-making – and, as far as we know from the existing literature, our systematic overview represents a novelty. We argue, furthermore, that the problems that occur are not marginal, but problems that may confront us frequently, if not regularly, in real-world governance settings. In this connection, we draw examples from European Union (EU) economic governance. Our treatment on this point is very far from being a full-fledged explanatory analysis but does, we believe, shed light on how it can be that the EU has not succeeded in transforming its "structural openness" into a similar openness when it comes to agenda-setting and policy-making.

However, the fact that problems with expert disagreement, biases and mistakes are noteworthy, including in EU economic policy, does not imply that the reliance on economic expertise in policy-making is ultimately misguided, or that it is impossible to institutionalise expert bodies so they deal better with our listed problems. Economic analysis is no doubt a powerful tool in policy-making; it gives an understanding of economic trends and relationships and the effects of political measures. The concerns over "econocratic" tendencies in governance need to be recognised but should not be overstated or conceived of as non-addressable. In this connection, we introduce three mechanisms tailored to tackle the epistemic uneasiness that the involvement of economic experts in policy-making has spurred. The mechanisms target (1) the behaviour of economic experts, (2) their judgement and (3) the conditions of their behaviour and judgement. Our approach adds to the existing proposals of EU economic governance reform that, as we will show, have given rather limited attention to epistemic parameters.

In the next section of the chapter, we present a more extensive version of our ten-point list with examples from EU economic governance. We go on to give an overview of the types of economic reform approaches and proposals that have been central in European Studies scholarship. We then outline our alternative reform approach, focusing on the three proposed mechanisms for ensuring the epistemic quality of economic expertise. The fourth part sums up and spells out some implications.

II Ten epistemic worries

(1) We cannot know who the economic experts are

Generally, experts are persons who know things that other people do not know within a certain domain, for example, about how the economy and economic policies work. Due to this epistemic asymmetry, non-experts or laypeople with regard to economic issues are often not in a position to know who among the putative economic experts are the "real" or the "best" experts, or to judge between competing claims when these experts disagree (for example, Hardwig 1985, 1991; Walton, 1997; Goldman, 2011; on disagreement among economists, see Machlup 1965 and Fuchs *et al.*, 1997)). In the absence of direct evidence, laypeople thus have to rely on trust in experts. This may be fair in many contexts – consider, for example, the interaction between patients and doctors – but there is an inevitable tension between the use of economic and other expertise *and* democratic politics, since the latter is based upon political equality. Hence, when democratic bodies authorise economic experts to influence political decision-making, they, at the same time, risk being subject to an authority that they themselves are unable to review and hold accountable. Delegating power to economists and other experts may then result in what has been referred to as "political alienation" (Dahl, 1985: 6–7).

It is not hard to detect cases from the EU economic governance context in which epistemic asymmetries are salient. For one thing, the expert knowledge provided is often technically complex. We see this, for example, in European Commission expert group reports in policy areas such as economic and monetary affairs, internal market, competition, external trade and taxation,[4] or in the working paper series of the European Central Bank (ECB)[5]. Recent examples are papers such as "Sources of Borrowing and Fiscal Multipliers," "Trading ahead of Treasury Auctions," "Fiscal Equalization and the Tax Structure" and "The New Area-Wide Model II: An Extended Version of the ECB's Micro-founded Model for Forecasting and Policy Analysis with a Financial Sector." It is no doubt hard for non-experts to evaluate the quality and soundness of the discussions and analyses of several of these reports and papers, and to make direct judgements as to whether the experts involved are truly knowledgeable in the relevant domains. Similarly, were putative economic experts to disagree on some of the conclusions made, it would require considerable expertise on the topics in question to formulate an informed and independent opinion on which of the competing claims to support. Consider for example the following questions recently discussed in an ECB working paper: the more exact relationship between monetary policy and inequality in income and wealth,[6] the implications of introducing a New Keynesian model in an argument on "interest-rate spreads and forward guidance"[7] or the risk of negative policy rates.[8]

(2) There are no moral experts

A democratic polity is characterised by pluralism; inevitably, there is disagreement about which political ends to pursue, and how to interpret and rank them. Questions about facts and the efficiency of means to ends are, of course, important. However, factual and technical considerations are often intertwined with norms and values. So, even if experts may tell us something about "*is*-questions," for example, about economic facts and mechanisms, and the effects of different economic policies, and if we, as novices, were able to identify the real or best experts with regard to such issues despite epistemic asymmetries, the question remains as to whether these experts would be able to deliver expertise on all the "*ought*-questions" involved, as well.

The default position in the literature on the question of moral expertise seems to be that there is no such thing. In democratic theory, this position has, for example, been put forward by Robert Dahl, according to whom (1989: 66) there is no moral knowledge, and hence no moral expertise, because there are no methods for demonstrating the intersubjective validity of moral judgements. Nevertheless, Dahl admitted that moral questions cannot be reduced to "subjective" questions pertaining simply to different "tastes"; there is scope for "argument drawing on human reason and human experience" (Dahl 1989: 67). This raises the question of whether there can be moral experts after all. Arguably, all accounts that consider normative questions to be possible objects of rational discourse open up, in principle, to the existence of moral expertise: if some moral arguments are more qualified than others, then some may be better able to make qualified moral arguments than others. On this premise, one could think of moral expertise, for example, in the following way (see, also, Gesang, 2010):

> Someone familiar with moral concepts and with moral arguments, who has ample time to gather information and think about it, may reasonably be expected to reach a soundly based conclusion more often than someone who is unfamiliar with moral concepts and moral arguments and has little time.
>
> *(Singer, 1972: 117)*

To talk about moral experts along these lines does seem to make it possible to identify someone as more competent in answering moral questions than others.

The problem of epistemic asymmetry would then reappear. For example, how should citizens approach arguments based upon highly complex theories of distributive justice? If they cannot assess them directly, they would again be dependent on trust in the epistemic communities to which the experts belong – be it, in this case, the community of moral and political philosophers or the more specialised epistemic communities connected to economic or other policy areas. Upon what basis can one as a non-expert deem whether this or that community should be recognised as having the competences that they claim to have?

If we return to the expert bodies of EU economic governance, a key observation that can be made is that several of them have, as a part of their mandate, to address not only questions of facts and the technical efficiency of policies, but also normative questions. We see this on several occasions in the European Central Bank and Eurosystem mission statements, and elaborating statements on "strategic intents" and "organisational principles."[9] For example, to ensure the "main objective" of the ECB and the Eurosystem – "the maintenance of price stability" – the ECB is mandated discretionary space to define "price stability for the common good," distinguished from price stability that is less "sound," and to interpret what it implies to show "due regard" to principles such as "independence," "decentralisation," "accountability" and "equal treatment." Similarly, we see in European Commission expert group mandates how economic and other experts are called upon to make judgements on distributive and other value-laden issues, for example, when the High-level Group of Experts on Pensions is asked "to identify and assess the main challenges related to the provision, adequacy and sustainability of supplementary (occupational and personal) pensions" in the light of "intergenerational balance" and other parameters, and to "develop policy recommendations at Union level and a potential roadmap for implementation,"[10] or when the Scientific, Technical and Economic Committee for Fisheries is to be "consulted, where appropriate, on matters pertaining to the conservation and management of living marine resources, including biological, economic, environmental, social and technical considerations."[11] The result is often discussions and recommendations that deal not only with issues which are technically complex, but also include complicated normative considerations, relying, for example, on arguments from welfare, environmental or development economics. We can add to this the many papers and reports produced by EU economic experts upon the basis of mandates which are seemingly purely technical, asking for "evidence," "mappings," "descriptions," "comparisons," "explanations" and/or "forecasts," but which will frequently involve deliberations on aims and goals and interpretation and ranking of standards and parameters, since the latter, as they occur, for example, in the EU treaties and regulations, will typically be under-specified and under-determined. In all these cases, it can quite easily be very hard for the untrained to grasp and assess the technical – and normative – claims involved, and even harder to review the relative merits of competing claims when putative experts disagree.

(3) Proper economic expertise requires "normal science" and political "well orderedness"

Even if we were able to know who the experts are, be they technical or moral – insofar as there are ways to identify relatively credible epistemic communities – there is the additional worry that this only applies under "normal' circumstances. We often see how fields or disciplines are characterised by competing paradigms or research programmes, and how, after periods of production of expert knowledge within the parameters of a certain cognitive framework, they undergo epistemic shifts that change the notions of what qualifies as expert knowledge. The sources of such shifts can be more or less internal to the epistemic community, spurred by theoretical or conceptual innovation, methodological breakthroughs or new technologies, but they can also be external and related to social and cultural changes, economic crisis or political ruptures. An example within economics is the rise and fall of Keynesian economics, as well as the renewed interest that it has attracted after the 2008 financial crisis (see for example Akerlof and Schiller 2009).

EU economic governance has been debated on the background of the different, and sometimes starkly opposed, accounts of what spurred the 2008 crisis, the role of the advice, models and predictions of economists and of the viable ways ahead. On the one hand, some analyses connected the Euro crisis to a shift in EU economic policy discourse "from pragmatism to dogmatism" rooted in "regulatory liberalism" and "monetary orthodoxy" (Mügge, 2011: 201; see, also, Jabko, 1999; McKay, 2005; Posner and Véron, 2010; Broome, 2013; and Heipertz and Verdun, 2004: 772, on the shift from Keynesianism to monetarism), and to institutional asymmetries and dysfunctional fiscal, monetary and finance regulation policies resulting from this orthodoxy (Jabko, 2010, Blankenburg et al., 2013; Mügge, 2013), rooted in deep trends and flaws in hegemonic economic thinking (for general arguments on the latter, see Reiss, 2008; Quiggin, 2008; Palley, 2012; and Schlefer, 2012). In short, according to this approach, economists and economic expertise were hugely responsible for the economic, social and political problems that Europe faced in the aftermath of the crisis. On the other hand, competing accounts emphasised how EU economic expertise, institutions and governance adapted and re-adapted in a relatively functional way before, during and in the aftermath of the Euro crisis (for example, Salines et al., 2012). Others focused more generally, arguing that it was not economics and economic expertise as such that were to blame for the bad policy choices which preceded the 2008 crisis, but possibly certain flawed economic models (on the pluralism of perspectives and positions among contemporary economists, see, for example, Stiglitz et al., 2008; Blanchard et al., 2012) and particular epistemic communities of economists, powerful stakeholders and politicians dogmatically relying on these models, or on academically sound models that were, however, applied selectively or mechanically, without a proper understanding of the models' assumptions and conditions (see, for example, Schlefer, 2012). Adding to the complexity, economic experts differed in their policy recommendations, where some spoke in favour of the austerity approach and "market conforming" measures, whereas others criticised austerity and emphasised the need for more "market shaping" measures (Jabko, 2010). In such situations, which of the experts and economists should the non-expert trust? How can the novice assess directly and independently which camp to side with? When competing epistemic cultures and approaches occur and expert standards and constellations shift, as we saw happening when the economic crisis hit, the question of who the "real" experts are, becomes, arguably, even harder.

(4) Ecomomic experts make cognitive errors

It is generally reasonable to assume that experts, *when* they are using well-established scientific methods and follow the rules of scientific reasoning, are less prone to making errors than laypeople. Nonetheless, the fact that experts do make errors is well known, and research in cognitive psychology has shown that expert judgements are more exposed to elementary fallacies stemming from the use of the intuitive "System 1" than we would like to think (Tversky and Kahneman, 1974; Tetlock, 2005; Kahneman, 2012). Experts have, for example, a dubious reputation as forecasters. In *Expert Political Judgment*, Philip Tetlock (2005) presents results from studies of the ability of experts to make economic and political predictions. The experts turned out to be overconfident; their answers to questions scored badly on accuracy, especially if they were "hedgehogs" who "know one big thing" in contrast to "foxes" who know "many things."

The problem of bad forecasting is generally a challenge for the many economic experts who develop and use models to produce predictions about economics and the effects of economic policy. Controversies surrounding the EU's economic forecasting endeavours, for example, the European Commission Economic Forecasts[12] or the ECB's Macroeconomic Projections,[13] are illustrative, and we see them occurring repeatedly, for example, in European news media. Forecasts and projections of the EU economic area and the Eurozone are criticised for being based upon uncertain, unlikely or even random estimates, resulting in poorly founded scenarios and recommendations, and, in the end, failed policies that affect business, public finance and the welfare of citizens all over Europe. One line of this criticism is addressed rather directly against economics and the economists who deliver "bad" advice. Another line of criticism is more indirect: the problem coming to the fore is maybe not so much that expert predictions are decisively false or flawed, but that economic experts tend to operate too confidently and exaggerate the certainty of estimates that are key to their problem framing and recommendations.

(5) Economists are one-eyed

There is an old saying that, for one who possesses a hammer, everything is a nail. Experts are, no doubt, often too confident of their own competence (Angner, 2006); they identify with their disciplines and are prone to frame problems so that they fall within their disciplinary matrices, paradigms or "epistemic cultures" (Buchanan, 2004; Lamont, 2009). For example, studies of environmental policy show how engineers, lawyers and economists tend to approach this policy area differently, focusing on technology, regulation and taxes/dues, respectively (Tellman, 2016). Not least in the aftermath of the 2008 Euro crisis, this line of critique against disciplinary bias has been frequently raised against economists in particular. Critics argue that what they see as key features of the epistemic matrix of economics – model building based upon idealised assumptions, unfounded forecasting, *etc.*, – unduly coloured the economic experts' advice before, during and after the crisis. This, for example, is a central line of argument among academic anti-econocrats (see, in particular, Earle, Moran and Ward-Perkins, 2017), who list the narrow problem-framing, along with the methodological rules and toolbox of economics, as one of several problems with this discipline's hold on policy advice. It was also one of the concerns for critics in the European Parliament and civil society when in 2013 and 2014 they accused the European

Commission of composing its expert groups with biased and "unbalanced" expertise (Holst and Moodie, 2015).

(6) Economic experts operate out of self-interest

Another general objection against experts is that they may be more or less biased by their self-interests. A statement from the philosopher Robert Spaemann in a 2008 German parliament commission on the permissibility of using human embryonic stem cells in research can exemplify this:

> I take the liberty of a final remark on the status of the 'experts' questioned. As an independent authority can only be considered whoever is not committed to a particular interest by his professional status. Thus, not researchers working with embryonic stem cells or representatives of research institutions under whose ceiling such research takes place. They are an interested party and must be viewed as competent lobbyists. Their (…) advice must be relativized and deserves no more hearing than that of a reflective nurse.
>
> *(quoted in Zenker, 2011: 362)*

In a well-functioning political system, conflicting interests are normally taken care of by the procedures for the selection of experts. Suspicions that the EU has not properly safeguarded against "corrupt" experts have, however, fuelled public demands for more transparency and better guidelines for expert selection. Moreover, even if there are no direct ties to parties who are interested in a certain outcome, experts may favour outcomes that are to their own advantage – for example, those that confirm positions which they have defended, be it in academic or more public settings, and so bolster their professional reputation. This worry arguably haunts EU debates and the role of experts in these debates all over Europe (see Holst and Molander, 2018, on this worry among Norwegian eurosceptics), and recently it has once more played out in the heated Brexit controversy. In this case, the Leave campaign accuses economic and other experts that they associate with the Remain camp of being unfit to give a balanced assessment of implications of Britain leaving the EU in the light of their previous analyses, research and advice which, according to Brexiteers, have been unduly EU-friendly.

(7) Economists are ideologically biased

A related and frequent charge about bias is that economic and other experts have ideological commitments or other deeper normative orientations that influence their judgements. We see this when experts explicitly embed their decisions or advice in a particular ideological or moral outlook. In addition, there are not so easily detectable cases. Numerous examiners of economics from Gunnar

Myrdal's classical examination of the value impregnation of classical and neo-classical economics ([1930] 1953) onward have noted how theoretical approaches may frame the problem in hand in such a way that some value options are tacitly favoured. For example, neoclassical economics is said to frame problems in a way that favours market solutions. In the EU economic governance context, we see this when EU expert bodies and economic advisors are repeatedly accused of introducing market-conforming measures and "neoliberalism" with their rec-ommendations and interventions. Sometimes, the charge is that the economists involved are politically conservative or committed "neoliberals." However, the more fundamental problem, according to many critics, is that the dominant approaches within economics have a systematic and inherent pro-market bias.

(8) Economic experts fail to speak truth to power

Yet another worry is that economists, along with other experts, belong and iden-tify with the societal or power élite, and that their élite position and frame of reference compromise their independence; experts are supposed to "speak truth to power" (Wildavsky, 1979), but their connections to the "establishment" tend to make them more affirmative than critical of the powers that be. This suspi-cion is a common ingredient in populist politics – debates over Brexit provide several examples – but is also fuelled by sober sociological scholarship on elite recruitment, formation and networks. Furthermore, despite its crudeness, the populist suspicion points to the circumstance that the duty of truth-telling (what the Greeks called *parrhesia*) requires courage because it may involve personal risks (Foucault, 2001).

Moreover, this worry is, no doubt, part of the criticism against EU "technoc-racy" and "expertocracy," for example, in the critique of the biased composition of the European Commission expert group system. Behind this criticism lies not only a democratic concern, but also a worry that élites of economists and other experts will reproduce convenient élite conceptions and prejudices ultimately in line with "corporate interests" instead of speaking up and speaking "the truth" in the interest(s) of ordinary people (Holst and Moodie, 2015: 39).

(9) Economists are bad at communicating their knowledge

Without doubt, experts are often bad at stating arguments in a comprehensible way:

> People have a hard time taking the perspective of a less knowledgeable individual, and the gap is only wider for experts addressing laymen.
> *(Mercier, 2011: 321)*

Because of élitist or arrogant/uncivil attitudes, experts may also be unwilling to communicate in ways that reach out more broadly to stakeholders and those affected. Such translation problems, be they due to experts' limited abilities or lack of adequate motivation, add to the already troublesome situation of epistemic asymmetry between experts and non-experts. Due to cognitive inequalities, it is hard for non-experts to hold experts to account. If experts are also bad communicators, then the situation will only worsen. This is also an issue in the EU economic governance context where economic policy expert reports are accused of being unnecessarily technical, and framed in ways that exclude the average citizen from their readership.

(10) Economic experts lack political judgement

The last objection is that experts lack an understanding of political processes and the ability to make political judgements, since they tend to view political questions as if they were questions of facts and logic. On the one hand, this may result in recommendations that are "right," in the sense that they are supported by solid evidence, but that lack political feasibility, at least in the here and now. A variant of this is when experts give unfeasible recommendations because they ignore the institutional political conditions for their implementation (Swift and White, 2008). On the other hand, experts may exaggerate the extent to which the space for political action is constrained by *Sachzwang*, by given circumstances and parameters. The result in the first case is some kind of utopian engineering; in the other, the result is adaptive, technocratic engineering that considers revisable facts and questionable concerns as "necessities." In the contexts of economists and EU economic governance, technocracy, in the latter sense, represents a rather persuasive problem. In particular, we often see how considerations that necessarily involve normative interpretation and ranking (for example, when an expert group recommends one policy over others) are presented as if they were purely technical or scientific questions.

Concluding, firstly, we believe to have shown that these ten outlined worries are real and not trivial in an EU context. To be sure, our claim is not that the selection of examples that we have provided is, in a strict sense, representative for how economic experts in the EU generally operate. However, our examples illustrate, we believe, that there are some genuine problems of an epistemic nature in this governance setting, and that these problems tend to occur and re-occur. Consequently, to address the puzzle stated in the introduction of this volume – why does segmentation take place, despite the EU's initial structural openness? – closure mechanisms of the kind that our list indicates should be investigated more systematically. Our claim is also not that the criticisms that are raised in the concrete controversies to which we refer, be it the controversy surrounding the European Commission expert groups or about Brexit, are altogether valid and beyond dispute. Nonetheless, we do not find any of them to be immediately unreasonable. Secondly, we should note how objections 4–10 are all about expert failures and inappropriate use of economic and other expertise, while objections 1–3 are of an epistemological nature and apply even under ideal conditions; if there is something akin to flawless expertise, objections 1–3 will still remain, since epistemic asymmetry represents an inherent problem in all use of expertise in policy-making. It follows from this that the challenge for non-experts to distinguish "real" EU economic experts from "fake" or quasi experts, or the "best" experts from the mediocre, is, to a certain extent, ineliminable. Yet, and thirdly, this does not imply that nothing can be done, that we either have to reject the use of economic and other expertise, or are completely subject to it in whatever shape it comes. There is room for taking measures in the design of export bodies and procedures so as to make the use of expertise compatible with requirements of epistemic trust and democratic delegation. As for objections 4–10, it would generally be a mistake to draw the conclusion that laypeople are as likely to be right as experts on issues of economics, or that relying on economic experts inevitably disturbs the logic of political discourse rather than enhances its quality due to the risks of expert biases and errors. What are called for, instead, are mechanisms that can prevent expert failures – and the "segmentation logics" that easily result from them – and secure against the misuse of expertise. The central question is thus how EU economic governance and similar institutions can be designed to ensure better that identified experts will perform their demo-cratically entrusted tasks in an acceptable way, and, preferably, in the best way possible.

III Approaches to EU economic governance reform

Interestingly, the academic community – and European studies in particu-lar – produced a set of proposals for reforming or adapting EU economic gov-ernance in the years before and after the 2008 shock and the economic stagnation and social crisis that followed. However, a review of the literature shows that the epistemic concerns raised played a rather limited role in these contributions.

In our search, we found, firstly, proposals with a *technocratic* orientation. The aim of these proposals is mainly to facilitate efficient political and administrative processes success on central macroeconomic variables and. An example can be found in Andrew Hallett and Svend Hougaard Jensen (2012), who propose rec-ommendations for smoother and more flexible fiscal co-ordination among EU member countries. They argue that "soft debt targets" should replace regulations based upon absolute limits of debt and deficits as those stated in the Stability and Growth Pact and the Fiscal Compact, and they propose a new fiscal policy com-mission that together with, among others, the European Central Bank (ECB), should have the central responsibility for the co-ordination of both Member State fiscal policies and the EU's fiscal and monetary regulation. Another example can be found in Marion Salines, Gabriel Glöckler and Zbigniew Truschlewski (2012). From the perspective of historical institutionalism, they analyse how the Commission, the Council, the ECB and other EU bodies involved in EU eco-nomic governance have adapted – functionally and gradually – to a crises-ridden environment, in accordance with institutional path-dependencies and with the aim of increasing both effectiveness and output. The point of these authors is not so much to recommend grand reforms as to make visible how EU institutions work, and how relatively well they work, even in times of crisis. Uwe Puetter's (2012; see, also, Puetter 2004 and 2007) technocratic reform agenda is also not so outspoken; he analyses EU economic governance as moving steadily towards "deliberative intergovernmentalism" with the Eurogroup, an informal forum for Eurozone finance ministers, in the front seat. Still, the virtues of this way of moving ahead in economic policy-making are emphasized. In particular, the Eurogroup, as a soft deliberative co-ordinating forum, is presented as enhancing decision quality and political stability in the Eurozone area.

These proposals and suggestions have a different flavour than those of our second category: reform proposals with a *social* focus. These proposals stress how economic regulation and institutions are supposed to serve a wider set of societal goals such as collective trust, equality and social justice. A clear example of this kind of proposal occurs in Dermot Hodson and Imelda Maher (2002). They argue that the ultimate success criterion of the Monetary Union (EMU) cannot be low and stable inflation. Rather, the EMU has to be transformed and re-institutionalised to ensure legitimacy more broadly speaking, and take into account a set of different standards linked to both "input, output, values and process," not only in the field of monetary policy but also in interconnected policy fields. A decisive factor to enhance legitimacy in this broad sense, according to these authors, is also to democratise decision-making procedures. In one of his articles, Nicolas Jabko (2010) argues along similar lines when he analyses the "duality of the euro," meaning both its "market conforming" and "market shaping" characteristics, and assesses the possibility and the possible virtues of an EU more concerned with "market shaping" and social concerns. Daniel Mügge (2013) also takes a closer look at the characteristics of EU finance regulation from a political-economic perspective, emphasising the similarities of European and US capitalism and regulatory regimes. Preferring a different and more social path, Mügge analyses how the characteristics of this regime contributed to the economic crisis in Europe, and accentuates, in particular, how a deeper democratisation of EU institutions is required to achieve this.

Finally, we can talk of the *democratic* reform proposals. As indicated, they sometimes overlap considerably with the reform proposals with a social focus. However, they primarily address the need for a basic democratic re-structuring of economic institutions, regulation and policy-making in the EU. In another article, Jabko (2003), for example, focuses more closely on democratisation, and argues that the relationship between the ECB and the European Parliament is insufficiently democratic, not least because the Parliament in different respects accepts a flawed conception of central banking as a purely technical, value-free endeavour. Jakbo's concerns overlap here with Robert Elgie's (2002) proposal to make the ECB more democratically accountable by introducing measures elaborated in principal-agent theory as "police patrolling" and "non-standard measures." Finally, Christopher Lord (2012) can exemplify a democratic proposal of reforming EU economic governance. He analyses the implications of the Eurozone crisis, the European Semester and the Fiscal Compact for democratic accountability and democratic equality. There is the increased use of the discretionary powers of – compared to other central banks – the extremely independent ECB, but also the transformation of "the European Commission and the Council of the EU into something of a common budgetary authority of the Euro-area. (…) On top of that, the European Council has assumed a role as an emergency decision-maker" (Lord, 2012: 46). All this paves the way for an unprecedented use of the community method in the fiscal area, according to Lord, something which calls for a much more committed democratisation of EU monetary and fiscal policy-making, including ensuring the European Parliament and the national parliaments have a pivotal role.

Yet, if we take seriously the epistemic worries spurred by the political role of economic experts and the pro-claimed rise of an "econocracy" in the EU, what is needed, in addition to these valuable technocratic, social and democratic reform proposals, is a conscious epistemically oriented approach; without an eye to the closure logics indicated by our ten-point list, attempts to effectively replace "segmentation" with "de-segmentation" will easily fail. Considering what commentators often argue about the key role of "output legitimacy" in the EU (see Scharpf, 1999, for the classical formulation), it is maybe somewhat surprising that scholarly contributions have had such a limited focus on epistemic parameters and the organisation of expertise (with some exceptions; see, for example, Mügge, 2011: 201–202),[14] factors that are known to influence decision and policy quality substantively. Given that expert arrangements in the area of economic policy need not only to be effective, democratic and integrated within a broader social agenda, but also to handle better the biases and mistakes of economic experts and take the problem of epistemic asymmetry into account, what requirements need to be in place?

IV Institutional mechanisms: An epistemic approach

With this in mind, we will sketch here some of the fundamentals of an epistemic approach to the reform of expert organisations, focusing on three sets of institutional mechanisms with different targets. One group of mechanisms targets expert *behaviour*, a second group is the *judgements* of experts and a third group is the *conditions* for expert inquiry and judgement.

To the first category belong the "dos and don'ts" of scientific communities aimed at guaranteeing the pursuit of truth through a fair competition between arguments. The adherence to such epistemic norms (on "the scientific ethos" see Robert Merton [1973]) is pre-supposed when political authorities and citizens appeal to expert opinion. In the end, the latter have to rely on the functioning of scientific communities (*i.e.*, that the norms of inquiry are enforced through mutual scrutiny and criticism). This is the predicament of epistemic asymmetry, but political authorities can have an influence on the conditions for their own trust. Decisions taken about the external organisation of science and research, and about the funding of research and the distribution of funds between different branches of research – for example, within different branches of economics, and between economics and other disciplines – may have considerable effects on the internal functioning of scientific communities. The way in which expert bodies and expert groups are organised may also be important for making the scientific *ethos* effective. In this connection, specific measures can be taken, such as checking scientific merit and past records (if the economic experts relied upon are supposed to contribute with a research-based view; what are their academic credentials?), but also their vested interests and political affiliations, in order to exclude unsuitable persons from assignments.

The second group of mechanisms aims at holding experts accountable by putting their judgements under review in different fora (Reiss, 2008: 38 ff). The primary forum for testing judgements and detecting fallacies and biases is the forum of peers; competent economic experts, for example, should review and control what other economic experts are doing. However, in a process of democratic decision-making, the testing of judgements and arguments must be extended from this forum to experts in other relevant disciplines to the legislature and other political bodies, and even to the public sphere at large. In these *fora*, economic and other experts can be asked to account for critical assumptions, explain the models used, specify their limits and present alternative models (see Schlefer, 2012: 280–281). Of special importance is to demand that they account for their specific area of expertise, that is, that the tasks with which they are entrusted lie within their domain of expertise. Mechanisms of this kind may influence to what extent experts are considered trustworthy, but may also counteract expert failures, for example, when experts fall victim to overconfidence or are insensitive to the evaluative, non-scientific dimensions of a problem.

The third group of mechanisms targets the conditions for expert inquiry and judgement. Epistemic self-constraint is closely related to the existence of cognitive diversity and an adequate intellectual division of labour. Experts who reason alone are exposed to *confirmation bias*, which is the tendency to look only for arguments that confirm their own ideas; and to *reason-based choice*, which is the tendency to pick the option for which reasons can be most easily gathered. Deliberating groups are less prone to these fallacies, and they may also enlarge the pool of ideas and information as well as weed out bad arguments (Mercier, 2011). However, the positive epistemic effects of deliberation are dependent on diversity. Without diversity – for example, when expert groups and agencies are crowded with like-minded economists alone – deliberation may work in the opposite direction and create groupthink (Sunstein, 2006; Sunstein and Hastie, 2015). Hence, organising expert work along team lines and deliberative lines, and providing for the necessary diversity and exposure to criticism from the wider epistemic community, are important ways of fostering epistemic modesty and improving the quality and conditions of expert inquiry and judgement. Crucially, cognitive diversity also involves co-operation between different disciplines and fields brought in to explain a subject matter from different angles.

V Conclusions and implications

In the end, the ten worries that we have presented and illustrated with the role of economic experts and examples from EU economic governance are, unfortunately, not unfounded. Our ten-point list refers to real challenges and drivers of "segmentation" that hearken back to the problem of epistemic asymmetries: how non-experts can trust that putative experts are real experts when these non-experts are not themselves in an epistemic position to assess the statements and justifications of experts directly. Given "the fact of expertise" in contemporary democracies (Holst and Molander, 2017), that is, that reasonable political decisions have to rely extensively on expert knowledge, epistemic concerns must be dealt with at the level of institutional design. What is called for are mechanisms that ensure that the performance of putative experts adheres to epistemic standards. We have tentatively sketched three groups of such mechanisms and showed how the epistemic approach from which they are derived supplement the dominant approaches in literature on economic governance reforms in the EU that have focused mostly on technocratic, social and democratic parameters. We believe this added approach, and the more stringent focus on the performance, interactions and organization of expertise that it inspires, is crucial for the triggering of "de-segmentation" logics. A fuller account of what this would imply more concretely in terms of reform for the economic policy area in the Union must, however, be left to another occasion.

Furthermore, even if mechanisms to check on the epistemic credentials of economic experts and improve on their performance can be put in place and made more effective, a problem remains that is not about epistemic trust. It is well known how politicians and officials often use expertise, not in the service of enlightenment and problem-solving, but selectively to consolidate organisational preferences or to legitimise pre-determined policy decisions, or symbolically to demonstrate competence and "epistemic authority" (Hunter and Boswell, 2015). This chapter has discussed and addressed epistemic concerns about the disagreements, biases and mistakes of economic experts. However, to address the larger problem of ensuring the epistemic quality of political outcomes, we not only need well-functioning expert bodies and experts who behave as good experts are supposed to, but also fully-fledged political systems – be they at national or EU levels – in which all central actor groups, from citizens, spokespersons and opinion leaders to party politicians, interest-group representatives, civil servants and ministers, show a concern for ensuring truth-sensitive decisions and policies.

Notes

1 This book chapter builds on two other co-authored articles by Holst and Molander: "Epistemic Democracy and the Role of Experts", (2019) *Contemporary Political Theory*, https://doi.org/10.1057/s41296-018-00299-4, and "Asymmetry, Disagreement and Biases: Epistemic Worries About Expertise", (2018) *Social Epistemology*, 32 (6): 358–371. Some sub-sections overlap across these pieces. This chapter's analysis of the role

of economic expertise and the case of EU economic governance is, however, unique. The analytical framework relied on in the two journal articles is also reframed and connected to debates on the role of economists in public policy, the idea of a "segmented political order" (see the introduction to this volume) and EU reform discourse in the aftermath of the 2008 crisis.

2 According to a popular argument, the power of economists would wither, since the economic crisis – assumed to be a direct result of the advice of economists – exposed the limitations of the competence of economists and the flaws of models of financial markets.

3 For the original formulation of an "epistocracy of the educated," see Estlund (2008).

4 The reports can be found in the Register of Commission Expert Groups, see http://ec.europa.eu/transparency/regexpert.

5 https://www.ecb.europa.eu/pub/research/working-papers/html/index.en.html.

6 The ECB working paper "How does monetary policy affect income and wealth inequality? Evidence from quantitative easing in the euro area" (No. 2190) studies the effects of quantitative easing on income and wealth of individual Euro-area households. It finds "that the earnings heterogeneity channel plays a key role: quantitative easing compresses the income distribution since many households with lower incomes become employed. In contrast, monetary policy has only negligible effects on wealth inequality."

7 The ECB working paper "Interest rate spreads and forward guidance" (No. 2186) introduces "a basic New Keynesian model" to replicate its finding. "This model predicts that output and inflation effects of forward guidance do not increase with the length of the guidance period and are substantially smaller than if liquidity premia were neglected," which "indicates that there are no puzzling forward guidance effects when endogenous liquidity premia are taken into account".

8 The ECB working paper "Life below zero: Bank lending under negative policy rates" (No. 2173) argues that "the introduction of negative policy rates by the European Central Bank in mid-2014 leads to more risk taking and less lending by euro-area banks with greater reliance on deposit funding," which suggests "that negative rates are less accommodative, and could pose a risk to financial stability, if lending is done by high-deposit banks."

9 https://www.ecb.europa.eu/ecb/orga/escb/html/index.en.html.

10 http://ec.europa.eu/transparency/regexpert/index.cfm?do=groupDetail. groupDetailDoc&id=36987&no=1.

11 https://stecf.jrc.ec.europa.eu.

12 https://ec.europa.eu/info/business-economy-euro/economic-performance-and-forecasts/economic-forecasts_en.

13 https://www.ecb.europa.eu/pub/projections/html/index.en.html.

14 Mügge is stressing the importance of including dissenting voices from "academia and the financial industry itself" in debates on future EU financial regulations, and "counter-expertise" that policy-makers should be "obliged" to address.

References

Akerlof, G. A., and R. J. Shiller (2009), *Animal Spirits: How Human Psychology Drives the Economy, and Why It Matters for Global Capitalism*, Princeton, NJ: Princeton University Press.

Angner, Erik (2006), "Economists as Experts: Overconfidence in Theory and Practice", *Journal of Economic Methodology*, 13 (1): 1–24.

Blanchard, Olivier, David Romer, Michael Spence, and Joseph Stiglitz (2012), *In the Wake of the Crisis. Leading Economists Reassess Economic Policy*, Cambridge, MA: The MIT Press.

Blankenburg, Stephanie, Lawrence King, Sue Konselmann, and Frank Wilkinson (2013), "Prospects for the Eurozone", *Cambridge Journal of Economics*, 37 (3): 463–477.

Brennan, Jason (2016), *Against Democracy*, Princeton, NJ: Princeton University Press.

Broome, André (2013), "The Politics of IMF-EU Co-operation: Institutional Change from the Maastricht Treaty to the Launch of the Euro", *Journal of European Public Policy*, 20 (4): 589–605.

Buchanan, Allen (2004), "Political Liberalism and Social Epistemology", *Philosophy and Public Affairs*, 32 (2): 95–130.

Caplan, Bryan (2007), *The Myth of the Rational Voter: Why Democracies Choose Bad Policies*, Princeton, NJ: Princeton University Press.

Cairney, Paul (2016), *The Politics of Evidence-Based Policy Making*, London: Palgrave Macmillan.

Christensen, Johan (2018), "Economic Knowledge and the Scientization of Policy Advice", *Policy Sciences*, 51 (3): 291–311.

Christensen, Johan, and Stine Hesstvedt (2018), "Expertisation or Greater Representation? Evidence from Norwegian Advisory Commissions", *European Politics and Society*, 20 (1): 83–100.

Christiano, Thomas (2012), "Rational Deliberation Among Experts and Citizens", in: John Parkinson and Jane Mansbridge (eds), *Deliberative Systems: Deliberative Democracy at the Large Scale*, Cambridge: Cambridge University Press, pp. 27–51.

Dahl, Robert A. (1985), *Controlling Nuclear Weapons: Democracy versus Guardianship*, Syracuse, NY: SUNY Press.

Dahl, Robert A. (1989), *Democracy and its Critics*, New Haven, CT: Yale University Press.

Douglas, Heather (2009), *Science, Policy, and the Value-Free Ideal*, Pittsburgh, PA: University of Pittsburgh Press.

Earle, Joe, Cahal Moran, and Zach Ward-Perkins (2017). *The Econocracy. The Perils of Leaving Economics to the Experts*, Manchester: Manchester University Press.

Elgie, Robert (2002), "The Politics of the European Central Bank: Principal-agent Theory and the Democratic Deficit", *Journal of European Public Policy*, 9 (2): 186–200.

Estlund, David M. (2008), *Democratic Authority: A Philosophical Framework*, Princeton, NJ: Princeton University Press.

Fourcade, Marion (2006), "The Construction of a Global Profession: The Transnationalization of Economics", *American Journal of Sociology*, 112 (1): 145–194.

Foucault, Michel (2001), *Fearless Speech*, Los Angeles, CA: Semiotext(e).

Fuchs, Victor R., Alan B. Krueger, and James B. Poterba (1997), "Why do Economist Disagree about Policy? The Roles of Beliefs about Parameters and Values". NBER Working Paper 6151, available at: www.nber.org/papers/w6151.pdf.

Gesang, Bernward (2010), "Are Moral Philosophers Moral Experts?", *Bioethics*, 24 (4): 153–159.

Goldman, Alvin (2011), "Experts: Which Ones Should You Trust?", in: Alvin Goldman and Dennis Whitcomb (eds), *Social Epistemology: Essential Readings*, Oxford: Oxford University Press, pp. 109–133.

Gornitzka, Åse, and Eva Krick 2018), "The Expertisation of Stakeholder Involvement in EU Policymaking", in: Magdalena Góra, Cathrine Holst and Marta Warat (eds), *Expertisation and Democracy in Europe*, London: Routledge, pp. 51–70.

Grundmann, Reiner (2017), "The Problem of Expertise in Knowledge Societies", *Minerva*, 55 (1): 25–48.

Hallett, Andrew Hughes, and Svend E. Hougaard Jensen (2012), "Fiscal Governance in the Euro Area: Institutions vs. Rules", *Journal of European Public Policy*, 19 (5): 646–664.

Hardwig, John (1985), "Epistemic Dependence", *Journal of Philosophy*, 82 (7): 335–349.

Hardwig, John (1991), "The Role of Trust in Knowledge", *Journal of Philosophy*, 88 (12): 693–708.

Heipertz, Martin, and Amy Verdun (2004), "The Dog that would Never Bite? What Can We Learn from the Origins of the Stability and Growth Pact", *Journal of European Public Policy*, 11 (5): 765–780.

Hodson, Dermot, and Imelda Maher (2002), "Economic and Monetary Union: Balancing Credibility and Legitimacy in an Asymmetrical Policy-mix", *Journal of European Public Policy*, 9 (3): 391–407.

Holst, Cathrine, and Anders Molander (2017), "Public Deliberation and the Fact of Expertise: Making Experts Accountable", *Social Epistemology*, 31 (3): 235–250.

Holst, Cathrine, and Anders Molander (2018), "Asymmetry, Biases and Biases: Epistemic Worries About Expertise", *Social Epistemology*, 32 (6): 358–371.

Holst, Cathrine, and Anders Molander (2019), "Epistemic Democracy and the Role of Experts", *Contemporary Political Theory*, forthcoming, available at: doi: 10.1057/s41296-018-00299-4.

Holst, Cathrine, and John R. Moodie (2015), "Cynical or Deliberative? An Analysis If the European Commission's Public Communication on Its Use of Expertise in Policy-Making", *Politics and Governance*, 3 (1): 37–48.

Hunter, Alistair, and Christina Boswell (2015), "Comparing the Political Functions of Independent Commissions: The Case of UK Migrant Integration Policy", *Journal of Comparative Policy Analysis*, 17 (1): 10–25.

Jabko, Nicolas (1999), "In the Name of the Market: How the European Commission Paved the Way for Monetary Union", *Journal of European Public Policy*, 6 (3): 475–495.

Jabko, Nicolas (2003), "Democracy in the Age of the Euro", *Journal of European Public Policy*, 10 (5): 710–739.

Jabko, Nicolas (2010), "The Hidden Face of the Euro", *Journal of European Public Policy*, 17 (3): 318–334.

Kahneman, Daniel (2012), *Thinking, Fast and Slow*, London: Penguin Books.

Lamont, Michèle (2009), *How Professors Think: Inside the Curious World of Academic Judgment*, Cambridge, MA: Harvard University Press.

Lord, Christopher (2012): "On the Legitimacy of Monetary Union", Swedish Institute for European Policy Studies, 2012: 3.

Machlup, Fritz (1965), "Why Economist Disagree?", *Proceedings of the American Philosophical Society*, 109 (1): 1–7.

Markoff, John, and Verónica Montecinos (1993), "The Ubiquitous Rise of Economists", *Journal of Public Policy*, 13 (1): 37–68.

McKay, David (2005), "Economic Logic or Political Logic? Economic Theory, Federal Theory and EMU", *Journal of European Public Policy*, 12 (3): 528–544.

Mercier, Hugo (2011), 'When Experts Argue: Explaining the Best and the Worst of Reasoning", *Argumentation*, 25 (3): 313–327.

Merton, Robert K. (1973), *The Sociology of Science: Theoretical and Empirical Investigations*, Chicago, IL, and London: University of Chicago Press.

Mügge, Daniel (2011), "From Pragmatism to Dogmatism: European Union Governance, Policy Paradigms and Financial Meltdown", *New Political Economy*, 16 (2): 185–206.

Mügge, Daniel (2013), "The Political Economy of Europeanized Financial Regulation", *Journal of European Public Policy*, 20 (3): 458–470.

Myrdal, Gunnar ([1930] 1953), *The Political Element in the Development of Economic Theory*, London: Routledge.

Palley, Thomas I. (2012), *From Financial Crisis to Stagnation: The Destruction of Shared Prosperity and the Role of Economics*, Cambridge: Cambridge University Press.

Pincione, Guido, and Fernand R. Tesón (2006), *Rational Choice and Democratic Deliberation: A Theory of Discourse Failure*, Cambridge: Cambridge University Press.

Porter, Theodore M. (1996), *Trust in Numbers: The Pursuit of Objectivity*, Princeton, NJ: Princeton University Press.

Posner, Elliot, and Nicolas Véron (2010), "The EU and Financial Regulation: Power without Purpose?", *Journal of European Public Policy*, 17 (3): 400–415.

Puetter, Uwe (2004), "Governing informally: The Role of the Eurogroup in EMU and the Stability and Growth Pact", *Journal of European Public Policy*, 11 (5): 854–870.

Puetter, Uwe (2007), "Providing Venues for Contestation: The Role of Expert Committees and Informal Dialogue among Ministers in European Economic Policy Coordination", *Comparative European Politics*, 5 (1): 18–35.

Puetter, Uwe (2012), "Europe's Deliberative Intergovernmentalism: The Role of the Council and European Council in EU Economic Governance", *Journal of European Public Policy*, 19 (2): 161–178.

Quiggin, John (2008), "Economists and Uncertainty", in: Gabriele Bammer and Michael Smithson (eds), *Uncertainty and Risk: Multidisciplinary Perspectives*, London: Earthscan, 195–204.

Reiss, Julian (2008), *Error in Economics: Towards a More Evidence-Based Methodology*, London-New York: Routledge.

Salines, Marion, Gabriel Glöckler, and Zbigniew Trchlewski (2012), "Existential Crisis Incremental Response: The Eurozone's Dual Institutional Evolution", *Journal of European Public Policy*, 19 (5): 665–681.

Scharpf, Fritz W. (1999), *Governing in Europe: Effective and Democratic?*, Oxford: Oxford University Press.

Schlefer, Jonathan (2012), *The Assumptions Economists Make*, Cambridge, MA: Harvard University Press.

Singer, Peter (1972), "Moral Experts", *Analysis*, 32 (4): 115–117.

Stiglitz, Joseph E., Aaron S. Edlin, and J. Bradford DeLong (eds) (2008), *The Economists' Voice. Top Economists' Take on Today's Problems*, New York: Colombia University Press.

Sunstein, Cass R. (2006), *Infotopia: How Many Minds Produce Knowledge*, Oxford: Oxford University Press.

Sunstein, Cass R. (2018), "The Most Knowledgeable Branch", *University of Pennsylvania Law Review*, forthcoming.

Sunstein, Cass R., and Reid Hastie (2015), *Wiser: Getting Beyond Groupthink to Make Groups Smarter*, Boston, MA: Harvard Business Review Press.

Swift, Adam, and Stuart White (2008), "Political Theory, Social Science, and Real Politics", in: David Leopold and Marc Stears (eds), *Political Theory: Methods and Approaches*, Oxford: Oxford University Press, pp. 49–69.

Tellmann, Silje M. (2016), "Experts in Public Policymaking: Influential, yet Constrained", Doctoral Thesis, Oslo and Akershus University College of Applied Sciences.

Tetlock, Philip E. (2005), *Expert Political Judgment: How Good Is It? How Can We Know?*, Princeton, NJ: Princeton University Press.

Tversky, Amos, and Daniel Kahneman (1974), "Judgment under Uncertainty: Heuristics and Biases", *Science*, 185 (4157): 1124–1131.

Urbinati, Nadia (2014), *Democracy Disfigured: Opinion, Truth, and the People*, Cambridge, MA: Harvard University Press.

Vibert, Frank (2007), *The Rise of the Unelected. Democracy and the New Separation of Powers*, Cambridge: Cambridge University Press.

Walton, Douglas (1997), *Appeal to Expert Opinion: Arguments from Authority*, University Park, PA: Pennsylvania State University Press.

Wildavsky, Aaron (1979), *Speaking Truth to Power: The Art and Craft of Policy Analysis*, London: Transaction.

Zenker, Frank (2011), "Experts and Bias: When is the Interest-Based Objection to Expert Argumentation Sound?", *Argumentation*, 25 (3): 355–370.

5

WHAT KIND OF CRISIS AND HOW TO DEAL WITH IT?

The segmented border logic in the European migration crisis

Espen D.H. Olsen

I Introduction

The European migration crisis is a crisis which, in popular as well as political discourse, is arguably addressed as a real crisis not only for the refugees living precarious lives, but also for political institutions and the receiving states. Indeed, the notion of what kind of crisis it "really" amounts to is highly contested. Moreover, the crisis is used for political purposes in the "everyday" struggle of electoral politics. In addition, it should be of interest to broaden the palette of research on the migration crisis to include reflections on the European Union (EU) as a form of political order, as a polity. Political orders are territorial communities marked by their politics of inclusion and exclusion. Managing migration is at the core of such politics. Policy proposals and bureaucratic measures geared to steer individuals, migration, and borders are thus interesting to study, not only from a sectorial vantage-point, but also as an example of what kind of political order is emerging in post-crises Europe.

In this chapter, I have chosen to discuss the European migration crisis as an example of the EU's *segmented political order*. The chapter first briefly reflects on the refugee crisis as a crisis in conceptual and political terms: What kind of crisis, and whose crisis is it? Whilst initially often referred to as a humanitarian crisis, focusing on the precarious situation for refugees, over time we see a certain shift in attention to issues of state security, border control, and the challenges facing both political institutions and the receiving states. Based upon this reflection, the chapter goes on to discuss the migration crisis and the efforts to craft solutions to it from the analytical framework of segmented political order. The focus is put on the recent policy proposals to reform and harmonise a Common European Asylum System (CEAS) in the wake of the refugee crisis as well as the launch of the European Border and Coast Guard (EBCG) within Frontex. In analysing the CEAS proposals from the European Commission and the background to the EBCG, the chapter uses a three-pronged analytical framework of segmented political order and puts a special *onus* on specific ideas and cognitive frames, the role of knowledge and expertise, and the institutional solutions chosen post-crisis.

The chapter proceeds as follows. In the next section, I briefly discuss the concept of crisis and the European migration crisis as a case. Following this, a section is devoted to the European migration crisis and its political and humanitarian background. After this, the chapter uses these conceptual reflections on the case of the migration crisis for an analysis of crisis politics as an example of the EU as a segmented political order. Finally, I give some concluding remarks, addressing the wider implications of the chapter and some suggestions for further research on crisis politics, not only in general, but also specifically for the EU.

II "Crisis" in conceptual and political terms: The European migration crisis as a case

The concept of crisis is much used in political language, in media stories, and even in everyday conversation/speech (Walby, 2015). The EU has, in the recent decade, undergone a series of deep institutional, economic, and legitimacy crises. In addition, the migration crisis of 2014 and 2015 exacerbated criticism of the EU's institutional abilities to deal with crises that are not only political or constitutional, but also affect individuals, EU citizens as well as non-citizen migrants. Debate on crises in the EU is nothing new (see, for example, Habermas 2012; Olsson, 2009; Trenz, 2016). In fact, crises have permeated European integration history from the "Empty Chair Crisis" in the 1960s onwards (see, for example, Kühnhardt, 2009). It is often argued that the EU has frequently invoked or used crisis situations as a means of fostering and even deepening European integration and the power of supranational institutions. The *politics* of crisis in the EU is, then, strongly associated with *how* the crisis is understood, not only as a crisis in and of itself, but also as part of the bigger picture of the ongoing process of integration. In macroscopic terms, the framing and handling of a given crisis may have tangible effects on the EU as a political system. In taking the European migration crisis as a case, the question is then the degree to which the political and institutional handling of the crisis has given added impetus to the development of the EU as a "segmented" political system, which is the core focus of this edited volume.

It is interesting to note, in this regard, that the conceptual historian Reinhart Koselleck (2006: 358) derives the etymological roots of "crisis" from Greek, as meaning, for instance, to "separate," "choose," "judge," or "decide." Moreover, it had the connotations of "measuring oneself," to "quarrel" or to "fight." In this sense, the concept of crisis became a central term in politics in the Greek understanding. In his more theoretical work on the concept of crisis, Koselleck argued that crisis is a moment of rupture, from which a *new reality emerges*. Crisis emerges in the moments when an old paradigm no longer works as it has *habitually* done over time. In this view, the crisis occurs when there is no longer any common ground upon which to communicate. Yet, in crisis, political actors seek to make sense of it and act to handle it. In so doing, an interesting query is whether they seek to define the situation based upon new concepts and solutions, or whether they "fall back" on already existing world views and logics. This is central for the argument of whether a given crisis bears the mark of *segmentation*, meaning the employment of dominating cognitive frames and certain logics of under-standing the problem and how to solve it. As will become clear in this chapter, the migration crisis quickly fell into a border logic based upon territoriality and sovereignty as the main frame for how to structure movement across borders, especially that which is deemed to be "irregular."

In political analysis, the concept of crisis became a source of some debate in the 1970s. After two decades of economic resurgence and the re-building of democratic institutions, Europe and the Western world were hit by what Habermas in *Legitimation Crisis* (1975) called a "late-capitalist crisis of legitima-tion." In this book, Habermas does indeed raise the question of how to define and understand the concept of crisis for social research and political analysis. Starting with an analogy with medical practice, crisis can be seen as something objective: crisis occurs in the phase when it is understood that the body cannot itself induce recovery. Taken more broadly, crisis can be associated with the "idea of an objective force that deprives a subject of some part of his normal sover-eignty" (Habermas 1975: 1). Yet, a crisis is not objective as such; it also fosters subjective responses and experiences. This co-existence of objective description and subjective meaning leads to a *normativity* of crisis: "the resolution of the cri-sis effects a liberation of the subject caught up in it" (ibid.: 1). More concretely, this means that, in order to make sense of crisis, political analysis must pay heed both to the "facts" of the crisis in *structural* terms, and the *agency* (or lack thereof) that follows in its wake. The migration crisis is a vivid example that there is a combination of structure and agency in any major political and/or societal crisis. In this book, structure and agency combine in an analytical framework that focuses on ideas, policy instruments, institutions and procedures, resources and patterns of dependence and vulnerability. The migration crisis is marked by individuals – citizens and non-citizens alike – that are heavily affected by it, in a physical, social, economic, and psychological sense. Crisis resolution, as we think of it in political science, is, however, focused on finding institutional and policy solutions.

A final point worth mentioning here is the notion of *steering*. Steering is inher-ently linked to the structure of society as a form of systemic integration – as the range of normative structures and goal values of, say, socio-cultural inte-gration, the economy, or political institutions. These are not set and can vary between political entities and societies. The important point to highlight here is the notion that a crisis is a crisis of *steering* when the different sub-systems of society cannot sustain the normative structures required for them to remain legitimate (Habermas, 1975: 6–8). In other words, a crisis in a *political* meaning must then be analysed in a way that renders visible the connection between normative structures (say, rule of law in the constitutional-democratic state) and steering problems (say, breaches of individual rights for short-term gains). In research on migration in a globalised and Europeanised setting, the potential conflict between, for instance, individual human rights and measures to control and/or reduce the numbers of migrants at the polity's border is clearly at the core. Different logics that stem from different sub-systems of society, such as the legal system, political decision-making, or territorial security, may indeed come into conflict, especially in the short- and mid-term handling of a given crisis. Yet, as migration has a profound linkage to the issue of borders, the issue of sovereignty may become a common denominator for handling a perceived crisis of *control* of the territory at the border. Jackson (2007) has usefully highlighted how sovereignty as *the* constitutive principle of statehood has created a *logic* of sovereignty whereby the integrity of state territory becomes a core concern of politics (see, also, Fossum, 2019; Chapter 2 in this volume).

In order to understand and make sense of a given crisis, I argue that we need to ask two inter-related questions. Firstly, there is the issue of *what kind* of crisis we are dealing with. In asking this, we need to discuss what is at stake in the crisis, for instance, which kinds of institutions, policies, and principles it affects or may affect. Moreover, the "what kind" question requires us to probe where the causes of the crisis originate. What are the factors preceding the crisis? What were the political conditions in the period before the events and actions that led to the calling of a "crisis"? And what are the visible cleavages in different political and institutional solutions? Are the understanding and subsequent handling of the crisis premised on openness to solutions or rather contingent on certain logics pertaining to the issue at stake, say migration?

Secondly, there is the issue of *whose crisis* it is. What does this entail? There are numerous actors that are involved in any crisis, but who faces the consequences? Moreover, there is a need to settle what kind of consequences they face and how they can handle the effects of these. There will obviously be differences in how actors deal with the effects of a crisis. States, political parties, non-governmental organisations (NGOs), citizens, or migrants will necessarily relate to a given crisis in different ways, in part depending on the already existing cognitive frames and understandings of the field that is in crisis. In studying the particularity of a specific crisis, the discussion as to whose crisis it is will then serve to clarify the kind of crisis that unfolds and its potential political and societal effects. These two questions are, of course, related. For instance, in probing what kind of crisis is happening, we may find that it is first and foremost an institutional one. Moreover, the very same institutions will then be part of the answer to the "whose crisis" question. Yet, in keeping these analytically separate, the nuances of structure (what kind) and agency (whose) will be more readily available for scrutiny.

III EU migration policies: Between supranational goals and intergovernmental logics

The issue of borders, movement, and migration is a recurring theme in European integration. Crudely speaking, the EU has, since the first Treaties in 1951 and 1957, been based upon a more or less fragile compromise between national control (veto) and supranational solutions. In the field of migration, this compromise has been especially tenuous, as borders, control over territory, and the definition of citizenship have traditionally been strongly wedded to the idea and fact of the territorial nation-state. In short, borders are about control of access to state territory and ultimately about access to its political community. Historically, the EU has sought to relativise the role of borders, especially in intra-EU relations. Somewhat paradoxically, however, this strong aim of dismantling its internal borders *between* the Member States has simultaneously been complemented by aspirations to retain control over access to *their* (and EU) territory, that is to say, on immigration from so-called third countries. Moreover, the EU has pursued an internationalist agenda based in part upon the value foundation of the principles of free movement, non-discrimination, and rule of law, efforts that are subsumed under the umbrella of the EU as a *normative power* (Manners, 2002).

The EU's "home affairs" policy on the migration field was therefore slow in the making. Nevertheless, while it started out as an intergovernmental engagement *outside* the Treaty framework, it has developed into a complex mix of intergovernmental and supranational arrangements now within the Treaty, and a constant source for legislative acts and political debate (see Lavenex, 2006). The catalysts for increased co-operation on migration were the growth in intra-EU mobility as well as the enthusiasm after the Single European Act, which would finally emerge with a "real" internal market for Europe. There have been three main "target groups" for EU policy-making on migration: mobile EU citizens, long-term residents from non-EU countries, and lastly, so-called third country nationals. It is the latter category of citizens from outside the EU that is at the core of the migration crisis.

Since the first efforts at policy co-ordination in the Trevi Group from 1975, EU migration policy has gone through a transformation towards broader policies and more supranational decision-making. Moreover, the EU has sought to regulate not only the way in which asylum applications should be handled, but also increasingly to secure its outer borders towards third countries. The so-called Dublin System has been in place since the 1990s and stipulates which country should process the asylum application from an asylum-seeker through the so-called first country principle. This was put in place, in official language, to stop secondary movements or "asylum shopping" further on in the EU when asylum is denied in the receiving state (European Commission, 2018). On the outer borders, the EU formed a border agency called Frontex in 2002. This agency was set up to aid and guide Member States in securing their borders, and thus EU territory. The complexity of EU migration politics is, however, not only linked to concrete policies, institutional constructions, or technical management. It is a system involving both vertical and horizontal relations between institutions and jurisdictions, including human-rights jurisprudence, that also go beyond the EU's legal and political institutions. The right of asylum is enshrined in the United Nations Declaration of Human Rights from 1948 and the Convention on the Rights of Refugees from 1951. As UN members and signatories to the 1951 Refugee Convention, all EU Member States are bound by this right to asylum. There are, however, no international legal options for individuals if they are mistreated according to the UN conventions, making the obligation as much moral as legal. Finally, it involves EU citizens as well as the individuals seeking entry into European territory.

This system faced a complex institutional and decision-making crisis, especially in 2014 and 2015. There was a strong increase in asylum applications from 2014 to 2015 from about 562,000 to 1.2 million.[1] To apply for asylum is a right of individuals according to the 1951 Refugee Convention, yet the organisation of how to receive, handle, and process such applications can vary between countries, not least due to different legal systems and bureaucratic capacities. The EU, in principle, has an outer border with free movement within through the Schengen agreement. This caused asymmetrical burdens on certain Member States such as first countries with borders towards third countries and liberal countries which have traditionally received more migrants than other more restrictive countries. All this transpired at a time where much of Europe has still not recovered from the economic crisis, and where there are low levels of trust in EU institutions and an increase in the support of political parties that harbour scepticism towards immigrants and multicultural society.

IV The migration crisis in the European Union: What kind of crisis and whose crisis is it?

The migration crisis has been, from the outset, clearly an institutional crisis. This is the common understanding of the crisis. It has rocked the foundations of European integration itself. The Schengen Agreement system is increasingly questioned, for instance, through unilateral decisions by Member States to suspend their open borders temporarily. As a consequence, it is frequently asked whether the whole idea of free movement is, in fact, under threat. In other words, a first cursory look at what kind of crisis the migration crisis amounts to immediately highlights that there are competing principles and goals at play in the European integration architecture: on the one hand, the fundamental principle and right of free movement for persons; and, on the other, policies and technologies of border controls. Moreover, border controls exhibit a duality in the EU, which concerns the issue of tearing down the *internal* borders *between* the Member States as well as the issue of controlling the EU's *external* border.

As Habermas pointed out, failures of goal attainment in the sub-systems, such as the political institutions of the state, leads to ruptures of social integration, and

then we have a crisis on our hands. The European migration crisis was arguably *not* an institutional crisis until supranational co-operation floundered, and
several Member States staked out their own course of action, which put new
and heavier burdens on other Member States. Arguably, this indicates a certain segmental logic of sovereignty at play, in which the territoriality of migration issues became apparent, triggering measures such as the closing of borders
and, eventually, suspension of the Schengen Agreement. These transformations
of discourse on mobility and border policies highlight, then, the institutional
responses. In this way, the crisis was real as an institutional fact as Member States
chose measures to handle the crisis, although they may be understood in terms
of effective policies. This mode of action was, however, more geared towards
short-term measures which safeguarded the Member States in question. As such,
the unilateral decisions by several Member States point towards a certain logic
of European responses to ruptures in the migration system. Migration is about
mobility across borders. Someone crosses the border between two territorial
polities. This creates a new relationship between the individual and host state,
but it is also a state-to-state relation. Within the EU, this relation has been structured as acts of opening up borders since the first treaties. Yet, perhaps due to
a logic of sovereignty, Member States not only sought to handle migration at
the outer borders of the EU, but also against *other* Member States of that same
supranational institutional framework. This is a first sign that crisis management
in the migration crisis navigated in the form of what may be called a segmental
logic of borders bent on sovereignty. As Jackson (2000: 24) highlights, the idea
of sovereignty creates certain expectations of state behaviour that "statespeople"
abide by. He calls this "reasons of state," meaning that the integrity of the state
in the interstate system depends on the demonstration of sovereign acts on its
behalf. When a border exists, this can be more or less "porous" or not. The logic
of the border from a standpoint of sovereignty is still that it can be closed at the
order of state authority and used as a gatekeeper instrument on outsiders. This
exclusionary logic of borders in modern states is arguably also a strong part of
the European migration crisis. Indeed, it can be understood as a certain cognitive frame and idea of how to manage the population of a state's territory. In the
migration crisis, many Member States of the EU used this cognitive frame to
manage it by closing their borders. In terms of what kind of crisis this was, then,
I would argue that, in addition to an institutional one, it was one of borders and
territorial control.

This is related to the fact that steering in the EU is complex. Institutions, rules,
and policies are all marked by the multilevel character of the decision-making
system. In addition, the EU is a mixed polity comprised of already existing,
sovereign nation-states, which, over the course of 50 years, have come together
in a project of integration. In this way, the nation-states have, as Bickerton
(2012) pointed out, become Member States. Yet, in the EU, the membership
status is different from "ordinary" international organisations. There are certain legal principles and "constitutional" rules, which have led to the veritable

transformation of the nation-states or Member States that comprise the EU (Eriksen and Fossum, 2012). They are no longer mere members, but are, in fact, ingrained into a common legal and political system of rules and decision-making. From such an understanding of the EU as a political order, an expectation of some form of unity and solidarity in times of crisis emerges. The migration crisis has seen different consequences across the EU, with the Member States at the external border facing the strongest consequences. This has, indeed, been the case since a common asylum and migration policy was forged in the 1990s. From this perspective, the institutional crisis of handling refugees at the border of the EU becomes even more vivid.

The EU is unique in the sense that it is an international organisation harbouring an idea of constructing a community of citizens *and* well-established nation-states. Through deepened integration and the widening of membership, the EU has expanded the space for politics. Between the "extremes" of European federalism and a Europe of the nation-states, there is a continuum of different ideas on the extent to which political community can become Europeanised or not. It is clear, however, that, in terms of legal integration, the basic principles of free movement and non-discrimination have created a supranational institution in which citizens and Member States are increasingly interwoven with decisions and structures emanating from "above" the nation-state. European citizenship has been argued by the European Court of Justice (ECJ) to be a "fundamental" status of EU citizens (Kochenov, 2013), and the Court's jurisprudence has highlighted how interconnected citizens and states have become within the remit of European integration (Kostakopoulou, 2005). Out of this "constitution," some community has clearly developed.

This peculiar political community has been termed a "community of strangers" (Castiglione, 2009). In a crisis such as the one on migration, this is arguably a very thin community. The question is further one of whether it is "sustainable" when faced with heightened pressure on both supranational and Member State institutions. It seems clear that the migration crisis is, in some way, a crisis also of the community, made even more profound through the sovereignty game played by single Member States. Faced with a surge in the numbers of refugees and asylum-seekers, many Member States did not think of the EU as a political community, but rather as being comprised of several communities, adhering more or less to their borders. In institutional terms, this was visible in the lack of effective, concerted action in which the Member States could agree to common measures. Rather, they argued over who was to blame for the new surge in migration flows and over what humane handling of refugees should look like. In terms of political community, this was visible in the sense that notions of Europe as *one* political space floundered when met with the realities of political and legal disagreements at Member State level. The "ever closer" union between citizens and Member States professed by the EU treaties has arguably not morphed into a political community in which solidarity and burden-sharing are at the core (Michailidou and Trenz, 2019; Chapter 7 in this volume). Had this been the case, the EU could counterfactually have been seen as *one* community in which all citizens and Member States were responsible for migration policies in Europe as a whole. Contrary to this, it emanated as a set of more or less insulated communities, which, in different ways, sought to safeguard their own interests before the European interest. In terms of migration and the management of EU territory, then, Europe was 28 communities, rather than one common territorial space. This created co-ordination problems and unequal burdens between the Member States in facing the crisis.

The question of *whose crisis* links to the question of *what kind* of crisis. Yet, as I focused on the institutional, political, and communal aspects to the migration crisis in the preceding section, in reflecting on the question of whose crisis, the focus is shifted towards what can be called the human consequences. This is a matter of interpretation, of course. Institutions can also be said to be part of the crisis register in terms of *who* the crisis, in agency terms, affects, and how it affects different entities. In shifting focus to the "human consequences," the aim is more specifically to shed light on how EU institutions and policies have dealt with the individuals and their rights in the handling of the crisis.

V Managing the migration crisis: EBCG and CEAS from a segmented order perspective

Frontex has been an EU agency with the task of aiding the Member States in border management against third countries since 2005. In the midst of the refugee crisis, the Commission launched an initiative to bolster the supranational traits of Frontex and create what could be called a more "unified" approach to the management of the EU's outer borders. The initiative from the Commission was directly linked to the migration crisis. I use the reform of Frontex into the European Border and Coast Guard Agency (EBCG) and the policy package on the Common European Asylum Policy (CEAS) as examples of segmented traits in the policy field of migration in EU politics (see, also, Jozef Bátora, Chapter 8 in this volume). These segmented traits are manifested most clearly in what I will highlight as a tangible *border* logic in how the EU – and specifically the Commission – seeks to handle the migration crisis. I also show how the issue of migration, and, concretely, migration "control," is closely wedded to borders in conceptual terms also at the supranational level. There is seemingly a paradox in this, as the process of European unification has been conceived to no little extent as a project of *eliminating* borders, not re-building them.

The EBCG and CEAS were initiatives of institutional and policy change framed in large part as reactions to the migration crisis which peaked in Europe in 2014–2015, but which had been looming for some years, especially with the precarious situation in the Mediterranean. The EBCG was officially launched in October 2016 (European Commission 2016d). The regulation that forms the EBCG was legislated in record time, highlighting its importance for EU decision-makers.[2] The regulation posits the EBCG as a multilevel and complex response to the migration crisis. The policy package on the CEAS was initiated in 2016 (European Commission 2016d). The aim of the CEAS was to harmonise European asylum policy across the EU Member States, to secure conditions for the asylum-seekers present on EU territory, and to clarify the rules for the processing of asylum applications. Moreover, the rights of asylum-seekers were also part of the package.

V.1 Ideas and cognitive frames

Migration is part of the human condition and modern society. People have at all times left their homes and traversed physical, social, cultural, and political borders to settle *elsewhere*. In pre-modern times and early modernity, borders were relatively porous and migration was not "managed" to the extent to which it is today. With the post-war welfare state and citizenship as membership in social-security communities, the need for control over territory became stronger. Moreover, the territorial, political, and social community often followed the same borders, even in multinational and federal states. European integration has been seen as a break with this system, not least through the principle of the free movement of persons and the de-construction of internal borders in the EU (Olsen, 2012).

Despite this notion of a "border-free" Europe, I will argue that both the EBCG and the CEAS have been marked by specific ideas and cognitive frames that structure EU migration policy and management in crisis mode. What is most important to note here is the fact that both initiatives are steeped in what can be called a territorial *border* logic. Migration, and especially migration *in* crisis, is framed from an understanding that there is an *external* EU *border* that needs to be both managed and safeguarded when confronted with migratory flows. Moreover, territoriality has, paradoxically from a post-national perspective (see, for example, Kostakopoulou, 2008), made a comeback *within* the circumstances of supranational policy efforts.

To exemplify this, the three Directives and Regulations making up the proposal for a new CEAS are steeped in an effort to harmonise and streamline the efficacy of asylum policies and procedures. In so doing, the CEAS should lead to common guarantees for asylum-seekers and extended rights for minors (European Commission, 2016a, 2016b). Yet, at the same time, a more rigid and obligatory sanctions regime for all EU countries is instituted when the system is abused by asylum-seekers (European Commission, 2016a). This locks asylum-seekers more closely to the first country, which, according to the Dublin Regulation, should be in charge of the asylum processing. Not only that, the territorial logic comes full circle with the proposal on harmonised standards and rights, which, in practice, institutes a "no movement" rule for asylum-seekers (European Commission, 2016c). They should remain in the country of first instance, and any breach of this rule may be sanctioned. In other words, the effort to "supra-nationalise" migration policy is nevertheless based upon a "national" logic of territoriality. It is not unlikely that such a territorial logic may then in the end pre-empt other efforts to reach a more equitable asylum system, such as quota arrangements to alleviate undue burdens on some EU Member States.

It is almost banal to highlight that a border logic is of quintessential essence for the EBCG, which, after all, is the EU's external border agency. In a borderless world, such agencies would clearly be redundant. The regulation that forms the EBCG argued that this new agency was part of the answer to a migration crisis that EU institutions understand as both complex and multilevel. In so doing, the *onus* is put on the need to safeguard "internal security" on EU territory, the management of the EU's external borders, to assess future threats to EU's borders, and to ensure the functioning of the Schengen Area. It is relatively clear from this that, under the remit of the main EU institutions, the migration crisis is at its core both an *internal* and an *external* crisis. As such, the emphasis on the need for a concerted effort at border management for internal and external purposes, with Europeanising solutions that can potentially undercut Member State sovereignty, is an example of supranational core formation in the EU as an answer to crisis. Moreover, it is interesting that policies and institutionalisation, such as EBCG, point to legal solutions to the migration problem while, to a large extent, eschewing socio-economic issues and the geopolitics of the EU neighbourhood, as well as the moral and ethical dimensions (see, for example, Olsen, 2018). Notwithstanding this, the EBCG is also assigned with the task of safeguarding what are called "fundamental" rights and the rights of certain specific groups, such as unaccompanied minors among the refugees. It remains, however, a question of whether the "managerial" logic of border protection trumps this focus on humanitarian issues. In a segmental logic of borders, the primary commitment is to safeguard the territorial integrity of a political entity. If there is a perception of threat and/or disorder at the border, so to speak, actions based upon such logic will most likely first focus on retaining *control* of the border, and not necessarily on alleviating the immediate causes of the disorder.

In this regard, the *onus* on the internal security of EU territory when facing the entry of migrants is interesting. As Huysmans (2006) has shown in his work on the link between security concepts and migration, a logic of "securitisation" has become increasingly prevalent. Securitisation means that issues which, from the outset, do not fit with a narrow and traditional concept of (internal) security in a military or physical sense, may still link to a security discourse. Migration is the mobility of persons from one territory to another, in which a border is traversed. When a territorial logic enters the picture, this can lead to the idea that entry into the territory needs to be (better) controlled. Arguably, this is what has transpired in the EU setting, where policies, rules, regulations, and institutions in the field of migration have been furnished to *control* the entry of migrants and thereby *secure* EU territory.

V.2 Institutional framework

The EU has been marked by an "accommodationist" mode of governing, rule-making, and institution-building since its inception. In debates on the EU, it has often been argued that it is either intergovernmental or supranational. This is of course a rather crude description, yet the thrust of the argument is that of either a Europe of nations or a United States of Europe. But, much research is increasingly pointing out the fact that EU principles and institutions have been straddling the distinction between these two modes of integration ever since the first treaties (see Bátora and Fossum, 2019; Introduction in this volume). In structural terms, the particular combination of these two principles – inter-governmental and supranational – is a key reason for the EU being a segmented political order, as highlighted in several chapters of this book (see also Fossum, Chapter 2 in this volume). The EU has been marked by constant negotiation between different visions and understandings of the project of European unification, and in the migration crisis, we can see some of the same phenomenon. It cannot be depicted merely as a fragmenting crisis in which any effort at common policies and practice has fallen prey to recalcitrant Member States and unilateral decision-making. It is also marked by efforts to come together and manage the crisis. Yet, here we can see some of the peculiarities with migration policy in the EU. In legislative terms, as was the case with CEAS, it has become increasingly "normalised," that is, with qualified-majority decision-making surpassing the veto power politics of unanimity. But, the word *manage* is important here. The EBCG is part of Frontex, which is a governmental *agency* at EU level, charged with the broad-reaching object of securing the EU's external borders. The EU is, however, not a state, and, as such, the EBCG is dependent on resources and personnel from the Member States. These come from different national traditions of border control. Some recent research argues that the EBCG has become "expertified," with an ever-increasing focus on the need for better co-ordination and technical procedures when encountering asylum-seekers and refugees that make it to the border of EU territory (see Olsen, 2018: 120). Arguably, then, the territorial border logic is amplified by a focus on the technicalities of border control and migration management. This is interesting, as migration and asylum links not only to the numbers of asylum-seekers received or the administrative arrangements to welcome them, but also more fundamentally about individual rights and how those who are already members perceive migration and their own political community. When the *onus* is put on expertise and "physical" problem-solving, there is a possibility that the issue of migration is understood more through a technical than a political lens. In the EU, the rise of experts and expertise has been visible for some time (Gôra et al., 2018; see, also, Boswell, 2008). Expertise is indispensable in most complex policy areas, as it is thought to ensure decision-making based upon sound reasoning and empirical knowledge (Boswell, 2008: 471). Yet, does this potentially de-politicise issues that are fundamental to the political life of a polity as well as to individuals who are in a precarious state? The migration and asylum issue is highly complex, both in terms of the external relations and the internal policies of states. Relying on expertise and problem-solving may be prudential, but what happens to the European *politics* of migration in the mid- to long-term? There may be a danger that, when politicians lose sight of the details as well as the bigger picture, the policy field is abducted by more extreme viewpoints, preying on the "experts" and putting individuals and their rights at further risk.

I have argued in this chapter that the migration crisis is first and foremost seen and debated as an institutional crisis in the EU. This does not mean that EU policy is devoid of humanitarian foundations. The policy preparations of the EBCG, for instance, exhibited some moves to bring the human-rights issues of migrants more to the fore in the work of Frontex. Crucially, there were pleas from Member State experts for better human-rights standards from the EU (European Commission, 2016d). Human rights are, however, a thorny issue in the politics of migration, as most state institutions tend to balance them against some notion of internal security in a territorial sense, based upon the principle of state sovereignty. Huysmans (2006) argued that European migration policies – both in nation-states and EU institutions –are framed by a "politics of insecurity" driven by a fear of what we can call "otherness." Huysmans argued that this was a general trend in European migration politics from the 1990s onwards, but especially in the aftermath of the 9/11 terror attacks in 2001. Arguably, this securitisation logic was no less important in the handling of the 2014–2015 migration crisis. While human rights and the individuality of asylum claims were acknowledged in the CEAS policy package, the bigger picture is still one of control, both at the external EU border and at the internal borders between the Member States. Take, for instance, the *onus* placed on what the Commission calls "operational measures," "managing inflows of migrants and refugees," and "targeting migrant smuggling" (European Commission, 2016e). Such issues are directly linked directly to the monitoring of migrants and refugees through technologies such as fingerprinting and databases (ibid.: 4–5). The plight of individual migrants in states of precariousness or the safeguarding of their rights as asylum-seekers is very much in the background or not dealt with at all, while "enhanced security measures" in countries such as Greece and Italy are very much in the foreground, as is the underlining of the importance of "strong borders" (ibid.: 9–12).

As mentioned earlier, EU migration policy has, over time, developed towards a more supranational form of decision-making and with less veto power for the Member States. Yet, this does not necessarily mean that migration in the EU has become more easily managed. Majority decisions create minorities and the potential for grievances among the "losing" parties. Migration is a policy field which is very closely wedded to the container idea of the sovereign nation-state, even in European integration (see Hansen and Hager, 2012). While the EU has moved in the direction of supranational decision-making, national logics still seem to prevail. In terms of the CEAS, this becomes evident. The post-crisis effort to institute more harmonisation and common rules in all areas of migration policy, including the reception and processing of asylum-seekers and migrants, has not yet led to a real *common* policy across the Member States. Rather, the territorial logic of borders plays out also *internally* in the EU. One obvious example here is the temporary, but prolonged, suspension of "border-free" Europe in the Schengen Agreement. One Member State after another chose to go it "alone" in the midst of the problems of managing new flows of migrants in 2015. The territorial community based upon state sovereignty trumped the need for supra-national policy co-ordination at EU level. Another example can be found in the problem of (re-)distribution in the migration field. Mechanisms for the settling of asylum-seekers have been passed by the Council, but several Member States still have not accepted the decisions. It seems, then, that the policy instruments available in EU migration policy encounter a logic that prevents the full realisa-tion and implementation of the decisions taken. It may be that the rule-based approach to policy-making in the EU meets an obstacle that is too high in this field, as issues of migration link with profound issues of political community and identity in the nation-states.

V.3 The role of knowledge and expertise[3]

The first part of the initiative to bolster Frontex was a feasibility study launched by DG Migration and Home Affairs on the creation of a "European System of Border Guards to control the external borders of the Union (ESBG)" (European Commission, 2014). In this study, the Commission utilised expertise at different levels of the political system to gauge different possible models for the proposed ESBG. The experts who were interviewed and surveyed mostly originated from domestic institutions or various stakeholders, typically from NGOs and civil society organisations, as well as from the European Parliament. Frontex experts were heavily involved in this process, attesting to a focus on handling the crisis through an increased *onus* on practical problem-solving for the EU as a territorial entity (Olsen, 2018: 117 et seq.).

The complexity of migration attests to the possibility that several kinds of expertise could be at work in the handling of a migration crisis, be it moral, technical, or problem-solving. How political actors and the main institutions understand the crisis is, moreover, relevant for the role of knowledge and exper-tise. I have highlighted that the migration crisis is first and foremost understood as an institutional crisis bent on issues of steering. The segmented logic of bor-ders arguably also comes into play in the role of expertise in the migration crisis. Borders are physical and create further boundaries socially, politically, and cul-turally. The physical fact of borders (or the potential of erecting them) has had a strong impact on the handling of the European migration crisis. Immediately after the crisis "erupted" in a public sense[4] and gained the attention of the media, the institutional answer from the EU as well national governments was to revert to the re-building of borders. Knowledge and expertise in the handling of the crisis also attest to this. The border narrative highlighted in the previous section was also in full swing in terms of the role of expertise. The institutional (and, to some extent, "existential") crisis of migration led to a clear focus on technical knowledge and solutions in the crisis resolution. But, what is "technical" about a migration crisis? When the reality of borders comes into play, notions of con-trol become prevalent. This means that knowledge and expertise are utilised/

employed (or conceptualised in an initial phase) to bring out facts and possible solutions to the problem. In the case of Frontex and the EBCG, issues of the management of external borders and the safeguarding of the internal security of the EU were at the forefront (Frontex, 2015: 9). In other words, through such "securitisation," expertise could provide knowledge about how to *manage* and *control* migration. Some form of "technology" thus enters the picture, predicated by the cognitive frame of (physical) borders between sovereign territories and polities (see Huysmans, 2006: Chap. 3). The border logic is, indeed, biased in this direction, as the management of borders will always require some form of physical structuring of entry into the territory under protection. Borders are physical in the structure of gatekeeping with respect to who are the insiders and the outsiders in relation to a specific political community. Moreover, this is at the core of sovereignty in the modern understanding of the territorial state. In this sense, as I have argued, the border logic of EU policies in the migration crisis is part of a "migration segment" premised on borders and their management as the "first mover" in migration politics.

In the framing of the CEAS, the Commission (European Commission, 2016d) had a clear focus on the management of borders, the control of migration, and the effective handling of asylum seekers (Olsen, 2018: 121). The CEAS was also marked by more efforts to deal with the crisis from the vantage point of "whose crisis" it was in a humanitarian sense. The Commission documents and legislative proposals do not shy away from, say, human rights or the safeguarding of individual asylum-seekers or refugees: "(we) need to enhance legal and safe pathways to Europe" (European Commission, 2016d: 3). Nonetheless, the Commission President, Jean-Claude Juncker, argued that "Europe needs to manage migration better, in all aspects" (ibid.: 20). In other words, the steering of the crisis in terms of problem-solving and technical expertise was very much at the forefront of the CEAS. It is interesting, then, to note that the CEAS is based around several proposals to limit the movement of asylum-seekers on EU territory, attesting to a strong *nationalised* border logic concerning migrants *within* a strong *supranational* policy framework (see Menéndez and Olsen, 2019). This is, then, indicative of an overall politics of migration which is neither intergovernmental nor supranational, but rather something in-between the two main modes of EU governance. In other words, the migration field fits the notion of a segmented political order exactly as a certain cognitive frame of borders as the *core* of the migration issue had prevailed, especially in the policy proposals and institutional solutions geared towards the handling of the crisis. The perception of what kind of crisis decision-makers faced was, to large extent, linked to the border logic that permeates this migration segment. The EU and the Member States clearly base their handling of the migration crisis on an inward-looking notion of *border security*, bent on the need for knowledge and expertise to aid in the *management* of the EU's external borders and thus to manage the influx of migrants to the national territories of the Member States.

VI Concluding remarks

EU migration policy has been heavily debated in the first two decades of the twenty-first century, and this debate has clearly amplified since the migration crisis on European soil and in international waters since 2014. In this chapter, the migration crisis has been analysed as a case of the EU as a segmented political order. The discussion has centred on how different aspects of the crisis, such as *what* kind of crisis and *whose* crisis it is, have mapped onto a certain cognitive frame and idea concerning migration. The chapter found that there is a prevalence for a specific logic of borders in the creation of the EBCG and the policy package on the CEAS. This is paradoxical from the viewpoint of European integration history, as the tearing down of borders has been at the forefront of its professed politics of mobility.

There is clearly a need for more in-depth research on the ramifications of this border logic, not only on the issue of migration, but also more generally for the EU as a political order. From this chapter, it seems clear that there is a form of "re-nationalisation" of political discourse in the EU on the migration issue. The idea that an ever-closer union of citizens, peoples, and states would also lead to unification of political identity and community seems to have become shattered in the aftermath of the migration crisis. This surge for re-nationalisation is often linked to issues of national identity or Member State reticence towards EU institutions (see Olsen, 2013). Yet, this chapter has highlighted that the border logic which underpins re-nationalisation is also at work at the supranational level. The answer, in policy terms, has been to address the need for a common European asylum system as well as to examine the renewed institutional *management* of the EU's physical borders, both internally and externally.

A drive towards a more common border control of the EU's borders points towards a form of "stateness" in the making. This form of core formation is, however, only a partial answer to the crisis, as it focuses more on containing the pressure on the actual, physical borders, rather than responding to the root causes of new migration flows. Strengthening borders is, furthermore, a return to the classical doctrine of the territorial state, where the protection of the borders and the security of the national people is at the core. It can be asked, then, at what cost does this border logic come. It is not given that it will alleviate intra-EU conflicts over the causes of migration, or of what kind of "normative power" the EU can be, or the nature of its political community "beyond the nation-state." The individual is, after all, at the core of migration. Refugees, asylum-seekers, and EU citizens are all individuals and those that bear the most vivid burdens of the migration crisis. As EU migration policy continues to be framed through such logic of borders, it is not unlikely that the humanitarian plight of migrants and refugees will continue to be pushed to the back of the policy agenda. This highlights, then, that, while the EU has professed to be a kind of cosmopolitan vanguard, it is at its core yet another form of polity bent on different forms of inclusion and exclusion of citizens and non-citizens.

Notes

1 Eurostat (2015), Asylum in the EU Member States, News release, 44/2016, 4 March 2016, available at: https://ec.europa.eu/eurostat/documents/2995521/7203832/3-04032016-AP-EN.pdf/790eba01-381c-4163-bcd2-a54959b99ed6, last accessed 28 January 2019.
2 Regulation (EU) 2016/24 of the European Parliament and of the Council of 14 September 2016 on the European Border and Coast Guard Agency, OJ L 251/1.
3 This part is indebted to Olsen (2018).
4 A point often forgotten in the debate on the migration crisis is the fact that it has been a crisis long in the making, finding its roots in the post-war settlements on refugee policies in Europe and the "asymmetric" integration of the EU's common asylum policy since the 1990s (see Menéndéz 2016).

References

Bátora, Jozef, and John Erik Fossum (eds) (2019), *The EU Post-Crises: The Rise of a Segmented Political Order*, London: Routledge.
Bickerton, Chris J. (2012), *European Integration: From Nation-States to Member States*, Oxford: Oxford University Press.
Boswell, Christina (2008), "The Political Functions of Expert Knowledge: Knowledge and Legitimation in European Union Immigration Policy", *Journal of European Public Policy*, 15 (4): 471–488.
Castiglione, Dario (2009), "Political Identity in a Community of Strangers", in: Jeffrey T. Checkel and Peter J. Katzenstein (eds), *European Identity*, Cambridge: Cambridge University Press, pp. 29–51.
Eriksen, Erik Oddvar, and John Erik Fossum (eds) (2012), *Rethinking Democracy and the European Union*, London: Routledge.
European Commission (2014), Study on the Feasibility of the Creation of a European System of Border Guards to Control the External Borders of the Union (ESBG), DG Home, Final Report, version 3.0, 16 June 2014, available at: https://ec.europa.eu/home-affairs/sites/homeaffairs/files/what-we-do/policies/borders-and-visas/border-crossing/docs/20141016_home_esbg_frp_001_esbg_final_report_3_00_en.pdf.
European Commission (2016a), Proposal for a Regulation of the European Parliament and of the Council Establishing the Criteria and Mechanisms for Determining the Member State Responsible for Examining an Application for International Protection Lodged in one of the Member States by a Third-country National or a Stateless Person, COM (2016) 270 Final, 4 May 2016, available at: http://ec.europa.eu/dgs/home-affairs/what-we-do/policies/european-agenda-migration/proposal-implementation-package/docs/20160504/dublin_reform_proposal_en.pdf.
European Commission (2016b), Proposal for a Directive of the European Parliament and of the Council Laying Down Standards for the Reception of Applicants for International Protection (recast), COM(2016) 465 Final, available at: https://ec.europa.eu/home-affairs/sites/homeaffairs/files/what-we-do/policies/european-agenda-migration/proposal-implementation-package/docs/20160713/proposal_on_standards_for_the_reception_of_applicants_for_international_protection_en.pdf.
European Commission (2016c), Proposal for a Regulation of the European Parliament and of the Council on Standards for the Qualification of Third-Country Nationals or Stateless Persons as Beneficiaries of International Protection, for a Uniform Status for Refugees or for Persons Eligible for Subsidiary Protection and for the Content

of the Protection Granted and Amending Council Directive 2003/109/EC of 25 November 2003 Concerning the Status of Third-country Nationals Who Are Long-term Residents, COM(2016) 466 Final.

European Commission (2016d), Towards a Reform of the Common European Asylum System and Enhancing Legal Avenues to Europe, Communication, COM (2016) 197 final, available at: https://eur-lex.europa.eu/legal-content/EN/TXT/?uri=COM:2016:197:FIN.

European Commission (2016e), The State of Play of Implementation of the Priority Actions Under the European Agenda on Migration, Communication, COM(2016) 85 Final, available at: https://eur-lex.europa.eu/legal-content/EN/TXT/HTML/?uri=CELEX:52016DC0085&from=EN.

European Commission (2018), "Managing Migration in All Its Aspects, Commission Note ahead of the June European Council 2018", available at: https://ec.europa.eu/commission/sites/beta-political/files/euco-migration-booklet-june2018_en.pdf.

Fossum, John Erik (2019), "The Institutional Make-up of Europe's Segmented Political Order", in: Jozef Bátora and John Erik Fossum (eds), *The EU Post-Crises: The Rise of a Segmented Political Order*, London: Routledge.

Frontex (2015), Risk Analysis for 2016, available at: https://frontex.europa.eu/assets/Publications/Risk_Analysis/Annula_Risk_Analysis_2016.pdf.

Gôra, Magdalena., Cathrine Holst, and Marta Warat (eds) (2018), *Expertisation and Democracy in Europe*, London: Routledge.

Habermas, Jürgen (1975), *Legitimation Crisis*, New York: Beacon Press.

Habermas, Jürgen (2012), *The Crisis of the European Union: A Response*, Cambridge: Polity Press.

Hansen, Peo, and Sandy Brian Hager (2012), *The Politics of European Citizenship: Deepening Contradictions in Social Rights & Migration Policy*, New York: Berghahn Books.

Huysmans, Jef (2006), *The Politics of Insecurity: Fear, Migration and Asylum in* the EU, London: Routledge.

Jackson, Robert (2000), *The Global Covenant: Human Conduct in a World of States*, Oxford: Oxford University Press.

Jackson, Robert (2007), *Sovereignty: The Evolution of an Idea*, Cambridge: Polity Press.

Kochenov, Dimitry (2013), "The Essence of EU Citizenship Emerging from the Last Ten Years of Academic Debate: Beyond the Cherry Blossoms and the Moon?", *International and Comparative Law Quarterly*, 62 (1): 97–136.

Koselleck, Reinhart (2006), "Crisis", *Journal of the History of Ideas*, 67 (2): 357–400.

Kostakopoulou, Dora (2005), "Ideas, Norms and European Citizenship: Explaining Institutional Change", *Modern Law Review*, 68 (2): 233–267.

Kostakopoulou, Dora (2008), *The Future Governance of Citizenship*, Cambridge: Cambridge University Press.

Kühnhardt, Ludger (ed) (2009), *Crises in European Integration: Challenges and Responses, 1945–2005*, New York: Berghahn Books.

Lavenex, Sandra (2006), "Shifting Up and Out: The Foreign Policy of European Immigration Control", *West European Politics*, 29 (2): 329–350.

Manners, Ian (2002), "Normative Power Europe: A Contradiction in Terms?", *Journal of Common Market Studies*, 40 (2): 235–258.

Menéndez, Agustín José. (2016), "The Refugee Crisis: Between Human Tragedy and Symptom of the Structural Crisis of European Integration", *European Law Journal*, 22 (4): 388–416.

Menéndez, Agustín José, and Espen D.H. Olsen (2019), *Challenging European Citizenship. Ideas and Realities in Contrast*, Basingstoke: Palgrave Pivot.

Michailidou, Asimina, and Hans-Joerg Trenz (2019), "European Solidarity in Times of Crisis: Towards Differentiated Integration", in: Jozef Bátora and John Erik Fossum (2019) (eds), *The EU Post-crises: The Rise of a Segmented Political Order*, London: Routledge.

Olsen, Espen D.H. (2012), *Transnational Citizenship in the European Union: Past, Present, and Future*, New York: Bloomsbury.

Olsen, Espen D.H. (2013), "European Citizenship: Toward Renationalization or Cosmopolitan Europe?", in: Elspeth Guild, Cristina Gortázar Rotaeche and Dora Kostakopoulou (eds), *The Reconceptualization of European Union Citizenship*, Leiden: Brill, pp. 343–360.

Olsen, Espen D.H. (2018), "The Role of Expertise in the European Refugee Crisis", in: Magdalena Góra, Cathrine Holst and Marta Warat (eds), *Expertisation and Democracy in Europe*, London: Routledge, pp. 108–125.

Olsson, Stefan (ed) (2009), *Crisis Management in the European Union: Cooperation in the Face of Emergencies*, New York: Springer.

Trenz, Hans-Jörg (2016), *Narrating European Society: Toward a Sociology of European Integration*, Lanham, MD: Rowman & Littlefield.

Walby, Sylvia (2015), *Crisis*, Cambridge: Polity Press.

6

TOXIC ORDOLIBERALISM ON THE EU'S PERIPHERY

Slovakia, the Euro and the migrant crisis

John Gould and Darina Malová

I Introduction

In this chapter, we trace aspects of Slovakia's relationship with the European Union (EU) from its accession in 2004 to the present, and we query what this tells us about segmentation in the EU's post-crises order. We focus on four political inflection points: the brief exchange rate (non-)crisis of 2006, the Great Recession of 2008–2010, the early Euro crisis of 2010–2012, and the migrant crisis of 2015–2016. We argue that the relatively strong position of the EU in domestic politics prior to 2009 was something of an illusion; in the absence of a real crisis requiring that Member States make extraordinary material contributions towards collective EU norms and goals, EU legitimacy had never really been tested. Since 2009–2010, however, this test has been repeatedly administered, with Slovakia receiving a lower grade each time. Slovak co-operation is no longer assured – particularly in the recent refugee crises.

Much of the reason, we argue, can traced back to what this volume's editors have called a "segmented" order in finance, and, in particular, the convergence of Slovak and EU financial policies around principles of German ordoliberal finance, an overriding commitment to fiscal restraint. Slovakia is an open, trade dependent small state that is highly vulnerable to international shocks to its export markets and to capital flight. Such vulnerability should promote policy convergence with the core, robust political support for the EU norm of solidarity, and a weary eye towards EU fragmentation (Keohane, 1969). To an extent, we find verification for this, but in a way that helps demonstrate this volume's concern with the post-crises segmentation of the EU. As we shall see, Slovakia's pre-Eurozone vulnerability to flight of capital helped socialise its politicians almost universally to embrace the ordoliberal norm of fiscal restraint. With the exception of the Great Recession of 2009–2010, Slovakia's governments have made it a policy to adhere as best they can to the fiscal expectations of the Eurozone. They have also supported International Financial Institutions' (IFI) initiatives to impose fiscal restraints elsewhere, particularly in Greece. Indeed, this socialisation has been so complete as to produce the occasional tension with core policies, as in the Slovak foot-dragging on the Greek assistance package of 2010 at the height of the Eurozone crisis.

Slovakia's politicians now confuse the "necessity" of fiscal restraint (as demonstrated in the pre-euro period of 2002–2008) with an objective virtue that should be applied everywhere in the Eurozone and almost always. They thus engage in "a segmental logic," as described in the introduction to this volume by Bátora and Fossum, "a form of 'closing of the mind' to segment-external ideas and influences."

This should be a cause for some concern. Traditionally, Slovakia has one of Eastern Europe's most pro-EU electorates. Yet, segmental thinking in finance has led Slovak political actors, such as Richard Sulík of the *Sloboda a Solidarita* (Freedom and Solidarity Party) (SaS), to stake their political identity on resisting "Brussels" when policy breaks from ordoliberal principles. Worse, "segmental logic" limits, or closes off entirely, discussion about periphery-centred heterodox policy alternatives that could benefit what we will call "Slovakia's internal periphery" – those areas that that benefit least from the Eurozone's ordoliberal policies. Voters from these perennially "distressed" regions have proven more likely to vote for populist and/or racist or xenophobic actors who pose an existential challenge to a liberal, unified Europe. Slovakia's emerging combination of fiscal rectitude and EU scepticism thus makes it a good case study of how a segment has become embedded in a national political establishment and why this matters for the future of the EU.

II Core formation and the brief exchange rate crisis of 2006

Slovakia's political élite today share a commitment to the Eurozone norm of fiscal restraint. While this has been a Slovak policy goal since 2002 at least, the national-populist left was not fully committed to it until Robert Fico's party, *Smer – sociálna demokracia* (Direction – Social Democracy) (Smer-SD) took power in 2006. The Smer's roots date back to the defeat of Prime Minister Vladimír Mečiar in the parliamentary election of 1998. Former Mečiar supporters who found themselves on the losing side of the economic reforms, who were tired of corruption, and who were worried about Slovakia's place in an open Europe abandoned the national-populist parties of the 1990s and drifted towards Fico's Smer after he broke away from the reformed communists in 1999 (Rybař and Deegan-Krause, 2008: 505). As a member of the parliamentary opposition (2002–2006), Fico built his political identity by questioning the market-oriented reforms of the parliamentary majority, led by Prime Minister Mikuláš Dzurinda of the *Slovenská demokratická a krest'anská únia – Demokratická strana* (Slovak Democratic and Christian Union) (SDKÚ-DS). The most substantial reform measure was

Slovakia's adherence to the "Maastricht convergence criteria" in preparation for the Slovak accession to the Eurozone (Fisher, Gould and Haughton, 2007).

The restrictions of Maastricht sought to avoid destabilising, short-term capital flows amongst Member States and aspirant states by limiting arbitrage opportunities for capital. In addition, once state macro-economies converged around low inflation and restrictive fiscal policies, policy-makers reasoned, it would be easier to surrender state-level monetary policies to the European Central Bank (ECB). The Bank's single monetary instrument could then more aptly apply to all Member States, since their voluntarily co-ordinated fiscal policies would ideally ensure that all members shared the same basic macroeconomic conditions. This would prevent imbalances between Member States that would put the ECB in the difficult position of having only one instrument to deal with inflation in one part of the Eurozone and deflation in another.

The Maastricht requirement of fiscal restraint, however, had distinct distributional effects in Slovakia. The country's central and eastern regions – its "internal periphery" – had Europe's highest unemployment rates; an embattled Roma population seeking deep, but nuanced, assistance; an underdeveloped infrastructure; and inadequate state services. Yet, the 2002–2006 Dzurinda government's commitment to "converge" fiscally with Northern Europe's surplus nations – most notably, Germany – ensured that these regions did not receive the fiscal attention that they sought.[1] European structural funds were made available to make up some of the shortfall. However, administrative incompetence and corruption reduced their impact and increased the popular perception that the system was rigged to serve the interests of the political élite in Bratislava.

Rather than establishing a regional development policy, Dzurinda's team of neoliberal economic advisors passed an investor-friendly flat tax, enabled firms to hire and fire workers more easily, stiffened the criminal code, privatised many public services, and began efforts to shift more of the burden for health and higher education from the state to the individual. Development would be driven by attracting foreign direct investment (FDI) through low wages, taxes, and regulations (Fisher, Gould and Haughton, 2007).

Dzurinda's development model and the Maastricht Convergence criteria made more sense in the inflation-prone Vah River valley of Slovakia. After the year 2000, an inflow of FDI into medium-skilled export-oriented manufacturing in the car industry and flat-screen TVs, among other things, created a strong demand for Slovak labour. However, further east, unemployment levels topped 20 and even 25 per cent – dominated by the region's marginalised Roma population. Indeed, Slovakia still has the EU's highest level of regional disparity (Machlica, Žúdel and Hidas, 2014: 40).

These areas needed (and still need) greater fiscal transfers, more educational opportunities, and heavier public investments into the sorts of infrastructure projects that would encourage FDI. But Maastricht's relentless pressures to tighten fiscal policy all but precluded a robust regional policy to address these issues in a comprehensive way. Instead, the internal periphery was subjected to another decade of outward migration as the most talented, educated, and entrepreneurial youth fled for jobs elsewhere. This too fed into the neoliberal model; unemployed migratory Slovak workers from the east provided international corporations with a reserve labour force – helping keep wages and inflation down in western Slovakia as the region benefitted from the FDI boom.

Moreover, as investors demanded local labour and products, they drove up demand for the Slovak *koruna* (crown), allowing the Slovak National Bank to revalue the crown against the Euro. With heavy foreign investments in manufacturing technology, productivity gains kept pace and ensured that the real wage impact on corporations did not increase. Between 2000 and 2009, the purchasing power of the Slovak crown nearly doubled. This made the Slovak middle class wealthier, but for those in the East and in non-traded sectors, whose productivity and wages failed to keep pace, everything rapidly became more expensive (Fisher, Gould and Haughton, 2007; Gould, 2009).

II.1 The non-crisis of 2006

Fico prevailed in the June 2006 parliamentary elections, in part because, as a nominal social democrat, he could speak for the concerns of this "internal periphery" and others around the country who felt the pressure of rising prices, stagnating fixed incomes, and stories of corruption. His economic message was often incoherent and populist, and it initially provided a poor alternative to the neoliberal *status quo*. Yet, his rhetoric spoke to those excluded from the FDI boom.

As Fico made electoral promises in the campaign, he began to question Maastricht's fiscal straitjacket. Forming a coalition government, Fico briefly spooked markets by forming a cabinet with Vladimír Mečiar's *Ľudová strana – Hnutie za demokratické Slovensko* (The People's Party – Movement for a Democratic Slovakia) (Ľ'S-HZDS) and the *Slovenská národná strana* (Slovak National Party) (SNS) – the latter led by the openly anti-Roma racist, homophobe Ján Slota. The coalition of left-leaning populists with right-leaning nationalists reminded observers of the authoritarian, fiscally profligate, and allegedly corrupt Mečiar cabinet of 1995–1998. The down-to-earth and often politically incorrect rhetoric of coalition party leaders Fico, Slota, and Mečiar spoke to those feeling challenged or left behind by Slovakia's rapidly integrating economy.

In July 2006, investors holding crown-based assets became concerned that the new Fico government would run larger fiscal deficits to meet Fico's promises of more re-distribution policies. Many exchanged their crown holdings for the euro on the assumption that the crown would soon lose value. The Slovak National Bank prevented a rout with a costly re-purchase of the crown to ensure that the crown–euro peg remained within its 15 per cent fluctuation band.

This was enough to get Fico's attention. On 12 July, he met with National Bank president Ivan Sramko to discuss the run on crown and, allegedly, to receive a quick primer on the pitfalls of capital mobility and the benefits of a strengthening currency. Following the meeting, Fico firmly re-emphasised his government's commitment to fiscal discipline and the January 2009 target for adopting the euro. The ensuing government programme declaration and budget were notable for their fiscal rectitude, further calming the markets (Malová and Dolný, 2016: 303).

With crown asset-holders firmly re-assured, Slovakia's investment boom continued unabated. In 2006 and 2007, Slovakia ranked among the world's best-performing economies. GDP growth topped 10 per cent in 2007. Fico's brief assault on the fiscal norms of Maastricht was a mere crack in a growth model that disproportionately benefited the west of the country. Between 2000 and the end of 2006, a cumulative total of 18.6 billion dollars (USD) of foreign investment produced the infrastructure for export-led development. Slovakia's currency peg appreciated from 48.6 SK/USD in the year 2000 to 21.4 SK/USD at the end of 2009, which meant that one crown could now buy over twice what it did at the turn of the century. Foreign investment in local technology and regional infrastructural investments (mostly in the west) ensured that productivity more than kept pace. Despite unprecedented demand for Slovak products in 2007, inflation only reached 2.8 per cent – a level made possible by revaluation, technology-enabled workers, and the country's rapidly dropping, but still significant, 11 per cent unemployment rate. Unemployment was still disproportionately located in the internal periphery (Eurostat, 2018) and primarily amongst the Roma and young people.

Fiscal discipline was easy to deliver under these conditions. Despite Fico's promise to undo Slovakia's neoliberal arrangements, the government did not tinker significantly with the Dzurinda government's basic capital-friendly measures (Gould, 2009). Slovakia adopted the euro as scheduled by his predecessors in January 2009. Fico took the credit.

The brief 2006 episode had put Fico's populist rhetoric norms in opposition to the Eurozone norms of fiscal convergence. Yet, when faced with the prospect of a flight of capital, a sharply de-valued Slovak crown, and the inflation that would certainly follow, Fico quickly abandoned his intention to develop the internal periphery *via* greater deficit spending. Rather than venturing into a full-blown systemic challenge, Fico backed down and resolved the crisis by committing the country fully to core adherence to the Eurozone.

III The Great Recession, 2008–2010: An external shock, but not (yet) an EU crisis

The July 2006 Slovak exchange crisis was the last time a ruling leader in Slovakia challenged the core Eurozone *norm* of fiscal convergence. This is perhaps a controversial statement because, from 2009 to 2012, the Slovak leadership failed to maintain Slovakia's formal Eurozone commitments. Why this was, and why Slovakia's participation in the collective departure from the fiscal rectitude was not a *legitimacy* crisis for the EU, merits some explanation. It also helps us to see better where Slovakia's other challenges to EU norms really mattered.

The global financial crisis of 2008–2010 challenged the formal terms of the Treaty of Maastricht. Yet, it would be hard to argue that Slovakia's response – to join other Eurozone members in running deep counter-cyclical deficits through to 2012 – was a challenge to Eurozone norms. Indeed, given that Slovak actions were part of a collective response to a deep recession, they were, arguably, consistent with core adhering behaviour.

After seven years of Slovak fiscal restraint, the EU welcomed Slovakia to the Eurozone in January 2009. Yet, in autumn 2008, just as the Slovak National Bank prepared to formalise the surrender of its monetary policy to the ECB, demand for Slovakia's exports in Germany and elsewhere collapsed and FDI flows stopped. Ironically, Slovakia's Visegrád 4 (V4) partners (Hungary, Poland, and the Czech Republic) had all kept their national currencies and thus remained free to devalue. The flip side was that, starting in 2009, both the Slovak government and investors could benefit from financing in euros and hence borrow free from the threat of a future currency devaluation that would raise the cost of debt repayment (Malová and Dolný, 2016). In addition, thanks to years of fiscal prudence, Slovakia's debt-to-GDP ratio was only 27.9 per cent (Eurostat, 2018), well below the 60 per cent limit set by Maastricht.

Slovakia was thus in good shape to fund a larger deficit in order to cover its automatic stabilising mechanisms and to pay for a controversial anti-crisis plan. Some of Fico's anti-crisis measures – like a used car buy-back scheme – were a blatant waste of money. Other measures, however, directly helped alleviate the burden on the poor, including an increase in the level of income that was exempt from the flat income tax. In 2009, the government began to provide financing and tax breaks to encourage high-value added investment. However, as a small, very open economy, there was very little else the government could do but assist its citizens with transfer payments while waiting for its export markets and internal demand to recover (Gould, 2009).

Admittedly, Fico presided over counter-cyclical spending that drove the deficit far beyond the convergence criteria expectations. Nonetheless, one would be hard pressed to call this a real challenge to the Eurozone. Germany, France, and Italy had all transgressed the 3 per cent deficit threshold earlier in the decade. Moreover, from 2009 through to 2012, Slovakia's annual deficit closely tracked that of France, and even Germany failed to meet Maastricht deficit criteria in 2009. In 2008 – before the stimulus efforts of 2009–2012 – both France and Germany had debt-to-GDP ratios of around 68 per cent. Slovakia's ratio never came near to this. A plunge into robust counter-cyclical spending in 2009 was the *dominant response* of virtually all Eurozone members – including those with extraordinarily high public debt-to-GDP ratios, such as Greece (Eurostat, 2018).

In this context, Slovakia's response to its export market failure of 2008–2009 was relatively uncontroversial in Brussels. As 2009 came to a close, the Commission merely challenged Slovakia (along with Slovenia and the Czech Republic) to *begin* the process of budget consolidation with a target of converging within the three per cent Maastricht deficit by 2013 (Rehn, 2010) – *a target that Slovakia subsequently met despite two changes in the governing party.* Slovakia's rapid return to fiscal restraint – even in the face of a return to high unemployment – demonstrates the degree to which Slovakia's political élite were fully socialised into the norm of fiscal discipline.

IV The Euro crisis and Slovakia's partial challenge to the EU

Slovakia's response to the ensuing Euro crisis of 2010–2012, however, was more nuanced and frequently out of line with the needs of the Eurozone and the preferences of both the zone's core and peripheral members. While Slovak élites were universally committed to collective fiscal restraint, they split over the equally important norm of Eurozone financial crisis solidarity. Some opposed EU demands that Slovakia help out its neighbours as a way of defining themselves as Slovak patriots on the domestic political spectrum. Chief amongst these was Richard Sulík of the SaS party. He was an ordoliberal market fundamentalist who was openly sceptical of Brussels, the Eurozone, and the Greek bail-out. Sulík was the first Slovak political actor explicitly to construct a party identity in opposition to the EU attempts to co-ordinate collective responses to collective financial problems. The result was a range of inconsistent Slovak responses that raised the cost of the EU's collective response to the Euro crisis.

Much of the reason for this lay in segmentation – a desire to see Greece and other high debtor states pay for their failure to embrace the ordoliberal norm of fiscal rectitude. A growing competition developed amongst Slovakia's political actors, who made two rhetorical claims. First, they framed calls for financial solidarity between Eurozone members as an attempt to shift the disproportional burdens of the crisis response to the Slovak taxpayer. Second, several Slovak politicians framed the Greek debt implosion as the product of immoral, Greek profligacy. To be fair, this rhetoric followed similar statements from German Chancellor Angela Merkel in early 2010. Sulík pointed out that, while Slovakia's government had restrained fiscal spending between 2002 and 2009, the "richer" Greeks had not. Why should Slovakia now be asked to carry the burden of an assistance package?[2] These arguments opened the door for a politics of resentment that challenged the core EU norm of solidarity that lay at the very heart of the EU project.

For those unfamiliar with the details of the Euro crisis, it began as the deep recession of 2009–2010 drove down tax revenue in Greece, leading banks to question the wisdom of re-financing Greece's growing debt (Henning, 2017: 74–100). As Greek debt-to-GDP rose from 100 per cent in 2008 to 129.7 per cent in 2009 (Eurostat, 2018), the rating agency Fitch downgraded long-term sovereign Greek debt from an A- to a BBB+ rating – the lowest Greek rating in a decade. The ECB demanded the Greeks undertake "courageous measures" to cut their budget deficit from over 12 per cent GDP to a balance (Smith and Seagar, 2009). Greek public workers responded with a strike which led to violent confrontations with the police in Athens. Meanwhile, EU leaders convened at the bi-annual EU summit to discuss a potential assistance package. Yet, Merkel took a hard line, asserting that the Greek government would have to resolve the crisis without assistance. Greek sovereign debt tumbled to "junk status" and private capital inflows to re-finance it stopped (Wachman and Fletcher, 2010).

The Greek fiscal crisis revealed the deep exposure of mostly northern European banks to a default, not only by Greece, but by other distressed Eurozone debtors as well. Worries about their health convinced EU leaders to correct for the lack of a bail-out mechanism in the Eurozone institutional architecture. As a stopgap measure, they agreed to a short-term 110 billion USD rescue fund and a temporary European Financial Stability Fund (EFSF) of 500 billion USD to help highly leveraged Eurozone members experiencing difficulty, to sell their sovereign debt (Inman, 2012). The EFSF was an *ad hoc* executive policy innovation to deal with a problem that the EU's treaty-based institutional architecture had not foreseen (Henning, 2017: 91–2).[3]

Fico supported the May 2010 summit package, but, led by Sulík, the opposition wanted to debate Slovak support for the package in parliament before the 2010 parliamentary election. Facing an election and economic populism from the opposition, Fico postponed the vote pending the outcome of the June 2010 parliamentary election (Balogová, 2010a).

Fico lost the election. In his place, former academic Iveta Radičová of the SDKÚ formed a centre-right coalition. Most importantly for this story, the new government included Sulík and his party, the SaS, as junior coalition members. But many other political actors played on the perennial Slovak anxiety that its leaders were somehow being duped by outsiders – including, in this case, the European Commission. Being tough with Brussels quickly became a theme of many of the main players in the Radičová government.

In August, the new coalition approved Slovakia's participation in the EFSF in the hopes of ensuring future stability in the Eurozone (a 3-year, 4.4 billion euro commitment). However, pushed by Sulík, parliament also refused to contribute to the Greek assistance package. The EU Commissioner for Economic and Monetary Affairs, Olli Rehn, regretted Slovakia's "breach of solidarity within the Eurozone" (Rehn, 2010). Predicting a Greek default despite the assistance, Sulík stated that Slovakia did not need solidarity, nor did it need the euro, really; fiscal restraint would suffice to provide stable growth. Incoming finance minister, Ivan Mikloš (SDKÚ), added, "When solidarity of the poor with the rich, or the responsible with the irresponsible, or taxpayers with bank owners or managers is the question, I do not consider it solidarity" (Balogová, 2010b).

Slovakia's refusal to contribute to the first Greek assistance package was little more than a "speed bump" from the EU perspective (*Business Blog*, 2011). Slovakia's proportionally allotted payment was an insignificant part of the package's success, so the break with solidarity was merely symbolic. However, as an equal, sovereign player within the EU, a Slovak veto could derail the EU treaty ratification process. This soon presented the EU with a real crisis, as the Greek debt-payment problems spread to Ireland, Iceland, and Portugal (Newman, 2015: 122). In the autumn of 2010, Ireland required EFSF loans, followed by Portugal in May 2011, and Greece again in August 2011 (Inman, 2012).

But it was the threat of Spanish and potentially Italian defaults that most frightened financial officials. Spain was a fiscal superstar compared to Greece, and compared well with France and even Germany. As the Greek, Irish, and Portuguese debt crises developed, however, bankers discovered that they were deeply vulnerable.[4] With the sharp fall in Spanish real-estate prices, the leveraged real-estate investments of private investors emerged as a systemic threat to over-leveraged European banks. Europe's financial system now had a financial collective action problem in which the efforts of all exposed banks to deleverage at once would lead to a systemic, European-wide banking crisis (Blyth, 2013). In a response widely considered to be illegal, the ECB purchased sovereign Spanish and Italian debt and recapitalized European banks with unlimited 3-year loans (Henning, 2017: 131–139).

IV.1 Austerity in lieu of core formation

The EFSF was a stopgap measure that would have been insufficient had it not been for IMF assistance, sovereign debt buy-backs, and the public acquisition of private bank debt (Henning, 2017: 99; 139). Most, now belatedly, agreed that the EU needed significant institutional re-structuring. Federalists and other advocates of deeper EU core formation argued that the way forward was a Eurozone fiscal union and the corresponding transfer of the scope of citizen sovereignty from the Member States to the EU (Habermas, 2012). Politically, however, solving the crisis by further federalisation was not on the agenda – reflecting the cognitive bias of the élites within a segmented financial order that excluded alternatives to ordoliberalism; indeed, in lieu of more union, the ECB, the European Commission, and the IMF (often referred to as the "*Troika*") chose to adopt fiscal restraint across the EU, regardless of the damage that this would do to the local economies of the peripheral debtor states.

Austerity had a long heritage in Slovakia, and, indeed, in Central Europe. What changed over time was the national discretion to manage it. In addition there was a cognitive shift from seeing austerity as a useful policy tool to the segment-internal idea that fiscal restraint was a virtue both *in* and *of* itself. In the 1990s, local governments had used currency devaluation, monetary restraint, and a sharp curtailment in government spending to make the transition from communist economies towards the market, and to manage rapid integration into the European markets. In the first decade of the 2000s, euro-candidate states such as Slovakia tried to mimic what it would be like to be part of a currency union by co-ordinating fiscal and monetary policies using the Maastricht exchange rate mechanism (ERM) convergence criteria. Notwithstanding this, Slovakia both retained and utilised significant local discretion – most notably by revaluing the

Slovak crown to absorb local inflationary pressures and encourage investments in labour productivity.

Within the Eurozone, ECB policy was designed to keep inflation low in the fully employed economies of the core. This did not meet the needs that the under-performing peripheral Eurozone members had for stimulus, but the growing cognitive pre-disposition of the financial élites to value fiscal restraint as being *morally* superior to looser fiscal policy ensured that this need was never taken seriously (Blyth, 2013). With monetary expansion and currency devaluation no longer an option, the response of the peripheral countries was to take advantage of low-rate, euro-denominated debt and expand their economies through heavy borrowing. Much of this occurred under the radar thanks to Greek/Wall Street obfuscation and to municipal and – as we saw with Spain – private-sector bor-rowing, which, at the time, was of no concern to international financial observ-ers. Yet, thanks to the global financial crisis of 2008, that model was now in full-blown crisis (Bird, 2010: 44–5).

Once again, austerity emerged as the solution. Rather than seek a differenti-ated counter-cyclical policy backed by stimulated spending in the core, and gen-erous lending from the core to the periphery, the *Troika* demanded that countries in crisis cut consumption and squeeze savings in order to reimburse the northern banks (Stiglitz, 2016). Slovakia's leading politicians backed this prescription. In 2011 and 2012, the *Troika* remained firmly committed to conditioning crisis aid on the distressed country's commitment to fiscal austerity. The *Troika* even forced the Greek government to increase taxes in the midst of a recession – a form of economic malpractice that left many observers dumbfounded (Blyth, 2013; Stiglitz, 2016).

Equally problematical was Germany's commitment to importing the sav-ings of others. Far from serving as the lender of last resort and/or a market for goods and services from distressed countries, Germany was amongst the first to reduce its fiscal deficit below 3 per cent (in 2010) and ran a current account sur-plus. This came at exactly the time when recession-damaged periphery econo-mies – including Slovakia's – could have used a good boost of German spending. Instead, the German leaders chose to put the entire Eurozone on a starvation diet. They then professed confusion when no one gained weight.

The May 2010 "bail-out" package thus – quite predictably – produced neither Greek recovery nor a resolution to the crisis. Following a 5.5 per cent contraction in 2010, Greece posted an additional 9.1 per cent tumble in 2011 (World Bank, 2016a). By late spring, it was clear that the IMF's earlier forecasts had been badly off. Slovakia had also tightened its belt after the 2010 vote, raising the VAT by 1 per cent and capping government salaries. But it was Germany's self-imposed contraction (and, hence, lower demand in Slovakia's primary export market) that hurt the most. In 2010, German demand stimulus helped drive Slovakia to a robust, export-fuelled 5.1 per cent recovery. With Germany's return to fiscal restraint in 2011, Slovak growth dropped to 2.8 per cent in 2011 and levelled off around 1.5 per cent in 2012 and 2013 (World Bank, 2018b). From 2012 to 2016,

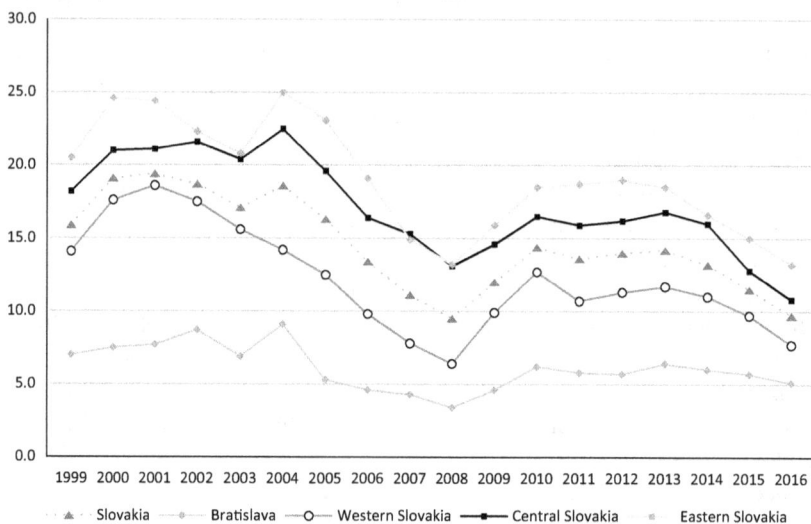

FIGURE 6.1 Per cent unemployed in Slovakia by region. Eurostat, 2018.

Slovakia increasingly relied on domestic demand to generate growth. Moreover, while growth has returned, unemployment remained in the double digits outside of western Slovakia through the 2016 election, with youth unemployment ranging from 23 to 30 per cent (European Commission, 2016b).

IV.2 The Treaty crisis of 2011

In March 2011, a Franco-German agreement led to a modification to the Lisbon Treaty creating the European Stability Mechanism (ESM) with the authority to loan up to 500 billion euro to distressed Eurozone members (Jabko, 2015: 79-84). As a Lisbon Treaty amendment, however, the ESM needed all EU Member States to be ratified. The subsequent Slovak ratification discussion brought down the Radičová government.

At the heart of the crisis was Richard Sulík of the SaS. His junior coalition party had enough seats to veto any coalition legislation. Rhetorically, Sulík was deeply wedded to a pejorative neoliberal narrative accusing Brussels of forcing Slovakia to subsidise Greek leisure while saddling the cost of "socialist"-style bail-outs on EU members. Without the SaS, however, the Radičová coalition government had to turn to the opposition for support. Fico's Smer was in favour of ESM ratification but strategically chose to withhold opposition support until Sulík and the rest of the government gave the treaty unanimous backing. Under intense pressure, Radičová upped the ante on Sulík by linking a vote in favour of ESM to a vote of confidence in the government. Sulík refused to back down, the vote failed, and the coalition government collapsed. His brief self-congratulations for saving the European taxpayer billions in "needless waste" was cut short after Radičová secured Fico's opposition support for the Treaty amendment in exchange for early parliamentary elections.[5]

IV.3 Slovakia doubles down on collective fiscal restraint

On 9 December 2011, Radičová joined EU leaders in "augmenting" the new ESM facility with a "fiscal compact." The pact, ratified on 2 March 2012 as the "Treaty on Stability, Coordination and Economic Governance" (TSCEG), attempted to achieve fiscal collective action without directly challenging the sovereignty of states. Specifically, treaty adherents promised to pass domestic constitutional measures guaranteeing fiscal restraint.

In many ways, this was worse than a fiscal union. A centralised federal fiscal union would have allowed for robust anti-downturn measures that would stimulate the economy where needed through regionalised demand management techniques. The Treaty, by contrast, sought to ensure fiscal restraint everywhere and at all times (Jabko, 2015: 78–84). Again, debate over the TSCEG in Slovakia (also referred to as the "fiscal pact") did not delve into the pact's collective economic implications, for example, that it made little sense to expect a slowing EU to accelerate growth by *restricting* fiscal spending across the EU. All six parliamentary parties supported the fiscal pact, and on 8 December 2012, the parliament passed the TSCEG-compliant constitutional amendments prescribing a series of increasingly painful penalties for government budgets as they grew closer to a debt-GDP ratio of 60 per cent. At 60 per cent, the Slovak constitution required a no-confidence vote to be taken in parliament.

In the March 2012 campaign, Fico's party, the Smer, won an unprecedented, outright majority in parliament, enabling Fico to rule with a one-party cabinet. In its government manifesto, the Smer remained committed to low, long-term public debt and collective Eurozone fiscal convergence at 3 per cent of GDP. Rhetorically, this required violent twisting of the Smer's nominal commitment to social solidarity. For example, the body charged with overseeing the deficit reductions below 3 per cent was called the "Council of Solidarity and Development." Few remarked on the blatant doubletalk (*The Slovak Spectator*, 2012).

Darina Malová has argued elsewhere that élite support for EU fiscal norms from both the Radičová and Fico governments has helped strengthen domestic support for the EU (2016: 308). Indeed, it is our judgement here as well, that, in the area of Eurozone policy, Slovakia's responses to the Great Recession of 2009–2010 and the ongoing Eurozone crisis have not fundamentally challenged the legitimacy of the Eurozone's norm of collective fiscal restraint. Nonetheless, Slovakia continued to resist honouring the norm of financial solidarity with the periphery – both at home and abroad. This, as the next section will argue, has contributed to the significant stress faced by the communities that were bypassed by Slovakia's great economic boom. Not surprisingly, these areas have been more open to supporting populist politics that pose a significant challenge to EU legitimacy, politics that echo the politics of Brexit and the recent trend towards resurgent continental nationalism and Euroscepticism. Thus, segmented thinking and policy in EU's financial regime has contributed to segmented thinking about the EU's liberal mission at the local level.

V The refugee crisis of 2015

The refugee crisis of 2015–2016 reveals the extent to which Slovakia's neglected internal periphery has contributed to a crisis in other areas, and it exposes the pressures that potentially threaten the long-term survival of the EU in its current form. The refugee crisis has done this by providing the losers of Slovakia's post-communist transformation with a broadly appealing narrative through which they can express their frustration, resentment, and anger at the long-term neglect of Slovakia's internal periphery. Slovakia's political élite have exploited this new narrative for political gain, but, as the rise of the ultra-nationalist *Ľudová strana – Naše Slovensko* (People's Party-Our Slovakia) (ĽSNS) demonstrates, they are not entirely in control. Indeed, the 2016 election witnessed a sharp shift from the incumbent ruling party, the Smer, towards nationalist parties of all sorts. Perhaps the only consistent explanation for the shift was a general desire on the part of voters outside of Bratislava to send a message to incumbent politicians and politics as usual. This was particularly true amongst first-time voters (Gyárfášová, 2017). It is entirely possible that we were witnessing many of the same dynamics that we have seen in Brexit and in the election of Donald Trump as the president of the United States.

Ironically, the arrival of the refugees in Europe created a crisis in Slovakia despite the fact that most refugees consider Slovakia, at best, to be a transit state, and, at worst, a country to be avoided. This has led to the popular quip that Slovakia has had a "refugee crisis without refugees" (Kusá, 2015). Nevertheless, with the March 2016 elections looming, Prime Minister Fico made rhetorical use of the issue wherever possible, putting himself directly at odds with the European Commission's efforts to devise a collective response to the tragic situation that was unfolding.

In May 2015, the European Commission proposed that the burden of taking in refugees be spread across the Member States according to a quota system. The Commission assigned Slovakia just over 800 refugees, which Fico promptly rejected, along with other Central European EU Member States. Fico responded over the course of the summer with Christian-chauvinist and xenophobic statements that put him in a leadership position on the issue. He argued that, although he did not wish to challenge the EU norm of solidarity, the migrants would divert scarce resources from needy Slovaks, raise the risk of terrorism in Slovakia, threaten Slovakia's Christian culture, and pose a lasting assimilation problem (O'Grady, 2015).

This hostility towards the European Commission put Fico rhetorically in league with the extreme xenophobe and fascist-nostalgic Marián Kotleba and his Banská Bystrica-based party, ĽSNS. At the time, ĽSNS was a regional Central

Slovakian party, and only a few saw it as a major threat. But, on 20 June 2015, Kotleba staged a violent demonstration in Bratislava under the slogan, "Stop the Islamisation of Europe! Together against the dictate of Brussels; Europe for Europeans!" In an incendiary speech, he wished his followers "a beautiful and nice white day" (*The Slovak Spectator*, 2015a). Kotleba was part of an alarming, quite probably Russian-supported, trend directed at the deliberate fragmentation of the EU, which fused radical nationalism with Euroscepticism (ČTK, 2017). But he also claimed to speak for those on the internal periphery and received disproportionate support amongst young, first-time voters in his region.

In the lead-up to the election, Fico co-opted much of the far right's rhetoric, all the while repeating support for the norm of EU solidarity upon the basis of a Christian conception of Europe. Other mainstream parties followed suit, essentially depriving Slovaks of a liberal, pro-EU, and refugee-centred alternative to vote for in the March 2016 election.

In summer 2015, Fico sought out regional V4 partners for support in resisting Commission quotas, and he threatened a referendum on the issue. Eventually, he conceded that he could accept some refugees, but would do so "voluntarily" while restricting their numbers to only 100 Syrian Christians, who would not "threaten our entity and cultural essence." The European Council called this "blatant discrimination."[6]

Facing "furious opposition" from EU member states, the European Council voted to make the refugee resettlement programme voluntary. This did little to solve the problem of burden-sharing, and it expected that both transit states such as Croatia, Greece, Italy, and Hungary and final settlement states such as Germany and Sweden would take on most of the burden themselves. Hungary, whose Prime Minister Viktor Orbán echoed Fico in rejecting resettlement on civilisational grounds, built a border fence to re-direct migrants from Serbia into another EU Member State, Croatia. Meanwhile, countries began to introduce border checks within the Schengen area, threatening freedom of movement.

As the EU descended into name-calling and uncoordinated burden-shifting country-level policies, some commissioners considered linking EU structural funds to EU-compliant policies on the refugee issue (Stevens, 2015). In mid-September 2015, EU interior ministers returned to the quota solution, agreeing to take in 120,000 refugees, to be distributed proportionally among the EU Member States. Slovakia was again assigned 802 refugees – in addition to the now-150 Iraqi Christians they had already accepted. Under the new plan, non-compliant countries would face stiff fines.

Fico joined Hungary, the Czech Republic, and Romania in voting against the measure on the Council, but lost to a binding super-majority (Traynor, 2016). He nevertheless promised to disobey the policy and in December challenged the quotas in the Court of Justice of the European Union (*Reuters*, 2015b). Meanwhile, Fico's party, the Smer, continued to exploit the refugee issue for political gains in the parliamentary election campaign. The terrorist attacks in Paris and the alleged migrant-led sexual assaults in Germany on New

Year's Eve were used to justify Slovakia's anti-quota policies and to "beef up" or strengthen Slovakia's own security apparatus, including an alleged surveillance policy on "every Muslim" in Slovakia (IntelliNews, 2015d). The Smer posted campaign posters across the country promising "We will defend you!" The Party of European Socialists (PES) (which, tellingly, had never objected to Fico's embracing of fiscal convergence) now put the Smer on notice, with a threat of suspension from the party club of the European Parliament for its rhetoric (IntelliNews, 2015c).

The Smer's electoral strategy was insufficient to preserve its parliamentary majority in the elections of March 2016. Thanks, in part, to Fico's leadership, polls indicated that 70 per cent of Slovak citizens were against hosting refugees, while 63 per cent considered them to be a security threat (Malová, 2016: 309). Accordingly, most pro-EU parties found it prudent to validate – fully or partially – Fico's rhetoric, essentially removing his advantage. As Malová has commented elsewhere, Fico's ethno/xenophobic and anti-EU rhetoric "let the genie out of the bottle." (2016)

Most parties pledged to keep Slovaks "safe" in some way. However, a Eurobarometer poll in summer of 2016 placed migrants only fifth on a prioritised list of voter issues. Unemployment was the major concern of those polled, followed by worries about health and social security. All four of the *most* mentioned issues related to the economic well-being of the recipients (2016: 11). Thus, Fico's decision to stoke the fears of the voters around immigration failed, in part, because other parties followed the same strategy, thereby annulling his advantage; and, in part, because voter concerns about economic insecurity remained paramount. As the incumbent party, the Smer now bore more responsibility for the economy. Slovaks thus spread their votes more broadly in 2016 than they had in 2012. The Smer won more votes than its rivals, but still had to enter into coalition with an odd constellation of right-wing conservatives, Slovak nationalists, and, paradoxically, Most-Híd (the Slovak and Hungarian words for "Bridge"), a moderate, pro-EU mixed Hungarian-Slovak party. Sulík's deeply Eurosceptic SaS shared the opposition with Kotleba's ĽSNS.

Studies show that many of those who supported Fico in 2012 fled to the SNS and the ĽSNS in 2016 in a vote that many considered to be an anti-systemic rejection of centrist parties. The ĽSNS easily crossed the parliamentary threshold. Meanwhile, Slovakia's long-standing nationalist party, the SNS, returned to parliament after having fallen short of the threshold in 2012 (Vražda, 2016). According to Marek Hlavac, the Smer, the SNS, and the ĽSNS secured proportionally more support from those areas with lower education rates and higher unemployment, which were, arguably, the best proxies for distressed regions in his data set (Hlavac, 2016: 40–41). This does not mean that the unemployed drove the populist vote; Slovakia's deeply underemployed Roma population rarely voted, and when they did, rarely voted nationalist. As in other European and US regions where populist electoral uprisings have shaken the established order, much of the vote came from "blue-collar workers," insecure in their futures and stressed by the conditions of stagnating wages and competition from technological change and globalised production. It is also notable that about one in five young first-time voters supported the ĽSNS, according to Olga Gyárfášová. Asked why, few would admit to racism or fear of migrants, but instead emphasised their desire to send a clear message to an indifferent, unresponsive political élite (2017). Arguably, then, it was persistent economic distress, low personal advancement opportunities, and frustration with Bratislava's corruption and political unresponsiveness that drove the nationalist shift in 2016.

VI Conclusion

Slovakia's electorate has lost its ranking as one of Europe's most EU-friendly, and today it could be called a typical, qualified supporter of EU institutions and initiatives (European Commission, 2016a). With politicians competing amongst themselves to capture the mantle of "reasonable EU-scepticism" against a background of regional economic disparity, this trend towards qualified support for EU institutions and policies is likely to continue. The two major institutional EU innovations in response to the Euro crisis – the ESM and the TSCEG – do not promise to solve the problems which they were designed to address. They build on ideas that carry what the editors of this volume call a "segmental logic" – a technocratic lack of imagination that is typical of segmented orders. Perhaps more worrisome for the future is that, by committing Slovakia to Eurozone-driven fiscal policies that limit the ability to stimulate its internal periphery, they are arguably contributing to the sort of Brexit-like politics of resentment that emerged during the refugee crisis. The segmental logic of financial élites is reinforcing conditions that strengthen political élites with distinctly segmental ideas about human rights, democracy and cultural diversity, and tolerance.

Indeed, Slovakia and other fiscal pact-compliant countries have created constitutional rules that collectively limit the opportunities of differential development policies, benefiting the EU core over its internal peripheries. As an institutional fix, the TSCEG is inferior to a federalised, central fiscal union which would allow more regionally nuanced fiscal policies. Indeed, additional core building – in the form of a supranational fiscal union – could offer solutions which would enable regionally specific counter-stimulus packages to assist the EU's many peripheral regions. However, given the cognitive binders of policy-makers and the resulting ordoliberal institutional fixes, such core-building initiatives appear unlikely in the near future. Given the post-crises appeal of resentment politics in Slovakia's distressed communities – and the distressed regions throughout Europe – greater segmentation, not less, appears to be the political direction in the EU.

Prime Minister Fico's xenophobic turn in 2015–2016 is symptomatic of segmentation. His actions in the migrant crisis directly challenged some of the EU's most fundamental norms. While he channelled his protest against the EU quota decision through the courts, his effort sought to shift the burdens of the refugee crisis disproportionately to select EU Member States, deepening internal EU tensions and discord just as the United Kingdom planned to depart from the integration project. Similarly, while Fico sought to bolster the EU's external borders,[7] he also sought to preserve the Schengen Treaty by limiting the overall inflow of migrants. This response favoured greater intra-EU co-ordination, if not federal integration, by boosting Frontex. But Fico simultaneously contributed to segmentation by joining right-wing politicians in a rhetorical assault on the basic principle of a multicultural Europe. This exacerbated the tensions between the EU's liberal norm separating church and state and the nationalists' desire to preserve Europe's "Christian character" within a "fortress Europe" (Malová, 2016: 309). Should democratic electorates choose a segmented path of ethno/cultural exclusion over the EU's inclusionary, democratic charter, the European experiment in democracy, human rights, and freedom of movement will effectively be over. The implication of exclusionary Christian cultural rhetoric is thus existential.

Notes

1 Maastricht expected Slovakia to limit fiscal deficits to no more than 3 per cent of GDP, maintain a debt-to-GDP ratio of less than 60 per cent, and ensure that interest rates and inflation rates converged with the three EU lowest-rate Member States.
2 Under pressure from the *Troika* and the capital markets, Greece contracted its domestic demand significantly after 2009, enabling Slovakia to converge rapidly with the declining Greek GDP and even surpass the Greeks in GDP PPP *per capita* in 2012 (World Bank, 2018a, 2018b). Purchasing Power Parity (PPP) is an economic theory that compares prices in different countries through a common basket of goods.
3 Before 2010, the ECB explicitly avoided any provisions for either financial assistance or a bail-out mechanism for fear of creating a moral hazard problem (Bird, 2010: 50). Yet, as Graham Bird has pointed out, "Moral hazard arguments are frequently acknowledged before a crisis but are usually overlooked in the midst of one" (Bird, 2010: 59). With Europe's largest creditors potentially at risk, the *Troika* quickly overcame its scruples. In addition, the ECB began to buy back Greek sovereign debt and to allow countries to use it (despite its junk status) to collateralise new loans from Eurozone banks (Bird, 2010: 47).
4 Local governments had also been borrowing heavily on international markets.
5 This was not the first time that domestic political actors had used an EU Treaty to secure government concessions. In 2009, Radičová's colleagues in the SDKÚ had held the Treaty of Lisbon hostage to obtain the reversal of the perceived illiberal provisions of Fico's press law (Malová and Dolný, 2016: 303). We should not dismiss Sulík's position as pure political grandstanding. As Gál has demonstrated, Slovakia's obligations, both direct and indirect, in the event of a Member State default are significant. A Greek default alone could cost Slovakia between a few hundred million and two billion euro (Gál, 2013:347).
6 In August, the Slovak government reframed its language to assert that it would "prefer" the mere 100 refugees that it was willing to resettle to be Christians. As Ivan Netik, Interior Minister Spokesman asserted, "we don't have any mosques in Slovakia so how can Muslims be integrated if they are not going to like it here?" (IntelliNews, 2015a).
7 Fico sent 50 Slovak police to help patrol the Hungarian border with Serbia (IntelliNews, 2015b), 20 to Slovenia, and an additional 100 to Frontex in January 2016, where they patrolled in Macedonia (IntelliNews, 2016).

References

Balogová, Beata (2010a), "Slovakia's New Election Issue: Greece", *The Slovak Spectator*, 17 May 2010, available at: http://spectator.sme.sk/c/20036195/slovakias-new-election-issue-greece.html, last accessed 6 September 2016.

Balogová, Beata (2010b), "Slovakia Backs Eurozone Plan, Rejects Greek Bailout", *The Slovak Spectator*, 23 August 2010, available at: http://spectator.sme.sk/c/20037151/slovakia-backs-eurozone-plan-rejects-greek-bailout.html, last accessed 6 September 2016.

Bird, Graham (2010), "The Eurozone: What Now?" *World Economics*, 11 (3): 41–59.

Blyth, Mark (2013), *Austerity: The History of a Dangerous Idea*, Oxford: Oxford University Press.

Business Blog (2011), "Slovakia and the European Debt Crisis – As it Happened", *The Guardian*, 12 October 2011, available at: www.theguardian.com/business/blog/2011/sep/26/european-debt-crisis-live, last accessed 31 August 2017.

ČTK (2017), "Odhalenie nemeckej televízie: Kotlebovci dostávali peniaze od prokremeľského podnikateľa", *HN* (*Hospodarsky noviny*), 30 May, available at: http://hnonline.sk/svet/969022-odhalenie-nemeckej-televizie-kotlebovci-dostavali-peniaze-od-prokremelskeho-podnikatela, last accessed 31 May 2017.

European Commission (2016a), "Public Opinion in the European Union", Standard Eurobarometer 86.

European Commission (2016b), "Country Report Slovakia 2016", Commission Staff Working Document, Brussels, 26 February 2016.

Eurostat (2018), "Unemployment Rates by Sex, Age and NUTS 2 Regions (%), Eurostat, European Commission", available at: https://ec.europa.eu/eurostat/web/products-datasets/-/tgs00010, last accessed 16 November 2018.

Fisher, Sharon, John Gould, and Tim Haughton (2007), "Slovakia's Neoliberal Turn", *Europe-Asia Studies*, 59 (6): 977–998.

Gál, Zsolt (2013), "Farwell to the Carpathian Tiger: Impact of the Global Crisis on Slovakia", in: Attila Ágh and László Vass (eds), *European Futures: The Perspectives of the New Member States in the New Europe*, Budapest: Budapest College of Communications and Business, pp. 337–364.

Gould, John (2009), "Slovakia's Neoliberal Churn: The Political Economy of the Fico Government, 2006–2008", Institute of European Studies and International Relations, Faculty of Social and Economic Sciences, Comenius University, Bratislava, Slovakia.

Gyárfášová, Olga (2017), "The Rise of Radicalism among Young People in Slovakia: Causes and Consequences", *Aspen Review*, Issue 2, available at: www.aspen.review/article/2017/the-rise-of-radicalism-among-young-people-in-slovakia-causes-and-consequences, last accessed 20 March 2018.

Habermas, Jürgen (2012), *The Crisis of the European Union: A Response*, Cambridge: Polity Press.

Henning, C. Randall (2017), *Tangled Governance: International Regime Complexity, the Troika, and the Euro Crisis*, Oxford: Oxford University Press.

Hlavac, Marek (2016), "Performance of Political Parties in the 2016 Parliamentary Election in Slovakia: Regional Comparisons and District-level Determinants", *Regional and Federal Studies*, 26 (3): 433–443.

Inman, Philip (2012), "Greek Debt Crisis: Timeline", *The Guardian*, 11 March 2012, available at: www.theguardian.com/business/2012/mar/09/greek-debt-crisis-timeline, last accessed 2 January 2017.

IntelliNews (2015a), "Slovakia Now 'Prefers' Christian Asylum Seekers", *IntelliNews – Slovakia This Week*, 21 August 2015, available through Lexis-Nexis Academic, last accessed 16 November 2016.

IntelliNews (2015b), "Slovakia to Send Police to Hungarian-Serbian Border", *IntelliNews – Slovakia This Week*, 14 October 2015, available through Lexis-Nexis Academic, last accessed 16 November 2016.

IntelliNews (2015c), "Visegrád: Fico Told to Take His Trousers Down", *IntelliNews – Slovakia This Week*, 25 November 2015, available through Lexis-Nexis Academic, last accessed 16 November 2016.

IntelliNews (2015d), "Slovakia to Hand Police Draconian Powers", *IntelliNews – Slovakia Today*, 28 October 2015, available through Lexis-Nexis Academic, last accessed 16 November 2016.

IntelliNews (2016), "Slovakia to Help Patrol Macedonian Border", *IntelliNews – Slovakia This Week*, 5 January 2016, available through Lexis-Nexis Academic, last accessed 16 November 2016.

Jabko, Nicolas (2015), "The Elusive Economic Government and the Forgotten Fiscal Union", in: Matthias Matthijs and Mark Blyth (eds), *The Future of the Euro*, Oxford: Oxford University Press, pp. 70–89.

Keohane, Robert O. (1969), "Lilliputians' Dilemmas: Small States in International Politics", *International Organization*, 23 (2): 291–310.

Kusá, Dagmar (2015), "Conversation with John Gould", 16 November 2015.

Machlica, Gabriel, Branislav Žúdel and Slavomir Hidas (2014), "Unemployment in Slovakia", Economic analysis, no. 30, Ministry of Finance, Bratislava.

Malová, Darina (2016), "How to Get from the Periphery: Compliance with the Maastricht Rules in Slovakia", Department of Political Science, Comenius University, Faculty of Arts.

Malová, Darina, and Branislav Dolný (2016), "Economy and Democracy in Slovakia during the Crisis: From a Laggard to the EU Core", *Problems of Post-Communism*, 63 (5–6): 300–312.

Newman, Abraham (2015), "The Reluctant Leader: Germany's Euro Experience and the Long Shadow of Reunification," in: Matthias Matthijs and Mark Blyth (eds), *The Future of the Euro*, Oxford: Oxford University Press, pp. 117–135.

O'Grady, Siobhán (2015), "Slovakia to EU: We'll Take Migrants – if They're Christians", *Foreign Policy*, 19 August, available at: https://foreignpolicy.com/2015/08/19/slovakia-to-eu-well-take-migrants-if-theyre-christians, last accessed 16 November 2018.

Rehn, Olli (2010), "Press Conference Speaking Points: Excessive Deficit Procedure – Effective Action", European Commission for Economic and Monetary Policy, Strasbourg, available at: http://europa.eu/rapid/press-release_SPEECH-10-313_en.htm, last accessed 3 December 2018.

Rybář, Marek, and Kevin Deegan-Krause (2008), "Slovakia's Successor Parties in Comparative Perspective", *Communist and Post-Communist Studies*, 41 (1): 497–519.

Smith, Helena, and Ashley Seager (2009), "Financial Markets Tumble after Fitch Downgrades Greece's Credit Rating", *The Guardian*, 8 December 2009, available at: www.theguardian.com/world/2009/dec/08/greece-credit-rating-lowest-eurozone, last accessed 2 January 2017.

The Slovak Spectator (2012), "Government Manifesto Passed", *The Slovak Spectator*, 15 May 2012, available at: http://spectator.sme.sk/c/20043429/government-manifesto-passed.html, last accessed 16 November 2018.

The Slovak Spectator (2015a), "Protest against Migrant Quotas Paralyses Downtown Bratislava", *The Slovak Spectator*, 22 June 2015, available at: https://spectator.sme.sk/c/20058267/protest-against-migrant-quotas-paralyses-downtown-bratislava.html, last accessed 16 November 2018.

Reuters (2015b), "Slovakia Files Lawsuit against EU Quotas to Redistribute Migrants", Reuters, 2 December 2015.

Stevens, John (2015), "EU Could Slash Funding for Countries Who [sic] Don't Take In More Migrants", *The Daily Mail*, 2 September 2015.

Stiglitz, Joseph (2016), *The Euro: How a Common Currency Threatens the Future of Europe*, New York: W.W. Norton.

Traynor, Ian (2016), "EU Braces for Turbulent Summit after Divisive Deal on Refugee Quota", *The Guardian*, 23 September 2016.

Vražda, Daniel (2016), "Odkrývame nové bašty Kotlebovej ĽSNS. Ako vyrástla tam, kde bol roky dominantný Smer", *Denník N*, 6 April 2016, available at: https://dennikn.sk/427550/kotleba-vyrastol-tam-bol-roky-dominantny-smer, last accessed 20 March 2018.

Wachman, Richard, and Nick Fletcher (2010), "Standard & Poor's Downgrade Greek Credit Rating to Junk Status", *The Guardian*, 27 April 2010, available at: www.theguardian.com/business/2010/apr/27/greece-credit-rating-downgraded, last accessed 2 January 2017.

World Bank (2018a), "GDP Growth – Annual %, Greece", World Bank, Washington DC, available at: http://data.worldbank.org/indicator/NY.GDP.MKTP.KD.ZG?locations=GR, last accessed 16 November 2018.

World Bank (2018b), "GDP Growth – Annual %, Slovakia", World Bank, Washington DC, available at: http://data.worldbank.org/indicator/NY.GDP.MKTP.KD.ZG?locations=SK&name_desc=false, last accessed 16 November 2018.

7

EUROPEAN SOLIDARITY IN TIMES OF CRISIS

Towards differentiated integration

Asimina Michailidou and Hans-Jörg Trenz

I Introduction

References to the principle of solidarity are found at several places and with shifting meaning in the Treaty framework of the European Union (EU) (for example, Articles 2, 3(3), 21(1), 24(2) and (3), 31(1); "Treaty on European Union" [TEU], the formal name for the Treaty of Maastricht). With the Treaty of Lisbon, the legal construction of the concept was given a three-dimensional definition: solidarity between Member States, between generations, and international solidarity (solidarity and mutual respect among people (Article 3(3) TEU). Moreover, the Lisbon Treaty established the Charter of Fundamental Rights of the European Union of the year 2000, which contains a "Solidarity" chapter outlining the social dimensions of the economic internal market, part of primary law (Article 6 (1) TEU). Nevertheless, the concept of solidarity remains largely general, if not vague, in the Treaties. The Treaty does not, for instance, make explicit reference to the principle of solidarity when referring to the relationship between the EU and the citizens or the Member States and individuals. Solidarity is also not listed among the core values of the EU (Art. 2 TEU) but is only introduced into the legal text through a side reference ("These values are common to the Member States in a society in which pluralism, non-discrimination, tolerance, justice, solidarity and equality between women and men prevail."). The society (in the singular!) which serves as a reference-point, remains undefined, and the meaning of "values" that "prevail" is also open to interpretation. In the Treaty of the Functioning of the European Union (TFEU, the Treaty of Lisbon 2007) *solidarity* is instead only very narrowly defined with reference to the obligation of EU Member States to act jointly in the event of a terrorist attack or a natural or man-made disaster (Art. 222 TFEU). This so-called "solidarity clause" is, in fact, to be understood as a kind of emergency mechanism. Mutual support in the "spirit of solidarity" is meant as an altruistic relationship between donors and receivers and not as a relationship of reciprocity among equals. This provision thus entrenches the distinction between the inclusive solidarity of the nation (reciprocity among a community of equals) and the open and flexible solidarity of Europe as a community of non-equals. Solidarity in Europe thus becomes a flexible arrangement that is open to constant re-negotiation and contestation.

The direct implication of this arrangement is that Europeans cannot draw on an *a priori* settlement of the question of to whom solidarity relationships apply and what these relationships entail, not only in legal terms (Domurath, 2013; Sangiovanni, 2013), but also in terms of moral duties and responsibilities. This is relevant from a sociological perspective in which claims for solidarity have always been intertwined with claims for democracy and the strong identity of citizens, and belonging to a community of equals. In the case of the EU, it remains difficult to see how such an inclusive notion of solidarity as a marker of a European *demos* can apply. In the European context, the linkage between solidarity and identity remains contested. At the same time, the EU faces numerous challenges which intensify such disputes about the notion of solidarity and its application. Appeals to solidarity are raised in times of crisis and drive the politicisation of the EU in terms of questions of re-distribution, burden-sharing, and justice (Closa and Maatsch, 2014; Jones, 2012).

To understand such solidarity-driven contestation and its effects on integration/disintegration, we do not only need to enter a normative debate about what it means to be solidary in the EU. We also need to develop, above all, the conceptual tools that help us to understand the politicised dynamics of EU solidarity contestation and its differentiating effects on integration. To this end, we relate differentiated integration to what Pieter de Wilde *et al.* (2016: 3) term as "differentiated politicisation across times, countries and settings." We argue that a politics of differentiated solidarity in the EU is driven by three inter-related factors. Firstly, restricted resources available for re-distribution in times of economic crisis and austerity bring into question the existing provisions for solidarity, not only across EU countries but also within national constituencies. Secondly, the new dynamics of differentiation have *de facto* fragmented the European space of solidarity, leading to adverse effects and visible negative impact on social cohesion and deepening social and structural inequalities among and within Member States (which, in the introduction to this volume, is assessed as the transition to a segmented EU political system). In the search for solutions to the EU's multiple crises, differentiation is, however, also increasingly promoted as a new paradigm, one which subverts the Community method of integration and shifts the focus from integration as centre-formation to differentiation, whereby Member States constantly (re-)negotiate their relationships to the EU along territorial and sectoral lines. Thirdly, the entrenchment of a "Europe of unequal living conditions" fuels the politicisation of the EU *across* countries. While politicisation could be beneficial for the democratisation of the EU, as it carries the potential to raise awareness and to mobilise Europe's citizens (de Wilde *et al.*, 2016; Statham and Trenz, 2015), its differentiated manifestations across Member States hinder democratic will formation. EU politicisation is, in this sense, not unifying (*i.e.*, improving the conditions for public control, political equality, and justification within the EU political system), but differentiating and creating unequal opportunities for democratisation between the Member States (de Wilde and Lord, 2016: 159).

In the remainder of the chapter, we unpack our argument in three steps. We first outline three modes of establishing solidarity relationships that rely on different justificatory repertoires ranging from charity (pity), egalitarian (contextualised) justice, and humanitarian (global) justice. We secondly re-construct how these different notions are translated into a politics of European solidarity and taken up by different actors (EU actors, national governments, and civil society). We thirdly discuss the salience of these politics of European solidarity in the current EU framework and its implications for differentiation and the process of segmentation of the EU's political order.

II Establishing solidarity relationships among strangers: From charity to global justice

Solidarity, in most general terms, connotes a posture of benevolence towards the vulnerability of others. It establishes a social relationship between a *benefactor*, someone who provides (or considers providing) a particular service of aid, and the *recipient* of such service. We can distinguish between cases where solidarity is "unreflected" and informed mainly by feelings or emotions of pity and cases in which solidarity is reflected with reference to particular norms and interests. It further makes a difference whether a solidarity relationship is established *in-group* (within the family or between friends) or *out-group* (between strangers). By looking at how these roles are differentiated over time, applied to specific cases, and translated into policies and legal-institutional frameworks, we can trace changes in communicative practices through which appeals for solidarity are made salient and justified. Accordingly, we distinguish between:

1. **Solidarity as charity:** In the most elementary situation, solidarity finds expression in the private act of providing assistance to people in need. A solidarity relationship is established at an inter-personal level to resolve an emergency situation. As such, it typically results from the casual encounter of a passer-by who confronts the suffering of an unknown person. Casualness and anonymity are often found in charity, which is meant as an exceptional help that does not need to result in an established social relationship. This form of solidarity as charity or benevolence is often criticised as being non-political. Detached from any political agenda, it avoids raising underlying questions of justice and is often applied in an arbitrary way, that is, depending on the goodwill of the benefactor and not institutionalised or legally guaranteed.[1] Solidarity as benevolence helps us, however, to identify

a primary (or genuine) form that becomes important as a reference point for the differentiation of other derivative political notions of solidarity. It is of significance, first of all, that this genuine relationship of solidarity is built without considerations of "groupness" or the identity of the persons involved. The distinction between in-group and out-group solidarity does not apply. Witnessing other people's suffering requires some form of intervention, irrespective of the question of the origin of the person in need. This situation is described in the parable of the Good Samaritan: the Samaritan casually passing-by assists precisely because he is a stranger to the person in need (and not a member of the in-group, like the other two passers-by in the story who refused to provide assistance). Solidarity is thus distinct from identity and generalised as an absolute ethical obligation to overcome strangeness in a situation of emergency. As an act of grace, solidarity is also detached from considerations of reciprocity and justice. Solidarity remains a private act; it is like an impulse to relieve suffering and that applies only to a direct, often casual, and unique inter-personal relationship that is informed by a morality of altruistic benevolence (Boltanski, 1999). The altruistic behaviour of benevolence is typically nourished by the emotion of pity, which is only possible if some notion of "fraternity" applies, not as a brother of kinship but as a stranger-brother, who shares basic human traits despite the misery of the one and the fortune of the other. This form of solidarity survives in the present world in the universal obligation to provide assistance as a witness to the misfortune of others. Refusing this basic aid to strangers can be costly and result in punishment.

2. **Egalitarian solidarity within a community of equals:** In the second case, solidarity is confined to the identitarian space of a community of equals. This situation is derived from the case of charity (the Good Samaritan) in the sense that a differentiation is introduced between a passer-by in need and a person in need that belongs to one's own community. Solidarity towards strangers is perceived as impulsive and exceptional, while solidarity towards members of the same community is seen as based upon shared values and self-interest. This includes a concern with the roots of the suffering of the other and a commitment to invest in his or her future well-being. Will Kymlicka outlines this difference as follows:

> If someone has a heart attack in front of us on the street, we have a humanitarian obligation to assist, whether they are tourists or citizens, but in the case of citizens, we also have an obligation to identify and address factors (such as economic insecurity) that make some people much more vulnerable to heart attacks than others.
>
> *(Kymlicka 2015: 4)*

For Kymlicka, as for many defenders of the national welfare states, such as Claus Offe or Fritz Scharpf in Germany (Offe, 2000; Scharpf, 2012), social justice depends on bounded solidarity. It ultimately relies on an ethic of membership, that is, on identity and its institutionalised form of citizenship. As a member of the national community, you still have the humanitarian obligation to assist a person in need, but you also have the additional option to engage with others in a debate about justice, for example, to raise the question about underlying inequalities that have caused the person in need to end up in an emergency and about measures that could prevent future misfortune. The contextualisation of the question of social justice within a community of exclusive solidarity further helps us to establish a relationship of reciprocity between the donor and the receiver of welfare. Reciprocity includes a notion of paying back and is thus combined with certain moral obligations on the part of the receiver of benefits. Usually, such pay-backs are displaced in space and time, which makes it possible to add a temporal dimension to solidarity, which is crucial for building a community of shared interests. The role model for this idea of solidarity through reciprocity is the family, in which each part has both rights and duties. Children have the right to receive care but also the duty to pay back when they are older. By introducing the moral duty to return services, solidarity is further linked to particular sanctioning mechanisms, which are justified by assumptions of deservingness. Children must be deserving of receiving benefits from their parents, but also parents must have a proven record as care-givers in order to expect benefits in later life from their children. Solidarity relations within the nation follow this model of reciprocal solidarity within the family by posing expectations of return payments to future generations. This comes at the price of conflating solidarity with collective identity: the nation as a kinship relationship of reciprocity among equals.

3. **Humanitarian solidarity as global justice:** The choice of containing the political struggle for social justice is rejected by cosmopolitans, who follow a different trajectory of "solidarity as revolution," which encompasses humanity and a vision of emancipation from any kind of domination that is perceived as unjust (Chouliaraki, 2013: 11). The same morality of social justice and reciprocity among equals that became contextualised and confined to particular groups in the previous model is thus projected upon the inclusive and non-discriminatory solidarity of humanity (as defended, for instance, by Marxism). Here, the notion of solidarity returns to its original meaning as solidarity with strangers, but provides a generalised account of the moral implications of such an encounter with strangers. Solidarity not only implies assistance (as in the first model), but also conceives of the possibility of building a reciprocal relationship with the stranger. The donor and the receiver are thus bound together by their engagement with questions of justice and the desire to overcome the inequalities that persist between them. Solidarity among strangers is built, as noted by Hauke Brunkhorst (2005), on the universalistic extension of the notion of *fraternity*, which is not a kinship relationship within a closed group but a principle that binds all humans

together as equals. Such a notion of universal brotherhood has been made possible by the monotheist religions which conceive all humans as children of the same and unique God, thus turning them into brothers and sisters, or, in other words, as *equals* before God. *Fraternity* as universal brotherhood is the basis upon which we can feel solidarity towards strangers. The humanitarian movements which, in the contemporary world, rely on this construct again detach solidarity from collective identity. By exposing the arbitrariness of any confined social justice arrangements, they base solidarity not upon distinction but upon the recognition of the commonalities of shared humanity (Glick Schiller, 2016:6).

III Differentiated integration and European solidarity

The European Union has, arguably, embraced elements from all three notions of solidarity and has turned them into specific policies and legal arrangements. It has shown a willingness to go beyond solidarity as charity and has entered – together with its citizens – into a post-national experiment, which, in parallel to the freedoms of the Common Market, introduced the principle of non-discrimination by nationality (Favell, 2014). European citizenship builds on the formal equality of citizens to be treated as equals when deciding to live in another country and when relying, for instance, on the solidarity services of the welfare state. The EU has further entered the field of humanitarian politics, which promotes an agenda of global justice and cosmopolitan solidarity and which advocates strong supranational institutions with the power of human-rights enforcement (Sjursen, 2007). The EU has thus successfully occupied the entire field of solidarity politics: in its capacity as a foreign policy actor and norm-setting actor, the EU promotes humanitarian solidarity; in its capacity as a domestic, law-enforcing actor, the EU imposes egalitarian solidarity among EU citizens, albeit not consistently (Domurath, 2013).

By embracing all three types of solidarity, the EU inevitably has to face the so-called "progressive dilemma" of solidarity (Kymlicka, 2015): the need to enter a trade-off between humanitarian solidarity towards outsiders and egalitarian solidarity towards insiders. According to this idea, there are limits with regard to what a family can share with others without running the risk of losses for its members. The efforts to create equal living conditions for all Europeans might result in rising inequalities at national level. In other words, there would be a trade-off between an inclusive, social justice-based, and re-distributive solidarity in Europe with the equally inclusive and re-distributive agenda of social solidarity among co-nationals. From the perspective of humanitarian solidarity towards outsiders, such a trade-off also works in the other direction: Western countries could show more solidarity towards refugees and admit more migrants and refugees if they were less committed to offering them rights and benefits. The "number *versus* rights dilemma" (Bauböck, 2016: 2) also applies to EU migrants, for example, when Denmark discusses cuts in study grants to be able to accommodate the higher number of foreign EU students. The necessity to enter such trade-offs has nourished the fear among electorates that European-solidarity transfers would come at the cost of eroding existing services at national level or downgrading services and standards for all.

Supporters of European integration have, for a long time, believed that such solidarity trade-offs could be avoided. The promotion of European solidarity would be a win-win constellation for all. Under conditions of economic growth, the common market would automatically create the equal living conditions of "an ever closer Union." Positive integration measures for re-balancing existing inequalities (for example, through structural funds) could be kept to a minimum or would be temporary. EU actors and institutions thus embraced a strong notion of egalitarian solidarity among EU citizens as equals. European solidarity was the secondary outcome of a much bigger project: the building of a European identity, the integration *telos* of a community of belonging that embraced citizenship, democracy, and re-distributive justice (Bottici and Challand, 2013; Schulz-Forberg and Stråth, 2010; Trenz, 2016). The progressive reading of European solidarity was thus ultimately coupled to the project of European identity-building, and thus an inclusive and re-distributive notion of European solidarity was conceived in the framework of inclusive citizenship as nationhood.

Differentiated integration in the EU can be measured by the degree that identity and solidarity become de-coupled. The unitary notion of a European identity has been increasingly replaced by a repertoire of differentiated solidarity discourses: ambivalence ranging from charity to humanitarian assistance, but increasingly blending in equality of rights. Such a repertoire of differentiated solidarity discourses has the advantage that it can be flexibly linked to various policies that are used to address inequalities within the Common Market and in the EU's external relations with third countries. By emphasising solidarity as a flexible principle over identity, such inequalities are increasingly treated as structural, that is, as inbuilt in the relationships between the Europeans (Hadjimichalis, 2011). Solidarity is then no longer the bond of a community of equals, but a driver of differentiation among non-equals (for example, those who have and can share, and those who do not have and claim their share). In a Union based upon differentiated integration, assumptions of equality and shared identity between the donors and the receivers of solidarity might ultimately be abandoned. In appealing to European solidarity, the differentiated parts are no longer driven by the quest for equality among the Member States and populations of the EU, but are instead looking for *ad hoc* solutions in emergency situations.

The notion of European solidarity has thus been gradually de-coupled from struggles for social justice, which remain the prerogative of national welfare states. Solidarity is primarily envisaged as case-specific salvation and no longer as system-related revolution. There is, in other words, one justice-promoting form of solidarity that remains bound to the nation-state and one form of solidarity as humanitarian assistance that applies to external relations or relations between the Member States. European solidarity is no longer progressive, but merely auxiliary. Solidarity as a principle of differentiated integration is softer than the internally inclusive and externally exclusive solidarity within a community of equals. European and transnational solidarity can, for instance, be claimed for, based upon a notion of unequal reciprocity: the differentiated parts that seek a solidarity relationship are not necessarily considered as equals; on the contrary, power and hegemony are crucial to the way in which European and transnational solidarity relationships are established. Shifting from egalitarian solidarity to differentiated solidarity makes it possible to de-couple the humanitarian from the social-justice agenda. While egalitarian solidarity within an identitarian community requires sustainable solutions and legal codifications, solidarity to strangers can be stretched and linked to flexible solutions and policies that remain non-institutionalised, non-legally binding, unique, and exceptional.

It is thus important to emphasise that solidarity relationships in the EU are established based upon the perceived *differences* between the Member States and the populations of Europe, for example, not only differences of income, of life chances, of welfare, and of economic growth, but also cultural differences and differences of power that constitute the differentiated space of the EU and no longer the Europe of equal living conditions. These perceived differences are now to be considered as the primary reason for the need to act in solidarity. The solidarity agenda becomes necessary because others are perceived as different, and not as equals to be embraced by an encompassing identity.

An outlook of what this vacillation between egalitarian solidarity within an identitarian space of equals and differentiated solidarity and humanitarian assistance among un-equals can mean has been presented in a joint statement issued by the four Visegrád countries on the occasion of the Bratislava EU summit meeting of September 2016, which proposed to introduce the new principle of *flexible solidarity* to the EU's refugee relocation scheme. Calls for policy and institutional reforms of the EU refugee allocation scheme have since then been debated controversially, with no reform – to date – being adopted or implemented. As noted by Biermann et al. (2019: 246) the differentiated and often ad-hoc responses to the refugee crisis "resembles a 'Rambo' game situation." The refugee crisis as an external shock had a clear differentiating effect on member states' willingness to cooperate and to address the critical lack of solidarity and absence of centralised institutions to deal with these issues. Should other Member States accept the new principle of flexible solidarity, this would mark a clear turn from the idea of solidarity as mandatory and imposed by supranational authority. Flexible solidarity should enable Member States to decide on specific forms of contributions which take their experience and potential into account. It further stressed that any refugee distribution mechanism should be voluntary. This would imply that "solidarity" and "responsibility sharing" need to be negotiated case by case, and that Member States would ultimately have veto power to decide about degrees of involvement in humanitarian assistance. Solidarity is thus reduced to an act of charity that entirely depends on the goodwill of the donor. The principle of sharing with others is no longer absolute; instead, decisions need to be taken case by case and depend on current power and interest constellations (such as the availability of side payments).

With this notion of flexible solidarity, the EU has recognised the necessity of entering into solidarity trade-offs. It has also renounced the possibility of providing a legal and institutional framework to settle such inevitable solidarity conflicts, but has, instead, agreed on the solution of negotiating such trade-offs on an *ad hoc* and case-specific basis. It is thus recognised that the promotion of European solidarity would not be a win-win constellation for all, but rather that the costs of European-solidarity transfers need to be calculated upon a case-by-case basis and closely scrutinised.

From the progressive perspective of egalitarian justice, the new differentiated European solidarity agenda can be easily denounced as a de-politicised form of solidarity, as it blends questions of social justice and of re-distribution without providing an institutional setting to settle such questions, either internally or externally. The EU measures of humanitarian assistance can be further accused of remaining selective and incomplete and of perpetuating suffering instead of providing sustainable solutions (see, for example, Langford, 2013; McDonough and Tsourdi, 2012; and Joly, 2016, on the issues of refugees and asylum-seekers during the latest crisis and over time). On the other hand, the requirement of case-by-case negotiation of transfer payments is likely to enhance conflicts between the governments of the Member States and to lead to a politicisation of solidarity-related issues both in domestic politics and across Member States. Appeals to European solidarity become more easily politicised as Member States seek to balance the option of confining solidarity as exclusive to nationals with that of expanding it to other Europeans or non-Europeans in need. European solidarity politics are, in this sense, different from a private version of charity, as solidarity action is heavily contested in terms of deservingness and questions of re-distributive justice. In line with the argument of differentiated politicisation, such a differentiated politics of solidarity would empower some actors over others, enhance international polarisation, and ultimately lead to the re-invigoration of exclusive notions of national solidarity that are further fragmenting the EU political space and damaging the democratic legitimacy of the EU. In the following, we are going to outline the contours of such a politics of differentiated solidarity by looking at different manifestations of charity, national closure, and re-distributive conflicts within the EU. We then discuss these examples of differentiation as evidence of the segmentation of the EU political order.

IV Solidarity under threat: The mutations of differentiated solidarity in Europe

To ground our approach to differentiated solidarity in Europe in empirical examples, we focus on the cases of the migration/refugee crisis and the Euro crisis, both of which have been several years in the making. Both of these crises have fostered social discontent, have fuelled (and been fuelled by) deep socio-economic changes, and have subsequently challenged traditional sources of identity, unleashing unprecedented cross-country solidarity mobilisation but also equally unprecedented (in the history of the EU) waves of xenophobia and nationalism (Brunkhorst, 2011; Closa and Maatsch, 2014; Delanty, 2008; Trenz, 2016). We particularly focus on the public expressions and justifications of solidarity, that is, the ways solidarity is both performed and contested in public debates among the Europeans. Such an approach is different from measuring public attitudes on solidarity in the sense that it takes into consideration the performative force of solidarity and the way in which dispositions of solidarity are shaped by public discourse (Boltanski, 1999). Appeals to European solidarity follow specific narrative threads, and actors who move within the contentious European space draw on such narration to engage with each other meaningfully. Crucial to such an approach is the role of the media in staging the vulnerability of others as an object of our empathy as well as of critical reflection and deliberation (Chouliaraki, 2013:22). Although EU media – the press especially, as it is mostly newspapers that have received the attention of researchers – have frequently opted to frame the coverage of the Euro crisis or the refugee crisis in terms of solidarity, they have often done so in a negative context, that is, to show why solidarity is neither necessary nor merited (Michailidou, 2017; Mylonas, 2012; Tzogopoulos, 2013). As Kontochristou and Mascha (2014: 57) put it, referring to the coverage of the Euro crisis by the media in Germany and France, "blackmail tends to but should not replace solidarity as a mentality." Thus, the theatricality of solidarity communication in the media creates a distinct virtual space of morality that links the spectators of suffering to vulnerable others and thus divides the roles of the potential donors and receivers of solidarity. The virtual media sphere creates the selective visibility for the subjects of solidarity (both the donors and the distant others), where they can be seen and heard, and also where we can consider the question of why we should act collectively in solidarity with others, strangers. The performance of solidarity through mediatised debates is currently changing the European space for humanitarian politics in important ways. In the current constellation of crisis-ridden Europe, solidarity contestations not only involve the governments of the Member States but also increasingly embrace confrontations between the citizens. This new politics of contested and mediatised solidarity can be traced along the dimensions explored in the following three subsections.

IV.1 The exceptionality of charity: The Europe of fragmented spheres of privatised solidarity action

The first dimension of European solidarity contestation regards the selective view on human suffering that was applied in the course of the refugee crisis of 2015 and gave rise to *ad hoc* mobilisations of solidarity as privatised forms of charity. In facing humanitarian disasters, we observe how charity is currently redefined by the members of Western publics who pay highly selective attention to the needs of strangers. Solidarity relationships are increasingly built through our selective media gaze that connects us to the suffering of others. Emotions of pity and compassion are often shared through social media and mobilise individuals who do not necessarily wish to occupy a political agenda but nevertheless support humanitarian action in exceptional circumstances. According to Chouliaraki (2013), such a depoliticised solidarity (what she calls *post-humanitarian* solidarity) becomes the dominant form on social media, which facilitates self-expressive forms of communication and blocks out the agenda of social justice. Solidarity is communicable through social media formats in a non-political from that builds on the shared compassion of the community of users with the victims, who are made visible often through icons (such as the drowned Syrian boy found on a beach in Turkey), but often disregards controversial issues of responsibility and justice. This form of solidarity is often criticised as a private and individual morality of "feel-good activism" that is part of consumerist behaviour. Such practices of post-humanitarian solidarity can be detected, for instance, in the social media morality displayed in collective user responses to the iconic images of refugee children (Mortensen and Trenz, 2016).

This is not to say that such practices of selective and individualized solidarity remain without effect and do not bear political consequences. It can, for instance, be claimed that Angela Merkel's move to open Germany's borders to refugees entering from other Schengen countries was backed by strong emotional campaigns, such as #RefugeesWelcome, that appealed for compassion towards war victims and mobilised many Germans, not only online but also in the streets, to provide first aid to refugees. At the same time, the exceptional character of this unique form of solidarity towards refugees was emphasised (Holmes and Castañeda, 2016). It was made possible precisely because questions of justice (*e.g.*, the fair distribution of refugees over the Schengen area) and political consequences of the decision (*e.g.*, long-term political support, integration hurdles, the financial burden, and/or the rise of xenophobia) were momentarily disregarded. This returns to the original notion of solidarity as an absolute principle of assistance. Like the Good Samaritan, many Europeans who witnessed the suffering of Syrian civil war refugees felt an impulse to assist. Such forms of "first aid" can be powerful, but they also remain ephemeral and often have no lasting impact on how solidarity issues are framed in the long run.

There is, indeed, ample evidence already available that this depoliticised solidarity of "feel-good activism" was only short lived (for example, Greussing and Boomgaarden, 2017; Berry *et al.*, 2015; Vollmer and Karakayali, 2018). In the context of a new politics of solidarity in Europe, it is important to understand how charity as exceptional solidarity is, in itself, highly politicised and open to constant contestation. In Sweden and Germany, for example, the two countries where empathy and solidarity still dominated the discursive landscape on the arrival of the refugees in September 2015, we could observe how the exceptionality of charity towards strangers led to a sharpening of identitarian struggles about the location of one's kin and ultimately led to the strengthening of right-wing populist parties (Dahlgren, 2016; Vollmer and Karakayali, 2018).

At the European level, we find that unilateral decisions of charity taken in one country remain highly contested in other countries and bear consequences for the fragile solidarity construct of the whole continent and its relationship to the world. This shows the limits of differentiation through unilateral actions of solidarity (segmented solidarity) in the field of humanitarian policies, which ultimately require collective solutions and not emotional national reactions. Uncoordinated charity politics are therefore coupled to power politics and serve to ferment a non-reciprocal relationship between the donating and receiving countries and a sharper delimitation of spaces of solidarity (Western Europe) *versus* spaces of vulnerability (the Global South, but also increasingly Southern Europe). In the absence of institutionalised mechanisms of reciprocity, acts of solidarity among EU Member States become the subject of a bargaining process and enhance the inability (or, more precisely, the difficulty) of EU leaders to identify their interest in helping other EU members (Fernandes and Rubio, 2012:20; Langford, 2013; Wodak and Boukala, 2014). What the refugee crisis has shown is that a Europe of fragmented spheres of privatised solidarity action is not sustainable and can only account for short-term, exceptional, and privatised altruistic support actions that mobilise parts of the population while polarising the others.

IV.2 The exclusivity of egalitarian solidarity: Europe as an exclusive space of solidarity

The second dimension of European solidarity contestations regards the re-distributive conflicts that have been triggered by the so-called Euro crisis since 2008. As an effect of the Euro crisis and in parallel to the appeals to transnational solidarity, the egalitarian solidarity of the nation-state becomes more exclusive. This new exclusivity, which pits the generosity of the so-called creditor countries against the deservingness of the debtors, has been the subject of fierce contestation in public debates throughout the Euro crisis and post-crisis period (Michailidou and Trenz, 2015). As shown by Stefan Auer (2014), in such a climate of heightened media and public attention, appeals to the "spirit of European solidarity" can become counter-effective. In his comparative analysis of public debates in the previously pro-European states of Germany, Slovakia, and Ireland, Auer (2014) shows how the bail-out funds granted to counter the Euro crisis were (falsely, or, at least, inaccurately) justified by both the EU and national governments as measures of solidarity towards fellow EU member States. However, these measures have required such efforts or sacrifices from EU Member States that

> their European projects [have been] put on a collision course with their political traditions, expectations and material interests. Slovaks can no longer be confident in strengthening their post-communist democracy

through its engagement with Europe. The pressure to demonstrate more 'transnational solidarity' with nations far richer than themselves contributed to Slovakia being ruled by a populist, who simply proved more compliant with the EU demands rather than his pro-western and significantly more liberally minded predecessors. In Germany, people are concerned that they can no longer trust their currency, the euro, let alone see it as the bedrock of economic and political stability. Perhaps more than citizens in any other nation, Germans are also profoundly worried about having both their own as well as the EU Rechtsstaat eroded through euro rescue measures, which are yet to prove their effectiveness. In Ireland, people who had experienced European integration as hugely beneficial both economically and politically have been forced to question their commitments. Their primary aim after the collapse of the Celtic Tiger is not just to restore the solvency and the economic viability of their nation, but reclaim as much self-government as possible.

(Auer, 2014: 331)

The exclusivity of national welfare regimes is often defended by new populist parties which explicitly oppose the EU and advocate the re-nationalisation of social and economic policies. This is done in such a way that foreigners (including EU citizens) are increasingly excluded from social welfare services. National welfare chauvinists also categorically disregard questions of fairness of re-distribution between nations, often by negating history and obscuring the sources of national wealth. Exclusive solidarity among nationals is often also defended based upon notions of superiority or based upon acclaimed entitlements that have been earned by "us and not by others." This includes increasing references to the notion of deservingness in the distribution of wealth, which stabilises existing regimes of inequality. Such notions of deservingness are especially evoked in dealing with the European South (see Hepp *et al.*, 2015, for citizens' perspectives on solidarity; and Vaara, 2014, on discursive legitimation strategies more broadly). Being undeserving is justified by references to alleged failures of the past or by reference to current governments which are seen as deviating from shared European values and therefore subject to official or unofficial sanctioning. In the north of Europe, such notions of deservingness often come close to the promotion of a new racialised superiority with reference to forms of cultural racism, which sees the Protestant, solidary and "naturally democratic" communities of the Northern welfare states as superior to the more individualised, self-interested, and often corrupt societies in the south of Europe (*e.g.*, Mylonas 2012). Welfare chauvinism is often paired with *nativism*, which defines belonging along "native" and "non-native" lines with the primary goal of excluding immigrants from the national community of solidarity (Guia, 2016). At the same time, one could argue that the manifestations of welfare chauvinism indicate a crisis of national solidarity, as it is often supported by increasingly dispossessed citizens who are themselves exposed to high levels of insecurity, which makes them gather behind the national flag in the name of exclusive solidarity and xenophobia (Brunkhorst, 2011). The crisis of European egalitarian solidarity is therefore also related to the demise of re-distributive welfare programmes at the national level. It shows that differentiated solidarity might be a direct result of enforced EU market integration and the failure of the market's promise to create equal living conditions for all in Europe.

IV.3 The new power politics of European solidarity: Towards reciprocity among non-equals?

The third dimension of European solidarity contestation follows from the two crises and their politicising effects, which are displayed as a new politics of power among EU Member States, who, although non-equals, are still bound to cooperate. In such a politicised environment, both humanitarian solidarity as unconditional assistance and reciprocal solidarity as formalised distribution of wealth become contested. Humanitarian solidarity, one could argue, works best in a de-politicised environment, when solidarity trade-offs and the costs of re-distribution are not thematised by the partners. This is often the case in EU external action and humanitarian assistance in third countries, where the EU has a (limited) mandate to build an image as a solidarity actor whereby the mandate and (restricted) scope of its solidarity action is seen as consensual by all the partners involved. The situation is quite different in the politics of European solidarity, which is meant to establish egalitarian relationships and to settle re-distributive conflicts among the Member States of the EU. The attempts to settle such conflicts about the reciprocity of solidarity relationships among Europeans result in differentiated politicisation with a dominant focus on conflicting national demands and an empowerment of national political institutions (de Wilde and Lord, 2016; de Wilde *et al.*, 2016). Differentiated politicisation of the conditions for reciprocal solidarity in the EU results *de facto* in differentiated solidarity. In times of crisis, when increasingly exclusive solidarity communities enter a process of negotiating solidarity relationships between themselves, solidarity politics become intrinsically related to power politics. To make solidarity negotiable among unequal partners, the solidarity–identity linkage that is constitutive to the egalitarian solidarity within national-welfare states needs to be broken. Only under the assumption that there is no legal and moral obligation of equality that "binds me to my partner" can the costs and benefits of solidarity be re-negotiated.

Solidarity towards the European partner is then different from the altruistic solidarity of charity, but it is also different from the reciprocal solidarity in egalitarian welfare states. European solidarity is neither seen as exceptional assistance nor as a legal duty. Instead, it is discussed as a form of payment that is linked to particular expectations. In the politics of European solidarity, these expectations need to be made explicit. Reciprocity is established in the sense that each part in the European solidarity relationship has rights and duties, yet these rights and duties are not derived from formal legal and constitutional entitlements but from inter-governmental arrangements. These inter-governmental settlements of solidarity relationships differ and are open to constant re-negotiation, enhancing the role of individual government leaders, as, for example, in the case of the Greek so-called bail-out agreements (McDonnell, 2014: 87–88). The net-contributing countries give, but can also legitimately expect, a return. As there is, however, a power dis-equilibrium between the contributing and the receiving countries, the contributor can then also set the conditions of return and set up the rules of compliance. Solidarity politics thus becomes intrinsically related to questions of power and hegemony in a relationship among non-equals (Nicoli 2015). This power dis-equilibrium is both the root of and the outcome of the legal ambiguity that surrounds solidarity in the EU Treaties (McDonnell, 2014: 87–88). It is precisely this ambiguity that has allowed the concept of flexibility to be attached to that of solidarity, which points directly to differentiated solidarity solutions. In the case of the Euro crisis and the Greek bail-outs, the ambiguous nature of differentiated solidarity creates a situation whereby the same grounds that allow for solidarity in the first place could also enable Member States to withhold solidarity (segmentation of solidarity): "If solidarity implies making necessary arrangements to allow even those States which are in severe difficulties to remain within the Eurogroup, the polemics implied that its opposite pole—flexibility, in its structural sense, whereby different groupings of Member States can make arrangements to cooperate, according to their wishes, and also their capabilities—could even go so far as to allow a forced 'exit'" (McDonnell, 2014: 87–88).

Solidarity provisions in relation to the asylum and refugee services that Member States ought to offer are similarly vague, or at least open to interpretation and conditionality. McDonough and Tsourdi, already in 2012 – well before the dramatic surge in the numbers of mostly Syrian refugees arriving in Greece in 2015 – pointed to some of these ambiguities (even though the authors themselves do not classify these as ambiguous):

> In a December 2011 communication, the Commission linked solidarity and trust. It acknowledged an EU responsibility to assist Member States under pressure to ensure 'adequate reception of asylum seekers and refugees and access to protection', and that 'the Union has a duty not only to its Member State[s], but also to asylum applicants'. Council conclusions of March 2012 affirmed that 'the framework for genuine and practical solidarity is a flexible and open "tool box" compiled of both existing and possible new measures'.
>
> *(McDonough and Tsourdi, 2012: 76)*

The key phrases in this excerpt are "linked solidarity and trust" – which makes solidarity, in the case of the refugee crisis, conditional upon other Member States identifying the member in need as trustworthy enough *without* providing *any* quantifiable/measurable criteria as to what would render a Member State trustworthy; and "the framework for genuine and practical solidarity is a flexible and open 'tool box'". Here again the words "genuine" and "flexibility" remain open to interpretation, this time also from the point of view of the recipient of solidarity.

European politics thus ends up implementing a scheme of differentiated solidarity. What is meant as a reciprocal relationship among equals becomes differentiated. The deservingness of the receivers of solidarity is not pre-defined by belonging to the inclusive community of co-nationals but instead needs to be constantly negotiated. Thus, solidarity becomes again optional, not a moral duty, but a political choice and, as such, needs to be claimed, defended, and justified. The positions are themselves negotiable; some might think that Germany has an economic interest in showing solidarity to others as a way to stabilise markets, while others might claim that Germany has a moral obligation to European solidarity, because it has profited most in the past. Solidarity relationships which are not based upon legal guarantees of reciprocity among equals are, in this sense, not only more political, they also turn to a more archaic situation of solidarity that applies in a stratified social context (*e.g.*, Bieler and Erne, 2015). Many of the so-called solidarity policies and measures are negotiated outside of EU jurisdiction, and their implementation is controlled by new triumvirate power arrangements such as the *Troika*. So-called solidarity packages are not structural policies, but emergency measures which are negotiated *ad hoc*, made conditional, and backed by disciplining measures or punishment. The differentiated regime of EU solidarity can, in this sense, be said to solidify not only a segmented political order, but also a segmented social space of unequal living conditions. Segmented solidarity raises with new vigour an old problem of structural injustice, which the European Communities were supposedly once meant to overcome (Eriksen, 2017).

V Conclusion

European solidarity has become a contested notion. EU solidarity policies reach beyond the consensual scope of humanitarian assistance in international relations, but, at the same time, are not backed by egalitarian welfare. EU solidarity contestations are, however, not simply displayed as a power game between the governments of the Member States, but are increasingly also amplified through public and media debates, which confront the people of Europe in a situation of structural inequality. In this sense, differentiated solidarity is, on the one hand, to be seen as the outcome of solidarity trade-offs between competing welfare regimes. On the other hand, it also results from the mutations of solidarity discourse and solidarity policies as implemented by the EU, with a notable shift from the unitary approach of an inclusive and egalitarian solidarity principle to more flexible approaches of humanitarian aid programmes (the old notion of inter-national solidarity) and *ad hoc* negotiations of schemes for re-distribution among the European partners ("solidarity among non-equals").

In the Europe of unequal living conditions, solidarity relationships are no longer defined in relation to questions of belonging (identity) but are nurtured by anxieties over security, jobs, and welfare (Delanty, 2008). As the EU has no response to these anxieties, and the demands and expectations of citizens are still mainly addressed to national governments, the European solidarity contestations are translated into differentiated patterns of politicisation.

One might ask why the re-scaling of EU solidarity relationships from egalitarian partnerships to differentiation is necessarily problematical. After all, solidarity, in any form, should be welcomed, particularly in times of crisis and in cases where the national/egalitarian framework of welfare is absent. This is in line with Rainer Bauböck (2016:5), who argues that a re-scaled solidarity in a multi-national and multi-level unit might also be a normatively attractive solution; differentiated solidarity can more easily fit the functional needs of the receivers of solidarity benefits, if cities, nations, and the EU divide the different tasks and do what each unit can do best. This chapter has, however, contended that differentiated solidarity in the EU does not follow the needs of different territorially confined solidarity communities but points, instead, to a problem of structural injustice (Eriksen, 2017). As such, it follows the "segmental logics" identified in the Introduction to this volume, which applies, however, not simply to the political architecture of the EU but also to the emerging cleavages within the EU's social space. European solidarity that is detached from a notion of egalitarian justice operates through highly moralising notions of deservingness. It thus becomes fragile and conditional, solidifying the unequal relations between the donors and the receivers, and takes it for granted that some will inevitably profit more from European integration than others. There is no way to preclude, therefore, that differentiated solidarity is not experienced as humiliation by those who, as the recipients of solidarity side-payments, are kept not only in structurally disadvantaged but also in morally inferior positions (Offe, 2015; (Eriksen, 2017). Both the crises that we have discussed in the second part of this chapter illustrate how, precisely, the mutations of solidarity are intrinsically linked to the rise of a segmented political order. Conditional forms of solidarity have followed the segmentation logic of the EU political order in its attempts to face the challenges of financial stability and burden-sharing. Solidarity discourse, in the context of the refugee crisis, has moved justifications from the initial humanitarian solidarity to forms of solidarity that are conditioned and constrained by securitisation, broadly speaking (for example, border controls, terrorist threats, the limiting of the number of asylum seekers and immigrants). In a similar manner, the differentiated and conditional forms of solidarity that we find in the Eurozone are entirely compatible with the marketisation logic that propels segmentation. The politicisation of the respective EU policy responses has, in turn, triggered further segmentation, not only along territorial lines, but, increasingly, also along social and identitarian lines, by breaking the linkage between national welfare states and the citizens. The EU's segmented character is thus helping to shape what we observe as increasingly differentiated forms of solidarity within and across Member States. In a politicised EU, differentiated solidarity remains highly conflictual and is not able to address properly the challenges to social justice which contemporary Europe is facing.

Note

1 See Boltanski (1999:XX) for the tradition of the (mainly Marxist) critique of what he calls a "politics of pity."

References

Auer, Stefan (2014), "The Limits of Transnational Solidarity and the Eurozone Crisis in Germany, Ireland and Slovakia", *Perspectives on European Politics and Society*, 15 (3): 322–334.

Bauböck, Rainer (2016), "Why Liberal Nationalism Does Not Resolve the Progressive's Trilemma: Comment on Will Kymlicka's Article: 'Solidarity in Diverse Societies'", *Comparative Migration Studies*, 4 (10): 1–6.

Berry, Mike, Inaki Garcia-Blanco, and Kerry Moore (2015), "Press Coverage of the Refugee and Migrant Crisis in the EU: A Content Analysis of Five European Countries – Report prepared for the United Nations High Commission for Refugees", *Cardiff School of Journalism, Media and Cultural Studies*, available at: http://orca.cf.ac.uk/87078/1/UNHCR-%20FINAL%20REPORT.pdf.

Bieler, Andreas, and Roland Erne (2015), "Transnational Solidarity? The European Working Class in the Eurozone Crisis", *Socialist Register*, 51: 157–177, available at: http://socialistregister.com/index.php/srv/article/view/22099/17941#.WCmomtUrK5s,last accessed 3 September 2016.

Biermann, F., N. Guérin, S. Jagdhuber, B. Rittberger, and M. Weiss (2019), "Political (non-)reform in the Euro Crisis and the Refugee Crisis: A Liberal Intergovernmentalist Explanation", *Journal of European Public Policy*, 26 (2): 246–266.

Boltanski, Luc (1999), *Distant Suffering: Morality, Media and Politics*, Cambridge: Cambridge University Press.

Bottici, Chiara, and Benôit Challand (2013), *Imagining Europe: Myth, Memory, and Identity*, Cambridge: Cambridge University Press.

Brunkhorst, Hauke (2005), Solidarity: From Civic Friendship to a Global Legal Community, Cambridge MA: The MIT Press.

Brunkhorst, Hauke (2011), "Solidarity in Crisis. Is This the End of a United Europe?", *Leviathan*, 39 (4): 459–477.

Chouliaraki, Lilie (2013), *The Ironic Spectator: Solidarity in the Age of Post-Humanitarianism*, Cambridge: Polity Press.

Closa, Carlos, and Aleksandra Maatsch (2014), "In a Spirit of Solidarity? Justifying the European Financial Stability Facility (EFSF) in National Parliamentary Debates", *Journal of Common Market Studies*, 52 (4): 826–842.

Dahlgren, Peter (2016), "Moral Spectatorship and Its Discourses: The 'Mediapolis' in the Swedish Refugee Crisis", *Javnost – The Public*, 23 (4), 343–362, special issue on "Global Moral Spectatorship in the Age of Social Media", edited by Mette Mortensen and Hans-Jörg Trenz.

Delanty, Gerard (2008), "Fear of Others: Social Exclusion and the European Crisis of Solidarity", *Social Policy & Administration*, 42 (6): 676–690.

de Wilde, Pieter, and Christopher Lord (2016), "Assessing Actually Existing Trajectories of EU Politicisation", *West European Politics*, 39 (1): 145–163.

de Wilde, Pieter, Anna Leupold, and Henning Schmidtke (2016), "Introduction: The Differentiated Politicisation of European Governance", *West European Politics*, 39 (1): 3–22.

Domurath, Irina (2013), "The Three Dimensions of Solidarity in the EU Legal Order: Limits of the Judicial and Legal Approach", *Journal of European Integration*, 35 (4): 459–475.

Eriksen, Erik Oddvar (2017), "Structural Injustice and Solidarity. The Case of the Eurozone Crisis", ARENA Working Paper 4/2017 University of Oslo, ARENA, Centre for European Studies.

Favell, Adrian (2014), "The Fourth Freedom: Theories of Migration and Mobilities in 'Neo-liberal' Europe", *European Journal of Social Theory*, 17 (3): 275–289.

Fernandes, Sofia, and Eulalia Rubio (2012), *Solidarity within the Eurozone: How Much, What For, For How Long?*, Report, number 51, Notre Europe, available at: www.notre-europe.eu/uploads/tx_publication/SolidarityEMU_S.Fernandes-E.Rubio_NE_Feb2012.pdf, last accessed 9 November 2013.

Glick Schiller, Nina (2016), "The Question of Solidarity and Society: Comment on Will Kymlicka's Article: 'Solidarity in Diverse Societies'", *Comparative Migration Studies*, 4 (6): 1–9.

Greussing, Esther, and Hajo G. Boomgaarden (2017), "Shifting the Refugee Narrative? An Automated Frame Analysis of Europe's 2015 Refugee Crisis", *Journal of Ethnic and Migration Studies*, 43 (11): 1749–1774.

Guia, Aitana (2016), "The Concept of Nativism and Anti-Immigrant Sentiments in Europe", EUI Working Paper MWP 2016/20, available at: www.mwpweb.eu/1/218/resources/news_970_1.pdf.

Hadjimichalis, Costis (2011), "Uneven Geographical Development and Socio-spatial Justice and Solidarity: European Regions after the 2009 Financial Crisis", *European Urban and Regional Studies*, 18 (3): 254–274.

Hepp, Andreas, Swantje Lingeberg, Monika Elsler, Johanna Möller, Anne Mollen, and Anke Offerhaus (2015), "'I just Hope the Whole Thing Won't Collapse': 'Understanding' and 'Overcoming' the EU Financial Crisis from the Citizens' Perspective", in: Graham Murdock and Jostein Gripsrud (eds), *Money Talks: Media, Markets, Crisis*, Bristol-Chicago IL: Intellect, The University of Chicago Press, pp. 189–208.

Holmes, Seth M., and Heide Castañeda (2016), "Representing the 'European Refugee Crisis' in Germany and Beyond: Deservingness and Difference, Life and Death", *American Ethnologist*, 43 (1): 12–24.

Joly, Danièle (2016), *Haven or Hell?: Asylum Policies and Refugees in Europe*, New York and Basingstoke: Palgrave MacMillan, in association with Centre for Research in Ethnic Relations, University of Warwick.

Jones, Erik (2012), "The JCMS Annual Review Lecture: European Crisis, European Solidarity", *Journal of Common Market Studies*, 50 (s2): 53–67, special issue.

Kontochristou, Maria, and Evi Mascha (2014), "The Euro Crisis and the Question of Solidarity in the European Union: Disclosures and Manifestations in the European Press", *Review of European Studies*, 6 (2): 50–62.

Kymlicka, Will (2015), "Solidarity in Diverse Societies: Beyond Neoliberal Multiculturalism and Welfare Chauvinism", *Comparative Migration Studies*, 3 (1): 17–39.

Langford, Lillian M. (2013), "The Other Euro Crisis: Rights Violations under the Common European Asylum System and the Unraveling of EU Solidarity", *Harvard Human Rights Journal*, 26 (1): 217–264.

McDonnell, Alison (2014), "Solidarity, Flexibility, and the Euro-Crisis: Where Do Principles Fit in?", in: Lucia Serena Rossi and Federico Casolari (eds), *The EU after Lisbon: Amending or Coping with the Existing Treaties?*, Cham: Springer, pp. 57–91.

McDonough, Paul, and Evangelia (Lilian) Tsourdi (2012), "The 'Other' Greek Crisis: Asylum and EU Solidarity", *Refugee Survey Quarterly*, 31 (4): 67–100, available at: http://rsq.oxfordjournals.org/content/31/4/67.full.pdf, last accessed 10 September 2016.

Michailidou, Asimina (2017), "'The Germans are Back': Euroscepticism and Anti-Germanism in Crisis-Stricken Greece", *National Identities*, 19 (1): 91–108.

Michailidou, Asimina, and Hans-Jörg Trenz (2015), "The European Crisis and the Media: Media Autonomy, Public Perceptions and New Forms of Political Engagement", in: Hans-Jörg Trenz, Carlo Ruzza and Virginie Guiraudon (eds), *Europe's Prolonged Crisis: The Making or the Unmaking of Political Union*, Basingstoke: Palgave Macmillan, pp. 232–250.

Mortensen, Mette, and Hans-Jörg Trenz (2016), "Media Morality and Visual Icons in the Age of Social Media: Alan Kurdi and the Emergence of an Impromptu Public of Moral Spectatorship", *Javnost – The Public*, 23 (4): 343–362, special issue on "Global Moral Spectatorship in the Age of Social Media", edited by Mette Mortensen and Hans-Jörg Trenz.

Mylonas, Yiannis (2012), "Media and the Economic Crisis of the EU: The 'Culturalization' of a Systemic Crisis and Bild-Zeitung's Framing of Greece", *tripleC: Communication, Capitalism & Critique*, 10 (2): 646–671, available at: www.triplec.at/index.php/tripleC/article/view/380, last accessed 24 October 2016.

Nicoli, Francesco (2015), "Eurocrisis and the Myths of European Redistribution: Illegitimate, Unsustainable, Inefficient?", *Perspectives on Federalism*, 7 (3): 19–48.

Offe, Claus (2000), "The Democratic Welfare State in an Integrating Europe", in: Michael Th. Greven and Louis W. Pauly (eds), *Democracy Beyond the State?: The European Dilemma and the Emerging Global Order*, Lanham MD: Rowman & Littlefield, pp. 63–90.

Offe, Claus (2015), *Europe Entrapped*, Oxford: Wiley.

Sangiovanni, Andrea (2013), "Solidarity in the European Union", *Oxford Journal of Legal Studies*, 33 (2): 213–241.

Scharpf, Fritz W. (2012), "The Double Asymmetry of European Integration", MPIfG Working Paper 09/12, Max-Planck Institute for the Study of Societies.

Schulz-Forberg, Hagen, and Bo Stråth (2010), *The Political History of European Integration: The Hypocrisy of Democracy-through-Market*, London and New York: Routledge.

Sjursen, Helene (2007), *Civilian or Military Power? European Foreign Policy in Perspective*, London: Routledge.

Statham, Paul, and Hans-Jörg Trenz (2015), "Understanding the Mechanisms of EU Politicization: Lessons from the Eurozone Crisis", *Comparative European Politics*, 13 (3): 287–306.

Trenz, Hans-Jörg (2016), *Narrating European Society: Toward a Sociology of European Integration*, Lanham MD: Rowman and Littlefield-Lexington Books.

Tzogopoulos, George (2013), *The Greek Crisis in the Media: Stereotyping in the International Press*, Farnham: Ashgate Publishing.

Vaara, Eero (2014), "Struggles Over Legitimacy in the Eurozone Crisis: Discursive Legitimation Strategies and Their Ideological Underpinnings", *Discourse & Society*, 25 (4): 500–518, Special Issue on "From Grexit to Grecovery: Euro/Crisis Discourses".

Vollmer, Bastian, and Serhat Karakayali (2018), "The Volatility of the Discourse on Refugees in Germany", *Journal of Immigrant & Refugee Studies*, 16 (1–2): 118–139.

Wodak, Ruth, and Salomi Boukala (2014), "Talking about Solidarity and Security in the Age of Crisis: The Revival of Nationalism and Protectionism in the European Union – A Discourse-Historical Approach", in: Caterina Carta and Jean-Frédéric Morin (eds), *EU Foreign Policy through the Lens of Discourse Analysis: Making Sense of Diversity*, London and New York: Routledge, pp. 171–190.

8

INTERSTITIAL ORGANISATIONS AND SEGMENTED INTEGRATION IN EU GOVERNANCE

Jozef Bátora

I Introduction

The EU's response to a series of existential crises in recent years has been marked by high degrees of adaptability and resilience. This chapter addresses a particular aspect in these adaptation processes – the formation of what is termed here as *interstitial organisations* in the EU's governance system. These organisations re-combine resources, rules, organisational norms and structures across various policy fields and institutional spheres to set up new organisational forms in order to address newly emerging and cross-cutting policy issues (Bátora, 2013, 2017, Korff et al., 2015). With the emergence of interstitial organisations such as the European External Action Service (EEAS), the European Stability Mechanism (ESM) and the European Border and Coast Guard (EBCG), the EU establishes instruments and mechanisms to support co-ordinated action in complex policy areas. At the same time, though, their unorthodox forms and ambiguous roles deepen EU complexity and generate new co-operation and co-ordination problems. Arguably, this development is different from the process of "agencifica-tion" in the EU (see, e.g., Everson, 1995; Egeberg and Trondal, 2011; Pollak and Puntscher-Riekmann, 2008; Rittberger and Wonka, 2011; Schout and Pereyra, 2011; Egeberg et al., 2015; Egeberg and Trondal, 2016) as these new organisa-tions do not easily fit into the category of agencies. The notion of "*de novo* insti-tutions," as suggested by Bickerton et al. (2015), may be a useful first step in a quest to understand this burgeoning of new EU governance organisations, but, as is argued here, such a concept is far from satisfactory in actually explaining the development which we see emerging. Indeed, the new bodies are hybrid amal-gams "in between EU institutions and member states," and we still lack a proper understanding of their nature and role (Everson et al., 2014).

To fill this gap, this chapter draws on organisation theory literature on the emergence of new organisational forms (Padgett and Powell, 2012). The main argument proposed here has two steps: I argue, first, that the new organisations set up in response to the crises in the EU could be usefully conceptualised as *interstitial organisations* (INTOs). Second, the formation of INTOs, such as the EEAS, the ESM and the EBCG, supports the functioning of policy segments in EU governance, including the EU's foreign and security policy, Eurozone governance and Schengen-zone governance in the area of external border protection. Third, they also operate as bridges and "integrative platforms" across policy fields, connecting multiple functional realms and combining functions and rules from them. They are established and used to gain action capacity and improve co-ordination in a situation of political, legal and institutional constraints in the EU's system of governance. Hence, the presence of INTOs in EU governance is possibly an indicator of an emerging pattern in the development of the EU's political order – segmented integration – developing alongside and in parallel to intergovernmental and supranational modes of integration.

The paper proceeds as follows. First, it reviews the literature on agencification and the new intergovernmentalism in the EU. Second, it reviews the organisation theory literature on the emergence of new organisational forms and introduces the concept of INTOs. Building on this, it proposes a framework for understanding the crises-driven development of the EU's system of governance and the formation of interstitial organisations. Third, it illustrates the concept by studying the formation of three new organisations: the EEAS, the ESM and the EBCG. Finally, it discusses the systemic implications of these developments for the formation of EU governance as a segmented order.

II Recent perspectives on the re-organisation of EU governance: Agencification and *"de novo* institutions"

In recent decades, EU governance has been characterised by a growing trend of agencification, which encompasses various degrees of delegation of regulatory capacity by Member States to EU-level agencies (Everson, 1995; Dehousse, 1997, 2008; Egeberg, 2006; Pollak and Puntscher-Riekmann, 2008; Egeberg and Trondal, 2011; Rittberger and Wonka, 2011; Schout and Pereyra, 2011; Egeberg et al., 2015). This phenomenon has been studied from at least three perspectives (Egeberg and Trondal, 2017). First, from an intergovernmentalist perspective, agencies have been seen as Member State instruments or agents for regulation, with the purpose of achieving greater joint-action capacity. Second, approaches which see EU agencies as hubs of transnational regulatory networks emphasise their independent role in soft forms of standard-setting at various levels of EU governance. Third, from a supranationalist perspective, EU-level agencies are seen as instruments at the disposal of the European Commission, and thereby as the building-blocks of an increasingly centralised EU administration. While these three broad perspectives provide different interpretations of the role and function of EU-level agencies, there are, arguably, several features that they all share (Egeberg and Trondal, 2017): they are set up at EU level as bodies which co-operate with key EU institutions, but are formally outside them; their mandates and powers are limited; usually, they are led by directors; their budget and work programmes are set by management boards consisting of blends of national officials and Commission officials; and their staff usually have temporary or *quasi*-temporary contracts.

Agencies constitute building blocks which connect the EU-level administration with national governmental administrations in what Trondal and Bauer (2017) term the *European multi-level administrative order.* The key assumption here is a hierarchy with EU-level institutions – most notably, the Commission – constituting the top level of the administrative order, and national-level agencies complementing the work of the former. Indeed, Egeberg and Trondal (2017) argue that there is growing (albeit sometimes creeping) supranationalisation of the EU's regulatory networks due to the growing influence of the Commission in the administrative and political running of EU agencies.

Yet, developments in the structures of EU governance in recent decades also show that, in an increasing number of functional areas, such as border protection or financial governance, EU Member States have been developing tailor-made solutions and structures between governments, with only a limited role being accorded to the European Commission. Indeed, in the post-Maastricht period, the nature of EU integration has, arguably, been developing away from the original Community method towards what Bickerton et al. (2015) term the *new intergovernmentalism.* In principle, this means that the traditional mode of an "ever closer Union" and the increasing empowerment of supranational institutions (most notably, the Commission) has given way to a somewhat unstructured growth of new types of organised responses to various functional needs. In the view of Bickerton et al. (ibid.), this entails the rise in influence of *de novo institutions* – intergovernmental bodies that emerge in various parts of the EU's institutional landscape and do not necessarily fall under the European Commission's jurisdiction or portfolio (ibid., 10–11). This includes Frontex, Eurojust, the EEAS, the ESM and a number of others. The characteristic feature of such *de novo* institutions is that they include a strong intergovernmental imprint by having representatives of the Member States' governments in their steering bodies. This makes them different from the classic types of supranational governance institutions of the EU (ibid., 32). Legally, they also differ from classic EU agencies, which have been operating under the so-called Meroni-doctrine, which states that EU agencies should not be granted discretionary powers in areas where such powers are not foreseen in the Treaties to rest with the EU. In the case of the *de novo* bodies, such as the ESM or the EEAS, the Commission has tolerated their role with discretionary powers of their own (ibid.).

While the volume by Bickerton et al. (2015) remains one of the few available sources to analyse systematically what the authors have labelled as the new inter-governmentalism and its consequences for the formation of the EU's governance system, the conceptualisation of what they term *de novo* institutions remains under-specified. Starting with the term "*de novo* institutions", it is not clear what this term actually means. From the description that Bickerton and his colleagues provide, it captures the rise of "new" institutions with newness defined by the intergovernmental set-up of the agencies. As they point out, these are "newly created institutions that often enjoy considerable autonomy by way of executive or legislative power and have a degree of control over their own resources." Yet, as is obvious, these *de novo* institutions are hardly a coherent group. Between the ESM, Frontex, the EEAS, Eurojust – one could go on – there are quite profound differences when it comes to their legal status, organisation, mode of emergence and operation. Arguably, though, what they do have in common is that they are hybrids – they combine the organising models and resources of multiple institutions. As an illustration, my previous analysis of the EEAS (Bátora, 2013) shows that it emerged as an interstitial organisation and has traits that it shares with the institutions that Bickerton et al. label as *de novo* institutions. Indeed, in order to get an analytical grip on the so-called *de novo* institutions and what this category tells us about the nature and workings of the EU, we may usefully apply the concept of interstitial organisations.

III Interstitial organisations: Institutional innovation through re-combination

When thinking about the development of the EU's governance order, it is useful to remind ourselves that the EU may *not* be fundamentally different from other kinds of political integration projects and/or other kinds of political entities. As such, we can build on established theories and methods of social scientific inquiry that we would otherwise apply when studying the formation of political or other social orders (Olsen, 2010, Fossum, 2015). Building on this, the starting point of the theoretical argument proposed here is hence that institutional innovation in modern societies is socially embedded. New organisations emerge in relatively dense webs of established institutions and social relations. The organisation theorist Arthur Stinchcombe (1965: 142) described this as the "social structure" of organisations, that is, "groups, institutions, laws, population characteristics, and sets of social relations that form the environment of the organization." Standard institutionalist explanations of how new organisations enter the social world discuss various modes of engaging with the social structure characterised by the adoption of established institutionalised models and various processes of socialisation and fitting in (Hannan and Freeman, 1977; DiMaggio and Powell, 1991). Adopting the established standards, structures, procedures and functions or standard features of organisations in a given institutional field is a specific way for new entrants to gain legitimacy. Yet, since ancient times, processes of institutionalisation entail the formation of dissenting elements and anti-systems (Eisenstadt, 1964). In any institutional system, there are multiple, parallel and sometimes contradictory models or logics of proper organising and proper behaviour (Friedland and Alford, 1991; Thornton et al., 2012). Indeed, political and social orders are characterised as "genetic soups" with multiple principles, rules, norms, resources and abilities to exploit these by actors in any given field (Olsen, 2010). As John Padgett's research on the rise of banking in medieval Italy shows, new organisational forms and new functions in organisations may be the result of re-combination, re-balancing and the transposition of rules, norms and various kinds of resources across institutional fields (Padgett and Ansell, 1993; Padgett, 2012). To understand the innovation and emergence of new organisational forms, it is hence crucial to capture how organisations and individuals are embedded in a social environment, how they draw upon the resources available there and how these are re-combined to generate new patterns of organised action, new practices, new structures and new norms (Padgett and Powell, 2012). The growth of new organisational forms by re-combining resources, rules and norms across institutional fields has been termed "interstitial emergence" (Mann, 1986; Morrill, 2004). An interstice is "a mesolevel location that forms from overlapping resource networks across multiple organizational fields in which the authority of the dominant resource network does not prevail" (Morrill, 2004: 6).

A key proposition in this chapter is that interstitial emergence may lead to the formation of what may be termed *interstitial organisations* (INTOs). Building on the author's previous work on the subject (Bátora, 2013, 2017), this chapter defines interstitial organisations as organisations that emerge in interstices between various organisational fields and re-combine the physical, informational, financial, legal and legitimacy resources that stem from organisations which belong to these different organisational fields. They feature combinations of rules, norms and practices drawn from the organisational fields that they span. Also, by operating *within* multiple institutional fields but not belonging fully to any of the fields, they increase heterogeneity and ambiguity in the fields that they span. This in turn leads to innovation as "standard" organisations from conventional fields need to explore ways how to relate to, accommodate and interact with the interstitial organisations (see, also, March 1991). This can be associated with de-segmentation, as INTOs which span various organisational fields re-combine the practices and rules from these fields. At the same time, INTOs may also be carriers of specific segmental logics by *organising in* certain solutions and providing access to certain participants while *organising out* other solutions and excluding other participants (see, also, the introductory chapter in this volume and Fossum 2019). They may thus be organisational carriers of segments in EU governance.[1]

In sum, there are three key features characterising INTOs: a) they are located in interstitial spaces between fields, and, at the same time, partially belong to these institutional fields, that is, they are only partially covered by existing institutional categories; b) they blend and re-combine practices from different institutional fields into innovative patterns and thereby generate innovation across institutional fields; and c) they are *new organisational forms* which require updates in the established categorisations of organisational forms, rather than mere adaptations of existing organisational forms and categories.

What, then, are the conditions under which interstitial organisations emerge? The literature on interstitial emergence suggests several such underlying conditions. First, it is a situation when established institutions fail to provide rules and procedures for emerging patterns of co-operation and social interaction beyond formal institutional frameworks (Eisenstadt, 1964; Mann, 1986; Morrill, 2004). Secondly, there are situations when there is an institutional performance crisis, when changes in the environment are so rapid that established institutions cannot adapt and profound institutional change is imminent (Olsen, 1995). Thirdly, it may be situations when established institutional structures face inherent constraints – these may be legal, organisational or political – and they cannot accommodate new functions and new goals within their own structures (Bátora, 2013; Korff et al., 2015). In sum, the conditions for the emergence of interstitial organisations include the following factors: institutional performance crisis, structural constraints, political constraints and functional needs – all in the light of the changing environmental conditions and/or the new interaction patterns beyond the established structures and rule-sets.

Arguably, such conditions represent profound institutional crises in governance orders. The EU is no exception here. One of the forms of adaptation is the setting up of different kinds of interstitial organisations. In the following section, the processes regarding three such organisations in the system of EU governance are reviewed: the EEAS, the ESM and the EBCG.

IV The EEAS as an INTO

Since the 1960s, the European communities – as a major economic player – have been gaining an increasing role in global affairs. This development has been accompanied by a steady growth of competences in the area of diplomacy and foreign affairs. The EC's diplomatic presence around the globe has grown steadily more professional and organisationally, and, in terms of diplomatic practices, has increasingly emulated states (Bruter, 1999; Dimier and McGeever, 2006; Bátora and Hynek, 2014). In the early twenty-first century, the EU was a key player in diplomacy and defence, contributing decisively to global trade regimes, development aid and, indeed, to crisis management operations around the globe. Indeed, in recent decades, the need for the EU to have an effective set of organised capacities at EU level capable of supporting the EU's global foreign policy actorness has been growing. Yet, while this has been the case, the organisational capabilities set up in support of the EU's actorness in diplomacy and global security have been evolving with serious limitations. The limits were, firstly, legal, as the EU is not a sovereign state and hence it cannot establish the standard organisational tool-kit which characterises the diplomatic capabilities of states, such as a foreign ministry or embassies (de Baere and Wessel, 2015; Wouters and Duquet, 2015). Secondly, the limits were political, as the EU Member States have either voted against the Constitutional Treaty proposal containing provisions on diplomatic action capacities (France and the Netherlands) or put up fierce resistance to attempts to strengthen EU-level capacity of diplomatic representation (the United Kingdom [UK]). Thirdly, limits were also related to what may be termed institutionalised notions of diplomacy as a marker of sovereignty (Bátora 2005, 2008). The diplomatic establishments of the Member States as robust and well-entrenched institutions have been resisting attempts to transfer competences and symbolic power to the EU's diplomatic organisational capacities (Adler-Nissen, 2014). The result of these pressures for effectiveness and parallel limits was the creation of the European External Action Service (EEAS) as an interstitial organisation tapping into the resources of multiple institutions and spanning the fields of diplomacy, defence, development aid, trade promotion and intelligence analysis (Bátora, 2013; Spence and Bátora, 2015). One of the primary purposes of the establishment of the EEAS was to break down the "silos" of the institutional set-up of the EU's external relations and to deliver a more integrated conduct of external policies. At the same time, though, the EEAS has also arguably become a carrier of a segmental statehood-cum-security logic by combining organisational features and functions of foreign ministries, defence ministries/military staff and intelligence agencies (ibid.; see, also, Fossum, 2019). This would underline the EEAS' interstitial nature in its organising of the EU's external relations in state-like ways without the EU actually being a state (Bruter, 1999; Bátora and Hynek, 2014).[2]

IV.1 The organisational resources of the EEAS and its interstitial nature

The organisational resources of the EEAS include the EEAS headquarters in Brussels and a network of EU Delegations in 139 countries and international organisations. By the end of 2018, it had 3,585 staff members, with 1,617 employed at the EEAS Headquarters and 1,968 in Delegations.

The EEAS is considered both to belong in the institutional field of diplomacy and to be different from the prevalent organizational form organizationally sustaining the field – the foreign ministries (Bátora, 2013; Adler-Nissen, 2014; Spence and Bátora, 2015; Onestini, 2015; Wouters and Duquet, 2015; de Baere and Wessel, 2015; see, also, Bruter, 1999; Dimier and McGeever, 2006). As High Representative of the Union for Foreign Affairs and Security Policy, Catherine Ashton pointed out in 2013, following the first two years of operations of the EEAS, that the service "seeks to add value by being more than a foreign ministry – combining elements of a development and of a defence ministry. The EEAS can be a catalyst to bring together the foreign policies of Member States and strengthen the position of the EU in the world" (EEAS Review 2013: 2). The

EU also considers the EEAS an "institutional innovation" that should help to bring about a more joined-up and comprehensive delivery of external affairs services to the EU institutions and to the Member States' governments (EU Global Strategy 2016). The EEAS taps into the personnel, rules and organisational models of EU institutions (the European Commission, Council Secretariat) and of the Member States' governments. The organisational models encompass foreign affairs administrations, defence ministries, development aid agencies and intelligence services. Also, it taps into the legal diplomatic resources such as diplomatic passports of the Member States (Wouters and Duquet, 2015). Given its interstitial nature, the EEAS has been able to bring together various kinds of resources from the EU's foreign policy tool-box and deliver comprehensive solutions in a number of foreign policy fields. Examples of where this has worked include the processes of reconciliation and stabilisation in the Western Balkans, most notably, the "normalisation dialogue" between Kosovo and Serbia (Bátora et al., 2017), as well as the negotiations of the Iran nuclear deal in 2015. In other areas, most notably the Ukraine crisis since 2014, the usefulness of the combined EEAS resources and processes has been far less clear.

In sum, the EEAS is an INTO spanning different institutional fields. At the same time, the EEAS is a carrier of statehood-cum-security segmental logic that organises the EU's external relations in ways resembling states – with attention to diplomatic status, sovereignty and security – while it is not one. This re-combination of organisational models is similar to that of the ESM addressed in the next section.

V European Stability Mechanism (ESM) as an INTO

The context for the establishment of the ESM was an unprecedented financial crisis spilling over to the crisis of the very foundations of the Eurozone and the Euro as a currency unfolding in the years 2009–2012. In an attempt to ameliorate the effects of the sovereign debt crisis hitting several Eurozone Member States, most notably Greece, Portugal and Ireland, the EU Member States and the EU institutions faced a severe crisis. The established legal rules of the European Monetary Union (EMU) did not provide support for any measures that would help to address the crisis, such as either bailing-out or expelling a troubled Member State (Featherstone, 2011).[3] Given this legal *lacuna*, EU Member States faced a dual challenge of having to act quickly, given the pressures of the global financial markets; and, at the same time, having to act in accordance with the existing legal framework of the EU (Closa and Maatsch, 2014). The solution was the setting up in June 2010 of the European Financial Stability Facility (EFSF) – an interim arrangement set up by the Eurozone Member States as a mechanism to support collective action in dealing with the most imminent pressures on the Euro/single currency. It generated numerous heated debates and, in some cases, spilled over into domestic political crises, resulting in the collapse of governmental coalitions (*e.g.*, in Slovakia in 2011). To provide a more stable organisational basis for collective action in addressing the Eurozone crisis, 17 Member States of the Eurozone agreed in October 2012 to set up the European Stability Mechanism (ESM) by developing the organisational and financial resources available in the framework of the EFSF.[4] The decision to set up the ESM was taken explicitly to address the existing institutional performance crisis, as the established structures of the Union or the Eurozone did not provide support in terms of rules and procedures for the kinds of functions and operations that were needed to address the Eurozone crisis. As the managing director of the ESM, Klaus Regling, explained, the setting up of the ESM

> was the result of a decision 17 euro area Member States to create a permanent crisis resolution fund to provide financial assistance under strict conditionality, appropriate to the financial instrument chosen, to euro area countries in temporary need of assistance. In doing so, *they filled an important institutional gap* that would have left the euro area vulnerable, as evidenced in the beginning of the crisis.
>
> *(ESM Annual Report 2012: 7; italics added)*

The ESM as an interstitial organisation emerged in an interstitial area previously not covered by the EU-level institutions or by the governments of the Eurozone. This is further anchored in its legal status. The ESM is a separate legal entity under public international law with its seat in Luxembourg. In effect, it is an international organisation founded by the governments of the Eurozone Member States. It has a legal personality and is established *outside* the legal order of the EU (de Witte and Beukers, 2013). It is neither an agency, nor a body, nor an institution of the EU, and hence it does not fall under the Treaties of the EU. While the legal status remains a challenge, as relations between the ESM and the EU remain ambiguous, the ESM (and the EFSF) achieved clearly positive results in returning a number of troubled Eurozone Member States to normal market access over the last years. This was done by following an explicitly German-inspired ordoliberal approach (see, also, Tranøy and Schwartz, Chapter 3 in this volume). Arguably, this would be making the ESM a primary carrier and constitutive feature of an economic segment in the EU inspired by German ordoliberalism, preferring certain types of solutions while organising out other types of solutions (*e.g.*, those inspired by Keynesian approaches).

VI The ESM organisational resources and its interstitial nature

The ESM has its own capital reserves of €80 billion paid in by the currently 19 Eurozone Member States. This sum is used as a guarantee to issue bonds on behalf of the Eurozone as a whole and thereby raise money on the international financial markets. These resources are then lent at favourable rates to Eurozone

Member States working to restructure their public finances and thereby make substantial savings in public budgets.[5]

The governance of the ESM consists of three levels: 1) the Board of Governors (usually finance ministers) of Eurozone Member States; 2) the Board of Directors (usually state secretaries from economy ministries); and 3) the Executive Director (Klaus Regling). The Corporate Governance Department of the ESM organises an annual meeting of the shareholders (*i.e.*, the Eurozone Member States) where the Board of Governors (the Eurozone finance ministers) approves the annual report. Regular audits of activities are done by the ESM Audit Department, and the ESM Code of Conduct provides a clear set of guidelines and rules for the conduct of operations. It is at the level of the Board of Governors that the ESM has a certain degree of democratic scrutiny and political accountability. Yet, since it is outside of the EU's Treaty framework, this is also necessarily limited. As Ban and Seabrooke (2017) point out, this is a challenge, since the ESM bail-out programmes are based upon conditionality with wide-reaching effects on the sovereignty of Eurozone Member States administered by the programmes. As the situation in Greece shows, there are numerous challenges related to the interstitial nature of the ESM tapping into the resources and rules of a number of other organisations. First, EMS programmes in Greece are negotiated by the Commission in co-operation with the European Central Bank; monitored by the Quadriga;[6] and approved by the ESM Board of Governors, consisting of the Eurozone finance ministers. This leads to overlapping and unclear responsibilities as well as perceptions that the EU and its institutions, rather than the Eurozone, are responsible for the austerity programmes and measures in target countries (ibid., p. 7). Second, as the ESM is outside the EU Treaties, the usual forms of EU-level accountability are not applicable. When called upon, the Executive Director attends hearings in the European Parliament where he responds to questions regarding ESM programmes, although this is largely an informal and irregular practice (ibid.). Due to the legal status of the ESM, most of its decision-making processes are secretive and characterised by higher degrees of informality than is usually the case in EU institutions. As the former president of the Eurogroup Jeroen Dijsselbloem pointed out in a letter to the European Ombudsman, "the Members of the Eurogroup may meet in their capacity of Governors under the [ESM]", which is "of an intergovernmental nature and hence, not covered by the EU Treaties' provisions on transparency" (quoted in Ban and Seabrooke, 2017: 8). Third, to stop impasses and enable effective action in bail-out programmes, the ESM's voting system is designed in such a way that it allows for a programme to pass if there is 85 per cent agreement among the Board members. In a situation in which the leverage of each country's vote stems from the level of its investment in the ESM (a system similar to, for instance, the IMF), there are virtually only three countries which possess veto rights (Germany with 26.96 per cent, France with 20.24 per cent and Italy with 17.79 per cent).[7] This leaves a number of smaller Eurozone Member States with rather limited possibilities of influencing decisions (Ban and Seabrooke, 2017: 7). In addition to this imbalance in influence among the Eurozone Member States, further challenges relate to the fact that Member States that are not part of the Eurozone may only take the role of observers and/or provide their views on specific lending programmes in which they may have contributed their resources. Important economies of the EU, such as the UK, Sweden, Poland and Denmark, are hence left out.

In terms of organisational resources, the ESM had 156 staff, secondees and trainees at the end of 2015. In 2017, the number of staff was 170 experts from 42 countries.[8] As an international organisation under international public law, the independence of the ESM is safeguarded by a number of traditional provisions which apply to most international organisations. Its senior representative and other senior staff are immune from legal proceedings pertaining to acts performed by them in their official capacity; their archives and documents, as well as their premises, are considered inviolable, protected by diplomatic immunity and hence safe from the interference of the authorities of Luxembourg. Also, as noted in the above, the ESM has full legal personality (ibid., 16). In this, the ESM is organisationally similar to international monetary institutions such as the IMF or the World Bank.[9] While all of these provisions provide the ESM with a high degree of independence as an organisation, its main governing bodies are merely extensions of the finance ministries of the Eurozone Member States, as they are manned by the political representatives and senior staff of these ministries (ibid.). The interstitial positioning of the ESM is also emphasised by its relations to non-EU institutions, such as EFTA. In October 2014, the ESM Board of Directors established the Administrative Tribunal of the ESM (ESMAT). The purpose of this administrative body is to ensure the ESM employees the right of access to justice regarding employment conditions. In December 2014, ESMAT signed a memorandum of understanding with EFTA Court, based upon which the latter provides the registry services to ESMAT.

In relation to the broader institutional architecture of the monetary and fiscal Union, the establishment and operation of the ESM as a first formal treaty-based intergovernmental institution uniquely for monetary union (and not for a broader group of EU members) has increased uncertainty in other institutions. The ECB, the European Commission and the European Parliament have been seeking to re-define their respective roles by taking into consideration the ESM and its new functions (Henning, 2017: 178). The ESM has been actively nurturing relations with experts in governments throughout the EU. One instrument here is its annual shareholder forum where ESM experts meet with officials from the Eurozone's Member State finance ministries (for example, 37 experts participated in such a forum in 2017).[10] In addition to this, the ESM organises research seminars, expert conferences, guest lectures and visitor groups. 150 such events were organised in 2017.[11] Arguably, many of these types of recurring interactions contribute to socialisation and institutionalisation of a segment by the ESM linking experts across the Eurozone Member States and beyond.

In sum, the ESM is an interstitial organisation tapping into the personnel, and legal and financial resources of multiple organisations, and re-combining organisational models into what seems to be a hybrid combination of an embryonic

Eurozone finance ministry; a nascent Eurozone version of the IMF and that of a Eurozone agency. Given its interstitial role, the ESM may also become a vehicle of de-segmentation tapping into rules and processes from multiple domains spanning EU-level monetary union and Member State level fiscal union. There are some suggestions that the ESM should be brought within the EU's Treaty framework by the year 2025 (ibid., p. 6). While this remains an option, it is useful to consider that the Eurozone Member States - in close co-ordination with key EU institutions - set up the ESM as an interstitial organisation *outside* the EU's legal framework helping the EU to address serious institutional gaps in dealing with the effects of the sovereign debt crisis on the Eurozone. A similar pattern could be seen in the establishment of the EBCG.

VII European Border and Coast Guard (EBCG) as an INTO

In 2015, the EU was hit by an unprecedented rise in the number of arriving immigrants. That year, there were about 1.5 million illegal border crossings into the EU. The national border management agencies of Member States such as Greece or Italy were overwhelmed, as was the EU's border management agency, Frontex, which, due to the limitations of its legal mandate, functions and resources, was unable to address the situation efficiently. In response to the crisis and the call issued by the EU's heads of state at their informal meeting on 23 September 2015 for improved management of the EU's external borders, the Commission worked out a proposal to set up the European Border and Coast Guard (EBCG).[12] The establishment of the EBCG was formally agreed upon by the Council of the EU on 14 September 2016, and it became legally operational in October 2016.

VII.1 The EBCG: Organisational resources and its interstitial nature

The EBCG was launched to deliver European integrated border management based upon a four-tier model comprising a) measures in third countries as part of the common visa policy; b) measures with neighbouring third countries; c) border control on the external borders of the Schengen area; and d) measures within the Schengen area, including return policies.[13] When it comes to its formal structure, the EBCG is composed of the *European Border and Coast Guard Agency* (Frontex as a body of the Union with a new expanded mandate) and national border management and coast-guard authorities involved in joint operations aimed at securing borders and coastal areas. As such, EBCG relies upon "the common use of information, capabilities and systems at national level and the response of the Agency at Union level."[14] Protection and management of borders and coastal areas are formulated as a "shared responsibility" of national border management agencies of the Member States and of Frontex. The role of the latter is to support national authorities in implementing standard measures throughout the Union's external borders. Moreover, Frontex is to reinforce, assess and co-ordinate measures implemented by national border management authorities.[15]

The functions of the renewed Frontex Agency are the following:

- to establish a technical and operational strategy for implementation of integrated border management at Union level;
- to oversee the effective functioning of border control at the external borders;
- to provide increased technical and operational assistance to Member States through joint operations and rapid border interventions;
- to ensure the practical execution of measures in a situation requiring urgent action at the external borders;
- to provide technical and operational assistance in the support of search and rescue operations for persons in distress at sea;
- to organise, co-ordinate and conduct return operations and return interventions.[16]

The EBCG Agency seeks to standardise the performance of border management on all the external borders of the Schengen area. This entails the secondment of Agency officials in places where there are risks – they are to be fully integrated into national information systems and provide relevant information to the Agency as well as perform regular *mandatory* risk analysis and vulnerability assessments. Also, the Agency will have *a right to intervene* to provide action on the ground in vulnerable spots in the Member States if the Member States concerned cannot or are not willing to address the situation effectively with their own resources. Such interventions are to be carried out even if the Member State concerned does not wish for this to happen.[17] Clearly, this would challenge the principle of the sovereignty of the Member States as well as third states in cases when the EBCG is deployed in operations in third countries' territories and, hence, the EBCG operates beyond the conventional role of EU agencies in the co-ordination and regulation of Member State policies (see Pollak and Slominski, 2009; Curtin and Egeberg, 2009). Also, the interstitial nature of the EBCG – that is, beyond well-established policy frameworks governing the protection of borders – raises particular issues relating to the democratic control and scrutiny of the new body (Monar, 2006; Ekelund, 2013; Campesi, 2018). At the same time, the focus on the protection of borders and the framing of these activities in terms of sovereignty and security contribute to the institutionalisation of a *securitisation segment* in the EU with EBCG as its key organisational carrier.

The EBCG arguably introduces a hitherto unusual model in relations between EU-level institutions and agencies and Member States, that is to say, it sets up a *hierarchy* with Frontex at the top, co-ordinating the network of national border management authorities of the Schengen area Member States (de Bruycker, 2016: 561; Rosenfeldt, 2016). Indeed, given this unusual set-up, de Bruycker (2016: 564) argues that the EBCG is "legal fiction." The EBCG spans EU institutions and Member States, leaving policy and strategy development in the area of the

EU's border security with EU institutions, and it uses a revamped Frontex as a tool in hierarchically co-ordinating the national border protection authorities of the Member States. In addition to the organisational expansion of Frontex, the EBCG has been co-ordinating the setting up of a reserve pool of 1,500 border guards from 19 EU Member States, who will be available to reinforce the Schengen area's external borders at 5 days' notice. Also, the EBCG is in the process of setting up a reserve pool of about 400 "return specialists" to assist Member States in managing the repatriation of migrants from the EU.[18] Not only is the EBCG heavily dependent on Member State resources, but these resources also come from different types of organisations, as some Member States have their borders and coasts guarded by paramilitary and military types of agencies (Carrera et al., 2017). In addition to tapping into various kinds of resources of EU institutions and EU Member States, the EBCG also spans various institutional domains related to border management (border protection, asylum policies, internal and external security). In doing so, it could potentially span across segments and, by creating structural openings, it could potentially contribute to de-segmentation in this sphere of EU governance.

When studying the emergence, operation and effects of the EBCG, one can identify practices underpinned by alternative institutional logics (*e.g.*, the logic of military missions to third countries, domestic police) and practices which break with the established norms in border agencies (*e.g.*, intrusion into the sovereignty of third states or the sovereignty of the EU Member States). As Léonard (2011) shows, the relatively soft, original mandate of Frontex has already enabled the agency to perform practices that excessively securitised the performance of the border patrolling functions. It is likely that, with the new mandate allowing the EBCG to operate both in third countries and inside the Schengen area, this will lead to further a transposition of rules from various institutional domains, including the military domain and the domain of domestic policing.

A number of innovative practices of Frontex have already been reported by Léonard (2011). This includes the setting up of a Frontex Risk Analysis Unit producing annual Risk Assessment Reports; the establishment of Frontex Situation Centre (FSC), which provides real-time information on ongoing migration flows towards the borders of the Schengen area members and associated members – information that is shared with the border authorities of the Member States;[19] the setting up of Rapid Border Intervention Teams (RABIT) and their deployment in Member States; the development of "data collection plans" with third countries, such as Russia, Ukraine and Moldova; and major operational manoeuvres such as joint naval task-forces operating in the Mediterranean Sea and seeking to stem migration flows (*e.g.*, EU NAVFOR MED *Sophia*). Such practices may be different from what is the usual pattern in national border and coast guards. It may be expected that the practices of Frontex as part of the newly established EBCG will be developed further and it is important to explore these to establish the nature of the practices.

Table 8.1 provides an overview of the three INTOs discussed in this chapter.

TABLE 8.1 Interstitial Organisations in EU Governance

	EEAS	ESM	EBCG
Established	2010	2012	2016
Legal status	Body of the EU anchored in the Lisbon Treaty	International organisation est. outside of the Treaties	Legal body comprising Frontex and Member State border protection agencies
Personnel	EU institutions (Council/ Commission) plus EU28 (diplomats, defence officials, development aid, intelligence)	Eurozone (19 MS)	Frontex and pool of officials from Schengen zone (26 Member States incl. N, IS, CH, & Liecht.)
Autonomous resources	HQ in Brussels; Organisational budget (approved by European Parliament); 139 diplomatic missions around the globe; Separate organisation	HQ in Luxembourg; Organisational budget (approved by Eurozone Member States); Separate organisation	HQ in Warsaw; Organisational budget approved by European Parliament and the Council; Separate organisation
Shared and externally accessed resources	Personnel (from EU Member States, e.g., heads of EU Delegations); Diplomatic passports (from EU Member States)	Financial resources from Eurozone Member States	EUROSUR intelligence (from Schengen Member States); Equipment (from Schengen Member States)
Spanning across institutional fields	Ministries of foreign affairs, defence ministries; development aid agencies; intelligence agencies	Finance ministries; EU agencies; international monetary organisations such as IMF	EU agencies; national border protection authorities; domestic law and order authorities; national military forces

VIII Conclusion: Interstitial organisations as a new crisis-driven mode in the development of segmented EU governance?

In order to address crises, the EU has developed interstitial organisations – bodies in support of EU governance which emerge between established institutional frameworks of EU institutions, EU agencies and Member State governments. This potentially constitutes a specific mode of formation of EU governance which has evolved in response to ongoing crises in the EU. INTOs provide organisational platforms for segments – constellations of actors sharing a segmental logic pertaining to a policy field (see Fossum, 2019 and the introductory chapter in this volume). Arguably, this may be indicative of an emerging pattern in the development of the EU's political order – segmented integration – developing alongside and in parallel to intergovernmental and supranational modes of integration. As this chapter sought to demonstrate, this is a process of change and adaptation that is not captured in the current literature on the evolution of the EU's political order, such as the body of contributions on "agencification" or on "*de novo* institutions" and the new intergovernmentalism. The organisation theory approach which was taken as a point of departure in this chapter emphasises the need to analyse the development of EU governance as just another example of a political order facing the pressure of a rapidly changing environment. This means that the EU is not special, and, rather than developing special new concepts to understand its evolution, we should employ the established social scientific approaches that are also used in other empirical contexts (see, also, Olsen, 2010). The notion of interstitial organisations is such a concept, one that is applicable to the EU and also to other contexts (Morrill, 2004; Bátora, 2017).

The newly set up INTOs, including the EEAS, the ESM and the EBCG, operate not only in different policy areas (diplomacy and defence, fiscal governance, border management), but also in different segments or fields of European integration. The EEAS is an EU-level institution which integrates and co-ordinates the diplomatic and defence capacities of the EU and of its 28 Member States and contributes to the formation of a sovereignty-cum-security segment. The ESM is an organisation set up and run by the Eurozone Member States and forming a fiscal policy segment informed by German ordoliberal ideas. Finally, the EBCG covers primarily the Schengen area countries, which includes the non-Member States of Norway, Iceland, Liechtenstein and Switzerland, but excludes the UK and the Republic of Ireland. This supports formation of a sovereignty-cum-security segment. The fact that organised arrangements which support the operation of these segments or fields have been developing in the form of interstitial organisations suggests several things:

First, the EU and its associated states can deliver and perform governance functions with the help of new kinds of organisational structures that we know neither from modern states nor from international organisations. Development of INTOs as the bearers of EU governance suggests that legal and political limits may bring about innovation in terms of governance forms.

Second, the fact that the three governance fields examined here are not co-terminous but tap into the same resources and rules suggests that development of organised governance capacities in a segmented EU order may lead to competition for scarce resources in terms of the time and attention devoted to these arrangements. It may also lead to tensions when it comes to the authority and responsibility shared between these governance INTOs in areas where their jurisdictions overlap. Examples include, for instance, overlaps between EBCG and EEAS in the countries of the EU neighbourhood or between the ESM and the EBCG in the reforms of Greece's public sector in the sphere of border management. In situations of such overlaps, there may be conflicts of priorities and procedures and, indeed, of authority.

Third, if we look at the different segments which the three INTOs discussed here co-constitute and which they span, it is clear that consolidation of these segments may also entail a particular co-ordination challenge in the system of EU governance. If, for instance, the Eurozone supported by the ESM and other institutional features emerges as a group of more integrated countries or an "inner circle" in the EU – a scenario promoted by the French president Emmanuel Macron – it would probably exclude the non-Eurozone Member States of the EU.[20] INTOs as carriers of particular segmental logics may, in fact, lead to various types of cognitive lock-ins in Cyert and March's sense as well as "trained incapacities" in Veblen's sense. An example here would be the sovereignty-cum-security segmental logic pertaining to the operations of the EEAS and the EBCG or the German ordoliberalism-inspired segmental logic of fiscal austerity inherent to practices and procedures promoted by the ESM. These kinds of segmentation processes may then narrow down the repertoires of the EU's actions and expose it to dangers of pathological adaptation and/or inability to use the full potential of its policy instruments. In the field of diplomacy, for instance, the EU has clearly capabilities and functions that make it operate differently than states (*e.g.*, external governance and enlargement processes). Yet, were the sovereignty-cum-security logic to gain the upper hand in the ongoing institutionalisation of the EU's diplomatic capabilities, such capabilities could easily be organised out and their potential would remain unused. The inherent danger of segmentation – or its illusion and lure – is that fosters collective action capabilities by generating bias and narrowing down policy options while at the same time limiting possibilities of institutional innovation and exploration. In March's (1991) sense, segmentation enhances processes of exploitation but puts a cap on exploration. In the EU's case, this is highly problematic, as the EU's success has been in setting up ways of governing that move beyond the limits of governance traditionally known in sovereign states. Indeed, a key *raison d'être* of the EU as a political project has been to allow sovereign states to co-operate and co-ordinate policies in ways that go beyond those usually operating inside sovereign states.

Finally, as this chapter shows, while INTOs in EU governance provide organised capacities for collective actorness of the EU and its Member States and may thereby contribute to increase the output legitimacy of EU actions, they also generate a number of challenges regarding input legitimacy (see Scharpf, 1997), democratic control and accountability (Olsen, 2017). Further research is needed into questions relating to procedures for ensuring accountability and democratic legitimacy of the newly established interstitial organisations in EU governance.

Notes

1 Following work by Christensen and Egeberg (1979), a *segment* can be defined as a pattern of linking participants, problems, solutions and choice opportunities in policy-making. Such patterns are stabilised by recurring interactions in consultative bodies such as committees or "remiss" systems. Participants in segments do not necessarily agree on every issue, but they do share a basic set of values and world views.
2 The uncertainty of the EU's status in diplomatic relations was demonstrated in November 2018 when the US State Department, without prior notification, downgraded the status of the EU Delegation to Washington, DC from that of a state to that of an international organization. Following criticism from both the EU and the US foreign policy establishment, this move was rectified by the State Department on 4 March 2019, and the EU Delegation again received recognition on a par with that given to a bilateral mission of a state (see *Immediate Change to the EU Delegation to the United States' Protocol Status*, available at: https://useu.usmission.gov/immediate-change-to-the-eu-delegation-to-the-united-states-protocol-status-2, last accessed 5 March 2019).
3 Article 125 of TFEU prohibits Member States from taking responsibility for each others' obligations and bailing each other out.
4 The EFSF and ESM remain separate legal entities sharing staff, facilities and operations. See https://www.esm.europa.eu/about-us/history#context, last accessed on 5 April 2017.
5 See https://www.esm.europa.eu/about-us/how-we-work#overview, last accessed on 5 April 2017.
6 Quadriga includes the European Commission, the European Central Bank, the International Monetary Fund and the ESM.
7 For an overview of ESM capital investment / votes distribution, see https://www.esm.europa.eu/esm-governance, last accessed on 5 April 2017. Germany's veto is further strengthened by the decision of the German constitutional court that ruled that no ESM programme can be agreed upon without the German Parliament passing it (Ban and Seabrooke, 2017: 7).
8 See ESM Annual Report 2017:16.
9 The IMF was established by the governments of 188 countries. It has a Board of Governors, an Executive Board (24 members), a staff of 2,600 from 147 countries and a HQ in Washington DC, but it has geographic units which cover the regions of the globe and a development focus. The World Bank was established by the governments of 188 countries. It has a Board of Governors and a Board of Directors (25 members) and it has geographic units that also cover all the regions of the globe and a development focus. By comparison, the ESM only covers the Eurozone, has a much smaller size in terms of staff and has no direct development focus. Its governance is, moreover, run by the finance ministers of the Eurozone convening in the Board of Governors.
10 See ESM Annual Report 2017, p. 61.
11 Ibid., p. 69.

12 See *A European Border and Coast Guard and Effective Management of Europe's External Borders. European Commission*, COM (2015) 673, 15 December 2015, available at: http://eur-lex.europa.eu/legal-content/EN/TXT/PDF/?uri=CELEX:52015DC067 3&from=EN, last accessed 10 January 2019.

13 See *Regulation (EU) 2016/1624 of the European Parliament and of the Council of 14 September 2016 on the European Border and Coast Guard*, Official Journal of the EU, L 251/2, available at: https://eur-lex.europa.eu/legal-content/EN/TXT/PDF/?uri=C ELEX:32016R1624&from=PL, last accessed 14 January 2019.

14 See Regulation (EU) 2016/1624 of the European Parliament and of the Council of 14 September 2016 on the European Border and Coast Guard, Official Journal of the EU, L 251/2,16.9.2016, point 5.

15 Ibid., point 6.

16 Ibid., point 11.

17 The Regulation (ibid.), Art. 24 specifies this: "In cases where there is a specific and disproportionate challenge at the external borders, the Agency should, at the request of a Member State *or on its own initiative*, organise and coordinate rapid border interventions and deploy both European Border and Coast Guard teams from a rapid reaction pool and technical equipment." (italics added) Furthermore, Art. 28 of the Regulation specifies that "Where control of the external border is rendered ineffective to such an extent that it risks jeopardising the functioning of the Schengen area, either because a Member State does not take the necessary measures in line with a vulnerability assessment or because a Member State facing specific and disproportionate challenges at the external borders has not requested sufficient support from the Agency or is not implementing such support, a unified, rapid and effective response should be delivered at Union level."

18 By the end of 2017, most of the operational needs of Frontex were met with Member States providing sufficient seconded personnel to Frontex operations (see Annual Information: Report on the Operational Resources; FRONTEX, 2018, available at: https://frontex.europa.eu/assets/Key_Documents/EBGT_TEP_Report/2017_ Frontex_Annual_Report_on_the_EBCGT_and_the_TEP_operational_resources. pdf, last accessed 25 February 2019).

19 EBCG and Frontex analyses build on resources collected via the Eurosur network. Launched in 2013, Eurosur connects a network of National Co-ordination Centres in Schengen zone Member States. Based upon the collected information, situational awareness on the external borders of the Schengen zone is generated by Frontex and provided back to the Member States' authorities. See http://frontex.europa.eu/intel-ligence/eurosur, last accessed 29 August 2017.

20 Steps in this direction have been taken, for instance, by the EU Member States agreeing to set up a budget for the Eurozone (see "EU Agrees to Create Budget for Eurozone", 14 December 2018, https://www.ft.com/content/2efa2276-ffbd-11e8-aebf-99e208d3e521, last accessed 14 January 2019).

References

Adler-Nissen, Rebecca (2014), "Symbolic Power in European Diplomacy: The Struggle between National Foreign Services and the EU's External Action Service", *Review of International Studies*, 40 (4): 657–681.

Ban, Cornel, and Leonard Seabrooke (2017), "From Crisis to Stability: How to Make the European Stability Mechanism Transparent and Accountable." Report. Brussels: Transparency International EU.

Bátora, Jozef (2005), "Does the European Union Transform the Institution of Diplomacy?", *Journal of European Public Policy*, 12 (1): 44–66.

Bátora, Jozef (2008), *Foreign Ministries and the Information Revolution: Going Virtual?* Leiden: Brill.

Bátora, Jozef (2013), "The 'Mitrailleuse Effect': The EEAS as an Interstitial Organization and the Dynamics of Innovation in Diplomacy", *Journal of Common Market Studies*, 51 (4): 598–613.

Bátora, Jozef (2017), "Turbulence and War: Private Military Corporations and the Reinstitutionalization of War-making", in: Christopher K. Ansell, Jarle Trondal and Morten Øgård (eds), *Governance in Turbulent Times*, Oxford: Oxford University Press, pp. 181–201.

Bátora, Jozef, and Nik Hynek (2014), *Fringe Players and the Diplomatic Order: The "New" Heteronomy*, Basingstoke: Palgrave.

Bátora, Jozef, Matej Navrátil, Kari M. Osland, and Mateja Peter (2017), "The EU's Crisis Management in the Kosovo – Serbia Crises", EUNPACK Working Paper, number 3, March 2017.

Bickerton, Christopher J., Dermot Hodson, and Uwe Puetter (2015), "The New Intergovernmentalism: European Integration in the Post-Maastricht Era", *Journal of Common Market Studies*, 53 (4): 703–722.

Bruter, Michael (1999), "Diplomacy without a State: The External Delegations of the European Commission", *Journal of European Public Policy*, 6 (2): 183–205.

Campesi, Giuseppe (2018), "European Border and Coast Guard (Frontex): Security, Democracy, and Rights at the EU Border", *Oxford Research Encyclopedia of Criminology & Criminal Justice*, Febuary 2018.

Carrera, Sergio, Steven Blockmans, Jean-Pierre Cassarino, Daniel Gros, and Elspeth Guild (2017), "The European Border and Coast Guard. Addressing Migration and Asylum Challenges in the Mediterranean?", *CEPS Task Force Report*, Brussels: CEPS.

Closa, Carlos, and Aleksandra Maatsch (2014), "In a Spirit of Solidarity? Justifying the European Financial Stability Facility (EFSF) in National Parliamentary Debates", *Journal of Common Market Studies*, 52 (4): 826–842.

Curtin, Deirdre, and Egeberg, Morten (2009), "Tradition and Innovation: Europe's Accumulated Executive Order", *West European Politics*, 31 (4): 639–661.

de Baere, Geert, and Ramses A. Wessel (2015), "EU Law and the EEAS: Of Complex Competences and Constitutional Consequences", in: David Spence and Jozef Bátora (eds), *The European External Action Service: European Diplomacy Post-Westphalia*, Basingstoke: Palgrave, pp. 175–191.

de Bruycker, Philippe (2016), "The European Border and Coast Guard: A New Model Built on an Old Logic"; European Papers, 1 (2): 559–569, available at: www. europeanpapers.eu, doi:10.15166/2499-8249/53.

de Witte, Bruno, and Thomas Beukers (2013), "The Court of Justice Approves the Creation of the European Stability Mechanism outside the EU Legal Order: *Pringle*", *Common Market Law Review*, 50 (3): 805–848.

Dehousse, Renaud (1997), "Regulation by Networks in the European Community: The Role of European Agencies", *Journal of European Public Policy*, 4 (2): 246–261.

Dehousse, Renaud (2008), "Delegation of Powers in the European Union: The Need for a Multiprincipals Model", *West European Politics*, 31 (4): 789–805.

Dimier, Véronique, and Mike McGeever (2006), "Diplomats without a Flag: The Institutionalization of the Delegations of the Commission in African, Caribbean and Pacific Countries", *Journal of Common Market Studies*, 44 (3): 483–505.

DiMaggio, Paul J., and Walter W. Powell ([1983] 1991), "The Iron Cage Revisited: Institutional Isomorphism and Collective Rationality in Organizational Fields", in:

Walter W. Powell and Paul J. DiMaggio (eds), *The New Institutionalism in Organizational Analysis*, Chicago IL: University of Chicago Press, pp. 63–82.

EEAS Review (2013), Brussels: EEAS, July 2013, available at: http://europeanmemoranda. cabinetoffice.gov.uk/files/2014/04/External_action_servive(_EEAS_Review: July_2013).pdf, last accessed 14 January 2019.

Egeberg, Morten (ed) (2006), *Multilevel Union Administration*, Basingstoke: Palgrave Macmillan.

Egeberg, Morten, Jarle Trondal, and Nina M. Vestlund (2015), "The Quest for Order: Unravelling the Relationship between the European Commission and European Union Agencies", *Journal of European Public Policy*, 22 (5): 609–629.

Egeberg, Morten, and Jarle Trondal (2011), "EU-level Agencies: New Executive Centre Formation or Vehicles for National Control?", *Journal of European Public Policy*, 18 (6): 868–887.

Egeberg, Morten, and Jarle Trondal (2016), "Agencification of the European Union Administration: Connecting the Dots", TARN Working Paper number 1/2016.

Egeberg, Morten, and Jarle Trondal (2017), "Researching European Union Agencies: What have We Learnt (and Where Do We Go from Here)?", *Journal of Common Market Studies*, 55 (4): 675–690.

Eisenstadt, Shmuel N. (1964), "Social Change, Differentiation and Evolution", *American Sociological Review*, 29 (3): 375–386.

Ekelund, Helena (2013), "The Establishment of FRONTEX: A New Institutionalist Approach", *Journal of European Integration*, 36 (2): 99–116.

ESM Annual Report 2012, available at: www.esm.europa.eu/sites/default/files/ esm2012annualreport.pdf, last accessed 5 April 2019.

ESM Annual Report (2017), European Stability Mechanism, Luxembourg: Publications Office of the European Union, 2018, available at: www.esm.europa.eu/sites/default/ files/ar2017final.pdf, last accessed 4 March 2019.

EU Global Strategy (2016), available at: http://eeas.europa.eu/archives/docs/top_stories/ pdf/eugs_review:web.pdf.

Everson, Michelle (1995), "Independent Agencies: Hierarchy Beaters?", *European Law Journal*, 1 (2): 180–204.

Everson, Michelle, Cosimo Monda, and Ellen Vos (eds) (2014), *EU Agencies in Between Institutions and Member States*. Alpen aan den Rijn: Wolters Kluwer.

Featherstone, Kevin (2011), "The Greek Sovereign Debt Crisis and EMU: A Failing State in a Skewed Regime", *Journal of Common Market Studies*, 49 (2): 193–217.

Fossum, John Erik (2015), "Democracy and Differentiation in Europe", *Journal of European Public Policy*, 22 (6): 799–815.

Fossum, John Erik (2017), "*Quo vadis Europa* – Segmentation, Consolidation or Fragmentation?", paper presented to the ECPR conference, Oslo, 7–9 September 2017.

Fossum, John Erik (2019), "The Institutional Make-up of Europe's Segmented Political Order", in: Jozef Bátora and John Erik Fossum (eds), *The EU Post Crises: The Rise of a Segmented Political Order*. Chapter 2 in this volume, pp. 22–46.

Friedland, Roger, and Robert Alford (1991), "Bringing Society Back In: Symbols, Practices and Institutional Contradictions", in: Walter W. Powell and Paul DiMaggio (eds), *The New Institutionalism in Organizational Analysis*, Chicago IL: Chicago University Press, pp. 232–263.

Hannan, Michael, and John Freeman (1977), "The Population Ecology of Organizations", *American Journal of Sociology*, 82 (5): 929–964.

Henning, C. Randall (2017), *Tangled Governance: International Regime Complexity, the Troika, and the Euro Crisis*, Oxford: Oxford University Press.

Korff, Valeska P., Achim Oberg, and Walter W. Powell (2015), "Interstitial Organizations as Conversational Bridges", *Bulletin of the American Society for Information Science and Technology*, 41 (2): 34–38.

Léonard, Sarah (2011), "EU Border Security and Migration into the European Union: FRONTEX and Securitisation through Practices", *European Security*, 19 (2): 231–254.

Mann, Michael (1986), *The Sources of Social Power: Volume 1, A History of Power from the Beginning to AD 1760*, Cambridge: Cambridge University Press.

March, John G. (1991), "Exploration and Exploitation in Organizational Learning", *Organization Science*, 2 (1): 71–87.

Monar, Jörg (2006), "The Project of a European Border Guard: Origins, Models and Prospects in the Context of the EU's Integrated External Border Management", in: Marina Caparini and Otwin Marenin (eds), *Borders and Security Governance: Managing Borders in a Globalised World*, Berlin: Lit Verlag, pp. 193–194.

Morrill, Calvin (2004), "Institutional Change and Interstitial Emergence: The Growth of Alternative Dispute Resolution in American Law, 1965–1995", in: Walter W. Powell and Douglas L. Jones, *How Institutions Change*, Chicago IL: University of Chicago Press, forthcoming.

Olsen, Johan P. (1995), "Europeanisation and Nation State Dynamics", ARENA Working Paper 9/1995, Oslo: ARENA.

Olsen, Johan P. (2010), *Governing through Institution Building*, Oxford: Oxford University Press.

Olsen, Johan P. (2017), "Democratic Accountability and the Terms of Political Order", *European Political Science Review*, 9 (4): 519–537.

Onestini, Cesare (2015), "A Hybrid Service: Organising Efficient EU Foreign Policy, in: David Spence and Jozef Bátora (eds), *The European External Action Service: European Diplomacy Post-Westphalia*, Basingstoke: Palgrave, pp. 65–86.

Padgett, John F. (2012), "Transposition and Refunctionality: The Birth of Partnership Systems in Renaissance Florence", in: John F. Padgett and Walter W. Powell (eds), *The Emergence of Organizations and Markets*, Princeton NJ: Princeton University Press, pp. 168–207.

Padgett, John F., and Christopher Ansell (1993), "Robust Action and the Rise of the Medici, 1400–1434", *American Journal of Sociology*, 98 (6): 1259–1319.

Padgett, John F., and Walter W. Powell (2012), *The Emergence of Organizations and Markets*, Princeton NJ: Princeton University Press.

Pollak, Johannes, and Sonja Puntscher-Riekmann (2008), "European Administration: Centralisation and Fragmentation as Means of Polity-building", *West European Politics*, 31 (4): 771–788.

Pollak, Johannes, and Peter Slominski (2009), "Experimentalist but not Accountable Governance? The Role of Frontex in Managing the EU's External Borders", *West European Politics*, 32 (5): 904–924.

Rosenfeldt, Herbert (2016), "Establishing the European Border and Coast Guard: All-new or Frontex Reloaded?", *EU Law Analysis*, 16 October 2016, available at: http://eulawanalysis.blogspot.sk/2016/10/establishing-european-border-and-coast.html.

Rittberger, Berthold, and Arndt Wonka (2011), "Introduction: Agency Governance in the European Union", *Journal of European Public Policy*, 18 (6) special issue: 780–789.

Scharpf, Fritz W. (1997), "Economic Integration, Democracy and the Welfare State", *Journal of European Public Policy*, 4 (1): 18–36.

Schout, Adriaan, and Fabian Pereyra (2011), "The Institutionalization of EU Agencies: Agencies as 'Mini Commission'", *Public Administration*, 89 (2): 418–432.

Spence, David, and Jozef Bátora (eds) (2015), *The European External Action Service: European Diplomacy Post-Westphalia*, Basingstoke: Palgrave.

Stinchcombe, Arthur L. (1965). "Social Structure and Organizations", in: James G. March (ed), *Handbook of Organizations*, Chicago IL: Rand McNally, pp. 142–193.

Thornton, Patricia, William Ocasio, and Michael Lounsbury (2012), *The Institutional Logics Perspective*, Oxford: Oxford University Press.

Trondal, Jarle, and Michael Bauer (2017), "Conceptualizing the European Multilevel Administrative Order: Capturing Variation in the European Administrative System", *European Political Science Review*, 9 (1): 73–94.

Wouters, Jan, and Sanderijn Duquet (2015), "*Unus Inter Plures*? The EEAS, the Vienna Convention and International Diplomatic Practice", in: David Spence and Jozef Bátora (eds), *The European External Action Service: European Diplomacy Post-Westphalia*, Basingstoke: Palgrave, pp. 159–174.

9

UNDERMINING THE STANDARDS OF LIBERAL DEMOCRACY WITHIN THE EUROPEAN UNION

The Polish case and the limits of post-enlargement democratic conditionality

Rafał Riedel

I Introduction

Given that the main question of this volume is what type of system has emerged out of the recent crises in Europe (2008–2014), this chapter specifically tries to position the most recent changes in Poland in the context of the consolidating segmented political system of the European Union (EU). Thus, it tackles a range of questions: In what sense does Poland's contemporary turn towards authoritarian populism contribute to EU segmentation? How, and to what extent, may we argue that the Polish government's view of the relation to and actions towards the EU contribute to EU segmentation? Or alternatively: How can we understand the Polish case of democratic backsliding as helping to push the EU towards a segmented political order? And – at the same time – how do the two dynamics, one at supra-national level and the other at nation state level (case study Poland), interact?

The logic of democratic backsliding is quite central to understanding the illiberal and de-Europeanisation trends that can be observed in Warsaw after the 2015 parliamentary elections. Looking at the criteria for a segmented political order that are elaborated on in the introductory chapter, it is legitimate to claim that the *PiS* (*Prawo i Sprawiedliwość* – the Law and Justice Party) government's contribution to EU segmentation unfolds along at least three closely related lines. First, the *PiS* government intends to reduce the scale and scope of the EU and to constrain its range of actions both at supranational and at domestic level (the Europeanisation pressure). Paradoxically, Poland is still interested in absorbing the largest share of the EU budget in the form of cohesion funds (and a large part of the agricultural funds). Under the slogan of territorial cohesion (eliminating inequalities for the benefit of the most underdeveloped regions of the EU), the solidarity principle was elevated to the top of *PiS*' European politics agenda. However, it very soon became clear that this solidarity was understood in quite a specific and very one-sided way. The Polish government seemed very attached to it when negotiating the EU budget and the long-term financial perspective, and treated it rather loosely when it came to sharing the risks and costs relating to the refugee allocation mechanism. This poses a series of legitimate questions: What type of EU does the *PiS* government want? What is the envisaged Polish position in it? And how does it affect the emerging segmented political order? Second, the democratic backsliding in Poland clearly has some ripple-effects, and, in so far as the *PiS* government also questions the EU's democratic credentials, we can associate democratic backsliding with undermining the credibility of what we refer to as the de-segmentation of institutions, notably, constitutional democratic ones: parliaments, constitutional courts (including citizens' rights), the media, and a free and vibrant democratic society. Thus, it is legitimate to argue that the *PiS* government fosters EU segmentation through weakening the overall credibility and legitimacy of the EU political system, both at the supranational and the domestic level. Third, the *PiS* government emphasises the national agenda so much that it could be claimed that it fosters EU segmentation through the re-assertion of the state or national sovereignty (especially through securitisation). It openly opts for a more intergovernmentalist Europe at the cost of supranational institutions (such as the European Commission or the Court of Justice of the European Union). On the ground, it manifests itself in various ways, for example, by taking a tough stance on asylum-seekers, seeking to halt immigration to the EU, labelling people terrorists, and opting for border controls.

The same emphasis on re-asserting national control can be found in other countries of the region, in such states as Hungary, which are actively involved in the process of "democratic erosion." The weakened commitment to internal EU law and order is closely associated with the context of an increasingly authoritarian Russia and a Trump-led United States (US), which are also bent on undermining multilateralism and international law. However, in the context of the European integration process, it should be noted that Brussels is framed by the (semi-)authoritarian governments in Warsaw or Budapest as an alien power trying to violate the will of the sovereign people. Such a simplistic understanding of democracy, limited to electoral procedures, is very often in conflict with the concept of liberal democracy that is supported by the EU's mainstream, as well as in conflict with other constitutional democratic principles, such as the protection of minority rights, to cite just one example. In consequence, and as a result of the accumulation of tension in various spheres (ecology, migration, solidarity, *etc.*), this conflict reveals the normative incompatibility of the cosmopolitan, multicultural and liberal political forces, in contrast to the nativist, conservative and nationalistic parts of the EU. Moreover, the illiberal forces in power in Poland and Hungary used this incompatibility as an excuse to marginalise the supranational institutions with their moralising attitude(s) (often portrayed in a neo-/post-colonial light).

As a result of this, we can observe the normative incompatibility of the afore-mentioned two sides of the EU, which could contribute to the even higher levels of differentiation in Europe. Moreover, it is correlated positively with the observable process of the emerging system of segmentation inside the EU. As it is understood in this volume, the notion of the EU as a segmented political system is a distinct form of differentiated system of governing. The Polish case analysis contributes to the debate on this type of segmentation because it shows how the post-crises EU has been imbued with a pathological form of differentiation, which is very clearly visible at the (semi-)peripheries of the EU.

II Vandalising liberal democratic institutions – The Polish case

Since the core institutions associated with de-segmentation are the liberal democratic institutions (which guarantee the rule of law, pluralism, transparency, openness and inclusiveness), it is essential to take a closer look at some EU Member States in which the constitutional democratic institutions have been devastated. The weakening of democratic institutions (by challenging them at the domestic or supranational level) may lead to the fostering of segmentation not only in normative terms but also institutionally. The EU consists of its Member States, and consequently, the vulnerability of the EU stems from its very dependence upon the Member States. This is a systemic vulnerability, and thus the democratic backsliding understood as the return to pre-transition practices and habits – in Poland (and in other Member States) contributes to the further segmentation of the system.

Prominent observers of democratisation processes in Central Europe characterise the last decade as a period of democratic recession, rollback, erosion, meltdown, setback or even decline. Others would prefer to say that it is a flawed understanding of the early post-Cold War transitions that generated over-optimistic expectations, which, not realised, produced exaggerated pessimism and gloom (Levitsky and Way, 2015). Philippe Schmitter, again in 2015, claimed that the developments in Central Europe do not mean the dismantling or destruction of democracy, but rather a change in the way it is being practised. This optimism was grounded on the assumption of better and better democratically educated citizens, who have access to vast sources of independent and critical information. At the same time, the charm of the West as the "promised land" has faded away – the collapse of the Soviet-style "people's democracy" has deprived Western democracies of one of their main bases of legitimacy, that is, an alternative and superior political system to that of their communist rivals. But reforms in the spirit of neoliberalism failed to produce the promise of continuous growth, fair distribution and equilibration. So, according to Schmitter, it is not democracy that is in decline, and it is certainly not backsliding that we are witnessing, but it is, instead, a crisis in the process of the transition from one type of regime to another, although it is not clear what the changes may bring about (Schmitter, 2015). At the dawn of the new century, the post-communist societies were disappointed with democracy and capitalism in its present form because of the lack of an effective modern state, which may lead (and often leads) to poor economic growth, poor public services, lack of personal security, pervasive corruption and so on. Francis Fukuyama points to the lack of proper institutionalisation as a main reason behind the democratic setback. It is the fact that the capacity of the state, in many new democracies, has not kept pace with the popular demands for democratic accountability. As he notes:

> It is much harder to move from a patrimonial or neopatrimonial state to a modern, impersonal one than it is to move from an authoritarian regime to one that holds regular, free, and fair elections. It is the failure to establish a modern, well-governed state that has been the *Achilles heel* of recent democratic transition.
>
> *(Fukuyama, 2015: 12)*

Others are equally pessimistic, although their mood is based upon a different set of arguments. Ivan Krastev claims that it appeared to be an illusion to consider the new democracies of Central and Eastern Europe (CEE) as consolidated. And the current process of backsliding is deeply rooted in the absence of a more value-based form of democratic politics. More precisely, it is not a crisis of democracy or democratisation, but a genuine crisis of liberal democracy. It is a backlash against globalisation, liberal cosmopolitanism and supranational politics (in Brussels) (Krastev, 2014). We may observe a kind of *"ersatz* liberalism" of the political mainstream in CEE. Liberalism in the region has rested not only on a narrow social base, but also on a narrow intellectual base. The proponents argue that the liberal values were not that much internalised by the wide spectrum of the society (&elites) but rather the acceptance of liberalism by the conditionality policy conducted by EU, NATO or IMF.

When most transitology scholars assumed that the leaders of democratic transformation (such as Hungary and Poland) were already in the phase of consolidating their liberal democratic systems, it became obvious that we may be witnessing not only de-consolidation but also de-democratisation tendencies in CEE. The year 2015 may be remembered as the year when Poland changed its democratisation trajectory.[1] This evolution was very dynamic, and the radical changes were already starting to be implemented in 2015 by the newly elected *PiS* government. From a democratic standards point of view, it proved difficult to legitimise the questions about their democratic nature right from the start. It does not happen very often that, after a mere 6 weeks of being in office (until the end of 2015), the ruling majority had violated so many democratic standards in such an open way that no independent observer had any doubts whatsoever about the undemocratic nature of the changes. After 3 years with the *PiS* in office (at the time of the submission of this chapter), Poland has already been downgraded in most of the democracy score rankings and is recognised internationally as a *defective* democracy (Bachmann and Hejj, 2018).

It is important to note that, very early on, the changes in Poland raised critical reactions from many international actors, including the EU officials – Luxembourg's foreign minister Jean Asselborn (Luxembourg held the Rotating Presidency in the Council of the European Union in the second part of 2015) and Frans Timmermans (vice-president of the EU Commission). Mark Toner, the acting spokesperson for the US Department of State, acknowledged that the American administration had questioned the Polish government about its actions regarding the Constitutional Tribunal. He added:

> USA cares very much about Poland, which is a valuable ally and a friendly democracy. This is why we observe the current developments with special interest.
>
> *(Zawadzki, 2015: 4)*

And Joschka Fisher (2015), in a text under the provocative title "The Fascism of the Affluent," openly wrote about Jarosław Kaczyński and his Law and Justice Party as being a quasi-authoritarian regime. The former German foreign minister and vice-chancellor from 1998 to 2005 writes about it in the context of European tendencies:

> The reasons for such parties' rise and success vary greatly at the national level. But their basic positions are similar. All of them are raging against the 'system,' the 'political establishment,' and the EU. Worse, they are not just xenophobic (and, in particular, Islamophobic), they also more or less unashamedly embrace an ethnic definition of the nation. The political community is not a product of its citizens' commitment to a common constitutional and legal order; instead, as in the 1930s, membership in the nation is derived from common descent and religion.
>
> *(Fischer, 2015)*

This reference to the 1930s, besides its symbolic power, speaks to the imagination of many observers and analysts who are critical about the tendencies in CEE. The experience of the interwar period, where unlimited majority rule paved the way for dictatorships, forced Western European decision-makers to strengthen institutions by limiting the sovereignty of the people, for example, with the introduction of a constitutional court. The new EU Member States, which are mostly post-communist regimes, have predominantly different post-World War II experiences. Here, quite a simplistic understanding of democracy dominated, one which prioritised the will of the people as the key to any governance process, despite the fact that democracy is not an arbitrary concept. As Jan-Werner Müller puts it, besides elections, there is need for a system of checks and balances, that is, the separation of powers, as well as strong protection of fundamental rights. (Müller, 2013: 39)

The central question has always been how to reconcile the genesis of democracy (the rule of the people) with what we may call the standards of democracy (the rule of law, accountability, engaged civil society, elections, *etc.*). Democracy has many facets, which concern its *leitmotivs*, its institutional design and its perception. Despite the many theories and concepts developed throughout time, certain aspects are undeniably intertwined with it, to wit, the rule of the people, the control of power and equality and freedom.

However, Poland, once a *wunderkind* of *Mittel Europa* transformation, changed its democratic trajectory in 2015. The undemocratic *djinn* had already been re-bottled a decade earlier, in 2005,[2] but Polish democracy had defended itself at the time. The period 2005–2007 was characterised, from the perspective of time, as a time of democratic success, not *malaise*. It was the democratic institutions which defended themselves and checked the ambitions of autocratic-leaning president Lech Kaczyński (Levitsky and Way, 2015: 56). Up to 2015, at least on the surface, Poland appeared to be the exception in the CEE democracy backsliding. It had enjoyed steady economic growth and had produced a strong, Christian Democratic, liberal party, in the form of Civic Platform (*PO – Platforma Obywatelska*). However, the status of the regional champion of liberalism might have been due to its party-electoral configuration, rather than to any deep cultural embracing of liberal norms. Like many pro-market parties in the CEE region, the *PO* pursued a narrowly defined technocratic programme based upon economic pragmatism. In opposition to the *PO*'s economic liberalism and social conservatism, the Law and Justice Party has long hoped to re-fashion Polish democracy into a "Fourth Republic" based upon much more conservative and Catholic values. They explicitly rejected the compromises made by the communist regime and the "Solidarity" (*Solidarność*) opposition at the beginning of the transition (in 1989). Until 2015, Poland was a case of illiberal conservative nationalism held at bay with rather gloomy prospects. Poland still remains a divided and polarised society (Dawson and Hanley, 2016: 29).

Just in its last session of the electoral year (2015), the Polish parliament – already with a *PiS* majority – legislated on many fundamental issues, including the media, finance and administration, reform of which would normally have taken years. The public discourse agenda was also filled with the following topics: the re-nationalisation of Poland or "re-Polonisation" of the media, and the "re-Polonisation" of the banks – one of the slogans of the winning *PiS* electoral campaign. The markets started to treat this plan seriously after May 2015 when Andrzej Duda won the presidential elections. *WIG-Banki* – the index of the Warsaw Stock Exchange – showed that the market value of the banks had dropped by 26.38 per cent (by the end of the year) (Frączyk, 2015). Clearly, the actions undertaken by *PiS* were colossal both in their weight and in their wide range. The depth and pace of the changes can be compared only to those of 1989 (the so-called "shock therapy"). The difference is that, after the collapse of communism, the legitimacy of the revolution was justified by the historical change, whereas, in 2015, Jarosław Kaczyński's party won only minimally (83 per cent of the Polish electorate did not vote for *PiS*) and the majority in the *Sejm* (lower house) was rather a coincidental effect of the other political parties not entering the parliament (the composition of votes gave *PiS* a simple majority of votes). Clearly, it was not a constitutional majority which would legitimise radical changes in a systemic manner. Thus, Jarosław Kaczyński – following the experience of his political ally from Budapest, Victor Orbán – attacked the Constitutional Tribunal, the guardian of the constitution.

Jarosław Kaczyński also revealed his motivations for the *PiS* actions against the Constitutional Tribunal by saying that it had the possibility to block any reforms, and that its members were dominated by the previous majority (mainly the *PO*), which had been de-legitimised. This is why, on 25 November 2015, the (newly elected) *Sejm* took the resolution, voted by the deputies belonging to *PiS* and *Kukiz'15*, which proclaimed that the October appointment (by the previous parliamentarian majority) of the five new judges was against the law. On 3 December 2015, the Constitutional Tribunal handed down the judgment that the October appointment was correct in the case of three judges but that two had been appointed illegally. In its justification, the Court argued that the previous *Sejm* could only appoint the (three) judges whose mandates were due to expire earlier. Despite this judgment, *PiS* elected its own five judges and refused to publish the official judgment of the Constitutional Tribunal.

Most independent commentators had no doubts that this moment should be remembered because it is the date when the democratic state of law (*Rechtstaat*) came to an end in Poland (Żakowski, 2015). President Andrzej Duda did not swear in the judges who had previously been appointed by the Constitutional Tribunal, because he claimed that they had been elected illegally. In addition, to strengthen the legitimacy of his decisions, he also added that it is the Parliament which is the emanation of the current will of the people (sovereign). At the same time, he ignored the role of the legal procedures at the highest – constitutional – level. Some constitutional lawyers claim that the three judges elected on 8 October 2015 could take part in Constitutional Tribunal sessions since they had been elected in conformity with the constitution. The fact that they had not taken the oath before the president did not disqualify them from being judges. The constitutional crisis was stimulated by *PiS* and is now developing into something worse. The constitutional institutions have become a mere *façade*. The *PiS* politicians justify the situation by speaking about the full autonomy of the parliament, which is curious. Deciding which Constitutional Tribunal judgments are valid and which are not – deciding on which to publish and which not to – seems like a Belorussian standard. To keep the Constitutional Tribunal in a position of defence, *PiS* decided to "reform" its legal status by practically paralysing its work. The new act was legislated in a "fast track" procedure, which was itself controversial. It was one of the reasons why Professor Małgorzata Gersdorf, the president of the Supreme Court, appealed on 30 December 2015, against the new law, claiming that it violated the principles of the democratic state of law (such as the separation of powers). Another problematical element of the new act was the lack of *vacatio legis* (the period between the promulgation of law and the time it takes legal effect), which was a way to "by-pass" the constitution. The Constitutional

Tribunal could not judge the act in any other way, as the newly legislated order had made the Constitutional Tribunal dysfunctional.

Such a demonstration of power was justified by *PiS* politicians with the argument that it was only a reaction to previous unconstitutional actions on the part of *PO*. It is true that it was *PO* which started the wrong-doing in the case of the Constitutional Tribunal in Poland, but the idea of improving the situation by doing even more evil is irrational (Kalukin, 2015). On 23 December 2015, Witold Waszczykowski, the foreign minister, sent a project for the reform of the Act on Constitutional Tribunal to the Venice Commission with a request for its opinion. For all those who were surprised by such behaviour, it very quickly emerged that it was just another trick by the new majority. The document sent to the Venice Commission (it was a rather soft version, before all the amendments implemented in the later work of the parliament) had nothing to do with the final version of the Act that was enacted a week later.

The problems surrounding the Polish Constitutional Tribunal may be judged differently depending on the particular context. Well-established democracies often operate more or less partisan procedures for appointing court judges. These procedures are often, to put it mildly, dominated by political expediency and do not represent clear examples of judicial independence. Yet, while appointing judges is often subject to intense negotiations between the government and the opposition, with far-reaching political consequences, recalling or impeaching judges is universally subject to the most stringent criteria and duly accorded exceptional constitutional safeguards. Lowering the threshold for the recall of judges may be taken as a serious violation of the spirit of the constitutional framework.

From a democratic standards perspective, perhaps the main issue is that *PiS* introduced a very strong element of informality that allows the party (and, above all, its leader) to wield power without constraints. It raises the spectre of arbitrary rule, which is in clear contrast to the checks and balances system. In the case of post-2015 Poland, the key problem has been the lack of constitutional responsibility of the key decision-maker – Jarosław Kaczyński. Formally speaking – apart from being the unquestioned leader of the *PiS* party – he does not hold any official state position but is merely a simple deputy in the parliament. He acts by utilising politicians, such as the president, Andrzej Duda, and the prime minister, be it Beata Szydło or Mateusz Morawiecki, who are totally dependent on him and his will. The relations between the newly elected president, Andrzej Duda, and the president of the *PiS* party, Jarosław Kaczyński, are very well reflected in one of the *PiS* party members' comments about the question of whether Kaczyński was satisfied with the behaviour of Duda with regard to the rapid swearing-in of the newly elected judges to the Constitutional Tribunal by *PiS*. The answer was both yes and no. Yes – because he obtained five judges of his own choice. No – because he noticed that Duda had hesitated for a moment. Duda, as a lawyer, knew that if he followed Kaczyński's instructions, he would – maybe in the future – be subject to an investigation by the Tribunal of State. If he did not follow his principal's expectations, however, it would mean an open war with Kaczyński, who does not seem to know the word *compromise* (at least that is what can be concluded from his political actions to date). Kaczyński, as the decision-maker, is sheltered from any constitutional accountability (Krzymowski, 2015).

Jarosław Kaczyński subordinated other politicians from his party, who resemble a disciplined military unit rather than a political party performing its basic functions in a democratic society, with representation or a transition belt translating the electorate will and preferences into a political decisions. By making the party members (including the prime minister and the president) co-responsible for the actions against the Constitutional Tribunal, he made them 100 per cent loyal to him and dependent on him. They can avoid political and legal responsibility only under Kaczyński's patronage (Wielowieyska, 2016). They are commonly referred to as just *marionettes* in Kaczyński's hands.[3]

Many, however not all, call this situation simply a *coup d'état* (Zoll, 2015). Others are more modest, claiming that it is instead pushing Poland towards an illiberal version of democracy (Sadurski, 2016). Donald Tusk coined an expression in which he called the non-*PiS* political camp *liberal-democratic*, in sharp contrast to the illiberal nature of *PiS* (Tusk, 2015). There are also other observers who ironise about what kind of revolution it is when the previous monarchs and rulers are not *decapitated*. Undoubtedly, the "good change" demolishes the previous order, questions its moral foundations and throws away all the elements of the past – including ideas and people (Olszewski, 2016). Jarosław Kaczyński calls it the "exchange of élites." He claims that the real goal of his party is to unveil the real picture, which is blurred by his political opponents. He uses the metaphor of the false movie which is displayed in front of the people and which they believe, even though the reality is different. This Plato's cave connotation reveals Kaczyński's attitude towards reality – it is constructed by "bad people," and the essence of his political existence is this battle between good and evil. He subjectively decides who is good and who is bad quite arbitrarily according to his own criteria (Migalski, 2015).

The populist fundaments of Jarosław Kaczyński's politics have been well investigated by social psychologists. Krystyna Skarżyńska, a political psychologist, claims that, in Polish society, there is a strong belief that Kaczyński wants "good for the ordinary people," which explains his anti-establishment and anti-élitist rhetoric. Others have revealed Kaczyński's personal features to be found in a strong feeling of moral superiority, in which he is a cold political player with no respect for other people or their feelings, convinced that the whole political world is against him (and, also, that they do not appreciate him), and *revanchist*. He also has many elements of an authoritarian personality, that is, a fascination with strength, a dreary perception of the world, cynicism, a marginalising of minorities, distrustfulness and aggression against ideas and people who oppose him, and he is determined – in a Machavellian way – to achieve his goals (Skarżyńska, 2016). For Kaczyński, the conflict is the essence of politics and also a method of governing. At the same time – and this is maybe the most problematical problem politically – he does not hold any constitutional responsibility. This is one of the consequences of steering the country from the back seat. Not only are the principles of accountability violated, the basic mechanisms of legitimacy are also disabled.

The political camp of *PiS* treats the majoritarian mechanisms of democracy as superior to the principles of the rule of law. According to the *PiS* leaders, it is the president who decides what is constitutional and what is not, instead of the Constitutional Tribunal. It is a usurpation of power. In Poland, there is a long tradition of superiorising the "reason of the state," the "will of the people," the "higher need," the "historical necessity" or "the judgement of democracy" above the law. Such situations happened in 1926 (with Piłsudski's *coup d'état*), in 1947 (with the establishment of the communist regime) and in 1981 (when martial law was implemented by General Wojciech Jaruzelski).

Theoretical and conceptual work in democratic studies has undergone a notable evolution in its endeavours to catch up with the democratic reality on the ground. There has always been some confusion about the teleological aspects of conceptualising the trajectories of post-communist regimes. There may be some merit in an analysis of the variables in order to explain the differences in regime transformation outcomes (Pop-Eleches, 2007). An inconsistence exists in general concerning the fundamental principles of democracy, for example, when political actors refer to the sovereignty of the people but try to eliminate the basic mechanisms of the control of power. The establishment of a defective democracy does not necessarily mean a direct transition (back) to autocracy. Regimes can foster this subtype for a longer period, without moving either in a democratic or in an authoritarian direction. This depends strongly on the external political, economic and social factors. The nature of the defective democracy is the dis-embedding of semi-democratic regimes (Merkel *et al.*, 2003). More "grey-zones" are identified, which are very diversified in their mixture of specific democratic standards and lead towards various gradations of democracy in the post-communist world.

Nevertheless, the general conception of a democracy founded on the rule of law has been disrupted in Poland. The year 2015 appears to have been critical in the contemporary history of Poland. After more than a quarter of century of being a poster-child for a pro-democratic transition, successful economic transformation and effective membership in the EU, Poland joined the club of the other troublesome countries of CEE. The whole region looks totally different now when compared with the situation in previous decades. Not only is the external context much less friendly, including such events as the refugee crisis, the Russian interventions in Crimea and Donbas, Brexit, the 2016 US presidential elections and the lasting consequences of the economic crisis, but also internally, in each of the EU countries, there is a growing Euroscepticism (France) and populism (Austria) and, very often, right-wing extremism (Holland) can be observed. Poland, as the largest country in CEE, seems critically important for the region, and lasted the longest in its pro-European orientation and its liberal democracy standards. Most observers have predicted that such a situation will continue due to the preferential determinants of the processes of democratisation, consolidation and Europeanisation. These included, among others, steady economic growth (sustained even in the times of the deepest economic crisis in Europe), and the enhancement of integration with the European market and active participation in Western structures (such as NATO and the EU).

Attila Mong, a Hungarian analyst, claims that the repetition of the Budapest scenario in Poland will be more difficult. The Poles are a bigger nation, much more diversified, with longer liberal traditions. And the tradition of the opposition is much stronger than in Hungary (Mong, 2015). Both nations had the fresh experience of functioning in a non-democratic regime. This experience was fresh enough in the 1990s, and was later on forgotten – or at least it did not function as an effective barrier in choosing non-democratic options. Besides, there are many other differences between the Polish and Hungarian situations. Victor Orbán's relations with the EU are full of realism. His party is a member of EPP (European People's Party) in the European Parliament, and he maintains good relations with Germany. Orbán shows himself to the Hungarian electorate as a friend to both sides (Germany and Russia), whereas Kaczyński prefers the rhetoric of "two enemies." Nevertheless, as of the end of 2018, both the Hungarian and the Polish governments are in conflict with the EU institutions, which regard democracy and the rule of law as being at risk in both states. Warsaw and Budapest reject such criticism and invoke their national sovereignty. Both governments view themselves as being democratically legitimised. They are of the opinion that the European integration project has gone too far, and they propose the strengthening of the nation states within the EU (Buras and Vegh, 2018).

Until the time of the EU enlargement, all the CEE states (which were subject to the conditionality mechanism) moved in the same general direction of the market economy based upon private ownership and liberal democracy, with the effective checks and balances system guaranteeing the rule of law. Victor Orbán's Hungary desperately worked to be the first of the post-socialist democracies to join the autocracy's club (Kornai, 2015). Since 2015, it has been accompanied by Poland, which means that more than half of the citizens of Central Europe do not live under the liberal democracy umbrella any more. The question of whether Poland and Hungary are still democracies at all is not an easy one to decide. Between democracy and authoritarian regimes, there is a continuum of various types of autocracy.

What made Polish politics explosive in and after 2015 was not the infringement of individual standards of democratic governance in isolation, but the interaction of circumstances and tendencies to disrupt or to re-frame the constitutional set-up of the country. Democracy backsliding – both in Poland and in the whole region – was not only expected, but also anticipated as a side-effect of the élite-driven (permissive consensus) and incentive-driven (Europeanisation) processes. Such forecasts rested on the assumption that the élites of the post-communist states had not internalised liberal-democratic values and would stretch (or even violate) constitutional norms if they could do so. Now, when the predicted democracy backsliding has actually begun, analyses are examining cross-national variations in the form and extent of the backsliding, and alternative ways of motivating élites to preserve liberal institutions. Democracy needs democrats and – predominantly – democratic citizens. The observed low levels of democratic activism and engagement on the part of citizens, as well as the weakly embedded institutions in the post-communist region's democracies, have been identified as, among others, the consequences of the legacies left by the previous systems (Dawson and Hanley, 2016: 22). However, the rule of law is a set of rules that are binding not just on citizens, but also (or predominantly) on the élites which wield coercive power. If the law does not constrain powerful authorities, it is tantamount to executive command, and the rule of law becomes an illusion. It is connected with the accountability principle, according to which the government acts in the name and interest of the whole community, rather than simply in the self-interest of the rulers or the narrow groups that they represent (or were elected by). Liberal democracy balances the potentially contradictory norms and institutions – on one side, the state generates and employs power, while on the other, the rules of law and accountability seek to constrain power and ensure it is used in the public interest. A state without constraining institutions is a dictatorship (Fukuyama, 2015). The *PiS* government has stripped away the formal checks and balances system in order to concentrate power in their own hands, motivated by exclusivist nationalism, with the intention of building an illiberal nation-state.

Illiberal nation states, which question and challenge the norms of the constitutional democratic order, are strongly committed to what is traditionally understood as sovereignty and are sceptical towards most EU policies, substantially contributing to the segmentation process of the whole EU system. Thus, the de-democratisation tendencies in Poland (and the region) undermine the democratic credentials of the Union as such. Together with the de-Europeanisation trends, they create a solid set of arguments which serve to de-legitimise not only specific EU policies, but also the EU polity in its entirety. The Union's systemic vulnerability stems from its Member States and their un-democratic qualities. Democratic backsliding in Poland, together with its strong Eurosceptic flavour, contributes to entrench further segmentation considerably. By rejecting the liberal democratic values, norms and institutions, Poland weakens the de-segmentation-immune system of the EU.

III The limits of post-enlargement democratic conditionality

This section aims to highlight the EU's role in defending democracy in its Member States. It shows the structural weakness of Brussels when faced with the challenge of some Member States that wish to devastate the liberal democratic order. Taking into account the salience of the liberal democratic norms and values that are fundamental for the functioning of constitutional democracies inside the EU Member States (as well as the EU's democratic credentials, as such), this section looks at the weakness of the immunity system of the EU with regard to its de-segmentation capacities.

This part of the chapter connects the literature on Europeanisation and conditionality with the discussion about the EU's contemporary legal instruments at the disposal of the Member States in order to defend democracy. The topic is highly valid from the point of view of the most recent developments in many CEE countries, which are scrutinised by the supranational institutions for their illiberal democratic practices. The European Union's transformative impact on its direct neighbourhood was obvious in the case of the waves of enlargement in 2004, 2007 and 2013. Both the political as well as the economic reforms of the CEE states were partly induced by the motivation stemming from the so-called "waiting room syndrome." Whether the EU can effectively defend the liberal democracy standards after the enlargement, when the accession motivation diminishes, is debatable. As the Polish case clearly shows, the post-enlargement conditionality hardly works and proves to be rather ineffective.[4] At the same time, the Europeanisation pressures appeared to be much more productive in the pre-accession period than after 2004 (Graziano and Vink, 2007). Thus, it is also possible to understand the particular EU (pre-enlargement) conditionality as "powerful tools to shape institutions in the CEECs which made policymakers choose EU models because of the incentives and constraints imposed by the EU accession process" (Grabbe, 2002: 262). However, doubts as to the precise understanding of conditionality were clearly expressed by James Hughes, Gwendolyn Sasse and Claire Gordon:

> If it is accepted that conditionality is an implicitly coercive instrument wielded by the Commission to secure compliance with certain desired policy or institutional outcomes, then we must also accept that the features of EU conditionality, in particular its rule-based prescriptive essence, are not well defined. Ambivalence and ambiguity are evident at both levels of conditionality identified above. In the case of the Copenhagen criteria it is obvious that the political conditionality for membership was highly politicized and operationalized in a selective manner. By the time enlargement negotiations accelerated from 1997, it is doubtful that the political conditionality as laid down in the Copenhagen criteria was a significant factor in the process, as the democratization of the CEECs was generally accepted as a reality and a starting-point for the other three Copenhagen conditions.
>
> *(Hughes, Sasse and Gordon, 2004: 525)*

Following these authors, the logic of EU conditionality is that it is not a uniformly hard rule-based instrument, but rather it is highly differentiated, with its nature shifting and transforming depending on the content of the *acquis*, the policy area, the country concerned and the political context to which it is applied. Particularly in the case of the 2004 and 2007 enlargements, the performance tasks set by the Commission were not easily devised, evaluated or benchmarked.

This ambivalence and vagueness across policy areas significantly weakened their impact.[5] Apart from this, clear causal relationships between the EU and domestic levels are difficult to trace since causation operates in both directions. Such processes are best studied as "an ecology of mutual adaptation" (Hughes, Sasse and Gordon, 2004: 526). Unfortunately, this kind of flexible method of case study (with all its imperfections) is assumed to be the most appropriate method for analysing the application of EU conditionality during enlargement.

Generally, EU policy towards the Central European candidate states was widely regarded as predominantly being a policy of conditionality. However, many authors recommend distinguishing (analytically) between the use of "conditionality" as a political strategy and its causal impact on domestic politics (Massey, 2004). It is impossible to hypothesise about the past, and we cannot answer the question of whether conditionality-driven change was the vehicle of transition, consolidation and the transformation of economy. This doubt underpins the main logic of EU conditionality understood as a bargaining strategy of reinforcement by reward, under which the EU provides external incentives for a target-government to comply with its conditions.[6] It is also possible to claim that these dominant features of conditionality might have been superseded by other mechanisms that could also lead to rule transfer. For example, in the process of the systemic political and economic transformation that the Central European states were undergoing, they might have considered EU rules as effective solutions to domestic policy challenges and thus adopted these rules independently of their EU conditionality and their desire to join. In addition, while the EU might provide incentives for the adoption of its rules, the mechanism through which the Central European governments adopt them might relate to the processes of persuasion and learning in which EU actors socialise with Central European actors rather than coerce them (Schimmelfennig and Sedelmeier, 2004: 626).

The primary law of the EU expresses very clearly the concept that democracy plays an important role in the treaties. It is a keyword concerning the EU's basic values, declared in the preamble, in the Union's functioning itself and in the character of the external actions and relations with third states (TEU, TFEU). The European Community had already existed for almost 30 years when the Single European Act mentioned the promotion of democracy for the first time in 1992. And, from that point on, the crucial position of democracy in its own development and enlargement was no longer neglected. In fact, there does not exist any official definition by the EU to clarify what is meant by this term. This is a fundamental problem; the EU proclaims democracy as a key element of its structures and demands it as a pre-condition for becoming a Member State and as a basic aim in its external activities, but in the end, the question still remains regarding which conditions have to be met in order to fulfil the Union's expectations regarding this concept. This raised a discussion within the EU about whether there was a need to define the basic aspects of a European understanding of democracy. At the request of the European Parliament (EP), the Office for the Promotion of Parliamentary Democracy (OPPD) identified the different definitions of international and regional organisations in order to underline their common key elements of democracy. Due to the danger of perceiving an EU-definition of democracy as a "unilateral imposition," it was argued that the EU should not adopt its own definition. Instead, the EU should "rely on an existing, comprehensive definition of democracy adopted by the largest possible group of countries, notably the UN General Assembly." (OPPD 2009) The following "essential elements" of democracy are emphasised:

- Respect for human rights and fundamental freedoms, inter alia, freedom of association and peaceful assembly, freedom of expression and freedom of opinion;
- The right to take part in the conduct of public affairs, directly or through freely chosen representatives, to vote and to be elected at a genuine periodic free elections by universal and equal suffrage and by secret ballot guaranteeing the free expression of the will of the people;
- A pluralistic system of political parties and organisations;
- Respect for the rule of law;
- The separation of powers and the independence of the judiciary;
- Transparency and accountability in public administration;
- Free, independent and pluralistic media. (OPPD, 2009: 6)[7]

Each enlargement signifies, for the Union, the spreading of peace and democracy in Europe by taking in new Member States. Within the accession process, in particular, thresholds concerning democracy and fundamental rights are stipulated. Article 49 TEU names, as a basic requirement for applying for membership, respect for and the willingness to promote the democratic values of the EU. Furthermore, the Copenhagen Criteria established in 1993 by the Council specify that possible candidates must provide stable institutions, which are able to guarantee democracy, the rule of law, human rights and respect for and protection of minorities (European Commission, 2014). Throughout the association process, the criteria are monitored and bound to a sharp conditionality. But these values are not only important during the enlargement time; they are also the basis for the existence and acting of the Union and the individual Member States. These shared values are anchored in Article 2 TEU and Article 6 TEU:

Article 2 (TEU) states that

> Union is founded on the values of respect for human dignity, freedom, democracy, equality, the rule of law and respect for human rights, including the rights of persons belonging to minorities. These values are common to the Member States in a society in which pluralism, non-discrimination, tolerance, justice, solidarity and equality between women and men prevail.

These are the values referred to in Article 49 TEU, which implies that the Member States are obliged to remain compliant to these fundamentals.[8] The EU clearly addresses its responsibility as a value community in cementing these fundamental principles into the Union's primary law. Indeed, they are the very basis for taking action in cases of infringement. Article 2 TEU demands the compliance of the Member States not only when they act on behalf of the EU, but also in any other – for example, national – contexts. As far as the outlined values are concerned, there is no distinction between the European level and matters of national sovereignty. In contrast, Article 6 TEU is limited to incidents that fall within the scope of EU law (EUAFR, 2013: 7–8).

The expression "community of values" is not just a European self-perception or a well-promoted image. The Union dedicates itself legally to democratic values and their defence. Since the developments in Hungary in 2010, it has become clear that the infringement of European values and the transformation of any EU Member State to an illiberal polity is not acceptable within the European context. The mechanism directly established for the protection of the fundamental values stated in Article 2 TEU is Article 7 TEU. It is frequently called the "nuclear option," as it is the severest instrument in defending fundamental rights.[9] Article 7 (2) TEU provides the pre-requisite for the sanctioning mechanism in Article 7 (3) TEU, which demands the identification of "the existence of a serious and persistent breach by the Member State." Only if these two steps are taken can political sanctions follow. These common provisions are clearly disconnected from EU legislative competences, as Member States are also liable under Article 2 TEU when they do not act under EU law. The three modes of intervention are bound to very demanding majority requirements, which could be one reason why the article has never been used to date. Until now, Article 7 TEU seemed "to be designed to threaten but not to actually apply" (EUAFR, 2013: p. 8).

Besides Article 7 TEU, there are three alternative instruments against democratic backsliding within the EU context:

- Use of the infringement procedures of the Articles 258 and 260 TFEU;
- Exert social pressure on the concerned Member State;
- Use of issue linkage. (Sedelmeier, 2014: 113)

In contrast to Article 7 TEU, the first instrument focuses on the infringement of obligations under the Treaties. In the context of fundamental rights, Article 258 and 260 TFEU can be applied when a Member State is non-compliant with specific values of Article 2 TEU that are separately anchored within the Treaty or EU secondary law, for example, non-discrimination on the grounds of gender, age, *etc.* The European Commission can launch such a procedures on its own, which can lead to a proceeding before the European Court of Justice (ECJ/CJEU), with the possibility of a financial sanction being applied to the Member State in question for steady non-compliance. These two instruments are the only ones explicitly mentioned in the Treaties in order to intervene against the breaching of liberal democratic principles. But another measure frequently used by international institutions is that of increasing social pressure on the country in question. This implies mainly public criticism and the shaming of the government in question for its non-compliance. This instrument can be used through the media or by means of open letters to the government. The actual threat of the opening an infringement procedure can also cause a change in the Member State's actions. Social pressure includes less public statements, too, such as, for example, an exchange between the EU institutions and the country in question in order to persuade the government of the "normative appropriateness of compliance" (Sedelmeier, 2014: 113). Issue linkage describes the connection between the demand to adhere to democratic standards with the possible suspension of rewards in another area. This can be expressed explicitly or in an indirect way. This is mostly effective if the Member State in question has strong preferences to obtain an agreement in a certain domain which requires high majority ratios. In contrast to the instruments mentioned to date, issue linkage is a rather unofficial means of enforcing compliance.

There are many suggestions for enlarging the EU toolkit in order to be more effective in reversing democratic backsliding. Jan-Werner Müller, for example, postulates a stronger role for national courts in order to protect fundamental rights, which mostly raises concerns about balancing out the relationship between the ECJ/CJEU and national constitutional courts and the primary legalistic responses to political challenges. Another possibility raised by Müller is to extend Article 7 TEU with a provision which makes it possible to expel a Member State completely (Müller, 2013a: 146-147). This would be a strong form of deterrent, but, considering that the European community is reluctant even to use the existing preventive mechanism of Article 7, this proposal is not very realistic. As Sedelmeier puts it, the main question concerning the effectiveness of all the actual and suggested instruments is whether the EU can anchor democracy from above. His comparative analysis of Hungary and Romania suggests a mixed result. The "EU might still have some hope of reversing democratic backsliding when faced with a pro-EU leadership with illiberal tendencies, but conversely, the EU's influence on Eurosceptic illiberal leaders might be especially limited" (Sedelmeier, 2014: 120).

In addition, it is worth mentioning that there are several traps into which researchers of the Europeanisation phenomena, and especially the conditionality mechanism, can fall. The first is connected to the democratic deficit debate. If we agree on the profound impact of Europeanisation beyond the EU's territory, we need to identify the key difference between the internal and the external dimension of governance. That is to say, while the former is concerned primarily with the *creation* of rules, as well as their implementation in national political systems, the external dimension is exclusively about the transfer of given EU rules and their adoption by non-Member States. One needs to see this phenomenon through the prism of the "democratic deficit problem," since transferring the rules outside and the impact of governance beyond the EU borders equates to exporting the "deficit problem" as well (Schimmelfennig and Sedelmeier, 2004: 661).

Secondly, even the famous Copenhagen criteria conditions are highly imperfect for a number of reasons. They are too broad, and what constitutes meeting them is open to interpretation, giving the EU considerable freedom in deciding upon what has to be done before compliance is achieved and membership (or even advancement in the application and accession procedure) granted. Certain functions or characteristics of governance are included in the third condition on the ability to assume the obligations of membership. This condition can be interpreted broadly by the EU. For example, the capacity to implement and enforce the *acquis* means that the EU is concerned with the entire judicial system. The necessity to administer EU regional aid means that the conditions include the creation of administrative units of subnational government equipped with a certain absorption capacity.[10] The very fact that Article 6 of the treaty confirmed the Copenhagen criteria (albeit with the exception of "respect for and protection of minorities") has been viewed as an attempt to reduce the sharp contrast between the rules for the existing members and the admission criteria for prospective newcomers (Pinelli, 2004). This may eventually generate frustration on the applicants' side especially, when confronted with the potential refusal of access.[11] In addition, the basic EU resource in external relations is its own credibility, and this capital is at risk in this context.[12] Certainly, not everybody who meets the criteria will be admitted, as the enlargement capacity of the EU is limited.

To date, the enlargement process, including the mechanism of conditionality, seemed to be the most effective transformative tool, mobilising the candidate and accession states to reform and meet the entrance criteria. However, the subsequent rounds of enlargement as well as the reform treaty negotiations have created not only external, but also internal, differentiation within the EU. Prior to the crises, the general assumption was that, whereas Member States would integrate at different speeds, they would all converge and end up at the same destination. Today, there seems to be a far greater acceptance that Member States may not end up at the same place, but may, instead, come to occupy permanently different statuses; some may be full members, others semi-members, quasi-members, former members and non-members. There appears to be a shift from a multi-speed Europe to a multi-status or structurally *differentiated* EU. And the neglect of the liberal, constitutional democracy values of some Member States cultivates this differentiation. Not only does it have profound economic and legal foundations, but the normative cleavages inside the EU are also more and more visible. As this text has shown, Brussels does not seem to have adequate instruments which would allow it to neutralise the illiberal tendencies in some parts of the EU's territory.

As is highlighted in the introduction to this volume, the story of the EU post-crises is one of a paradoxical mixture of openness and closure. It follows that a viable diagnosis of the EU polity post-crises must pay attention to the very factors that produced this mixture: the role of ideas and ideologies, the role of knowledge and cognition and the role of structural and institutional factors. Poland, as a representative case of the CEE region, exemplifies a normative shift in which certain ideas and concepts were neglected – such as liberal democracy (or liberalism as such). As a consequence of a cluster of countries following their own set of ideologies (for example, illiberalism or nationalism), we can observe the incoherence and maybe even the imbalance of the whole system (with the EU understood as a community of values). This creates the pre-conditions for a fragmented and segmented political order. Some parts of the political system challenge the entrenched ideologies, action logics and perceptions of how things ought to be done. Thus, the resulting incoherence challenges the de-segmentation capabilities at the very core of the EU system.

IV Conclusions

The year 1989 became a watershed for the CEE countries, when firstly Poland and Hungary, and then, in a "domino" effect, East Germany, Romania, Czechoslovakia and other states, including the Soviet Union in 1991, began their journey towards democratisation. However, from the perspective of time, we know that not all of them arrived at the final destination. The road from authoritarianism does not always lead to liberal democracies but sometimes leads to hybrid regimes or defective democracies. As the Polish and Hungarian cases show, neither is the road towards democracy a one-way street. After Orbán and Kaczyński took power, it soon became clear that de-democratisation is possible alongside de-Europeanisation, and that they interact with the other phenomena such as the crisis of 2007–2008 and its consequences, as well as the emerging fragmented political order in Europe.

An informal speech delivered on 26 July 2014 at a student campus in Baile Tusnad, Romania, by the Hungarian Prime Minister Viktor Orbán (2014) became a "baptizing moment" for CEE illiberalism. Orbán announced his vision of creating an "illiberal state," based upon the assumption that democracy and liberalism do not need to co-exist, even in the context of EU membership. Victor Orbán's concept of liberal democracy was defined in relation to the supposed failure of the Western liberal model. This pessimistic mood reflects the *Zeitgeist* of CEE, which is fuelled by transformation fatigue, on the one hand, and the end of Europeanisation conditionality, on the other. This lack of constructive co-ordinates brought about the democratic backsliding and worsening of the relationships with wider Europe. What we can observe is not only the incompatibility of values between the EU's core and its peripheries but also a paradigmatic shift in the way both sides perceive each other. On one side, countries like Poland and Hungary are seen as problematical cases, which threaten the fundamental values upon which the European integration project was constructed. On the other, the CEE states do not see in Brussels any solution, only a problem. Despite the in-flow of EU funds, the West is perceived as threatening the traditional values to which the region is attached, as the coloniser (in economic and cultural terms) and – what is worse from the perspective of the authoritarian governments in Warsaw and Budapest – as a scrutiniser of the standards of democracy in the governance process.

This illiberal turn, in political, economic, cultural and all other dimensions, creates a gap between the EU Member States devoted to pluralism, multi-culturalism and cosmopolitanism, on the one hand, and closedness, conservatism and nationalism, on the other. It also means a radical departure from the trajectory that the region took in 1989. As a result, it greatly contributes to the fragmentation of Europe – an important part of its political system questions the very norms and values upon which contemporary Europe was founded. Certainly, it co-exists with some of the trends present in the widely understood West (such as nativism in the US). Nevertheless the scale, depth and way in which the illiberalism observed in CEE articulates itself needs to be seen as a salient element of the emerging segmented political order in Europe.

In the introductory chapter to this volume, the editors formulated a set of assumptions and criteria for assessing the extent to which the EU is a segmented political system and how this concretely manifests itself. Contemporary Poland, governed by *PiS*, can be seen as a critical case which illustrates the emergence of such a segmentation in Europe's peripheries. The way in which the conservative-nationalist government in Warsaw perceives the EU (understood as Brussels, but also other capitals), the way in which it contests the fundamental values upon which the EU is based (for example, the rule of law), the way in which it promotes the hard Eurosceptic message, all serve intentionally to isolate itself from the EU's core. It contributes to the segmented political system by creating a cluster of EU Member States (together with Hungary and other CEE countries) that challenge the already existing normative order. And it is happening in the turbulent times in which the EU is itself undergoing radical changes as it tries to settle itself after the series of crises that it had to face in the last decade.

The new government in Warsaw has openly declared its preference for a more inter-governmental Europe. The supranational institutions (such as the EU Commission and the Court of Justice of the European Union [CJEU]) are treated as intrusive when they interfere with the domestic Polish constitutional order. It seems as though the *PiS* government has prioritised its missionary vision of Poland over the pragmatic compromise-building in everyday Brussels politics. It would preferably see a "scaled-down" EU in the future, instead of the intended deepening of the integration project. At a rhetorical level, this is also complimented by the traditional Germanophobic narrative, economic and political nationalism, as well as by neglecting the neoliberal order which brought so much social pain in the times of transition.

As a result, we can observe the *PiS* government contributing to the segmentation of the European political order on two levels: first, by demolishing the domestic institutions of constitutional democracy; and second, by questioning the supranational EU level of governance. At nation-state level, it violated the division of powers and the balance between them, and also destroyed many of the other standards of liberal democracy. It all happened in the face of Europe and with the broad acceptance of the Polish citizenry. At supranational level, it challenges the Commission's legitimacy in interfering in the constitutional systems of the Member States, it ignores the EU's decisions and actions in numerous spheres (for example, the Article 7 procedure) and, finally, it claims that it will not take into account the future judgments of the Court of Justice of the European Union taken against Poland. In the inter-governmental domain, it acts in a manner which is predominantly destructive or – at best – defensive, by trying to build "blocking coalitions," usually with the Hungarian or other delegations from the region. A cluster of countries is emerging on the EU's Eastern peripheries which is contributing to the construction of both differentiation and segmentation in Europe.

As has been already mentioned in the introduction to this volume, differentiated integration is associated not only with structural openness but also with cognitive and ideological openness. The analysts of EU differentiation underline the role of political conflict over interests, as well as over values and ideologies, as a major cause or driver of EU differentiation. The "big bang" enlargement of the Member States of the EU is highly diverse in cultural, linguistic, ethnic, economic, political, institutional and constitutional terms. Institutionally speaking, the internal structures of the EU Member States and the manner in which they organise their functions along territorial lines differ along a wide range of dimensions. All this leads to greater differentiation and also contributes to the emerging segmented political system in the EU.

Notes

1 Before going into detail on the post-2015 developments, it is important to point out that they are nothing new in Polish politics. Even between the parliamentary and presidential elections in 2005 and the parliamentary ballot in 2007, the Polish government was actively changing the constitutional set-up and interfered in the business of the independent media that expressed their fears for the fledgling democratic institutions in the country. Whether or not the actions of the *PiS* really amounted to a gradual undermining of Polish democracy is less and less debatable due to the growing consensus among scholars that it is democratic backsliding.

2 When *PiS* won the parliamentary elections for the first time and started participating in a coalition government.

3 When Viktor Orbán visited Poland on 7 January 2016, he only met Kaczyński – they spoke half-secretly in the South of Poland (in a region which historically belonged to Austro-Hungary). The absence of the foreign minister and the prime minister shows that, when the really important issues are discussed, it is Kaczyński who is the party to be met.

4 It is also important to remember that the term *conditionality* does not refer exclusively to the phenomena taking place within the EU's gravitational pull, but also, for example, in the case of states, and international and supranational organisations which require respect for human rights and democracy from third countries in development aid and trade. The recipients, in order to sustain the inflowing assistance, must take into account the donors' preferences. They may also prefer tied transfers because they do not want to be treated simply as poor relations. They prefer transfers justified by some higher purpose – for example, transition, innovation, adjustments to world standards, *etc*. It is rather rare for developed countries or their organisations to give support without conditions, more often taking the form of negotiated aid.

5 The argument supports Olsen's observation that the EU's effectiveness in institution-building and policy change, even within the Union, has varied across institutional spheres such as competition policy, monetary affairs, external and internal security and culture (March and Olsen, 1989).

6 It is argued that, among the applicants, only Poland had the luxury of being able to engage in hard bargaining, for Polish negotiators assumed that factors such as the country's size and geo-political importance would prevent the EU from excluding the country from the first group of accessions.

7 The definition is a normative one. There are no institutional or process-oriented components mentioned. This is logical, because the democratic systems within the EU are diverse but are still considered to belong to one form of government. "This suggests, that it is not the formal nature of the democracy but its practice that determines its characteristics" (OPPD, 2009: 7).

8 Article 6 TEU names three different legal sources resulting in obligations for the Member States. The first one is the Charter of Fundamental Rights of the European Union, which is not part of the Treaty of Lisbon but does have the same legal value. The second source mentioned for guiding the Union's actions is the European Convention on Human Rights. Finally, the common constitutional traditions of the Member States concerning fundamental rights is to be the general principles of EU law. It is outlined in this article that these provisions are not supposed to extend the competences of the Union.

9 The article provides the possibility for the Council to decide by qualified majority to suspend certain treaty rights of the Member State in question, including its voting rights. But before this option can be considered, two conditions have to be fulfilled. The preventive mechanism in Article 7 (1) TEU consists mainly of a warning by the Council to a Member State, where "a clear risk of a serious breach" has been determined.

10 On the other hand, the "club membership rules" were clearly settled not long before those of the Union itself. Reference to the principles of liberty, democracy and respect for human rights as the "grounds" of the EU was not included within EU primary law until the Treaty of Amsterdam.

11 After "consuming" the costs of adaptation, the potential lack of reward may create dissatisfaction both for the applicant's political élites as well as for its citizens.

12 The credibility of the EU's threat to withhold rewards in cases of non-compliance and, conversely, its promise to deliver the reward in cases of rule adoption (Schimmelfennig and Sedelmeier, 2004: 665).

References

Bachmann, Klaus, and Dominik Hejj (2018), "'Illiberale Demokratien' Bauplaene aus Ungarn un Polen", *Osteuropa*, 68. Jahrgang / Heft 3–5: 127–148.

Buras, Piotr, and Zsuzsanna Vegh (2018), "Stop Bruessel! Polen und Ungarn in der Europaeische Union", *Osteuropa*, 68. Jahrgang / Heft 3–5: 99–114.

Dawson, James, and Sean Hanley (2016), "East Central Europe: The Fading Mirage of the 'Liberal Consensus'", *Journal of Democracy*, 27 (1): 20–34.

European Commission (2014), European Commission, *Communication from the Commission to the European Parliament and the Council. A New EU Framework to Strengthen the Rule of Law*, 2014.

EUAFR (2013), "The European Union as a Community of Values: Safeguarding Fundamental Rights in Times of Crisis", available at: https://fra.europa.eu/en/publication/2013/european-union-community-values-safeguarding-fundamental-rights-times-crisis, p. 7.

Fischer, Joschka (2015), "The Fascism of the Affluent", Project Syndicate – The World's Opinion Page, available at: www.project-syndicate.org/commentary/affluent-fascists-western-politics-by-joschka-fischer-2015-12, last accessed 30 December 2018.

Frączyk, Jacek (2015), "Renacjonalizacja banków: Po spadkach kursów na GPW to możliwe. Pieniądze na to już są", available at: www.money.pl/banki/wiadomosci/artykul/renacjonalizacja-bankow-po-spadkach-kursow,181,0,1977013.html, last accessed 12 December 2018.

Fukuyama, Francis (2015), "Why is Democracy Performing so Poorly?", *Journal of Democracy*, 26 (1): 11–20.

Grabbe, Heather (2002), "European Union Conditionality and the Acquis Communautaire", *International Political Science Review*, 23 (3): 249–268.

Graziano, Paolo, and Maarten Vink (2007), "Introduction", in: Paolo Graziano and Maarten Vink (eds), *Europeanization: New Research Agendas*, Basingstoke: Palgrave Macmillan, pp. 8–9.

Hughes, James, Gwendolyn Sasse, and Claire Gordon, (2004), "Conditionality and Compliance in EU's Eastward Enlargement: Regional Policy and the Reform of Sub-national Government", *Journal of Common Market Studies*, 42 (3): 523–551.

Kalukin, Rafał (2015), "Po drugiej stronie lustra", *Newsweek Polska*, nr 50 / 7–13 December 2015, pp. 26–28.

Kornai, Janos (2015), "Hungary's U-Turn: Retreating from Democracy", *Journal of Democracy*, 26 (3): 34–48.

Krastev, Ivan (2014), "From Politics to Protest", *Journal of Democracy*, 25 (4): 5–19.

Krzymowski, Michał (2015), "Naczelnik testuje prezydenta", *Newsweek Polska*, nr 50 / 7–13 December 2015, pp. 20–25.

Levitsky Steven, and Lucan Way (2015), "The Myth of Democratic Recession", *Journal of Democracy*, 26 (1): 45–58.

March, James G., and Johan P. Olsen (1989), *Rediscovering Institutions: The Organizational Basis of Politics*, New York: The Free Press.

Massey, Andrew (2004), "Modernisation as Europeanisation. The Impact of the European Union on Public Administration", *Policy Studies*, 25 (1): 19–33.

Merkel, Wolfgang, Hans-Jürgen Puhle, Aurel Croissant, Claudia Eicher, and Peter Thiery (2003), *Defekte Demokratie. Band 1: Theorie*, Opladen: Leske + Budrich.

Migalski, Marek (2015), "Platonizm prezesa PiS", *Rzeczpospolita*, 8 December 2015, p. 12.

Mong, Attila (2015), "Polska na węgierskiej ścieżce. A teraz zapnijcie pasy", *Newsweek Polska*, nr 50 / 7–13 December 2015, pp. 30–32.

Müller, Jan-Werner (2013), *Wo Europa endet. Ungarn, Brüssel und das Schicksal der liberalen Demokratie*, Berlin: Suhrkamp Verlag.

Müller, Jan-Werner (2013a), "Defending Democracy within the EU", *Journal of Democracy*, 24 (2): 146–147.

Olszewski, Michał (2016), "Jakiś mały rozlew krwi", *Gazeta Wyborcza*, sobota-niedziela, 2–3 January 2016, p. 16.

OPPD (2009), "Democracy Revisited. Which Notion of Democracy for the EU's External Relations?", Brussels, 2009, p. 5.

Orbán, Victor (2014), Prime Minister's Office, Prime Minister Viktor Orbán's Speech at the 25th Bálványos Summer Free University and Student Camp, 26 July 2014, Tusnádfürdő (Băile Tuşnad), Romania.

Pinelli, Cesare (2004), "Conditionality and Enlargement in Light of EU Constitutional Developments", *European Law Journal*, 10 (3): 354–362.

Pop-Eleches, Grigore (2007), "Historical Legacies and Post-Communist Regime Change", *The Journal of Politics*, 69 (4): 908–926.

Sadurski, Wojciech (2016), In an Interview Entitled: "Autokracja w sercu Europy", *Newsweek Polska*, 2/2016, 4–10 January 2016, pp. 18–21.

Schimmelfennig, Frank, and Ulrich Sedelmeier (2004), "Governance by Conditionality: EU Rule Transfer to the Candidate Countries of Central and East Europe", *Journal of European Public Policy*, 11 (4): 669–687.

Schmitter, Philippe C. (2015), "Crisis and Transition, but Not Decline", *Journal of Democracy*, 26 (1): 32–44.

Sedelmeier, Ulrich (2014), "Anchoring Democracy from Above? The European Union and Democratic Backsliding in Hungary and Romania after Accession", *Journal of Common Market Studies*, 52 (1): 105–121, 113.

Skarżyńska, Krystyna (2016), In an Interview Entitled "Kruchość i siła", *Polityka* nr ½ (3041), 01–01, 12 January 2016, pp. 26–28.

TEU (2007), *Consolidated Version of the Treaty on the European Union*, Treaty of Maastricht.

TFEU (2007), *Consolidated Version of the Treaty on the Functioning of the European Union*, Treaty of Lisbon.

Tusk, Donald (2015), In an Interview Entitled: "Co mi zrobią, jak mnie złapią", *Polityka*, 51/52 (3040), 16–27 December 2015, pp. 24–29.

Wielowieyska, Dominika (2016), "Rewolucja rozpoczęta", *Gazeta Wyborcza*, nr 5 (8642), 8 January 2016, p. 1.

Żakowski, Jacek (2015), "Państwo siły i państwo prawa", *Wirtualna Polska*, available at: www.wp.pl, last accessed 9 December 2015.

Zawadzki, Mariusz (2015), "Ameryka niepokoi się sytuacją w Polsce", *Gazeta Wyborcza* czwartek-piątek, 31 December 2015 – 1 January 2016, p. 4.

Zoll, Andrzej (2015), In an Interview "Dziś Wieczorem", TVP Info, 9 December 2015.

10

NEWSPAPER PORTRAYAL OF THE EU IN CRISES IN THE CZECH REPUBLIC, SLOVAKIA AND HUNGARY

The Union's imagined linearity[1]

Max Steuer[2]

I Introduction

Are crises perceived as an opportunity for developing novel structures and institutions? The EU, in particular in the period from 2008 onwards, is certainly a case in point to study whether an "innovative potential" is recognised in crises, given that it is considered to have been marked by quite a few of them. To the extent that perceptions can shape realities, perceptions about the crises in the European Union (EU) can tell us something about how the EU's future is thought through by the actors in focus. Knowledge about these mosaics of perceptions can then be used to see what was omitted from the debates (and the way in which they were framed) or how these debates made some alternatives inconceivable as opposed to others. To bring us a step closer to such knowledge, this chapter looks at a particular amplifier for the discourse about the "crises" in the EU, that of quality newspapers. To the extent to which newspapers, as well as other media, can influence citizens' views and public opinion in the EU (De Vreese and Boomgaarden, 2006), including their reflections on the crises (Michailidou and Trenz, 2015: 239); channel the opinions of the political élites; and even trigger changes in support for particular political forces, their role is substantial for the development of relations between the citizens and the élites and, eventually, of a European public sphere (Koopmans and Statham, 2010). In turn, quality newspapers could be presumed to adhere to calmer, more evidence-based assessments than tabloids or the new media. Hence, they should be able to evaluate the alternative scenarios and trajectories for the Union in a more nuanced manner than other media, and the absence of such an approach in their framing of the debate might signal a deeper trend across the whole media environment.

This chapter looks at six Central European newspapers that, besides being seldom studied, bring the additional value of offering a better understanding of the sentiments towards the EU in relation to the crises in this region. The selection of the Czech Republic, Slovakia and Hungary includes one country which is in the Eurozone (Slovakia) and two countries which are not. Presumably, the portrayal of the crises in economic terms in relation to the EU would be stronger in a Eurozone Member State. Furthermore, the selection of a country that exhibits trends of democratic backsliding (Hungary) (*e.g.*, Greskovits, 2015) and two countries which display such trends less explicitly helps us to understand whether the Hungarian press, operating in a country with vocal anti-European élites and several restrictions on press freedom at that time, displayed more anti-European tendencies than their Czech or Slovak counterparts.

The analysis shows how the portrayal of the EU in crises during an almost nine-year period, from the outbreak of the financial crisis in the United States (US) (Fabbrini, 2017) until a few days after the referendum on Brexit at the end of June 2016, followed an imagined linearity, finding no space for the vocabulary of a multi-dimensional development of EU integration along the lines of the framework in this book. While this gives rise to the claim that the newspaper portrayal enhances cognitive segmentation by locking the debate into a set of simplified cleavages, the overall rareness of the perception that the EU will successfully overcome the crises and develop in ways that enhance public well-being points to potential fragmentation marked by significant polarisation and the readiness to search for "alternatives" that do not account for the EU at all. Viewing the data capturing the portrayal until a few days after the Brexit referendum from a "post-crises" perspective stimulates doubts about the capacity of public language to "catch up" with the actual developments of the EU, and, in relation to that, the capacity of the process of segmentation to at least retain, if not enhance, the current level of democratic legitimacy of the EU. The absence of an "imagination of segmentation" in the discourse about the crises reinforces the risks that this process poses for democratic legitimacy (Eriksen, 2018; see, also, Fossum in this volume).

The argument is developed in four steps. Firstly, the case for a dialogue between theory and data for the conceptualisation of crisis-framing in the EU when studying media discourse about this phenomenon is introduced. This is followed by a classification of three categories of crisis frames, which are applicable for an empirical analysis of a particular portion of media discourse. While the content analysis of six Central European newspapers here applies an inductive logic, the basic classification of crises, as well as the contexts in which they are likely to be presented, helps us to establish the main patterns in the empirical data. Thirdly, the summary of dominant frames shows not only how the EU has been portrayed as being in a complex crisis in the period under examination, but how the EU institutions represented by "European élites" have also come to be perceived as the actors responsible for it. The praise for opposition to the joint European solutions by the Visegrád Four Member States, which is visible in some portions of the data, remains at odds with the general desire to develop joint European solutions and to avoid the fragmentation of the Union.

Finally, the overreaching trend emerging in the images from the newspapers analysed is that of a linear portrayal of the EU's development both in relation to and after the crises.

II Constructing political orders as ways out of crises

Crisis is a signal word that can attract the attention of an audience, since it entails seriousness, urgency and a need for immediate, even drastic, changes to overcome it. As such, studying the portrayal of the EU in relation to this signal word captures a non-negligible portion of the portrayal of the EU as a whole, including the ideas related to its political ordering "post-crises." This section advocates the "liberation" of our inquiries into the EU's portrayal from approaches taking the crises as objectively given facts as well as those which attribute a predetermined, top-down content to this contested concept. In doing so, it paves the way for analytically studying the framing of the EU in crises and its ways out of the crises in the media selected. Clearly, this landscape underwent rapid developments in a very short time, including from the academic perspective. The edited volume by Kyriakos Demetriou (2015) was one of the first to put the crisis at the centre of attention in relation to the EU, although it connected it largely to economic terms[3] and largely omitted the discussion on phenomena such as crisis framing or multiple, mutually reinforcing crises. Shortly after, there was a terminological shift from speaking about an EU in "crisis" to an EU in "crises," emphasising their multiplicity (Fossum and Menéndez, 2014: 5; Laffan, 2016), but the justifications for using the term to capture particular political developments remained blurred. Even Jürgen Habermas, who offered a careful analysis of the process of emergence of a societal crisis more than 40 years ago (Habermas, 1975: 1–31), appeared to take the crisis for granted (Habermas, 2012, 2015, 2016).[4] Some interpreters of Habermas' work, among others, on the concept of the crisis (Genna and Wilson, 2016) also appeared to remain unconcerned about the determination of the criteria that "create a crisis" from a certain set of developments.[5]

This approach might look like a legitimate terminological shortcut, but it does not tell us about the process *through which* a set of developments becomes a crisis – in other words, how, by whom and for what purposes it is *constructed* as one. Crisis construction can become a powerful tool in the hands of those who prefer to emphasise the EU's weaknesses while remaining silent about its strengths. It can evoke the emotion of fear from uncertainty caused by unclear or unknown threats beyond the horizon (see Altheide, 2002; see, also, Cross and Ma, 2015a, 2015b). As crises are in contrast with the "normal" state of affairs (cf., Schmitt, 2006), they might be interpreted as a threat to the fundamental standards or values that a particular group considers as vital for their lives. Thereby, they can serve as a trigger for demands for substantial changes in various directions, and potentially become a means of demagogy and manipulation. While it is beyond the scope of this chapter to uncover the process of crisis construction fully, it is necessary to highlight how powerful a potential it has for "sensing" the EU today. Recent scholarly work has identified the complexities[6] in the concept of "crisis" (Runciman, 2016; Roitman, 2016) in abstract terms. However, less emphasis has been placed on crisis construction in the EU context, and the construction of *ways out of the crises* in particular. Thus, a gap emerges in observing to what extent certain developments in the political reality are more or less conceivable through the lens of the dominant frames portrayed in the public sphere. By stressing some possibilities as opposed to others, the scope of public imagination about the EU's development might, in turn, be narrowed.

Precisely because of the contested content of the concept of crises and the lack of criteria determining their start and finish, analyses interested in crisis construction should adopt a bottom-up approach. Here, crises are those that are talked about as such in the public sphere. In the context of the EU, crises have to be linked to it, assuming the EU as being (co-)responsible for their occurrence or influenced by them in its nature as an entity, in its decision-making processes, or in terms of deliverables. The bottom-up approach calls for empirical studies that capture the understanding of crises by the various political actors. The difficulty is that the scope of the public discourse has become broad and multifaceted, unfolding at various levels simultaneously. Analyses of the specific inputs of one group of actors would thus necessarily be biased towards their preferences and interpretations. This limitation is, to an extent, overcome when the portion of discourse subject to analysis is that in the media. While the media cannot be conceived as merely a channel of opinions of other actors, media discourse (Fairclough, 1995) encompasses the voices of many other actors. We have to be aware that these do not add up to a precise representative sample, because the media have their political positions as well (Eilders, 2002; Ho and Quinn, 2008), and can be subject to various biases (Entman, 2007; Kuypers, 2002). Even so, they are the most suitable actor for an analysis of the portrayal of the EU in crises because of the variety of other actors who channel their opinions through them, and the way in which they are linked to public perception. Such an analysis needs to be aware of the mechanism at play in the media portrayal of an issue area, known as *framing*. The next section fulfils this requirement by identifying a set of loose framing patterns that enable an empirical study of the portrayal of the EU in crises in quality newspapers.

III Reporting about the crises in quality newspapers: Framing patterns

The previous section outlined the significance of crisis construction and the capacity of the portrayal of the EU in crises to preclude certain forms of its further development as opposed to others. Framing, then, is the tool for crisis construction, and this section provides a way to capture how this tool has been used in (and possibly by) the selected media. In contemporary studies of issue portrayal, it has become clear that focusing descriptively on the content cannot provide an appropriate picture of its message, not to mention the implications that the message carries. Instead, messages are constructed through framing, "the process of culling a few elements of perceived reality and assembling a narrative that highlights connections among them to promote a particular interpretation" (Entman, 2007: 164). Frames can be created by emphasising selected facts over others and placing them into a certain context, but they can also create an "imagined reality."

In the discourse about crises, framing is of special importance, because crisis has a strong subjective element that can hardly, if at all, be determined in a precise form (see Roitman, 2013). Moreover, crisis can capture the attention of a target group in favour of some, as opposed to other, policy solutions, when these are argued to reduce or even eradicate the causes that are supposed to have brought it to life. In addition, in the chain at work between the (perceived) causes and consequences of the crisis, the capacity to produce associations with individuals' own lives (*e.g.*, through living conditions, security or the possibility that their political voices matter), it displays precisely some of those characteristics that Beate Kohler-Koch (2000: 528) deems necessary for a "concept to become a frame of reference."

The contemporary EU is strongly prone to crisis framing. Since the 1990s, writings about the EU in some kind of crisis have proliferated enormously. While, since 2008, the economic crisis (for which terms such as *euro, financial* or *(sovereign) debt crisis* are also used, not necessarily synonymously) has been an obvious example, the EU has been debated as being in various types of crisis, such as the enlargement crisis (Vobruba *et al.*, 2003) before that. Yet, the economic crisis marks the beginning of a "crisis period" in which no fewer than nine crises can be observed (Bengoetxea, 2015: 62–63). But does each of these crises share certain characteristics? Is there a unifying criterion, one that recognised them as crises? Or are these the crises that are being "talked about" in some form or another in various public *fora*? If so, what features can be identified in these discourses? To whom do these discourses attribute the responsibility for each crisis, and how do they understand the desirable resolution of the crises for the EU's future?

Existing research has identified that there is a widespread tendency in the international media to display crisis-related events in a negative setting, as an existential threat to EU integration (Cross and Ma, 2015a, 2015b). Cross and Ma note that "it would also be valuable to include local and other language media coverage within member states." Recent studies have gone deeper into the unpacking of the difference between crises in objective terms and their portrayal at the domestic level; however, they have been overwhelmingly restricted to one crisis (the frontrunners being the "Euro crisis" and the "refugee crisis") and have examined traditional or new media in Western or Southern Europe (Cock *et al.*, 2018; Fotopoulos and Kaimaklioti, 2016; Joris, Puustinen, and d'Haenens, 2018; Kaiser and Königslöw, 2017; Myria and Rafał, 2017).[7] In one case, the framing by transnational European media (but not restricted to crisis) was placed under scrutiny (Williams and Toula, 2017). As such, the possible interplay between the portrayal of different crises and their consequences in relation to each other remains in the shadow of scholarly attention.

While the frames themselves should not be pre-determined but should rather emerge from the data, three general categories for identifying them were chosen with the purpose of exploring, in particular, the interpretations of the EU's trajectories of development in relation to crises. Firstly, it is the category of "EU institutions *versus* Member States." This is present with emphasis on one or both as the actors in focus, or the evaluations of the EU institutions' (the Commission, the Parliament) as opposed to the Member States' (and the Council's) decisions in the context of crisis. The second category captures the performance of the EU in the crises. This shows to what extent there is pessimism which persists about the crisis, meaning whether the EU will break up or fail in some other form due to not being able to handle the crisis. While it can be assumed that more optimistic references are those that do not deal with the crisis at all, the depth of the "crisis-related pessimism" is still an open question. The final category addresses the future of the EU in crisis more explicitly. This includes frames on what the EU should or should not look like in terms of the distribution of decision-making powers and the depth of further integration. It also highlights what ideas about the structure and development of EU integration are present (if at all) in the media discourse. These categories have been considered for the major crises, the portrayal of which has emerged from the data (the economic crisis, the Ukraine crisis and the "migration/refugee crisis"). The next section explains how the data were collected and analysed, and discusses the value of looking at (some) Visegrád countries from a contemporary perspective.

IV Content analysis of newspaper portrayal: The Cases of the Czech Republic, Slovakia and Hungary

Media discourse on the EU in crises can be identified in the broad discourse about the EU in a simple way – if the media portray the EU in crises, they mention both in some form. While a keyword search allows us to identify the whole population in the dataset,[8] these keywords determine its scope. Thus, the frames identified with a bottom-up approach for the EU in crisis do not necessarily match with those for the EU in general.

This study analyses[9] an original dataset in three languages to identify the crisis frames at work in three countries of the Visegrád Four. These countries have recently become known as voices of an "alternative" to the "European mainstream" in certain EU policy fields, thus raising doubts about whether they still want to remain within the core of EU integration.[10] In the descriptive part, basic statistics are provided about the incidences of articles devoted to the various crises in the newspapers analysed. Then, the three frames are evaluated based upon their incidence in articles on the various crises. This shows which kinds of reactions are more common with the respective "crises" upon which the newspapers are focusing.

The population of 1,347 articles (Figure 10.1)[11] includes a variety of crises in relation to the EU. Out of the more than 50 types of crises identified here, three stand out, in accordance with the assumptions of this analysis: the economic crisis, the Ukraine crisis and the "migration/refugee crisis."[12] The fourth and fifth categories can be found in those of "crises" (when the multiplicity of crises was explicitly highlighted in the article) and "complex crisis" (when, instead of naming a sphere that is "in crisis," the article referred to an overreaching crisis of the EU). For example, Friss (2012) writes about a "double crisis" that emerged in the first decade of the twenty-first century in the EU, "one strand of which is economic-financial, and the other is institutional, affecting the Union and the European liberal parliamentary democracies to various degrees." Another example is that of a German political scientist (Stier, 2015a) who argues that

> Europe is in a deep crisis. At the beginning of the year [2015], it struggled with financial and economic problems, while the current crisis is political. It is also a moral crisis, as the basic values of the Union are being questioned.

The Slovak president Andrej Kiska (2015) has also been in favour of the interpretation of the "crises," voicing that

> In the last quarter-century, since the fall of the Iron Curtain, Europe and the global world experienced several serious crises. But, in its complexity

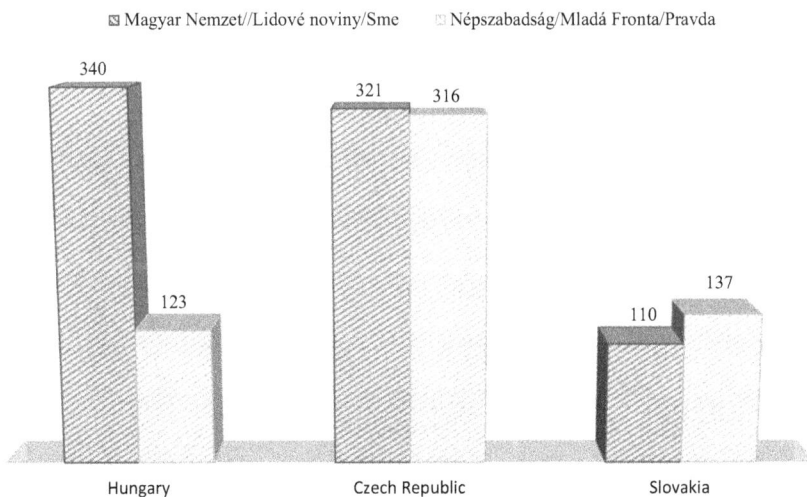

FIGURE 10.1   Number of articles in each newspaper.

Source: author

and uncertainty, the world is, in the present times, unsettlingly, more unstable than it has been during the lifetimes of most of us.

With over a hundred mentions, "complex crisis" and "crises" are powerful enough to be considered as distinct frames. On their own, however, they do not tell us much about the implications of such an interpretation of the crises for the future of the EU, about the relationship between Member States and EU institutions or about the attribution of responsibility for the causes of the crises. Figure 10.2 shows that references to the main "types" of crises are, for the most part, evenly distributed, with some small exceptions. Two can be pointed out. Firstly, the Czech press paid comparatively greater attention to the "(im-) migration/refugee crisis," while the Slovak and the Hungarian press gave greater prominence to the economic crisis in general.[13] Secondly, the Ukraine crisis was comparatively more referred to in the Hungarian newspapers than in the Czech and Slovak ones.

Importantly, the "migration/refugee" crises occupied the overall attention of the newspapers to a previously unwitnessed extent in the crisis discourse. With 557 (241 on the "refugee"/"humanitarian" crisis, and 329 on the "(im-)migra-tion" crisis) incidences, it outnumbered both the economic crisis (310 incidences) and the Ukraine crisis (171 incidences). Two newspapers (both Czech ones, see Editorial Board, 2016a, 2016b) created a separate category for articles on this "crisis," which frequently made it into the headlines as well. In contrast to the economic crisis, few clues were given to explain why the events that were being reported should be considered as a "crisis."[14] For these reasons, the "migration/

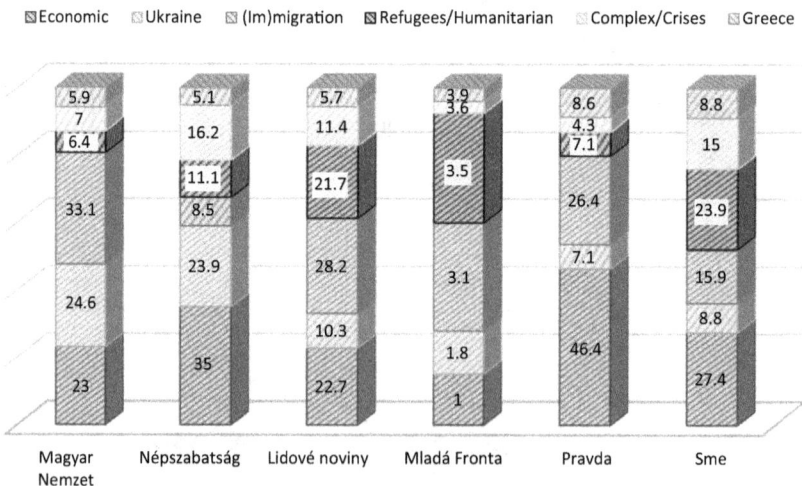

FIGURE 10.2 Incidences of the most common types of crises in the analysed articles (in %).

Source: author

refugee" crisis is an exemplary case of crisis construction, whereby the crisis emerges from the way in which certain events are reported, rather than by crossing a pre-determined line between the normal state of affairs and the point of crisis.

V Frame category 1: The EU versus Member States

Beyond the steep increase in the frequency of the portrayal of the EU in "crisis" in the last two years, new frames can be identified in some of the common dilemmas that the crisis discourse brings about, namely, which actor is at the centre of attention of the pieces reporting on crises, who is responsible for the crises in question and how the future of the EU is perceived in relation to the crises. In the first category, the population of articles allows us to distinguish between two common positions (see Figures 10.3 and 10.4), emphasising either the EU as a community of its Member States, or highlighting the actions of the EU institutions (particularly of the Commission). As these frames emerge from the overall tone of the articles rather than a particular dichotomy (as opposed to the infrequent, but present frame that explicitly contrasts the EU and Member States), both these frames can be considered to be weak (see Atikcan, 2015: 22–27).

In this category, there are several new frames, though, that gained prevalence in the context of the "migration/refugee crisis." Firstly, there is the frame of Turkey (see Figure 10.4), which presents the country's claims *vis-à-vis* the EU

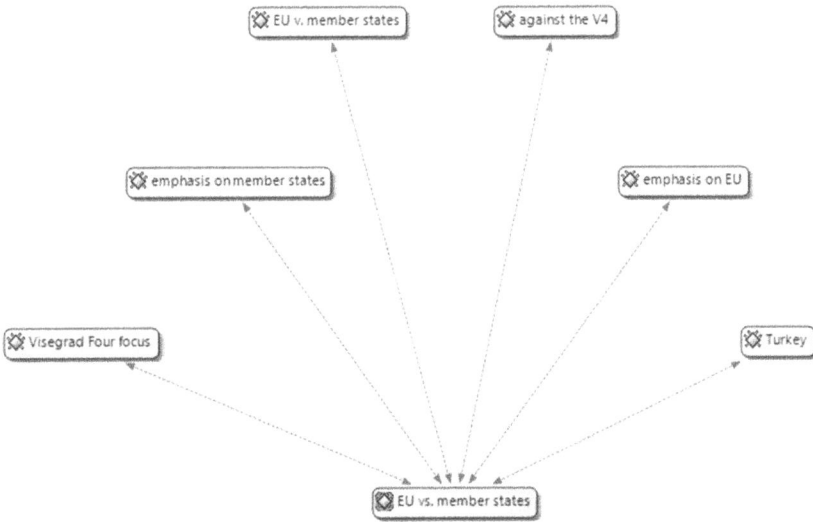

FIGURE 10.3 Frames in the first category – the actor in focus.

Source: author

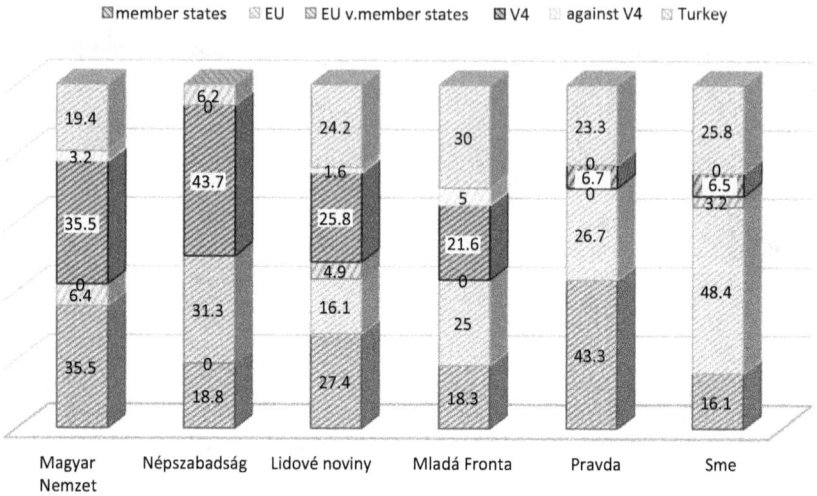

☒member states ☒ EU ☒ EU v.member states ☒ V4 ☒ against V4 ☒ Turkey

FIGURE 10.4 Incidences of the most common frames in the first category (in % of the total number of included articles into the category separately for each newspaper).

Source: author[15]

in exchange for it "stopping the refugees." For instance, an article entitled "The Turks can Come without Visas" (MTI, 2015b), reports about the "important question" of one of the European Council meetings: "with what kind of concessions they can reciprocate the help offered by Turkey in the refugee crisis."

Secondly, in a number of articles, a specific focus on Visegrád Four (V4) is present. Although this focus does not go beyond short descriptions of some of the V4's positions or actions in all of them, with 64 articles containing such a reference, it is strong enough to be considered a frame on its own. The core of this frame is in referring to the summits of the V4 in which they articulated their opposition to the "EU approach" the loudest. One example is a press release on the extraordinary V4 summit with the participation of Macedonia and Bulgaria on 15 February 2016, reproduced in *Mladá Fronta* (ČTK, 2016c):

> If control of the external European borders is not improved and the migration influx is not stopped, the situation could spiral out of control. Failure in this area could cast doubt upon the very foundations of the European Union.

Notwithstanding the few articles which explicitly criticise the V4's rebellion against the refugee re-location schemes, the majority does not praise them either, but remains at a descriptive level with no normative position. Hence, despite the undoubted presence of this frame, the articles (in this period analysed at least) generally do not argue for the Union's fragmentation. Another question is whether *the effect* of such a portrayal of the EU could manifest in greater acceptability of divergent voices about the future of EU integration, which is discussed in the subsequent categories.

VI Frame category 2: The performance of the EU

Turning to the perception of the EU's results in the crises, *i.e.*, what the Union can or cannot deliver to concrete target groups, there is a clear negative, linear evaluation emerging from the articles under study. The variations on the "failure," or at least the "weakening," of the EU as a result of the crises (Figure 10.5) clearly outweigh the positive notions of the EU's strength and resilience. This could be somewhat expected, given the type of framing that tends to accompany crises (including those which serve to produce and deepen fear). However, the absence of views of crises as an opportunity for renewal and positive reforms is striking. Moreover, a rather massive opposition against what is perceived to be the "European élite" or "European bureaucracy" is clearly visible from the articles, particularly in Czech media and in the Hungarian *Magyar Nemzet*.

A few examples of this negative framing, which creates a linear binary opposition between the citizens of the Member States and the "European élites," are as follows. In an interview with a pro-Russian political scientist in the *Magyar*

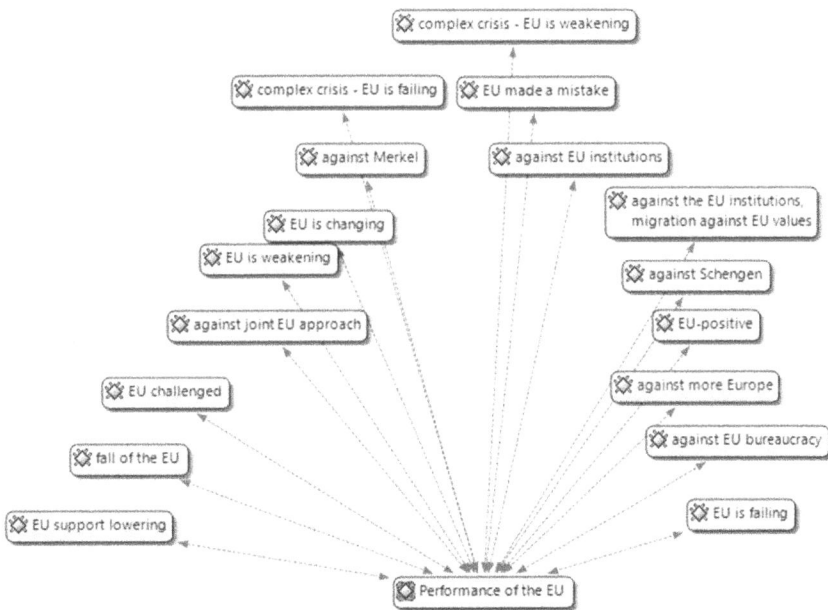

FIGURE 10.5   Frames in the second category – the evaluation dimension.

Source: author

Nemzet (*Hungarian Nation*), the interviewee vehemently argued that both the American and the European élite exert pressure on countries such as Russia and Hungary, allegedly for three reasons: "the economic relations with Russia, the striving for independence, and the questioning of the exclusiveness of liberal values" (Stier, 2015b). Furthermore, the opinion of Mr. Viktor Orbán that the "European political élite sits in an ideological bubble" (MTI, 2015a, with particular reference to the approach towards migration) made it to the headlines of the same newspaper. His view that "'Brussels makes a mistake' when it focuses on the re-location of refugees among the Member States instead of protecting its borders" (ČTK, 2016a) made it to the Slovak newspaper *Sme*.

Another example of the anti-European élite frame is that of the Czech philosopher Miloslav Bednář (2016), who, in *Lidové noviny*, referred to a view of Jiří Weigl, (the Head of Office of the former Czech President Václav Klaus) that is illustrative and worth quoting at length:

> The main ideological-political line of the EU has [...] intentional and substantial participation in the migration influx to Europe. [...] European élites see, in this migration, a new opportunity to use this crisis to exacerbate further the tension for an integrational transformation of Europe in accordance with their views. It is not just an effort to strengthen further the power of the bureaucracy in Brussels [...] with forced quotas for accepting immigrants. Progressive visionaries see in migration a core ally that can disrupt the homogeneity of nation-states and the national identity of their inhabitants [...].

Duhan (2015) argues along the same lines:

> The technocratic and moralising approach of European élites is telling about their crisis too. It shows their weak link to their societies, not only to populations, but also their culture, nation and civilisation. They ceased feeling solidarity with Europe and its legacy. [...]

This frame of attribution of responsibility for migration (portrayed in a hostile way) to the "European élite" is deepened by labelling it as a phenomenon that "plays alongside the lines" of this élite's plans. The mild element of a (European) conspiracy entailed in this frame makes it more attractive to anyone searching for seemingly plausible explanations for the above-average numbers of refugees arriving, which are an alternative to the mainstream explanations.

What Viktor Orbán is in the Hungarian press, the former Czech president Václav Klaus represents even more vividly in the Czech press. As an ardent opponent of the EU, Klaus managed to express his views in the press on numerous occasions. In an older interview, Klaus (then still president) clearly stated that

> I would defend Europe, I would not defend the EU. I think that it is an unfortunate development that took place in Europe; I would not wish

Europe anything wrong. And that it all plays out in the way it does, that is extremely sad. (Krist, 2009)

Klaus also found several followers whose voices are prominently reflected in the two Czech newspapers of the sample. Some of the most extreme positions in the course of the "migration/refugee" crisis were represented by MEP Petr Mach for the *Party of Free Citizens*, who claimed that the quotas are a "dictate of the EU" that, if not withdrawn, leave the Czech Republic with no choice but to exit the EU altogether (Havlická, 2015). Others, such as the chairman of the former party of Václav Klaus, and Petr Fiala, himself a professor of political science, use milder, but (as far as the position on quotas goes) similar rhetoric:

> We are being forced to [accept] solutions that are not good [referring to the Commission's proposal on relocation schemes].
>
> *(Kotalík, 2016)*

In Slovakia, former Prime Minister Robert Fico occasionally occupied the role of the critic of the European élites. In an interview for the Czech newspaper *Mladá Fronta*, which was reproduced/re-printed in the Slovak newspaper *Pravda*, he raised doubts that the EU "could stop migration."

> I am asking, are we really leading the Union to self-destruction?
>
> *(SITA, 2016a, see also Palata, 2016)*

One of his ministers at the time, and the chief of his party's election campaign, conveyed a similar message:

> if the EU does not enter into an open dialogue with its citizens, radicals will seize this initiative. For decades, things have been done in a stealthy way so that the EU becomes a super-state.
>
> *(SITA, 2016b)*

The representatives of the executive were supported in this rhetoric by some opposition leaders, such as the chairman of the Party of the Hungarian Community, who was especially outspoken in denouncing the quotas:

> the quotas could not work, and it is actually very undemocratic decision-making on the part of Brussels, that it wants to force the quotas upon respective states.
>
> *(Cuprík and Vrabcová, 2016)*

Some journalists offered similar opinions:

> If someone sets the states of the Union apart now, it is the Commission together with the similarly oriented European Parliament. They live in an

illusion about an all-European democracy, in which the people are supposed to vote for their president of the Commission, a kind of a European
government. The will of the democratically elected prime ministers is a
burden for them.

(Houska, 2016)[16]

Voices of experts such as the "political scientist, economics and publicist" Petr
Robejšek (2014)[17] can also be found arguing this way:

> As usual, the European élite attribute to themselves more capabilities than
> they have, and take on more powers than they are capable of exercis-
> ing. The incapability of the Union to resolve big questions is "compen-
> sated" for with an obsession with details. Brussels wants to neutralise the
> growing disparity of the association [in interests and development] with
> *gleichschaltung*.[18]

The handful of positions that support the ideas behind the EU and/or its capacity
to deliver valuable outputs lags behind in strength and intensity. In most newspapers, it is not prevalent or is missing altogether (*Magyar Nemzet*). It is more
commonly present in *Pravda* and *Népszabadság*, although, in both cases, it is made
up of fewer than ten articles in absolute numbers. Yet, it can still be considered
a "weak frame," comprising a set of positions, such as those of Zeeb (in Mánert,
2014),[19] Garton Ash (2012)[20] or Urban (2015).[21]

Overall, the performance of the EU is clearly negative in the six newspapers,
with small differences between the three countries (Figure 10.6). There is a

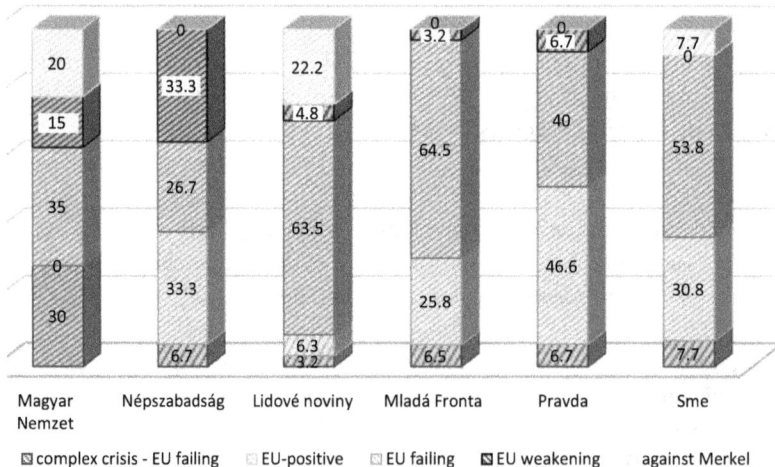

FIGURE 10.6 Incidences of the most common frames in the second category (in % of
the total number of included articles into the category separately for each
newspaper).

Source: author

strong frame attributing responsibility for the crises (especially the "migration/refugee" crisis) to an unspecified group of "European élites," which goes as far as to accuse them of causing the crisis, benefiting from it or, at least, preventing it from ending with appropriate solutions. These are sometimes viewed as infringing upon the rights of the Member States and the "national communities" within them, which creates a binary opposition and "clouds" other views. This frame is not countered by another similarly strong one that would emphasise the Union's resilience, the benefits that it provides and/or its capacity to endure in some, albeit segmented, form.

VII Frame category 3: The future of the EU

The last category of frames speaks to the implications of the portrayed crises for the optimal future configuration of the EU. It shows, firstly, the prevalence of linear thinking about the Union in relation to the crises through the traditional dilemma between more or less integration, and, secondly, the presence of a great variety of "ways forward," which are mostly vague and unclear on the structure that would emerge if this particular way (defined often through specific policies, such as joint EU solutions on migration) came into being (see Figure 10.7).[22]

After the frames are broken down into frequencies, a clear dominant frequency stems from the data, the one on the joint EU approach. With 123 incidences

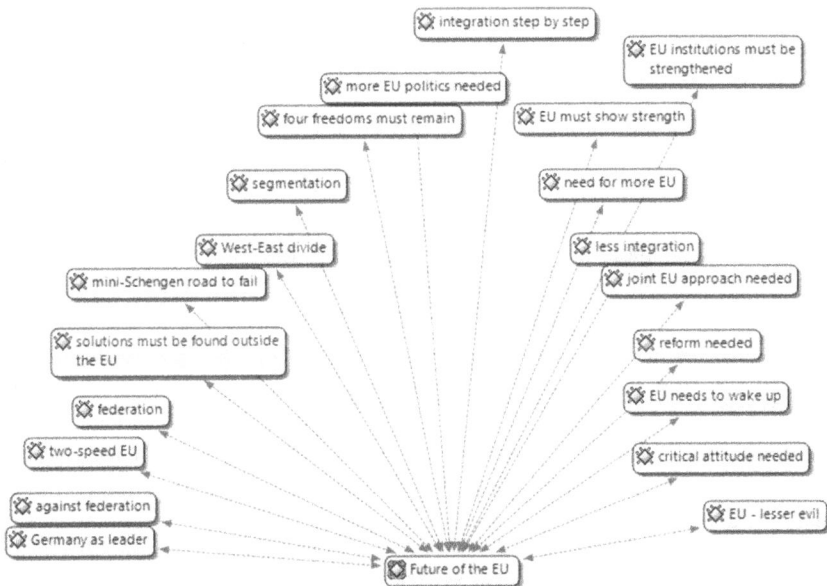

FIGURE 10.7 Frames in the third category.

Source: author

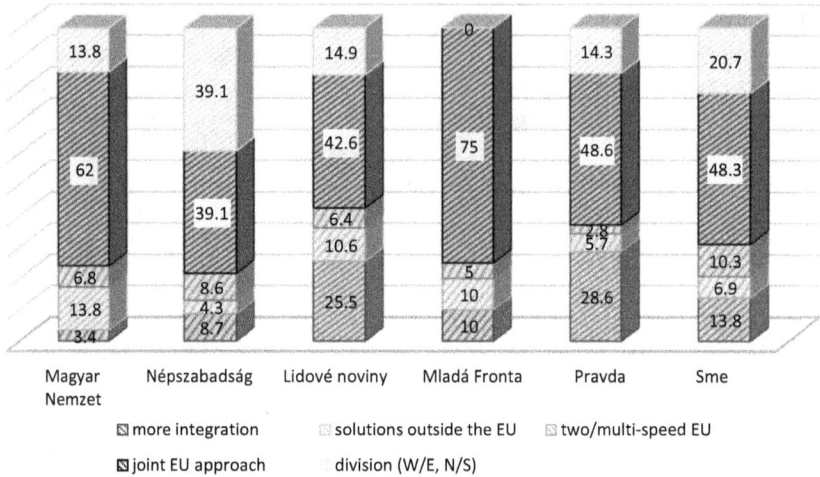

Values in the chart from left to right (Magyar Nemzet, Népszabadság, Lidové noviny, Mladá Fronta, Pravda, Sme):

Magyar Nemzet: 13.8, 62, 6.8, 13.8, 3.4

Népszabadság: 39.1, 39.1, 8.6, 4.3, 8.7

Lidové noviny: 14.9, 42.6, 6.4, 10.6, 25.5

Mladá Fronta: 0, 75, 5, 10, 10

Pravda: 14.3, 48.6, 2.8, 5.7, 28.6

Sme: 20.7, 48.3, 10.3, 6.9, 13.8

Legend: more integration; solutions outside the EU; two/multi-speed EU; joint EU approach; division (W/E, N/S)

FIGURE 10.8 Incidences of the most common frames in the third category (in % of the total number of included articles into the category separately for each newspaper).

Source: author

(see Figure 10.8), mostly in relation to the "migration/refugee crisis," it is by far the strongest frame related to the category of the EU's future. A closer look demonstrates that it encompasses different ideas on the substance of this joint approach. Positions range from that in which the joint approach should unfold among the *Member States* of the EU, with the larger states having a greater pool of responsibility (Pataky, 2016, interviewing the Croatian minister of foreign affairs Miro Kovac), through the emphasis on a *European* solution which is to be found in "increased border security and refusing refugees" (ČTK, 2016e), up to the call for an *EU solution* in which Member States need to participate (Krbatová, 2016).[23] Others again stress the need to "protect the joint Europe with joint efforts and find courage for major economic and social reforms [...]" (Dzurinda, 2016); and there is, of course, Angela Merkel, who referred to the joint EU approach on numerous occasions (ČTK, 2016b).

One noticeable frame is the one on the divisions (West/East, North/South) that persist or are deepening in the EU in relation to the crises. Critical comments are reproduced in the articles that object to such divisions, particularly in the context of the economic situation. One quite imaginative portrayal of the threat of deepening divisions is through a cartoon re-published in *Népszabadság* (Figure 10.9), in which the EU is "shifted" to the East, while the former Western European states are united in a different structure called "*Merkelreich.*" Without stating it explicitly and thus allowing the concept being captured by the content analysis, the cartoon is an example of the fragmentation of the EU.

FIGURE 10.9 The future of the EU according to a cartoonist. The term is reserved for the east, while the west is transformed to "Merkelreich." The "Czechs" and the "Hungarian Empire" form small but independent entities.

Source: Friss (2015)

Fragmentation appears to be the threat on the horizon in the views of others as well. An op-ed entitled "European United Dreams" is worried that

> the nation-states do not work in the ways they used to, and the societies of the European periphery can easily get trapped into the crisis of the nation-state. […] Thus, it is necessary to proceed further at the European level in some direction.
>
> *(Tamás, 2014)*

The greatest risk, in this columnist's view, is thus the intensification of the centre–periphery divide (which he does not precisely define, however). In connection with the "migration/refugee crisis," there have been concerns over the "tension between Central Europe and the rest of Europe" (Holkovský in Cuprík, 2015) or even an "open conflict at the next summit of the EU between German Chancellor Angela Merkel and the countries that refuse her plan to resolve the refugee crisis in co-operation with Turkey" (ČTK, 2016d). As Figure 10.8 shows, the frame on division is present in newspapers across the countries under study. Moreover, it is overwhelmingly perceived as negative for the EU's future.

This is a noticeable contrast to the frame on the V4, where the "separationist" attitude in the "migration/refugee" crisis was praised in most of the texts in which it appeared. As "separationist" attitudes are likely to deepen, their support can hardly be reconciled with the voice in favour of joint European solutions, regardless of their content. This is yet another form of opposition that may have contributed to segmentation in the Union through the creation of two lines of thought speaking *alongside, but not to*, each other.

VIII Conclusion: Towards a post-crises portrayal of the Union

What does the analysis of the newspaper portrayal of the EU in crises tell us about the development of the EU post-crises? For one thing, this chapter supported the standpoint that determining when there is a crisis, when it starts and when a "post-crises" era comes about is intertwined with its construction. Despite all the spatial and temporal limitations of the chapter's empirical analysis, it can be concluded that the crises live their own lives in the media, which is far from being based upon fact; this explains why a set of events has "earned" the right to be labelled as a crisis, upon the basis of what criteria the responsibility for its causes can be attributed and how its possible consequences can be evaluated. In a period of more than eight years, in six Czech, Slovak and Hungarian quality newspapers, a gloomy picture of a crisis-struck Union emerges, with a number of characteristics. Firstly, the responsibility for at least the latest and most anxiously perceived "migration/refugee crisis" is largely attributed to the EU institutions in Brussels and the "European élite," and a bright future for the EU can hardly be imagined at all. Secondly, it is a picture in which the joint approach of all EU Member States is still perceived to have power, but is difficult to achieve because of the persistent, or even deepening, divisions between their positions. Thirdly, the V4's prevalently praised position towards some issues within the "migration/refugee" crisis is at odds with the preference for a joint approach, and implicitly paves the way towards fragmentation of the EU. Finally, while there is clearly a frame that believes in European integration, sometimes explicitly in the form of "more EU" with a federation as its finality, in terms of the regularity of its appearance, it is far from one what could be evaluated as strong.

Despite some differences in specific frames,[24] this chapter has argued that all the newspapers under scrutiny share something in common: the *linear image of the EU's development*. By creating oppositions between the Member States and EU institutions, between the European élites and citizens and between nation-state sovereignty and deeper integration, they exemplify a linear thinking about the Union with hardly any space for a segmented political order. A possible explanation for this linearity is that the language of crises, as discussed throughout the chapter, supports radical changes with a capacity to overcome them, rather than some form of muddling through. The standpoints of the "Ever Closer Union" or the Union's fragmentation fit into this language better than that of segmentation. At the same time, the creation of opposing standpoints talking alongside each other but not *to each other*, that is, without the capacity to engage with the diverging views in order to generate a more overarching narrative, supports *segmented language*, characterised by cognitive and ideological closure (see the Introduction to this volume). Further empirical research, possibly including more types of media, could show the subsequent trends in the portrayal of the EU as well as whether the Czech Republic, Slovakia and Hungary will increasingly stand out due to the cementing of the idea of pursuing their own "Visegrád" approach while still remaining in the EU, or whether there will be increasing differences due to changing public discourse as well as the undermining of the very foundations of democracy. All in all, the crisis construction process seems to have left at least some segments of the public discourse about the Union unaware of the subsequent policy developments. With the entrenchment of linear views of the Union and the absence of a vocabulary that could account for what is happening, it is doubtful that EU citizenry would be able to understand and relate to the Union more post-crises than before them, even if the "crisis talk" does not continue with such intensity (see Steuer, 2017). Empirically, this seems to have created an environment in which segmentation can flourish. Normatively, this is not good news for building a democratic Union, whatever form it will take.

Notes

1 The work on this chapter was supported by the Slovak Research and Development Agency, Grant no. APVV-15-0732 (project "European Union's Recognition Order and the Small Member States").

2 All online sources cited as to 1 August 2016. All English translations of Czech, Hungarian and Slovak sources are by the author. The author is grateful to the editors of the book and participants of research workshops in Oslo (ARENA Centre for European Studies) and Bratislava (Comenius University, Department of Political Science) as well as the 2017 Interim Conference of the IPSA Research Committee 36 in Pavia for valuable comments on earlier drafts of the chapter. The usual disclaimer applies.

3 Several other analyses covering only one crisis, mostly the "economic" one, can be identified (*e.g.*, Berend, 2012; Talani, 2016; Bitzenis, Karagiannis and Marangos, 2015).

4 Interestingly, Heins (2016: 1, 7–9), based upon analysis of Habermas' writings, argues that "Europe's current crisis is also a crisis of its narratives, and hence a crisis of meaning." He identifies several narratives present in Habermas' work and confronts them in the "semiotic square" that includes "transnational democracy, democratic nation-state, executive federalism and European federal state." Thus, he helps us to understand the components of the "crisis of narratives."

5 Post-Brexit, the notion of crisis has received more attentive treatments, for instance, in a volume edited by Dinan (2017).

6 These include the difficulty of determining the *time frame* of the crisis (when it started, when and under what conditions it will end) (Runciman, 2016) but also "the ways in which it regulates narrative constructions, the ways in which it allows certain questions to be asked, while others are foreclosed" (Roitman, 2016: 30).

7 A report co-ordinated by Tamsin Murray-Leach of LSE (2014) argued that the crisis is framed almost exclusively in economic terms, and the EU plays the role of the "foreign other" in this crisis, as opposed to the Member States.

8 Two daily newspapers (on the relevance of newspapers, see Nossek, Adoni and Nimrod, 2015) were selected in each of the two countries, with the effort to choose the ones leading on the media market in the respective countries (as of summer 2016). The first category comprises *Sme* (We are) in Slovakia, *Lidové noviny* (People's Newspaper)in the Czech Republic and *Magyar Nemzet* (Hungarian Nation) in Hungary; the second category comprises *Pravda* (Truth) in Slovakia, *Mladá Fronta* (Youth Front) in the Czech Republic and *Népszabadság* (People's Freedom) in Hungary.

9 With the help of qualitative content analysis, designed "systematically [to] describe the meaning of qualitative material" (Schreier, 2012: 1).

10 The media environment in this region is undergoing substantial changes (see, *e.g.*, Bajomi-Lázár, 2018). Most notably for this analysis, both Hungarian newspapers that were included here are now defunct (*Népszabadság* ceased to be published in late 2016, *Magyar Nemzet* in early 2018), giving evidence to the point of the "colonisation" of the Hungarian media sphere (Bajomi-Lázár, 2014; see also 2017). On the one hand, this means that neither of the newspapers is a relevant actor in the post-crises Hungarian political discourse. On the other hand, these newspapers offer particularly unique sources for analysis during a transformative period when they increasingly faced the difficulties posed by the governmental control of the media environment. This could imply the tendency to position themselves more critically towards the governmental policies, and, in turn, more favourably towards the EU tackling its crises, given that the Union advocates for guarantees of free press and expressions. In the case of the absence of such a trend, a certain "blindness" of these newspapers in terms of their capacity to counter the dominant governmental narratives can be hypothesised.

11 Two Czech newspapers and one Hungarian newspaper together comprise three times as many articles as the two Slovak newspapers and the second Hungarian newspaper. To avoid biased results in favour of the three newspapers, percentages are applied in the subsequent charts.

12 An explicit distinction was made between the "(im-)migration" and "refugee" crisis to highlight the difference between the terminology. One article, therefore, could be categorised as including a reference to both the "migration" and the "refugee" crisis. In most articles referring to migration/refugees, one of the terms prevailed while the other was not used at all.

13 One of the Slovak newspapers, traditionally considered as a left-wing one, reported about the economic crisis in almost half of all articles according to this classification.

14 For example, Kain (2015) writes that "the EU is at the crossroads. How it deals with the current immigration and security crisis will decide, whether it remains liberal, open, but first and foremost united and resilient. Or whether we just quickly make up a castle from sand, that will be swept away by the next wave." He does not specify at all what the immigration and security crisis is.

15 The overall number of articles in *Népszabadság* included in this chart (16) does not allow a valid comparison to be made with its counterparts.

16 Another example coming from the period before the "migration/refugee crisis": "Even if a Nobel prize would be awarded for procrastination, it would be someone else instead of the European political class who would go for the Nobel price to Oslo this year. Indeed, in the first half of the year, practically nothing at all happened." See Vajs (2012).

17 "The pedants of Brussels on their way towards a messianic dictatorship."

18 The term in this context has origins in Germany under national socialism and denotes the subjugation of all aspects of life to the ruling ideology (see King and King, 2014).

19 "In the present age of global struggle, Europe must summon the courage and solidarity to elevate the concept of the union in a logical direction, towards a real Europe with the shape of a democratic federal state, that will be powerful enough to be able to face all the challenges mentioned above."

20 "And that [memory on war, Soviet threat, German unification, the 'return to Europe' of the Eastern states, and rising living conditions within 'Europe'] is the basis of a new argument for European unification."

21 "The nation state is for a crisis of such magnitude impractical to say the least. It was exactly the absence of other than national decision-making mechanisms that prevented Europe from recognizing the warning symptoms early on and via joint coordination prevent the very emergence of the refugee wave."

22 With respect to more sophisticated accounts of the developments, there is virtually no example of core formation around the Eurozone in the articles. The frame on the V4 includes some examples praising the V4's position towards migration/asylum policies; however, this is not in the sense that the V4 should form its own block within the Union, but that the Union *jointly* should adopt the V4's approach. A few notions of a two/multi-speed EU can be identified that could be most closely associated to segmentation. Fragmentation is the most commonly appearing frame (see on regional divisions below), but in a negative sense (*i.e.*, the EU needs to avoid it).

23 This was an interview with a Slovak MP, who said, among other things, that "Europe as an union but also as a continent faces a problem, that it can resolve only with joining forces. Even though the refugee wave does not arrive to us, Slovakia has to somehow participate in the problem."

24 Addressing the comparative questions from this chapter's Introduction, it cannot be said that the Eurozone membership would indicate a significantly different portrayal of the Eurozone crisis, or that in Hungary, facing significant democratic backsliding, the language of blaming the "European élites" would be more present.

References

Altheide, David L. (2002), *Creating Fear: News and the Construction of Crisis*, London and New York: Routledge.

Atikcan, Ece Özlem (2015), *Framing the European Union: The Power of Political Arguments in Shaping European Integration*, Cambridge: Cambridge University Press.

Bajomi-Lázár, Péter (2014), *Party Colonisation of the Media in Central and Eastern Europe: Modern Business Decision Making in Central and Eastern Europe*, Budapest: Central European University Press, available at: https://muse.jhu.edu/book/36150.

Bajomi-Lázár, Péter (2017), "Particularistic and Universalistic Media Policies: Inequalities in the Media in Hungary", *Javnost – The Public*, 24 (2): 162–172.

Bajomi-Lázár, Péter (ed) (2018), *Media in Third-Wave Democracies: Southern and Central/ Eastern Europe in a Comparative Perspective*, Paris and Budapest: Editions L'Harmattan.

Bednář, Miloslav (2016), "Migrační krize a Evropská unie jako evropský problém", *Neviditelný pes – Lidové noviny*, 30 May 2016, available at: http://neviditelnypes. lidovky.cz/svet-migracni-krize-a-evropska-unie-jako-evropsky-problem-pnc-/p_ zahranici.aspx?c=A160528_223906_p_zahranici_wag.

Bengoetxea, Joxerramon (2015), "The Current European Crises: The End of Pluralism?", in: Serge Champeau, Carlos Closa, Daniel Innerarity, and Miguel Poaires Maduro (eds), *The Future of Europe: Democracy, Legitimacy and Justice after the Euro Crisis*, London and Lanham MD: Rowman & Littlefield, pp. 57–74.

Berend, Ivan (2012), *Europe in Crisis: Bolt from the Blue?*, New York: Routledge.

Bitzenis, Aristidis, Nikolaos Karagiannis, and John Marangos (eds) (2015), *Europe in Crisis: Problems, Challenges, and Alternative Perspectives*, Basingstoke and New York: Palgrave Macmillan.

Cock, Rozane De, Stefan Mertens, Ebba Sundin, Lutgard Lams, Valeriane Mistiaen, Willem Joris, and Leen d'Haenens (2018), "Refugees in the News: Comparing

Belgian and Swedish Newspaper Coverage of the European Refugee Situation during Summer 2015", *Communications*, 43 (3): 301–323.

ČTK (2016a), "EÚ sa v migračnej kríze vydala na pospas Turecku, povedal Orbán ", Sme, 23 April 2016, available at: http://svet.sme.sk/c/20145748/eu-sa-v-migracnej-krize-vydala-na-pospas-turecku-povedal-orban.html.

ČTK (2016b), "Merkelová: Je potrebné znížiť počet utečencov v EÚ", *Pravda*, 16 March 2016, available at: http://spravy.pravda.sk/svet/clanok/386941-merkelova-je-potrebne-znizit-pocet-utecencov-vo-vsetkych-krajinach-eu.

ČTK (2016c), "Pokud nezvládneme migrační proud, situace se vymkne kontrole a ohrozí EU, shodli se lídři V4 na summitu v Praze", *Ihned.cz*, 15 February 2016, available at: http://zahranicni.ihned.cz/evropa-slovensko/c1-65164860-evropska-unie-musi-podporit-ochranu-hranic-v-bulharsku-a-makedonii-shodli-se-lidri-v4-na-summitu-v-praze.

ČTK (2016d), "Visegrád narúša Merkelovej plány", *Pravda*, 14 February 2016, available at: http://spravy.pravda.sk/svet/clanok/383453-visegrad-narusa-merkelovej-plany.

ČTK (2016e), "Zvažme uzavření německých hranic před migranty, říká bavorský ministr", *Idnes.cz*, 18 January 2016, available at: http://zpravy.idnes.cz/bavorsky-ministr-navrhuje-uzavreni-hranic-fkz-/zahranicni.aspx?c=A160118_101401_zahranicni_jj.

Cross, Mai'a K. Davis, and Xinru Ma (2015a), "A Media Perspective on European Crises", in: Hans-Jörg Trenz, Carlo Ruzza, and Virginie Guiraudon (eds), *Europe's Prolonged Crisis*, Basingstoke: Palgrave Macmillan, pp. 210–231.

Cross, Mai'a K. Davis, and Xinru Ma (2015b), "EU Crises and Integrational Panic: The Role of the Media", *Journal of European Public Policy*, 22 (8): 1053–1070.

Cuprík, Roman (2015), "Čo bolo podľa vás udalosťou roka a prečo? Odpovedajú slovenské osobnosti (anketa)", *Sme*, 30 December 2015, available at: http://domov.sme.sk/c/20069627/co-bolo-podla-vas-udalostou-roka-a-precoodpovedaju-slovenske-osobnosti-anketa.html#ixzz4NbsxtYsx.

Cuprík, Roman, and Marie Vrabcová (2016), "Šéf SMK: Maďari sú iná menšina ako utečenci", Sme, 1 February 2016, available at: http://domov.sme.sk/c/20084375/sef-smk-madari-su-ina-mensina-ako-utecenci.html.

De Vreese, Claes H., and Hajo G. Boomgaarden (2006), "Media Effects on Public Opinion about the Enlargement of the European Union", *Journal of Common Market Studies*, 44 (2): 419–436.

Demetriou, Kyriakos N. (ed) (2015), *The European Union in Crisis: Explorations in Representation and Democratic Legitimacy*, Cham: Springer.

Dinan, Desmond (ed) (2017), *The European Union in Crisis*, London: Palgrave.

Duhan, Andrej (2015), "Uprchlická krize je i důsledkem selhání evropských elit", *Česká pozice – Lidové noviny*, 18 October 2015, available at: http://ceskapozice.lidovky.cz/uprchlicka-krize-je-i-dusledkem-selhani-evropskych-elit-p21-/tema.aspx?c=A151015_162700_pozice-tema_lube.

Dzurinda, Mikuláš (2016), "Potrebujeme nové sebavedomie", *Sme*, 1 May 2016, available at: http://komentare.sme.sk/c/20152250/potrebujeme-nove-sebavedomie.html#ixzz4NbwTwYmp.

Editorial Board (2016a), "Keyword: Migration Crisis", *Lidové noviny*, 30 June 2016, available at: www.lidovky.cz/migracni-krize-011-/zpravy-svet.aspx?klic=218103.

Editorial Board (2016b), "Keyword: Refugee Crisis", *Mladá fronta*, 30 June 2016, available at: http://zpravy.idnes.cz/priliv-uprchliku-do-evropy-dfm-/zahranicni.aspx?klic=64244.

Eilders, Christiane (2002), "Conflict and Consonance in Media Opinion Political Positions of Five German Quality Newspapers", *European Journal of Communication*, 17 (1): 25–63.

Entman, Robert M. (2007), "Framing Bias: Media in the Distribution of Power", *Journal of Communication*, 57 (1): 163–173.

Eriksen, Erik Oddvar (2018), "Political Differentiation and the Problem of Dominance: Segmentation and Hegemony", *European Journal of Political Research*, 57 (4): 989–1008.

Fabbrini, Sergio (2017), "The Euro Crisis through Two Paradigms: Interpreting the Transformation of the European Economic Governance", *European Politics and Society*, 18 (3): 318–332.

Fairclough, Norman (1995), *Media Discourse*, London and New York: Bloomsbury Academic.

Fossum, John Erik (2019), "The Institutional Make-up of Europe's Segmented Political Order", Chapter 2 in this volume.

Fossum, John Erik, and Agustín José Menéndez (eds) (2014), *The European Union in Crises or the European Union as Crises?*, Oslo: Arena – Centre for European Studies.

Fotopoulos, Stergios, and Margarita Kaimaklioti (2016), "Media Discourse on the Refugee Crisis: On What have the Greek, German and British Press Focused?", *European View*, 15 (2): 265–279.

Friss, Róbert (2012), "A torta felosztása", *Népszabadság*, 16 July 2012, available at: http://nol.hu/velemeny/20120716-a_torta_felosztasa-1318405.

Friss, Róbert (2015), "Harmadik út", *Népszabadság*, 16 November 2013, available at: http://nol.hu/kulfold/20131116-harmadik_ut-1426543.

Garton Ash, Timothy (2012), "Prežije Európa vzostup zvyšku sveta?" *Sme.sk*, 10 September 2012, available at: http://komentare.sme.sk/c/6528186/prezije-europa-vzostup-zvyskusveta.html#ixzz4Nbp0j7gu.

Genna, Gaspare M., and Ian W. Wilson (2016), "Conclusion: European Identity, Crises, and Integration", in: Gaspare M. Genna, Thomas O. Haakenson, and Ian W. Wilson (eds), *Jürgen Habermas and the European Economic Crisis: Cosmopolitanism Reconsidered*, London and New York: Routledge, pp. 215–220.

Greskovits, Béla (2015), "The Hollowing and Backsliding of Democracy in East Central Europe", *Global Policy*, 6 (S1): 28–37.

Habermas, Jürgen (1975), *Legitimation Crisis*, translated by Thomas McCarthy, Boston MA: Beacon Press.

Habermas, Jürgen (2012), *The Crisis of the European Union: A Response*, Cambridge and Malden MA, Polity Press.

Habermas, Jürgen (2015), *The Lure of Technocracy*, Cambridge and Malden MA: Polity Press.

Habermas, Jürgen (2016), "Core Europe to the Rescue: A Conversation with Jürgen Habermas about Brexit and the EU Crisis", *Social Europe* (blog), 12 July 2016, available at: www.socialeurope.eu/2016/07/core-europe-to-the-rescue.

Havlická, Kateřina (2015), "Premiéři jsou víc než ministři, doufá Zeman ve zrušení kvót pro uprchlíky", *Idnes.cz*, 22 September 2015, available at: http://zpravy.idnes.cz/premieri-jsou-vic-nez-ministri-doufa-zeman-ve-zruseni-kvotpoq-/domaci.aspx?c=A150922_210910_zahranicni_kha.

Heins, Volker M. (2016), "Habermas on the European Crisis: Attempting the Impossible", *Thesis Eleven*, 133 (1): 3–18.

Ho, Daniel E., and Kevin M. Quinn (2008), "Measuring Explicit Political Positions of Media", *Quarterly Journal of Political Science*, 3 (4): 353–377.

Houska, Ondřej (2016), "Kam sa schováme, až sa rozpadne EÚ?", Sme, 26 February 2016, available at: http://komentare.sme.sk/c/20104288/kam-sa-schovame-az-sa-rozpadne-eu.html.

Joris, Willem, Liina Puustinen, and Leen d'Haenens (2018), "More News from the Euro Front: How the Press has been Framing the Euro Crisis in Five EU Countries", *International Communication Gazette*, 80 (6): 532–550.

Kain, Petr (2015), "Rozdělí imigranti Evropu? Z krize ale může vyjít i silnější", *Lidové noviny*, 7 December 2015, available at: http://byznys.lidovky.cz/rozdeli-imigranti-evropu-z-krize-ale-muze-vyjit-i-silnejsi-po3-/statni-pokladna.aspx?c=A151206_151639_ln-media_lvk.

Kaiser, Johannes, and Katharina Kleinen-von Königslöw (2017), "The Framing of the Euro Crisis in German and Spanish Online News Media between 2010 and 2014: Does a Common European Public Discourse Emerge?", *Journal of Common Market Studies*, 55 (4): 798–814.

King, Martha A., and Jonathan S. King (2014), "Gleichschaltung", in: Michael T. Gibbons et al. (eds), *The Encyclopedia of Political Thought*, Chichester: Wiley-Blackwell, pp. 1483–1484.

Kiska, Andrej (2015), "Prejav prezidenta Kisku v Národnej rade SR", *Pravda*, 7 October 2015, available at: http://spravy.pravda.sk/domace/clanok/369985-prejav-prezidenta-kisku-v-narodnej-rade-sr.

Kohler-Koch, Beate (2000), "Framing: The Bottleneck of Constructing Legitimate Institutions", *Journal of European Public Policy*, 7 (4): 513–531.

Koopmans, Ruud, and Paul Statham (2010), *The Making of a European Public Sphere: Media Discourse and Political Contention*, Cambridge: Cambridge University Press.

Kotalík, Jakub (2016), "Vláda neví, co má v migrační krizi dělat, kritizovali šéf ODS s Červíčkem", *Idnes.cz*, 28 April 2016, available at: http://zpravy.idnes.cz/plan-ods-k-reseni-migracni-krize-dn9-/domaci.aspx?c=A160428_100329_domaci_jkk.

Krbatová, Lucia (2016), "Šebej: Európa sa pára vo švíkoch, špekulácie o predčasných voľbách sú stratou súdnosti", Sme, 28 March 2016, available at: http://domov.sme.sk/c/20126392/sebej-europa-sa-para-vo-svikoch-spekulovat-opredcasnych-volbach-je-strata-sudnosti.html#ixzz4Nbw3AjXX.

Krist, Tomáš (2009), "Klaus: Vláda Mirka Topolánka byla zlobbovaná", *Lidové noviny*, 15 May 2009, available at: www.lidovky.cz/klaus-vlada-mirka-topolanka-byla-zlobbovana-fz2-/zpravy-domov.aspx?c=A090515_153653_ln_domov_mpr.

Kuypers, Jim A. (2002), *Press Bias and Politics: How the Media Frame Controversial Issues*, Westport CT: Greenwood Publishing Group.

Laffan, Brigid (2016), "Europe's Union in Crisis: Tested and Contested", *West European Politics*, 39 (5): 915–932.

Mánert, Oldřich (2014), "Federální Evropská unie je nutností, míní šéf proevropského think-tanku", *Idnes.cz*, 19 May 2014, available at: http://zpravy.idnes.cz/rozhovor-projekt-demokraticke-unie-benjamin-zeeb-fvp-/zahranicni.aspx?c=A140517_174645_zahranicni_ert.

Michailidou, Asimina, and Hans-Jörg Trenz (2015), "The European Crisis and the Media: Media Autonomy, Public Perceptions and New Forms of Political Engagement", in: Hans-Jörg Trenz, Carlo Ruzza, and Virginie Guiraudon (eds), *Europe's Prolonged Crisis*, Basingstoke: Palgrave Macmillan, pp. 232–250.

MTI (2015a), "Orbán Viktor: Ideologikus burokban ül az európai politikai elit", *Magyar Nemzet*, 19 December 2015, available at: http://mno.hu/kulfold/orban-viktor-ideologikus-burokban-ul-az-europai-politikai-elit-1319909.

MTI (2015b), "Vízum nélkül jöhetnek a törökök", *Magyar Nemzet*, 18 October 2015, available at: https://mno.hu/kulfold/vizum-nelkul-johetnek-a-torokok-1309714.

Murray-Leach, Tamsin (ed) (2014), "Crisis Discourses in Europe: Media EU-Phemisms and Alternative Narratives", London School of Economics and Political Science, available at: http://blogs.lse.ac.uk/eurocrisispress/2014/11/20/crisis-discourses-in-europe-media-eu-phemisms-and-alternative-narratives.

Myria, Georgiou, and Zaborowski Rafał (2017), *Media Coverage of the "Refugee Crisis": A Cross-European Perspective*, Strasbourg: Council of Europe.

Nossek, Hillel, Hanna Adoni, and Galit Nimrod (2015), "Media Audiences: Is Print Really Dying? The State of Print Media Use in Europe", *International Journal of Communication*, 9: 365–385.

Palata, Luboš (2016), "Obávám se, že Evropská unie migraci ani zastavit nechce, říká Fico", *Mladá fronta*, 26 January 2016, available at: http://zpravy.idnes.cz/robert-fico-rozhovor-05t-/zahranicni.aspx?c=A160126_104749_zahranicni_kha.

Pataky, István (2016), "A német nagylelkűség találkozása a realitással", *Magyar Nemzet*, 3 February 2016, available at: http://mno.hu/kulfold/a-nemet-nagylelkuseg-es-a-realitas-1326837.

Robejšek, Petr (2014), "Bruselští pedanti na cestě k spasitelské diktatuře", *Idnes.cz*, 4 May 2016, available at: http://zpravy.idnes.cz/komentar-evropska-unie-robejsek-diktatura-f2j-/domaci.aspx?c=A140503_142520_zahranicni_aha.

Roitman, Janet (2013), *Anti-Crisis*, Durham NC: Duke University Press Books.

Roitman, Janet (2016), "The Stakes of Crisis", in: Poul F. Kjaer and Niklas Olsen (eds), *Critical Theories of Crisis in Europe: From Weimar to the Euro*, Lanham MD: Rowman & Littlefield International, pp. 17–34.

Runciman, David. (2016), "What Time Frame Makes Sense for Thinking about Crises?", in: Poul F. Kjaer and Niklas Olsen (eds), *Critical Theories of Crisis in Europe: From Weimar to the Euro*, Lanham MD: Rowman & Littlefield International, pp. 3–16.

Schmitt, Carl (2006), *Political Theology: Four Chapters on the Concept of Sovereignty*, edited by Tracy B. Strong, translated by George Schwab. Chicago IL: University of Chicago Press.

Schreier, Margrit (2012), *Qualitative Content Analysis in Practice*, Los Angeles CA: SAGE Publications.

SITA (2016a), "Fico: Obávam sa, že EÚ nechce zastaviť migráciu", *Pravda*, 26 January 2016, available at: http://spravy.pravda.sk/domace/clanok/381254-fico-obavam-sa-ze-eu-nechce-zastavit-migraciu.

SITA (2016b), "Maďarič vidí v brexite stratu dôvery, Šebej apeluje na rozvahu", Sme, 26 June 2016, available at: http://domov.sme.sk/c/20200733/madaric-vidi-v-brexite-stratu-dovery-sebej-apeluje-na-rozvahu.htmlí.

Steuer, Max (2017), "Why the EU Needs 'De-Crisising'", *Crossroads Europe*, 2 October 2017, available at: https://crossroads.ideasoneurope.eu/2017/10/02/article-18.

Stier, Gábor (2015a), "A szabadság iránti vágy béklyójában Merkel", *Magyar Nemzet*, 11 November 2015, available at: http://mno.hu/kulfold/a-szabadsag-iranti-vagy-beklyojaban-merkel-1313386.

Stier, Gábor (2015b), "Szergej Mihejev a magyar–orosz viszonyról és a vazallus Európáról", *Magyar Nemzet*, 15 February 2015, available at: http://mno.hu/kulfold/szergej-mihejev-a-magyar-orosz-viszonyrol-es-a-vazallus-europarol-1272949.

Talani, Simona (ed) (2016), *Europe in Crisis: A Structural Analysis*, Basingstoke: Palgrave Macmillan.

Tamás, Pál (2014), "Európai Egyesült Álmok", *Népszabadság*, 21 March 2014, available at: http://nol.hu/kulfold/europai-egyesult-almok-1451589.

Urban, Jan (2015), "Česká hysterie uprchlická", *Neviditelný pes – Lidové noviny*, 3 October 2015, available at: http://neviditelnypes.lidovky.cz/spolecnost-ceska-hysterie-uprchlicka-d8v-/p_spolecnost.aspx?c=A151001_170352_p_spolecnost_wag.

Vajs, Miroslav (2012), "Eurosaprebiloťažkýmrokom", *Pravda*, 31 December 2012, available at: http://spravy.pravda.sk/ekonomika/clanok/253443-euro-sa-prebilo-tazkym-rokom.

Vobruba, Georg, Maurizio Bach, Martin Rhodes, and Julia Szalai (2003), "Debate on the Enlargement of the European Union The Enlargement Crisis of the European Union: Limits of the Dialectics of Integration and Expansion", *Journal of European Social Policy* 13 (1): 35–62.

Williams, Ann E., and Christopher M. Toula (2017), "Solidarity Framing at the Union of National and Transnational Public Spheres", *Journalism Studies*, 18 (12): 1576–1592.

11

EUROPEAN CRISES AND FOREIGN POLICY ATTITUDES IN EUROPE

Michal Onderco

I Introduction

Since 2008, the European public has been treated to a spectacle of multiple multi-faceted crises, both within the borders of the European Union (EU) and outside them. The institutional reaction to the crises was a proliferation of the supranational structures to deal with their fallout. At the same time, the legitimacy of such structures is being increasingly contested by the population – the democratic legitimacy of the EU is being challenged. Numerous scholars have studied the link between the impact of the economic crisis and individual preferences about the European project (Armingeon and Ceka, 2014; Hobolt and Wratil, 2015; Kuhn and Stoeckel, 2014; Polyakova and Fligstein, 2016).

If the crisis brought about the erosion of the legitimacy of the foreign policy of the EU, we can reasonably assume that a more extensive re-assessment of EU foreign policy preferences may take place. Fragmentation of public attitudes happens along two lines – vertical, of which Euroscepticism is one expression; and horizontal, which is about the rise of xenophobia (and general opposition to the "other" – whether the "other" are EU Member States, or fellow citizens of one's own country who happen to be somehow different). Forces tearing the EU apart, then, are much stronger than mere opposition to Brussels-centrism (Fossum, 2015). In particular, when it comes to relations with the United States (US), a long-term cornerstone of the European security order, the crisis had a serious potential to inflict damage. As Sophie Meunier (2013) explained, the crisis tarnished the image of the US as a global leader, damaged the credibility of capitalism as a system, and had the potential to exacerbate further the criticism of the US as a hypocritical power. This would damage the global image of the US, to which all the ills are pinned (Beyer and Liebe, 2014), and this was further exacerbated by the election of Donald Trump, who is nowadays deeply unpopular in Europe (Calamur, 2018) Trump's unpopularity is an extreme case of anti-Americanism, a long-known phenomenon (Chiozza, 2009; Fabbrini, 2002; Katzenstein and Keohane, 2007; Spiro, 1988) despite the close co-operation between European governments and the US. As Ulrich Krotz argues, the quest for "Europe-as-not-America" is one of the drivers of European integration (2009). At the same time, we can observe that the far-right Eurosceptics, on the rise in response to the crisis throughout Europe, are far more anti-American and pro-Russian than the established parties.

Moreover, we know that the voters of the far right and Eurosceptic parties[1] tend to have experienced the crisis (Hobolt and de Vries, 2016; Serricchio *et al.*, 2013), and we know that these parties have pro-Russian attitudes (*The Economist*, 2014). Despite the topical importance of understanding the effects of the European crises on public attitudes in the area of foreign policy in Europe, there has been very little research into it to date.

If we are to understand the emerging segmented order in Europe, we should understand what drives it. As the editors of this edited volume argue, weak or lacking legitimacy is one of the potential constraints on the system. This chapter looks at foreign policy preferences as a legitimacy constraint on the exercise of foreign policy by national actors. The impact of the financial crisis on the foreign policy attitudes in Europe is crucial for the study of the democratic legitimacy of European foreign policy. If the general public is becoming opposed to Western co-operation, it would be difficult for the governments to pursue a pro-Western foreign policy, which may, in the end, lead to the unravelling of the EU (*inter alia*) as we know it. The public support for foreign policy is an important aspect of the post-crisis EU, and provides an additional source of impetus towards internal segmentation.

The ambition of this chapter is two-fold: to look for theoretical arguments linking the Euro crisis and foreign policy attitudes, and to analyse empirical data about the effect of the crisis on foreign policy preferences. The goal of this enterprise is to gauge the influence of the financial crisis on public attitudes to foreign policy in Europe. Scholars who attempt to link the experience of crises in Europe to the attitudes towards European integration generally develop arguments which rest on different causal arguments: failed economic expectations, and nationalism (sometimes also called *identity threat*). Both of these have a potential to lead to similar outcomes *vis-à-vis* attitudes towards the European Union. If the "economic expectations" argument is true, we should see a dip in the support for the EU among individuals who have been economically impacted by the crisis, but not necessarily a change in attitudes towards other actors. If the "nationalism" argument is correct, we should see an overall dip in the support for all outside actors, and this should not be necessarily limited to the EU.

In this chapter, I look at the European citizens' attitudes towards the EU, the US, and Russia, using the data from the 2013 Transatlantic Trends Survey (TTS). In addition to the impact of the economic crisis, I look at the feelings of identity threat as potential explanations for the attitudes towards the three actors.

The results suggest that individuals who experienced the economic crisis are significantly less likely to hold positive views about the EU and are significantly more likely to hold positive views of Russia. The results also suggest that while individuals who experienced the economic crisis are significantly less likely to hold positive views about the EU, only citizens in the old EU Member States are significantly more likely to hold positive views of Russia. Perceptions of identity threat are associated with a decreased support for the EU but have no impact on attitudes towards the US and Russia in Western Europe. In Central and Eastern Europe, however, perceptions of identity threat are associated with more negative views of the US and more positive views of Russia. The results therefore confirm that the economic crisis in Europe had a wider impact on foreign policy preferences among Europeans than previously thought, and opens new avenues for the study of the knock-on effects of economic crisis in Europe.

II Crisis and foreign policy opinion

II.1 Economic impact and attitude towards foreign actors

The economic crisis that hit the EU in the aftermath of the 2008 credit crunch has led to widespread economic hardship in Europe, programmes of bail-outs, and austerity, which put a premium on European integration for all Member States and forced dramatic change in institutional developments in Europe (Hemerijck et al., 2009; Kuhn and Stoeckel, 2014; Scharpf, 2011; Schimmelfennig, 2014). The economic crisis has morphed into a legitimacy crisis, in which citizens question the accepted notions of the broader direction of their polities (Bátora and Fossum, forthcoming; Hemerijck et al., 2009; Streeck, 2013). European integration has become a hotly debated topic in domestic politics in the politicisation of European integration (Hooghe and Marks, 2009; Zürn, 2014), which gave rise to the emergence of public attitudes that question the very utility of such integration. The practical demonstration of the phenomenon manifests itself in the emergence of Eurosceptic parties throughout the EU in all the elections that have taken place recently. These parties are marked by pronounced nationalism, which rejects the supranationality of the EU.

A common explanation, spelt out by Braun and Tausendpfund (2014), is that being personally affected by the crisis means that individuals feel that they are under threat. Individuals feel that the promises of economic well-being are not being met, and, as a result, they withdraw their support from the EU. Such an effect is confirmed in the work of Polyakova and Fligstein (2016), who demonstrate that the population in the countries hit by the crisis became more Eurosceptical and more nationalistic. One of the rare existing country case studies that looks at the effect of the crisis on public opinion about the EU confirms the existence of such an effect (Dimitrova, 2012).

However, the architecture of post-Cold War Europe was squarely built on transatlantic co-operation, the institutional deepening of European integration, and the expansion of both European and transatlantic institutions to the countries of Central and Eastern Europe (Rynning, 2015). A decrease in support for European integration may therefore suggest that the support for the whole post-Cold War structure in Europe has been weakened. This is particularly relevant because, as Meunier (2013) rightly suggests, three of the six varieties of anti-Americanism mentioned by Katzenstein and Keohane (2007) are directly applicable to the crisis: the sovereignists would reject the American leadership of the global financial system; the ideological opponents would see the crisis as a consequence of American capitalism; and the liberals would see the American behaviour in the crisis as being hypocritical.[2]

The public trust in the EU has been systematically undermined by actors with a pro-Russia orientation – be they far-right parties with funding from Moscow, espousers of Russian propaganda, or political leaders who suggest a re-orientation towards Russia and Asia (Applebaum, 2015; Scenario Team Eurozone 2020, 2013). In fact, the new political parties – the Eurosceptics in the United Kingdom (UK), France, and Germany – argue for a thorough re-thinking of foreign policy, including re-consideration of broader foreign policy ties (Chryssogelos, 2010; Mudde, 2007). These actors point out the perils of supranationalism, which align well with Russia's focus on nation states as the *locus* of decision-making and the publicly professed focus on the country's independence from outside interference.

At the same time, if individuals are disappointed by the economic performance of their countries and those around them, they may find more inspiration in the countries in the East. For example, Hungarian Prime Minister Orbán in 2014 claimed that what he refers to as illiberal democracy based upon national standards, such as the one in Russia (Simon, 2014), should be adopted in Hungary, too. One can therefore expect that those who are disappointed by the direction of the post-Cold War development in Europe may hold positive attitudes about alternatives in the East. Upon the basis of these expectations, I have formulated the following hypotheses:

H_1 Individuals impacted by the economic crisis are more likely to hold a negative opinion about the European Union;

H_2 Individuals impacted by the economic crisis are more likely to hold a negative opinion about the US;

H_3 Individuals impacted by the economic crisis are more likely to hold a positive opinion about Russia.

II.2 Identity threats and attitudes towards foreign actors

If the economic crisis really turned Europeans into nationalists, then they would be less likely to develop positive images about other countries. This is similar to the results from marketing research, which has suggested that ethnocentric customers are less likely to buy foreign products or tend to buy only the products for which the country is famous – for example, German beer (Balabanis and Diamantopoulos, 2004; Cleveland *et al.*, 2009). Therefore, we can also hypothesise that, if individuals are becoming more nationalistic, they will be forming a more negative view of foreign actors.

Research has shown that citizens holding exclusive national identities feel threatened by European integration, which brings about foreign influence (Hooghe and Marks, 2005). This corresponds to research that has shown that individuals may oppose trade liberalisation because they feel culturally under threat (Margalit, 2012). In fact, such an understanding of European integration is in line with a long-standing argument among constructivists, who underline the identity dimension of European integration (Risse-Kappen, 1994; Risse *et al.*, 1999). Harald Schoen (2008) has shown that territorial identities (such as national or regional ones) help to explain attitudes towards European integration.

The supranational response to the financial crisis in Europe may have created a threat to individuals who value decision-making in their own country. These citizens may feel that their national identity is under threat from increasing Europeanisation, and may wish to withdraw their support from the EU (Kuhn and Stoeckel, 2014; Hobolt, 2016). However, if the Euro crisis led to an increase in nationalism, then the EU would not be the only actor impacted – there would be a steep fall in support for all foreign actors, be they in the EU or others. Some of the early research on the effects of the crisis suggests that public attitudes in Europe, in the wake of the crisis, *did* become more nationalistic (Fligstein *et al.*, 2012). If this is correct, it would suggest that the constraints on European public opinion in the wake of the crisis are not only vertical, but also horizontal. Therefore, the following may be hypothesised:

H_4 Individuals who feel their identity is threatened are more likely to hold a negative opinion about the EU;

H_5 Individuals who feel their identity is threatened are more likely to hold a negative opinion about the US;

H_6 Individuals who feel their identity is threatened are more likely to hold a negative opinion about Russia.

III Data and methods

To study these hypotheses empirically, I employ the data from the 2013 wave of the Transatlantic Trends Survey (TTS), an annual survey executed by Taylor Nelson Sofres for the German Marshall Fund of the United States and the Compagnia di San Paolo di Torino (2013). TTS is widely used in academic and policy literature as a reliable source for studying public opinion on security issues (see, e.g., Everts and Isernia, 2015; Everts *et al.*, 2014; Faust and Garcia, 2014).

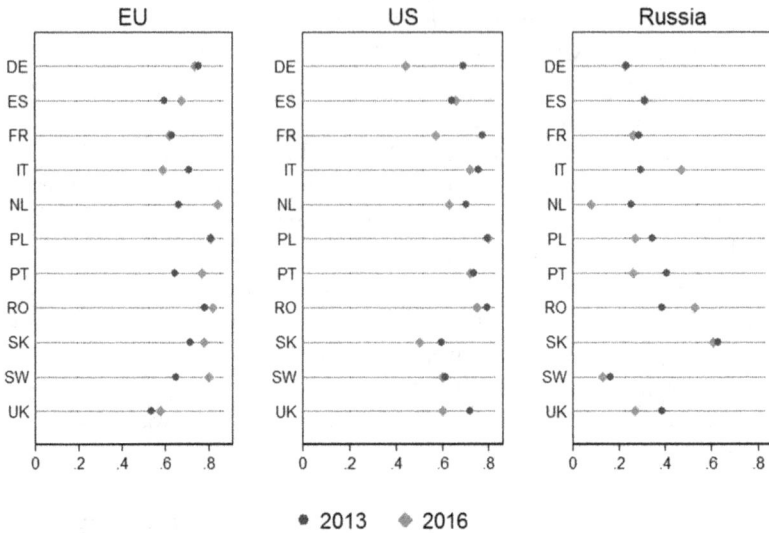

FIGURE 11.1 Share of population holding positive views of various foreign actors.

The year 2013 was selected because it preceded the war in Ukraine, in which Russia was heavily involved, and which may have influenced attitudes towards the country among EU citizens. Eleven EU Member States[3] were included in the survey in 2013, with the representative sample size being approximately 1,000 individuals per country. As is seen in Figure 11.1, the general trends of public opinion have remained by and large the same since then.

III.1 Dependent variable

To capture attitudes towards external actors (EU/US/Russia), I look at the following question: "Please tell me if you have a very favourable, somewhat favourable, somewhat unfavourable or very unfavourable opinion of the EU/ the US/Russia?" Original answers were then recoded on a dichotomous scale of "unfavourable/favourable."[4]

III.2 Independent variables

Crisis

To measure the individual impact of the economic crisis, I use the answer to the following survey question: "And regarding the extent to which you or your family has been personally affected by the current economic crisis, would you say that your family's financial situation has been…", and I dichotomise the responses into "not affected" (including "Not really affected/Not affected at all") and "affected" (including "Greatly affected/Somewhat affected").

Identity threat

The question asked respondents for their agreement with the statement "Immigrants are a threat to our national culture." I code these dichotomously as "agree" ("Agree strongly/ Agree somewhat") and "disagree" ("Disagree somewhat/Disagree strongly"). While not capturing the same phenomenon, prior research has shown that national identity and attitudes towards immigrants are, in fact, strongly correlated (Esses *et al.*, 2006; Sides and Citrin, 2007).

Control variables

In the individual model, I add additional controls to account for

- *Partisanship.* The scholarship on partisanship and foreign policy has demonstrated that right-wing parties tend to advocate more hawkish positions compared to left-wing parties (Arena and Palmer, 2009; Mello, 2014). In the area of European studies, it was shown that left-wing parties were strong opponents of European integration (Hooghe and Marks, 2009), but that the relationship started to change after the 1990s (Aspinwall, 2002; van Elsas and van der Brug, 2015). For these reasons, I measure for individual partisanship, and I measure partisanship on a self-reported scale from 1 to 7, where 1 means far left and 7 represents the far right.
- *Education.* One of the established findings in European studies is that a more educated population is more supportive of European integration (Gabel, 1998; Gabel and Palmer, 1995). The available evidence from the US also shows that college (university) education is associated with "more tolerant, pro-outsider views of the world" as a result of socialisation (Hainmueller and Hiscox, 2006:473). Furthermore, as research has shown that a lower education level is associated with support for Brexit (Goodwin and Heath, 2016; Hobolt, 2016), I measure whether the individual has elementary or no education, high-school education, or tertiary education.
- *Age and gender.* In line with previous research (Anderson and Reichert, 1995; Gabel and Palmer, 1995), I control for the age and gender of respondents. Not only has research into support for Brexit showed that age is an important predictor of support for Brexit (Goodwin and Heath, 2016), but research into gender attitudes towards the issue of foreign policy has also found systematic differences between men and women (Eichenberg, 2016; Everts and Isernia, 2015).

III.3 Method

I estimate six models – two for each foreign policy actor (US, EU, Russia), one looking at the "old" EU Member States and one looking at the "new" EU Member States.[5] Each of them looks at the same set of independent variables, and each of them uses logistic regression with country-clustered standard errors.

IV Results

Before delving into the multi-variate analysis, let us turn to the overall percentage of the population holding positive views of the EU, US, and Russia using the data from the 2013 TTS and from the European Commission (2016).[6] The most Eurosceptic country is the UK, where only 53 per cent of the population held positive views about the EU (58 per cent in 2016). On the other hand, in Poland, the most Euro-optimistic country under study, the share was 82 per cent in both 2013 and 2016, and Romania was a close second with 79 per cent of the population. When it comes to positive attitudes about the US, Poland and Romania are again the two countries with the most positive view of the country (in both cases, almost 79 per cent). Slovakia was the country in which individuals were most anti-American (only 59 per cent of the population had a positive view). Slovakia is also the most Russia-positive country in the sample; 63 per cent of the population had a positive view of Russia in 2013 and 61 per cent in 2016. This contrasts strongly with only 16 per cent in Sweden and 35 per cent in Poland. The results do not show significant differences between the East and the West but do show distinctive profiles in some countries, such as Slovakia, where Russia is far more popular than in any other country in the sample. The results also show that the Russian invasion of Ukraine did not have a dramatic impact on the attitudes of the general public towards Russia, with the exception of Portugal and the Netherlands (in the latter case probably due to the shooting down of the MH 17 aircraft over Ukraine, which has been widely attributed to Russian-controlled military forces).[7]

Using the data from Transatlantic trends between 2006 and 2014, we can look at public attitudes over time (The German Marshall Fund of the United States, and Compagnia di San Paolo di Torino, 2006; The German Marshall Fund of the United States, and Compagnia di San Paolo di Torino, 2007; The German Marshall Fund of the United States, and Compagnia di San Paolo di Torino, 2008; The German Marshall Fund of the United States, and Compagnia di San Paolo di Torino, 2009; The German Marshall Fund of the United States, and Compagnia di San Paolo di Torino, 2010; The German Marshall Fund of the United States, and Compagnia di San Paolo di Torino, 2011; The German Marshall Fund of the United States, and Compagnia di San Paolo di Torino, 2012; The German Marshall Fund of the United States, and Compagnia di San Paolo di Torino, 2014). We have to recognise that the beginning of the crisis in Europe coincides with the departure of the deeply unpopular (among Europeans) President George W. Bush and the entry into office of President Barack Obama, with whose rule the so-called "Obama effect" is associated (Pew Research Center, 2012). Having said that, there are three main groups of countries. One is formed by the UK, where the US is significantly more popular throughout the period, compared to the EU or Russia. Then, there is Slovakia and Bulgaria, where the EU is more popular than the US or Russia. Bulgaria is, in this respect, even more remarkable, because the US is the least popular foreign policy actor in this country (from those under study). The last group of countries consists of the rest of the countries (France, Germany, Spain, Italy, Portugal, Poland, and Romania), where the EU and the US are roughly similarly popular, and where the pattern of development over time is roughly the same. After the boost in 2009 (the Obama presidency), the popularity of the EU and of the US remains the same over time or decreases slightly. The only exception to the pattern is Romania, where the popularity of both the US and the EU drops significantly in 2012.

Indeed, the most recent data from the 2016 Eurobarometer does not show significant changes compared to the data from 2013.[8] With a *caveat* that we are looking at the data from two different sources (and hence using possibly two different sampling methods), we may see an increase in support for the EU in the Netherlands and Sweden, the growth of anti-Americanism in Germany and France, and an increase in support for Russia in Romania and Italy, coupled with a simultaneous decrease in the Netherlands and Portugal. By and large, however, we do not observe large-scale changes in public opinion.

Moving to the multi-variate results, instead of traditional presentation in the form of a table with co-efficients, I present the results of the multivariate analysis in a simple graph. Two explanatory variables are listed on the y-axis.[9] The interpretation of the graph is fairly straightforward. The x-axis denotes how much more likely individuals are to develop positive views of a given actor, if a variable (on the y-axis) is present. Therefore, a value higher than 1 means *increased* likelihood, whereas a value lower than 1 means *decreased* likelihood. The horizontal

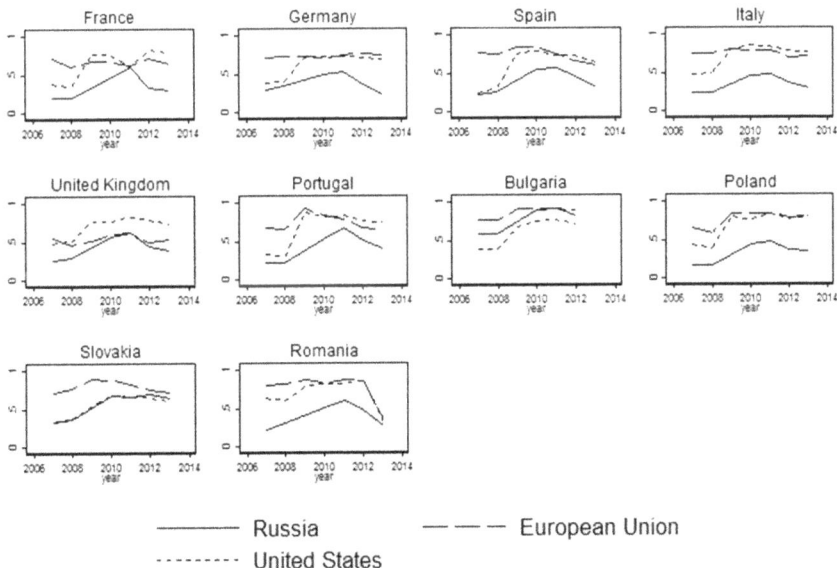

FIGURE 11.2   Share of population holding favourable opinion about actors (over time).

bars denote 95 per cent confidence intervals; if these cross the dashed line at value 1, the effect is not statistically significant.

In the old Member States, individuals (who consider themselves to be) affected by the economic crisis in Europe are more likely to hold more positive views of Russia and less positive views of the EU. Whereas the likelihood of holding positive views of Russia is, *ceteris paribus*, 0.26 for those not affected by the crisis, it is 0.30 for those affected by the crisis, while the probability of holding a positive view of the EU is, *ceteris paribus*, 69 per cent for those not affected by the crisis, and 64 per cent for those affected by the crisis. The situation is different in the new EU Member States. While the drop in the support for the EU is more pronounced (7 percentage points – 82 per cent *versus* 76 per cent), it is also statistically weaker. The crisis has had no effect on attitudes towards Russia.

This suggests that the public opinion in the old EU Member States, at an individual level, approximates partially the hydraulic press, a device where the downwards push of one piston results in an upwards push by another piston, with heightened strength. The experience of economic crisis, which accounts for the worsening of attitudes towards the EU, is associated with an improvement in attitudes towards Russia. This result confirms the results of earlier research that the crisis did not lead to the rise of anti-Americanism in Europe (Meunier, 2013), but it extends it to suggest that the opinion about Russia actually *improves* among the Western Europeans who feel that they have been negatively affected by the economic crisis. Western Europeans are more likely not only to be more critical

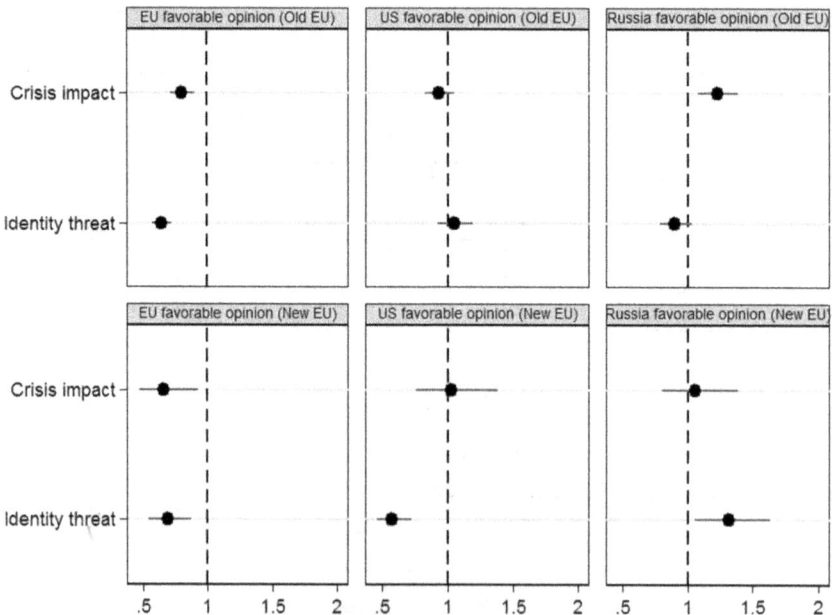

FIGURE 11.3 Effect of main variables on foreign policy.

of the EU but also to develop more positive views of other countries. In Eastern Europe, the experience of the financial crisis leads to some re-calibration of attitudes towards the EU, but overall, the EU remains rather popular.

While country fixed effects are not reported here, it is interesting to note that strong country effects persist. Compared to Germany (to which all Western European countries were compared), all other old EU Member States are much more Eurosceptic. When it comes to attitudes towards the US, citizens in Italy and France are 1.7 times more likely to develop positive views of the country, while the British and the Portuguese are twice as likely to have a positive view of Russia.[10] Among the new EU Member States, compared to Poland, Slovakia is the country that stands out in its attitudes towards both the US and Russia. While the Slovaks are only half as likely as the Poles to have a positive view of the US, they are almost three times as likely to have positive views of Russia. The persistence of these significant country-fixed effects warrants further study into origins of these strong national profiles, especially in the less-studied countries of Eastern Europe.

The threat to identity is, as expected, associated with lower support for the EU in both the old and new Member States. The effect of a threat to identity on attitudes towards the EU is exactly as hypothesised. The higher the proportion of the population who feel that the EU is a threat to their national culture, the lower is the share of those holding positive views of the EU. This adds to an existing body of literature which has found a similar impact of the threat to national identity attitudes towards the EU (Carey, 2002; Kuhn and Stoeckel, 2014; Kuhn et al., 2014; McLaren, 2004). Interestingly, however, the effect does not extend to attitudes towards Russia and the US among Western Europeans, presumably because the relations with these countries are not seen as threatening national identities. Among Eastern Europeans, citizens who feel under threat in terms of their identity tend to develop significantly worse images of the US and significantly better images of Russia (though the effect is statistically slightly weaker). This is probably because the US is associated with liberalism, which becomes associated with threats to nation and identity, whereas Russia is associated with direct opposition to liberalism. Given the relevance of liberal values and principles to the European project, this may actually underline a non-economic threat to support for the EU, in which internal constraints (and hence segmentation) may come not only because of unfulfilled economic promises, but also because of "dangerous" cultural ideas.

As for the other control variables, the results are not too surprising. When it comes to partisanship, support for the EU curiously copies the pattern of the positive view of the US. Citizens on the left tend to have more negative views of the EU as well as of the US, a fact that is not too surprising. Those on the centre-right are more likely to have slightly more positive views of the EU and of the US. Interestingly, those on the far right tend to be significantly more negative about the EU and tend to be more positive about Russia. Given the large amount of support Russia has given to the far-right movements in Europe, this may not be entirely surprising. Interestingly, the effect is present only among the Western European countries – among the Eastern European countries, partisanship plays little role. Though previous research has shown that large (and extreme) right-wing parties in the CEE (such as Civic Democracy in the Czech Republic, *Fidesz* [Hungarian Civic Alliance] in Hungary or *Prawo i Sprawiedliwość* [Law and Justice Party] in Poland) are, in fact, rather sceptical towards entanglement abroad (Kopecký and Mudde, 2002), this result may require future research and update.

Tertiary education is not associated with support for the EU among Western European citizens, in line with expectations from theory derived from previous research. It appears that Western European citizens reap the benefits of the European project, regardless of their education. The effect of age is as hypothesised: older Europeans are less likely to have positive views of any of the EU actors. Interestingly, the effect is statistically significant at all levels of age when it comes to opinions about the EU, but, when it comes to opinions about the US, only 55–64-year-olds are statistically distinguished from the rest of the sample, while, in the case of Russia, it is the population between the ages of 45 and 64. Curiously, Western European males are significantly more likely to hold positive views about Russia.

V Conclusion

In this chapter, I have looked at the extent of the internal constraints on national public policy as an expression of the segmentation of the European political order through the lens of the European public opinion on foreign affairs in the aftermath of the financial crisis. The existing research on the subject has been inconclusive and has focused exclusively on the EU. Theorists of European integration claimed that the governance crisis led to the breaking of the legitimacy of both domestic governments and of the European project, and that Europeans will stop seeing Europe positively (Scharpf, 2011; Schimmelfennig, 2014). Such findings were contradicted by empirical research which doubted such conclusions, or saw the effect of the crisis only as being conditional upon other factors (Hobolt and Wratil, 2015; Kuhn and Stoeckel, 2014). This chapter has focused on the overall impact of the crisis on foreign policy preferences among Europeans.

The results from the present research confirm that, on aggregate, the impact of the economic crisis on opinions about foreign policy in Europe was not particularly dramatic. Despite the potential that the crisis had to lead to a wider re-assessment of foreign policy beliefs among Europeans, the crisis is not associated with sharp upturns in foreign policy attitudes.

Crisis does influence attitudes towards the EU, but the effect is only moderate. Also, individuals impacted by the crisis do have a more positive view of Russia but not of the US. These results hint at the hydraulic press effect, in which downward pressure on one piston leads to upward pressure on the other piston. In the present case, this indicates that citizens improve their attitudes to (some) other entities as they decrease their support for the EU. This may be due to simple comparing – citizens see other entities not hit as strongly as themselves by the crisis (or coping with it better) and thus adjust their views of the EU. This result suggests that experiencing the crisis is not directly associated with the re-shaping of public attitudes, but that support for European integration may be somewhat instrumental.

One aspect not studied in this chapter is the impact on the views of Europeans of the election of Donald Trump as US president. It is likely that future studies, looking at Trump's election and its impact, will find that it did indeed have a significant negative impact and has led to a rise in anti-Americanism in Europe. This would not be the first time that Europeans turned to anti-Americanism in the face of the election of a Republican president (Chiozza, 2009; Revel, 2003), but it might be a particularly acute case. Compared to the latest bout of anti-Americanism in Europe, the European polity is currently experiencing multiple vulnerabilities – not only domestic constraints expressed through Euroscepticism, but also a resurgent Russia on its borders (as the editors of this volume mention in the introduction), and thus the impact of Trump's election might be stronger and more lasting.

On the other hand, confirming the results of the previous studies, a threatened identity is strongly associated with attitudes towards the EU and shapes attitudes both towards the US and towards Russia in Eastern Europe. It may be considered that Eastern Europeans take the US as a proxy for liberalism and Russia as the opponent to it. This finding underlines that the internal constraints on foreign policy-making might come not only from material considerations, but also from immaterial ones. One should take into account that the data upon which this analysis is based was collected *before* the 2015 refugee crisis. Given that the opposition to liberalism has been underlying the opposition to the EU's handling of the migration crisis, it should not be totally surprising if the further fracturing of attitudes towards foreign actors follows this line among Eastern (and also Western) European citizens.

The claims of those who state that the crisis led to changes in foreign policy attitudes in Europe need to be qualified. Individual experience of crises is associated with change in foreign policy preference. Such changes, however, are similar to the hydraulic press – crisis does not lead to a decrease of positive attitudes towards the post-Cold War Europe in general, but only to those of European integration. Such attitudes, however, provide further emphasis on the domestic constraints and the emergence of a segmented European political order. More research is needed to show whether there is a substitution effect, or whether it is a differential assessment based upon performance that affects attitudes.

The results also show that the nature of the constraints which stem from public opinion, which emerges as an aspect of the segmentation of the European political order, varies between the old and the new EU Member States. In particular, the results suggest that, while the economic cleavage is prevalent in the old EU Member States, the identity cleavage is clearly dominant in the new EU

Member States. Hence, the nationalism that many decry in the old EU members relates specifically to the attitudes towards the EU in the old EU, but is associated with wider foreign-policy attitudes in the new EU members. In particular, given the external sources of the segmentation of the political order in Europe, this finding is very relevant. Future research should further explore the origins, and "consequences," of such structuration.

Notes

1 Examples of such parties include the *Freiheitliche Partei Österreichs* (Freedom Party) in Austria, *Vlaams Belang* (Flemish Interest) in Belgium, or *Alternative für Deutschland* (Alternative for Germany). For a full list, see Table A.1 in Hobolt and de Vries (2016).
2 The other three varieties of anti-Americanism – jihadist, élitist, and legacy – are not applicable in this case.
3 Namely, France, Germany, Italy, the Netherlands, Poland, Portugal, Romania, Slovakia, Spain, Sweden, Turkey, and the United Kingdom.
4 All analyses have been re-run with the original (non-dichotomised) responses. The main results hold.
5 For the list of countries, see footnote 4.
6 I chose 2016 because the collection of the data preceded the election of Donald Trump, which might provide an additional motivation for adjustment of attitudes.
7 The Dutch attitudes towards Ukraine and Russia are complex, however; in 2017, for example, the Dutch rejected the EU-Ukraine Association Agreement in a referendum. See Jacobs *et al.*, (2018) for analysis of the motivations for that choice.
8 These numbers come from *before* the election of Donald Trump, and therefore do not reflect the dip in the views of the US that ensued.
9 An online appendix at the author's website provides the full table with all the results.
10 The Europeans' approval of sanctions is a result of their view of the EU as the sanctioning country. See Onderco (2017).

References

Anderson, Christopher J., and M. Shawn Reichert (1995), "Economic Benefits and Support for Membership in the EU: A Cross-national Analysis", *Journal of Public Policy*, 15 (3): 231–249.

Applebaum, Anne (2015), "The Fearful Foe That Ought to Unify Europe", available at: www.ft.com/intl/cms/s/0/32c10406-1b2d-11e5-8201-cbdb03d71480.html#axzz3uejHAI7l, last accessed 18 December 2015.

Arena, Philip, and Glenn Palmer (2009), "Politics or the Economy? Domestic Correlates of Dispute Involvement in Developed Democracies", *International Studies Quarterly*, 53 (4): 955–975.

Armingeon, Klaus, and Besir Ceka (2014), "The Loss of Trust in the European Union during the Great Recession Since 2007: The Role of Heuristics from the National Political System", *European Union Politics*, 15 (1): 82–107.

Aspinwall, Mark (2002), "Preferring Europe: Ideology and National Preferences on European Integration", *European Union Politics*, 3 (1): 81–111.

Balabanis, George, and Adamantios Diamantopoulos (2004), "Domestic Country Bias, Country-of-Origin Effects, and Consumer Ethnocentrism: A Multidimensional Unfolding Approach", *Journal of the Academy of Marketing Science*, 32 (1): 80–95.

Beyer, Heiko, and Ulf Liebe (2014), "Anti-Americanism in Europe: Theoretical Mechanisms and Empirical Evidence", *European Sociological Review*, 30 (1): 90–106.

Braun, Daniela, and Markus Tausendpfund (2014), "The Impact of the Euro Crisis on Citizens' Support for the European Union", *Journal of European Integration*, 36 (3): 231–245.

Calamur, Krishnadev (2018), "The World Has More Confidence in Putin Than in Trump", available at: www.theatlantic.com/international/archive/2018/10/global-opinion-of-trump/571870, last accessed 3 October 2018.

Carey, Sean (2002), "Undivided Loyalties: Is National Identity an Obstacle to European Integration?", *European Union Politics*, 3 (4): 387–413.

Chiozza, Giacomo (2009), *Anti-Americanism and the American World Order*, Baltimore MD: Johns Hopkins University Press.

Chryssogelos, Angelos-Stylianos (2010), "Undermining the West from Within: European Populists, the US and Russia", *European View*, 9: 267–277.

Cleveland, Mark, Michel Laroche, and Nicolas Papadopoulos (2009), "Cosmopolitanism, Consumer Ethnocentrism, and Materialism: An Eight-Country Study of Antecedents and Outcomes", *Journal of International Marketing*, 17 (1): 116–146.

Dimitrova, Anna (2012), "Public Opinion in Bulgaria with Regard to the EU Membership in the Context of the Economic Crisis", *L'Europe en Formation*, 364 (2): 289–304.

Eichenberg, Richard C. (2016), "Gender Difference in American Public Opinion on the Use of Military Force, 1982–2013", *International Studies Quarterly*, 60 (1): 138–148.

Esses, Victoria M., Ulrich Wagner, Carina Wolf, Matthias Preiser, and Christopher J. Wilbur (2006), "Perceptions of National Identity and Attitudes Toward Immigrants and Immigration in Canada and Germany", *International Journal of Intercultural Relations*, 30 (6): 653–669.

European Commission (2016), "Special Eurobarometer 451: Future of Europe", available at: http://ec.europa.eu/commfrontoffice/publicopinion/index.cfm/ResultDoc/download/DocumentKy/76431, last accessed 10 April 2017.

Everts, Philip, and Pierangelo Isernia (2015), *Public Opinion, Transatlantic Relations and the Use of Force*, Basingstoke: Palgrave Macmillan.

Everts, Philip, Pierangelo Isernia, and Francesco Olmastroni (2014), "International Security across the Atlantic: A Longitudinal Comparison of Public Opinion in Europe and the United States", available at: www.transworld-fp7.eu/?p=1502, last accessed 25 June 2015.

Fabbrini, Sergio (2002), "The Domestic Sources of European Anti-Americanism", *Government and Opposition*, 37 (1): 3–14.

Faust, Jörg, and Maria Melody Garcia (2014), "With or without Force? European Public Opinion on Democracy Promotion", *Journal of Common Market Studies*, 52 (4): 861–78.

Fligstein, Neil, Alina Polyakova, and Wayne Sandholtz (2012), "European Integration, Nationalism and European Identity", *Journal of Common Market Studies*, 50 (Special Issue 1): 106–122.

Fossum, John Erik (2015), "Democracy and Differentiation in Europe", *Journal of European Public Policy*, 22 (6): 799–815.

Gabel, Matthew (1998), "Public Support for European Integration: An Empirical Test of Five Theories", *The Journal of Politics*, 60 (2): 333–354.

Gabel, Matthew, and Harvey D. Palmer (1995), "Understanding Variation in Public Support for European Integration", *European Journal of Political Research*, 27 (1): 3–19.

Goodwin, Matthew J., and Oliver Heath (2016), "The 2016 Referendum, Brexit and the Left Behind: An Aggregate-Level Analysis of the Result", *The Political Quarterly*, 87 (3): 323–332.

Hainmueller, Jens, and Michael J. Hiscox (2006), "Learning to Love Globalization: Education and Individual Attitudes Toward International Trade", *International Organization*, 60 (2): 469–498.

Hemerijck, Anton, Ben Knapen, and Ellen van Doorne (2009), *Aftershocks: Economic Crisis and Institutional Choice*, Amsterdam: Amsterdam University Press.

Hobolt, Sara B. (2016), "The Brexit Vote: A Divided Nation, a Divided Continent", *Journal of European Public Policy*, 23 (9): 1259–1277.

Hobolt, Sara B., and Catherine de Vries (2016), "Turning against the Union? The Impact of the Crisis on the Eurosceptic Vote in the 2014 European Parliament Elections", *Electoral Studies*, 44: 504–514.

Hobolt, Sara B., and Christopher Wratil (2015), "Public Opinion and the Crisis: The Dynamics of Support for the Euro", *Journal of European Public Policy*, 22 (2): 238–256.

Hooghe, Liesbet, and Gary Marks (2005), "Calculation, Community and Cues: Public Opinion on European Integration", *European Union Politics*, 6 (4): 419–443.

Hooghe, Liesbet, and Gary Marks (2009), "A Postfunctionalist Theory of European Integration: From Permissive Consensus to Constraining Dissensus", *British Journal of Political Science*, 39 (1): 1–23.

Jacobs, Kristof, Agnes Akkerman, and Andrej Zaslove (2018), "The Voice of Populist People? Referendum Preferences, Practices and Populist Attitudes", *Acta Politica*, 53 (4): 517–541.

Katzenstein, Peter J., and Robert O. Keohane (2007), *Anti-Americanisms in World Politics*, Ithaca NY: Cornell University Press.

Kopecký, Petr, and Cas Mudde (2002), "The Two Sides of Euroscepticism: Party Positions on European Integration in East Central Europe", *European Union Politics*, 3 (3): 297–326.

Krotz, Ulrich (2009), "Momentum and Impediments: Why Europe Won't Emerge as a Full Political Actor on the World Stage Soon", *Journal of Common Market Studies*, 47 (3): 555–578.

Kuhn, Theresa, and Florian Stoeckel (2014), "When European Integration Becomes Costly: The Euro Crisis and Public Support for European Economic Governance", *Journal of European Public Policy*, 21 (4): 624–641.

Kuhn, Theresa, Erika van Elsas, Armen Hakhverdian, and Wouter van der Brug (2016), "An Ever Wider Gap in an ever Closer Union: Rising Inequalities and Euroscepticism in 12 West European Democracies, 1975–2009", *Socio-Economic Review*, 14 (1): 27–45.

Margalit, Yotam (2012), "Lost in Globalization: International Economic Integration and the Sources of Popular Discontent", *International Studies Quarterly*, 56 (3): 484–500.

McLaren, Lauren M. (2004), "Opposition to European Integration and Fear of Loss of National Identity: Debunking a Basic Assumption Regarding Hostility to the Integration Project", *European Journal of Political Research*, 43 (6): 895–912.

Mello, Patrick A. (2014), *Democratic Participation in Armed Conflict: Military Involvement in Kosovo, Afghanistan, and Iraq*, Basingstoke: Palgrave.

Meunier, Sophie (2013), "The Dog That Did Not Bark: Anti-Americanism and the 2008 Financial Crisis in Europe", *Review of International Political Economy*, 20 (1): 1–25.

Mudde, Cas (2007). "A Fortuynist Foreign Policy", in: Christina Schori Liang (ed), *Europe for the Europeans: The Foreign and Security Policy of the Populist Radical Right*, Aldershot: Ashgate Publishing, pp. 209–221.

Onderco, Michal (2017), "Public Support for Coercive Diplomacy: Exploring Public Opinion Data from Ten European Countries", *European Journal of Political Research*, 56 (2): 401–418.

Pew Research Center (2012), "Global Opinion of Obama Slips, International Policies Faulted. Drone Strikes Widely Opposed", available at: www.pewglobal. org/2012/06/13/global-opinion-of-obama-slips-international-policies-faulted, last accessed 1 June 2015.

Polyakova, Alina, and Neil Fligstein (2016), "Is European Integration Causing Europe to Become More Nationalist? Evidence from the 2007 to 2009 Financial Crisis", *Journal of European Public Policy*, 23 (1): 60–83.

Revel, Jean-Francois (2003), "Europe's Anti-American Obsession", available at: http://web.archive.org/web/20031204174924/http://theamericanenterprise.org/issues/articleid.17764/article_detail.asp., last accessed 3 June 2015.

Risse-Kappen, Thomas (1994), "Ideas Do Not Float Freely: Transnational Coalitions, Domestic Structures, and the End of the Cold War", *International Organisation*, 48 (2): 185–214.

Risse, Thomas, Daniela Engelmann-Martin, Hans-Joachim Knope, and Klaus Roscher (1999), "To Euro or Not to Euro?", *European Journal of International Relations*, 5 (2): 147–87.

Rynning, Sten (2015), "The False Promise of Continental Concert: Russia, the West and the Necessary Balance of Power", *International Affairs*, 91 (3): 539–552.

Scenario Team Eurozone 2020 (2013), "Future Scenarios for the Eurozone: 15 Perspectives on the Euro Crisis", available at: http://library.fes.de/pdf-files/id/ipa/09723.pdf, last accessed 18 December 2015.

Scharpf, Fritz W. (2011), "Monetary Union, Fiscal Crisis and the Preemption of Democracy", available at: www.lse.ac.uk/europeanInstitute/LEQS/LEQSPaper36.pdf, last accessed 1 June 2015.

Schimmelfennig, Frank (2014), "European Integration in the Euro Crisis: The Limits of Postfunctionalism", *Journal of European Integration*, 36 (3): 321–337.

Schoen, Harald (2008), "Identity, Instrumental Self-Interest and Institutional Evaluations: Explaining Public Opinion on Common European Policies in Foreign Affairs and Defence", *European Union Politics*, 9 (1): 5–29.

Serricchio, Fabio, Myrto Tsakatika, and Lucia Quaglia (2013), "Euroscepticism and the Global Financial Crisis", *Journal of Common Market Studies*, 51 (1): 51–64.

Sides, John, and Jack Citrin (2007), "European Opinion about Immigration: The Role of Identities, Interests and Information", *British Journal of Political Science*, 37 (3): 477–504.

Simon, Zoltan (2014), "Orbán Says He Seeks to End Liberal Democracy in Hungary", available at: www.bloomberg.com/news/articles/2014-07-28/orban-says-he-seeks-to-end-liberal-democracy-in-hungary, last accessed 15 July 2016.

Spiro, Herbert J. (1988), "Anti-Americanism in Western Europe", *Annals of the American Academy of Political and Social Science*, 497 (1): 120–132.

Streeck, Wolfgang (2013), *Gekaufte Zeit: die vertagte Krise des demokratischen Kapitalismus*, Erste Auflage 2013, ed., Berlin: Suhrkamp Verlag.

The Economist (2014), "Europe's Elections: The Eurosceptic Union", available at: www.economist.com/news/europe/21603034-impact-rise-anti-establishment-parties-europe-and-abroad-eurosceptic-union, last accessed 20 July 2016.

The German Marshall Fund of the United States, and Compagnia di San Paolo di Torino (2006), "2006 TransAtlantic Trends Survey [MCMISC2006-GMF]. Taylor Nelson Sofres [Producer]", Storrs CT: Roper Center for Public Opinion Research, RoperExpress.

The German Marshall Fund of the United States, and Compagnia di San Paolo di Torino (2007), "2007 TransAtlantic Trends Survey [MCMISC2007-GMF]. Taylor

Nelson Sofres [Producer]", Storrs CT: Roper Center for Public Opinion Research, RoperExpress.

The German Marshall Fund of the United States, and Compagnia di San Paolo di Torino (2008), "2008 TransAtlantic Trends Survey [MCMISC2008-GMF]. Taylor Nelson Sofres [Producer]", Storrs CT: Roper Center for Public Opinion Research, RoperExpress.

The German Marshall Fund of the United States, and Compagnia di San Paolo di Torino (2009), "2009 TransAtlantic Trends Survey [MCMISC2009-GMF]. Taylor Nelson Sofres [Producer]", Storrs CT: Roper Center for Public Opinion Research, RoperExpress.

The German Marshall Fund of the United States, and Compagnia di San Paolo di Torino (2010), "2010 TransAtlantic Trends Survey [MCMISC2010-GMF]. Taylor Nelson Sofres [Producer]", Storrs CT: Roper Center for Public Opinion Research, RoperExpress.

The German Marshall Fund of the United States, and Compagnia di San Paolo di Torino (2011), "2011 TransAtlantic Trends Survey [MCMISC2011-GMF]. Taylor Nelson Sofres [Producer]", Storrs CT: Roper Center for Public Opinion Research, RoperExpress.

The German Marshall Fund of the United States, and Compagnia di San Paolo di Torino (2012), "2012 TransAtlantic Trends Survey [MCMISC2012-GMF]. Taylor Nelson Sofres [Producer]", Storrs CT: Roper Center for Public Opinion Research, RoperExpress.

The German Marshall Fund of the United States, and Compagnia di San Paolo di Torino (2013), "2013 TransAtlantic Trends Survey [MCMISC2013-GMF]. Taylor Nelson Sofres [Producer]", Storrs CT: Roper Center for Public Opinion Research, RoperExpress.

The German Marshall Fund of the United States, and Compagnia di San Paolo di Torino (2014), "2014 TransAtlantic Trends Survey [MCMISC2014-GMF]", Storrs CT: Roper Center for Public Opinion Research, RoperExpress.

van Elsas, Erika, and Wouter van der Brug (2015), "The Changing Relationship between Left-Right Ideology and Euroscepticism, 1973–2010", *European Union Politics*, 16 (2): 194–215.

Zürn, Michael (2014), "The Politicization of World Politics and Its Effects: Eight Propositions", *European Political Science Review*, 6 (1): 47–71.

12

INTEGRATION THROUGH DIFFERENTIATION AND SEGMENTATION

The case of one Member State from 1950 to Brexit (and beyond)

Christopher Lord

I Introduction

This book makes the important distinction between differentiated integration, differentiation, and segmentation. Only by understanding all three can we understand the European Union (EU). Differentiated integration is self-evidently a form of integration. It denotes a process of coming together, albeit through institutions and policies which differ in terms of which Member States participate and with which commitments. It uses differentiation and flexibility to enable forms of integration that would not otherwise happen. Differentiation, on the other hand, denotes neither integration nor the lack of it. It is simply a term for any variation in authority relations, decision rules, administrative arrangements or substantive policy outcomes within a given political order. As such, differentiation is an almost universal feature of complex, modern political systems.

Segmentation, in contrast to both differentiated integration and differentiation, consists in ideological or cognitive variation in how problems and solutions are framed and understood within the same political order. Segmentation occurs when different policies within a polity depend on contrasting assumptions of fact and value about the economy and/or society; or on different normative justifications or standards of validity. Segmentation is cognitive where it involves biases in beliefs about cause–effect relationships, or, still more fundamentally, biases in what problems or solutions even receive the attention of actors with a political system (Jervis, 1976). Segmentation is ideological when it involves biases in how choices of value – and of economic, social, and political structures – are assumed to be foreclosed and without alternative. Both cognitive and ideological biases can even vary – policy by policy – within the same political order. For sure, segmentation is unlikely to be institutionally innocent. Actors are likely to select and adjust those institutions that support their ideological and cognitive biases.

But that, in itself, implies that the impact of segmentation is ideational – or to do with policy ideas and assumptions – before it is institutional.

Hence, taking the two preceding paragraphs together, we might anticipate three likely sources of variation within the EU's political and legal order: i) differences in institutional arrangements for making decisions common to all; ii) differences in the integration of members and even non-members to specific Union policies and institutions; and iii) differences in assumptions of fact and value within particular policy segments. I argue that all three have become important to the EU through the challenge of managing relations with just one of its Member States. All three have been used to manage incompatibilities between the United Kingdom's (UK) political and legal order and that of the Union. All three help answer the puzzle of how the EU combined UK membership with considerable further integration after 1973.

It is hardly a new interpretation to observe that the UK made much use of the scope for differentiation within the EU's polity (Leruth and Lord, 2015). More surprising is how far the UK contributed to differentiated *integration* and just how far it shaped some of the cognitive and ideological assumptions of some of the Union's policy segments. The argument proceeds as follows. Section II discusses incompatibilities between the UK's political and legal order and those of the Union. Section III analyses how differentiation, differentiated integration, and segmentation have helped manage those incompatibilities. Section IV discusses how those solutions were eventually insufficient to avoid a majority voting to leave the Union. Section V briefly speculates on differentiation after Brexit.

II Polity incompatibility

In setting out her approach to Brexit in her Lancaster House speech of January 2017, Theresa May repeated a claim, made by many since 1950, that the EU's supranational institutions are hard to reconcile with the UK's own political order:

> The principle of parliamentary sovereignty is the basis of our constitutional settlement … The public expect to be able to hold governments to account very directly, and, as a result, supranational institutions as strong as those of the EU sit very uneasily in relation to our political history and our way of life.
>
> *(UK Government, 2017)*

If, as Joseph Weiler (1997: 97) has argued, the primacy of Union laws is the "MS-DOS or Windows" of the EU's legal order, national parliamentary sovereignty is surely the DNA of the UK's polity.

In principle, there has always been a contradiction between the construction of the UK's political order around the unlimitable sovereignty of its national parliament and the construction of the Union around the priority of its own laws. Hence, Tony Blair's (2010: 604) "theory" that the British "problem with Europe" is that the UK "did not invent it" is not as "absurd" as he makes out. Had the UK invented them, it is a fair guess that the original European Communities would have included neither supranational institutions nor a seeming commitment to further integration over time. Indeed, for those who questioned the compatibility of the British and European political and legal orders, the problem was never just that the EU had supranational institutions. An even deeper worry was that those supranational institutions might be cumulatively entangling, and that membership might be taken as a commitment to ever-further integration. As soon as the French Government proposed a European Coal and Steel Community (ECSC) in 1950 with supranational institutions, the British Foreign Office cautioned that the UK should only participate if it was prepared to be "hustled along the road to full federation through the creation of supranational authorities controlling a widening range of functions."[1] Yet, it was Winston Churchill who most memorably expressed the view that the UK could only participate in European integration up to a point. As he put it, "we are with but not of Europe. We help, we dedicate, we participate, but we do not merge or forfeit our insular character."[2] Some even doubted that it would always be wise to "help." The permanent secretary at the Foreign Office was to scribble "embrace destructively" when confronted with an early proposal for a Common Market (Horne, 1988: 363). More than 60 years later, the UK's former permanent representative to the EU, Ivan Rogers (2018: 2), noted that, for some, any commitment by the Union to further integration over time could only mean that the UK would have to get off at some point. Hence, one of UK's last acts of membership was to seek the ultimate opt-out: from the treaty commitment to "ever closer Union" itself.

Even if not always moved by arguments about parliamentary sovereignty, an important element of the British public was open to the more general argument that EU membership was incompatible with what it was for the British public to govern itself as a democratic people. The roots of concerns about self-rule and identity are best understood by beginning at the end, with Brexit itself. It is often argued that Brexit is the product of an inconsistent coalition. And, in many ways, it is. Many of its strategists and policy entrepreneurs see Brexit as an opportunity to turn the UK into one of the most open and de-regulated economies in the world. Many of its voters, on the other hand, supported Brexit as a protest precisely against those forms of unregulated globalisation and free movements of labour that may be needed for the UK to prosper as a highly competitive and fully internationalised economy outside the EU.

Yet, whatever their contradictions, there are two factors common to many who voted for Brexit. First, many of them would probably agree that they voted in some way for the UK to "take back control of its own laws, money and borders." Failure to understand this risks failure to understand the June 2016 referendum (Weale, 2017). Second, many Leave voters are also older voters. As Anthony Barnett (2017) observes, opinion surveys find no majority for Brexit in any age group "under the age of 55." In a YouGov (2017) survey in March 2017, only 12 per cent of the 18–24 age group thought that Brexit was "right," while

65 per cent thought it "wrong." Just how generational differences intersected in the Brexit vote with beliefs about the incompatibility of EU membership with what it is for the British public to control its own laws comes out in a YouGov survey. When asked to pick "two or three of the most important issues when deciding on Britain's future relationship with the EU," 54 per cent of all Leave voters and 54 per cent of those over 65 chose "ensuring Britain has control over its own laws" as an answer. In contrast, this response was chosen by only 17 per cent of Remain voters and only 12 per cent of the 18–24 age group. It should be noted that this does not mean that younger voters consider the control of laws to be unimportant. It may just be that the younger are less likely than older voters to believe that the UK ever lost control of its own laws to the EU or – dare one say it - that they believe the EU is a broadly fair way of sharing out control of laws between countries which choose to make some of their laws together. It would seem, then, that Leave *versus* Remain is a generational cleavage and a legitimacy cleavage. Leavers and older voters believe that Brexit is "right" and justified by a need for the UK to regain control of its own laws. Remain and younger voters disagree that this is justification for Brexit.

Such a fundamental difference can only be explained by the very different experiences of generations of UK voters. No voter under the age of 50 has any political memory from a time in which the UK was not a member of the EU. No voter over 50 is likely to be unaffected by the profound influence of the Second World War on British politics and society. Those from that age group who did not directly experience the Second World War are the children of those who did. All were brought up during the long post-war period when – until well into the 1970s – the Second World War was famously the stuff of daily conversation and television in the UK. After 1945, many in Britain would find it hard to define their attitudes to European unification without recalling how close the UK had come to invasion from continental Europe in 1940–1941. Few would go as far as the government minister who was forced to resign in 1990 after claiming that the EU was achieving through peace what Adolf Hitler had failed to achieve through war. But concern about external domination was plainly a part of British Euroscepticism, whether that was scepticism about the very idea of European unification, British participation in it, or any EU policies or institutions that might corrode national identity or elude the control of individual Member States.

Moreover, the war reinforced older concepts of British statehood and identify. Fear of invasion was central to the formation of British identity (Colley, 1992). Preventing a concentration of power on the European continent was the main external purpose of the British state. Great power status and global presence were its main external characteristics. The sovereignty of its parliament and the supremacy of its laws were its guiding internal principles. The UK was one of the few European states that emerged from the crisis of 1914–1945 without being defeated, invaded, or discredited by war. Even the idea of parliamentary sovereignty weathered the storm. The UK was one of only five European states in which parliamentary democracy (more or less) survived uninterrupted between 1918 and 1945 (Hobsbawm, 1994: 111). After 1945, attachment to national parliamentary sovereignty only seemed to grow stronger. The Labour and Conservative parties both mythologised parliamentary sovereignty. In their own self-understanding, parliamentary sovereignty had enabled them heroically to transform their country in their own image: leftwards between 1945 and 1951; rightwards between 1979 and 1990. Fears that European integration would constrain parliamentary sovereignty – and, therefore, their own ability to pursue domestic political programmes of their own choosing – shaped opposition to the EU in both parties. Typical of the huge opposition that developed in the Labour Party to British entry to the Common Market in the 1970s was the leftwinger who told the House of Commons that joining the EU would "put the locks on socialism."[3] Typical of the deep Euroscepticism that later developed in the Conservative Party was the ex-chair of the Leave campaign, and Margaret Thatcher's former finance minister, who argued that, by recovering full parliamentary sovereignty, Brexit would remove the last obstacle to the completion of the Thatcher revolution. In a political system that punishes divided parties, both governments and the two main parties have had to reckon with even small pockets of opinion that can be mobilised around claims that the Union is a form of external domination that is incompatible with what it is for the UK public to govern itself as a democratic people.

III Managing polity incompatibility

Given all the foregoing, many worried that the British and European political and legal orders would prove incompatible with one another, and that the UK would, therefore, constrain and disrupt European integration if it became a member. In January 1963, the French president, Charles De Gaulle, memorably vetoed British accession on the grounds that the UK would be a "Trojan Horse." When, in 1969, the six original members re-opened negotiations with the UK, it was not without taking the precaution of first committing the UK to existing and further integration (Simonian, 1985), lest it should seek to unravel it. Nor did British governments altogether conceal their view that controlling the process from within was a reason for joining it (UK Government, 1971). Throughout its membership, the UK also supported the enlargement of the EU, in part, it was suspected, because a wider EU would be less likely to be a deeper one; or, as the joke went, if enough states could be persuaded to jump on board, the raft would eventually sink.[4] Then, when the UK joined in 1973, it seemed to confirm the fears that it would disrupt the Communities. It spent much of the first decade of its membership seeking to re-negotiate the terms of its accession. The first change of government in 1974 brought in a Labour administration committed to a wholesale re-negotiation. The next change in 1979 brought in a Conservative government which refused to agree to any major new initiative within the European Communities until it received a rebate on its budget contribution in 1984.

Yet, British membership after 1973 neither fragmented the Union nor constrained its development. To the contrary, I will argue later that the UK was the single most important supporter of the single most important act of centre formation in the history of the contemporary EU. Here, I take co-ordination and norms and obligations to consult and discuss to be one indicator of centre formation. But by far the most important indicator is, of course, how far the Union can (and does) over-rule and bind its component democracies in making decisions and laws.

So maybe all the historic conceptions of parliamentary sovereignty, identity, national self-rule, and great and global power status mentioned earlier had themselves to be adjusted to the need for a thoroughly modern economy, state, and society such as the UK to co-operate with its European neighbours? Adaptation to security contexts was crucial to the UK's acceptance of European integration even before British governments felt able to be a part of it. Opposition to any concentration of power on the near continent was quickly abandoned. By 1950, the British Foreign Office felt that intervening "to prevent progress to a West European Federal system" would "incur the utmost political odium."[5] The Ministry of Defence felt that "any failure to give effect to the Schuman proposals would amount to a setback in the cold war/Cold War."[6] If, at the start of the 1950s, British policy on European integration had to adapt to geopolitical competition, by the end of the 1950s, it began to adapt to changing patterns of global economic competition: first, to a growing propensity for developed economies to trade primarily with one another and their immediate neighbours; and, then, especially from the 1980s, to a perception that the UK and its neighbours needed to develop their competitive advantage in a shared internal market – free of any crazy patchwork of multiple laws and multiple fixes for favoured producers – if they were to cultivate the high-value added economies needed to sustain their expensive societies.

However, the UK did not just adapt to the external demands of economic and security systems. In some ways, the UK also adapted understandings of its own political and legal order – and, therefore, the very historic conceptions of self-rule mentioned earlier – to its membership of the Union. Take the example of a famous High Court judgment in which Lord Denning said of the EU Treaties:

> The Treaty is like an incoming tide. It flows into the estuaries and up the rivers. It cannot be held back. Parliament has decreed that the Treaty is henceforth to be a part of our law.[7]

This was grudging. Indeed, Denning would end his career a supporter of the Eurosceptic revivalism of the 1990s. Yet, Denning's judgment was an example of national courts working hard to adapt national law to Union law and to avoid conflicts between the two. As Peter Lindseth (2010) has argued, this is one of three ways in which Member States have evolved "mechanisms" that allow the Union to borrow the legitimacy of its component Member States and their democracies.

The UK has also promoted the other two, namely, national parliamentary scrutiny, and collective supervision of Union decisions by national executives. Together with the Danish parliament, Westminster pioneered practices of national parliamentary scrutiny of Community decisions, which had barely existed before 1973.

The UK's role in promoting the joint supervision of Union decisions by national executive actors was less original. However, the UK civil service was a famously thorough participant in this process. This was crucial. Even if it creates dangers of "executive domination," the intimate involvement of national actors in Union decisions is key to maximising alignment between the Union's polity and those of its Member States through a search for the greatest possible agreement between the elected governments of those Member States. Data on voting in the Council of Ministers demonstrates that, even where Qualified Majority Voting is available, almost all decisions are taken with the agreement of almost all Member States. Moreover, in this regard, the UK was just like other Member States. British Governments hardly ever felt any need to vote against Council decisions (Mattila and Lane, 2001). In sum, then, the UK has contributed to the development of EU Member States into states of a distinctive kind (Bickerton, 2012), namely, states that have adapted their own law, executives, and representative institutions to their shared membership of the Union. This is, both in and of itself, a huge contribution to integration.

However, my main interest is not in what the UK case tells us about the adaptiveness of a Member State to the EU, but, rather, in the adaptiveness of the Union itself to possible incompatibilities between its polity and that of one of its Member States. The remainder of this section shows how the Union adapted to UK membership through all three means mentioned earlier of differentiating a shared political order from within, namely, differentiation a) in common institutions; b) in the participation of members; and c) in the cognitive and ideological assumptions of policy segments. Indeed, the sometimes complex and creative solutions used to accommodate the UK demonstrated just how much scope there is within the Union's political order to use all three in combination. Sometimes, this constrained integration. Other times, though, it by-passed obstacles to integration or even catalysed it in ways that help to explain how UK membership was combined with continued integration after 1973.

III.1 Differentiation

Philippe Schmitter (2000: 21) once described the Union as, in some ways, "a plurality of polities at different levels of aggregation." For sure, some institutions – the Commission, Council of Ministers/European Council, and European Parliament – operate across the range of Union policies and decisions. Yet, there are important variations in the decision-rules, practices, and allocations of powers by which those institutions aggregate, or compound (Fabbrini, 2015), the powers and preferences of Member States and other actors. Sometimes, the Union merely co-ordinates the powers and preferences of Member States.

Sometimes, it socialises preferences of Member States through learning, deliberation, or experimentation (Sabel and Zeitlin, 2008). Sometimes, it combines preferences into binding majorities, albeit using powers conferred by each Member State, and using practices that emphasise a need to exhaust informal efforts to reach the greatest possible agreement before employing the formal powers of qualified majorities to outvote others.

The main way in which the Union has developed different ways of making decisions common to all is through the Community and Union methods (Bickerton *et al.*, 2015). Under the Community method, the Commission exercises an exclusive right of initiative. The Council formally decides by Qualified Majority. The European Parliament (EP) normally gets to co-decide. The Court of Justice of the European Union (CJEU) always has competence. In contrast, under the Union method, the Commission often participates in decisions, but it has no exclusive right of initiative. The Council normally decides by unanimity. The Parliament is only consulted or informed. The Court of Justice is often excluded from jurisdiction (ibid.).

Although the UK was far from alone in promoting the Union method, it, perhaps justifiably, claimed it as an important gain from the Treaty on European Union (TEU) (Patten, 2017). Before the TEU, earlier versions of the Community method more or less had a monopoly on Treaty formation. In other words, it was assumed that, in the interests of eventually building a uniform political and legal order within the Treaties, other forms of co-operation should occur outside the Treaties. Hence, the Union method has self-evidently frustrated the development through the Treaties of a single institutional order with a singular form of political authority based upon the Community method. But before that is dismissed as altogether negative for integration, it needs to be noted that the Union and Community methods do not usually compete with one another. Rather, they do different things. The Community method makes law in matters where the Union has competence. The Union method mostly co-ordinates national powers through the institutions of the Union. Whilst the Union method requires the unanimous agreement of Member States – and can do nothing else, given that it co-ordinates the powers of Member States – this unanimous agreement is crucially formed within European institutions: the European Council and the Council of the European Union. Moreover, the Union method is often also co-ordinated with decisions under the Community method. It often draws on the expertise and participation of the Commission.

The institutional configuration contained in the Union method has – with growing importance since 1992 – allowed the Common Foreign and Security Policy (CFSP) to co-ordinate security missions and security capabilities in ways that go beyond the largely declaratory character of early attempts at foreign policy co-operation. It has also allowed Justice and Home Affairs to develop ambitious forms of information exchange in matters of internal security. It has even permitted a hybrid of the Union and Community methods to be used by the European semester (Lord, 2017) to co-ordinate the budgets – and, therefore, the taxing, spending, and borrowing – of the Member States. All these are, as Philipp Genschel and Markus Jachtenfuchs (2014) argue, examples of how the EU now co-ordinates core state powers in ways that anchor the Union as a general-purpose polity in the co-ordination problems of its Member States. In sum, without a combination of monetary union which the UK did *not* shape and the Union method which it *did* shape, the EU would probably have remained the kind of "regulatory state" that Giandomenico Majone (1994) claimed it to be in the 1990s: a hugely powerful instrument of market regulation, largely confined, nonetheless, to market regulation.

III.2 Differentiated integration

Of the three ways of differentiating a polity internally discussed here, differences in how far members participate in particular policies and institutions are the best-known means by which British membership of the Union after 1973 was reconciled with continued integration. Monetary union, the Schengen *acquis*, and Justice and Home Affairs (now the Area of Freedom, Justice and Security [AFSJ]) are all forms of integration that have preceded with UK opt-outs. Indeed, in the latter two cases, the UK has both opt-outs and opt-ins. The UK also has a partial opt-out from the EU's Fundamental Charter of Rights.

At first, British governments did not seek differential participation. To the contrary, they feared complete non-participation in initiatives as much as they feared full participation in unwanted proposals for further integration. British governments believed that the main lesson of non-membership between 1950 and 1973 was that the UK should not allow itself to be marginalised from decisions by which it would be affected, or from policies to which it might one day have to adhere (Heath, 1970). Jacques Attali (1995: 876–7) recalls a conversation during the Maastricht negotiations during which, in response to François Mitterrand's observation that "Europe has got used to British opposition and to making plans without the UK in the expectation it would join later," John Major cautioned against always regarding the UK as a European integration laggard. As he put it, "Britain didn't just want to join the train. It wanted to be in the driver's cabin." UK governments may have been guarded about centre formation beyond the creation of the single market or co-operation using the Union method, yet, they were determined, nonetheless, to remain at the centre of the Union. For their part, the defenders of a uniform *acquis communautaire* feared that accommodating the UK (and others) by differentiating the participation, rights, and obligations of different members to different policies would fracture the Union.

However, the UK's opt-outs permitted, more than they constrained, integration. First, and most obviously, other Member States were able to integrate further without having to step outside the EU Treaties in order to circumvent a British veto. Indeed, the idea – pioneered in response to British membership – that differentiation is the way to reconcile disagreements between those who want to integrate further and those who do not, seems likely to outlast

British membership itself. "Coalitions of the willing" in which "new groups of Member States agree on specific legal and budgetary arrangements to deepen their co-operation in chosen domains" form one scenario in the Commission's (2017: 20) recent White Paper on "the Future of Europe" after Brexit.

Second, the British were often supportive from the outside. When the Exchange Rate Mechanism collapsed in 1993, it was the British finance minister who proposed the compromise of relaxing the mechanism but not abandoning it in ways which would have put the Treaty commitment to monetary union in question. Nor was this just an isolated example. The UK was too embedded in the Union's overall political economy for it not to have an interest in the stability and success of EU policies in which it did not participate. Much later, David Cameron's noisy veto in 2011 of the inclusion of the Fiscal Compact in the Union Treaties obscured the quieter assessment of his government that further integration of the Eurozone needed the UK's support, given the fragilities in its own banking system.

Third, the UK sought to compensate for its absence from some policies by commitment to others. By putting the UK at the core of the European Common Security and Defence Policy (CSDP), Tony Blair hoped to offset its absence from monetary union (Liddle, 2014: 113). By combining continued use of the monetary union opt-out with a commitment to CFSP/CSDP, the 1997–2010 government hoped to be an indispensable partner in a policy governed by the decision-rules which it felt most able to accept whilst abstaining from a policy governed by decision-rules most likely to provoke opposition within the UK, not least in the cabinet itself. Not only is CFSP/CSDP (mainly) governed by the Union method, but, crucially, from a point of view of domestic opposition to supranational institutions, monetary union establishes an even more supranational authority than the Community method.

As Kenneth Dyson has remarked (2000: 11), "The ECB has the potential to play an active role as a supranational 'executive' body that exceeds the autonomy of action available to the European Commission." Not only is the ECB "probably the most independent central bank in the free world" (European Parliament, 1998), it is unlike other – apparently independent – Union institutions. Most Union institutions are usually constrained several times over. First, they are often unable to take decisions on their own without other Union institutions. Second, they are, in any case, parts of a wider institutional order that rarely enjoys its own exclusive competence. This makes it difficult to take decisions without regard for what national and sub-national authorities are attempting to do in the same policy-field. Third, Union decisions are usually implemented by national or sub-national authorities, over which the Union only has limited coercive resources (Scharpf, 2009). In contrast, these constraints are weak, or even non-existent, in the case of the ECB. It acts in one of the few areas where the Union has exclusive competence. Within the Eurozone, the ECB has monopoly control over monetary policy. Moreover, it decides monetary policy on its own initiative and without having to concern itself with other veto holders among the other Union institutions. Finally, the ECB's implementing agents are not national governments. Rather, they are national central banks, themselves part of the epistemic community of independent central bankers.

There was, then, a certain coherence to the UK accepting the authority relations entailed by the Community method and the single market whilst rejecting those involved in the single currency. The former are more embedded than the latter both in the implementation of individual Member States and in their joint decision-rights in Union institutions. Moreover, differentiation avoided a breach. The Eurozone countries got their shared currency and shared central bank, and, crucially, they got them within European Treaties of which the UK remained a part. The treaty obligation to join the euro did not apply to the UK. The ECB's strongly supranational powers and decision-rules only applied within the Eurozone. To the extent, then, that it avoided what might have been earlier crises in the UK's membership – notably over the negotiation of the TEU in 1990–1991 – differentiated integration of Member States to specific policies was essential to the resilience of an EU that included the UK.

III.3 Segmentation

However, support for differentiation of the Union's overall institutional architecture into the Community and Union methods, together with abstention from some policies with supranational commitments, cannot explain everything about UK membership. Sometimes, the UK embraced supranational forms of integration with enthusiasm, whilst nonetheless insisting that some commitments should apply uniformly to all members. Other times, the UK constrained integration even of a kind governed by the Union method and even of a kind where co-operation was likely to take the form of differential participation through "coalitions of the willing."

To understand these further forms of variation in how the UK constructed its own membership of the EU, we need to turn to the third form of variation mentioned earlier: cognitive and ideological differences in how policies are believed to work and in what choices are assumed to be available in making them. Institutions that are otherwise objectionable may seem appropriate, given what are assumed to be limited alternatives, and limited means of achieving those alternatives, within a particular policy segment. Opposition can, conversely, be over-determined where it rests both on objections to institutions in themselves and on their suitability to a particular policy segment. This section shows how the single market was a policy segment where the UK put aside its normal opposition to supranational institutions. Security co-operation, on the other hand, was a policy where assumptions particular to that policy reinforced UK opposition to institutional development at Union level.

Thatcher wrote as follows in her memoirs:

> I had one overriding positive goal. This was to create a single market … What remained were so-called non-tariff barriers. The price which we would have to pay to achieve a single market with all its economic benefits

was more majority voting in the Community. There was no escape from that, because otherwise particular countries could succumb to domestic pressures and prevent the opening up of their markets. It also required more power for the European Commission.

(1993: 553)

The point was later reinforced by Ivan Rogers (2018: 13–14), the UK's permanent representative to the EU, who, throughout his career, followed and shaped the development of the single market on behalf of successive British governments:

a single market is not remotely like a free trade area. It is a much deeper and more fundamental trade liberalization tackling the stickiest … behind border barriers … and that *requires* (his italics) supranationalism … requires qualified majority voting … and requires tough supranational enforcement and adjudication: in other words a strong and activist Commission and a rigorous supranational Court … Both were consistently more UK friendly than the centre of gravity in the Council of Ministers on liberalization, internal and external … There is and can be no intergovernmentalist single market. This is a Unicorn.

Yet, for all the supranational institutions that a single market required, no Member State pushed harder for it than the UK. As Rogers (2018: 14) continues:

We were for our entire membership the biggest champion of single market initiatives … UK demonstrably had more impact in pushing the EU in a trade liberalization direction than any other player.

By pressing so hard for a single market, the UK made a decisive contribution to European centre formation, perhaps the most important act of centre formation in the construction of the contemporary EU. Although the European Communities were founded in the 1950s, there is much to the argument that there was little more to European integration before the mid-1980s (Bickerton, 2012). The single market initiative changed all that. It switched efforts from removing border barriers to trade to removing those behind boundaries. This required a massive volume of shared law-making. Whilst, then, the European Court of Justice had first claimed the supremacy of European Community law in 1964, it was only in the late 1980s that Member States began to use their shared membership of the European Community to legislate together on an ambitious scale. From the launch of the single market programme in 1986, the EU became a significant form of shared rule. From then on, Member States made large volumes of law together. The allocation of values in each Member State and the lives of the citizens of each Member State were now significantly affected by the laws that their governments made through their shared membership of the Union.

Hence, any expectation that the UK might constrain integration from within was overwhelmed by the UK's own appetite for one particular form of European integration, namely, the UK's own appetite for one particular form of European integration. Market integration was considered the one form of integration to which supranational institutions and law-making were considered appropriate. Indeed, this was one area where UK governments insisted – against their normal taste for differentiation and differentiated integration – that there should, indeed, be some obligations, some ways of thinking, and some ways of doing things that should apply to all 28 Member States, for example, as part of any uniform body of policies and laws that would eventually have to be swallowed whole by new members.

Although space does not permit full a discussion here, there were, perhaps, two reasons why British governments believed supranational institutions and law-making were uniquely justified in decisions on market integration. First, beyond the creation of the legal framework itself, market integration could be understood, in Hayekian terms, as a natural or spontaneous order rather than a planned or designed one. Second, the single market programme allowed British Governments to constitutionalise free market solutions both internally and externally. Once enacted as EU law, single market measures could only be changed on a proposal from the Commission, supported by an over-sized majority of the Council and a vote of the EP. Not only would this make it hard for subsequent British governments to reverse market liberalisation within the UK, but market liberalisation within the UK would also be more secure if its immediate economic neighbourhood was also a part of a single market that could not be easily altered by the normal decision rules and arrangements for political competition within any one Member State.

The Common Foreign and Security Policy (CFSP) was another policy segment whose guiding assumptions were profoundly shaped by the UK, although, in this case, British policy assumptions reinforced rather than over-rode concerns about institutions. Here, a core problem was that both the UK and France were *de facto* veto-holders over the development of security co-operation within a Union in which they were the only two large-scale security providers. Yet, as Jolyon Howorth (2018) has put it, the UK and France assumed contrasting answers to a "Euro-Atlantic security dilemma." "London feared … that too overt a European drive in the direction of autonomy (in security) would fuel US isolationism. Paris was confident that the US would welcome and take seriously allies that took themselves seriously … Nobody seemed sure whether" EU defence capacity would "weaken or strengthen the alliance." Richard Whitman (2016: 83) adds that France "has persisted with the idea of Anglo-French co-operation at the heart of a successful European foreign, security and defence policy," whilst, in contrast, the UK has tried to develop a bilateral Anglo-French defence relationship without that implying a wider commitment to European security co-operation.

The two governments came closest to framing the problem of European security in the same way in agreeing at the Saint-Malo summit (1998) to establish a Common Security and Defence Policy (CSDP) within the CFSP. The Saint-Malo Declaration assumed, first, that the Atlantic Alliance was best secured by Europe doing more; and, second, that European security co-operation could achieve some things that were unlikely to be done through NATO. NATO was a collective security guarantee against an actual aggression, but, short of that, a CSDP could usefully be tasked with "preventing, managing and resolving crises using both military and civilian resources." More recently, however, the UK policy has been more reluctant to frame a stronger CFSP and CSDP as solutions. As Whitman (2016: 82–84) continues, the UK has resisted improving the "effectiveness of CFSP via greater use of the EU's own financial resources and power as a trading block." It has also resisted the further development of the European Defence Agency and vetoed the creation of a permanent operational headquarters, with the result that the EU had to use headquarters borrowed from Member States and from NATO. Indeed, a clear indicator that it has preferred to frame European security co-operation as, at most, "civilian" can be seen from the fact that the UK "has been a very modest contributor to the military strand of CSDP operations. In contrast, it has contributed personnel to the majority of EU civilian missions."

IV Breakdown

I have argued that three forms of differentiation were used to reconcile UK membership with continued European integration after 1973. The UK sought to differentiate the Union's institutional methods. It abstained from some policies, and, where it did participate, it shaped and differentiated the assumptions of core policy segments to its own purposes. At the time of the 2004–2007 enlargements and the Convention on the Constitutional Treaty, few would have regarded the UK's complex relationship with the Union as a significant constraint on how far the British government could shape the membership, powers, and institutions of the Union (Lord, 2008). It was a measure of the UK's influence as much as of its awkwardness that, during the Convention, its president, Valéry Giscard d'Estaing, often asked the representative of the British Government to respond first to proposals (Norman, 2003). Far from being representatives of a failed Member State, British governments seemed to have a remarkable ability to get much of what they wanted from membership of the Union, whilst avoiding almost everything that they did not want. As seen, they secured both the single market initiative and the enlargement of the Union. Yet, when, invited to participate in monetary union, the UK secured an opt-out. Indeed, so extraordinary was the UK's ability to "have its cake and eat it" – to forge a relationship that was so "bespoke" as almost to amount to its own private form of membership – that it combined a general opt-out from large areas of Justice and Home Affairs (now the AFSJ) with opt-ins to 130 specific measures.

But could abstaining from some policies whilst setting the core assumptions of others be relied upon to reconcile EU membership with conceptions of what it was for the UK to govern itself as a democratic people? Was "pick and mix" a stable and sustainable approach to membership? Or did it contain the seeds of its own destruction? One obvious difficulty was that abstention from monetary union made the UK more detachable from its membership of the Union. Although much of British opinion would doubtless have hated participation in the Euro, Brexit would still have been more difficult if the UK had had to confront the risks and costs of re-substituting a national for a shared currency at the same time as exiting the EU's single market and customs union.

Another problem was the sheer volume of shared law-making that followed from developing the single market as the policy segment at the core of UK membership. This goal turned out to be much more than a once-off exception to the UK's more general opposition to supranational polity-building. Rather, creation of the single market was sufficient in itself to constitute the EU as a "regulatory state" (Majone, 1994). In significant part as a result of the single market, the Union now makes 20–30 per cent of the laws (depending on the Member State and on the methods of calculation) (Töller 2010) under which the 510 million citizens of the Union's 28 Member State democracies live their lives. Moreover, even laws of national and local origin have to be adjusted and interpreted so that they are compatible with EU law (Brouard *et al.*, 2012). Once again, Ivan Rogers (2018: 3) identifies the problem: membership left the UK with "a huge number of legal, institutional and regulatory arrangements which had become central to the operation of the British state … The UK's very immersion in these structures meant that its own state's capacity to resume sovereignty … was much diminished across large tracts of the economy."

Belief that the UK could participate with limited implications for the control of its own laws or its boundaries was then further challenged by the multiple crises in European integration after 2008, as was the idea that the UK could participate in some policies without exposure to the effects of others. In contrast to the Maastricht model, in which complete centralisation of monetary policy was balanced by near-complete fiscal de-centralisation, the euro crisis pushed the members of the monetary union into more fiscal co-ordination and into a banking union. Monetary union, it was now believed, would need to develop further if it was to survive at all. This, many in the UK feared, would either force the UK to join the euro or risk domination by a Eurozone majority in decisions on the wider EU. Here, the UK faced an acute dilemma. For it was, in a sense, anything but a monetary union "out." Since 1999, London has developed as the financial centre for the euro without being in the euro (Jones, 2015). It dominated both euro currency and bond trading. It headquartered most non-EU banks within the Union's single financial market. British governments, therefore, worried about institutional incongruence between the EU and its monetary union. Many rules that govern access to the euro's financial infrastructure (Armstrong, 2016: 34) – clearing and liquidity – can (unsurprisingly) be made by Eurozone actors alone. However, other financial regulations are made as single market rules by the EU-28. Amongst the EU-28, the 19 members of the Eurozone approximate on their own to a qualified majority of 55 per cent of Member States, representing 65 per cent of the Union population. It was a sign of how far it now feared domination by a Eurozone majority that, when asked to agree changes to the European Banking Authority (EBA), the UK insisted that the EBA should only be able to take decisions with a double majority of both Eurozone "ins" and "outs."

However, the financial crisis would not, on its own, have been fatal to UK membership. The prospect of a referendum being held on the UK's membership of the Union – made certain by the unexpected success of the Conservatives in securing an absolute majority in the May 2015 election – briefly turned opinion in favour of remaining within the Union. In June 2015, the Remainers led the Leavers by 61 per cent to 27 per cent in an IPSOS-Mori poll. Yet, by December 2015, that lead had disappeared again. An ICM poll had Remainers and Leavers almost tied at 42 to 40 per cent respectively. The migration crisis of summer 2015 undermined the majority for remaining in a way that demonstrated that the UK's differential participation in policies could not be relied upon to defuse opposition to membership overall. Abstaining from Schengen could not be presented as a knock-down argument that the UK remained in control of its own borders if migrants accepted into the EU could eventually end up in the UK under free movement. Complaints that the UK had lost control of its own laws could now be merged with complaints that it had lost control of its own boundaries, overwhelming all the elaborate defences that British governments thought they had constructed against claims that EU membership was incompatible with what was it was for the UK to govern itself as a democratic people.

Indeed, opposition to free movement within the EU, the crisis in migration from outside the EU, and the residual effects of the financial crisis came together in a deadly constellation. In a rare moment in which differentiated integration meant the UK integrating faster than anyone else, the UK government waived the 5-year transitions before extending free movement to the 2004 and 2007 enlargement countries. By 2016, around 4 million citizens from other Member States were resident in the UK. This coincided with a sharp decline in the real incomes of unskilled labour. Although this decline was caused by the financial crisis, it was easy to blame it on EU free movement. The Brexit vote was strong in areas where there had been "a sudden influx" of EU immigrants (Goodwin and Heath, 2016). Although the government tried to anticipate this difficulty by demanding still more differentiation – this time, even in the core principle of free movement – its failure to obtain a stronger emergency brake only illustrated a further difficulty in looking to differentiation in the rights and obligations of membership to sustain domestic support for that membership; differentiation depends on the agreement of other members who also have domestic constraints.

However, the UK's complex relationship with the Union was not just overwhelmed by the crisis. A form of membership that relied on differentiating the

Union's institutions and policies to fit the UK – rather than building domestic support and commitment to EU membership – was itself vulnerable to the crisis. UK membership was as much a domestic failure as it was an external success in negotiating exceptions and priorities. Domestically, the UK has probably never been a Member State in the sense that its public valued, supported, or even knew much about the EU. The Eurobarometer has often found low levels of identification with the Union and, above all, identified a public opinion that, in almost all its surveys, turned out to have the least knowledge of the EU. Then, of course, there was the relentlessly negative framing of the EU in the UK media. Pieter de Wilde, Asimina Michailidou, and Hans-Jörg Trenz show how "suggestive" reporting increases "cynicism" about the EU (2013: 180). But UK governments would probably have been more courageous in challenging misrepresentations of the EU had it not been for something else. In a system of just two main political parties that alternate in government, it mattered that those parties were never completely united, and were sometimes deeply divided, within and between themselves on the UK's membership. British governments often responded by obfuscating Union issues rather than explaining and justifying them (Lord, 1993).

The unwillingness of British governments to own up to EU policies which they had themselves agreed, shaped, and even encouraged made it more likely that Union decisions would be perceived as external impositions. Throughout, the Eurobarometer found that the British public was the least likely to have heard of the Council of Ministers. A public that does not know that there *is* a Council of Ministers is less likely to know that its own government participates in Union decisions, and, therefore, is more likely to perceive those decisions as external impositions. Moreover, domestic support for UK membership had always been transactional. Few identified with the Union or valued European integration as an aim. But many accepted that a body such as the Union might be needed to deal with interdependence and cross-border problems. Many also accepted that the UK needed a level of access to its largest and nearest market. It is a matter of taste whether an instrumental/transactional approach to political association is (un-)desirable. But it should not come as a surprise if it leads to a "pick and mix" form of membership, or, indeed, to a form of membership that comes and goes with (mis-)calculations of its costs and benefits.

V Differentiation without membership

Given the deep and complex human, economic, and security interdependencies with the EU, the UK may wish to continue to participate in some Union policies. Several Leavers have themselves variously supported continued market access, continued security co-operation, continued research collaboration, and even some continued labour and capital mobility. Hence, a final question is whether the UK will end up substituting external internal forms of differentiation.

However, it has, historically, been far easier to abstain selectively from inside the Union than to participate selectively from outside it (Eriksen and Fossum, 2015). As seen, as a member after 1973, the UK succeeded in many attempts to opt out and in. In contrast, as a non-member after 1950, it failed in several attempts, both unilateral and multi-lateral, to participate sufficiently in the European Communities from the outside, and consequently felt the need to join as a full member. Saying "no" to Monsieur Robert Schuman is not what the British government believed itself to be doing in 1950. It wanted to be "associated with the proposal"[8] and expected to be able to participate very powerfully without full membership. As a government working party put it, "even as non-members our bargaining power and goodwill would be considerable ... Some of the advantages of membership would come to us without being a member."[9] Whilst, however, an association with the ECSC was agreed, it contained little substance (Lord, 1996). Also unsuccessful were attempts to create a wider circle of "outs" by persuading the European Communities to develop their common market within a European free trade area.

Moreover, there are structural – and not just historically contingent – reasons why it may be harder to participate selectively in Union policies and institutions as a non-member than to abstain selectively as a member. First, Member States have formal veto powers. They can insist on selective rights of non-participation as a condition for not vetoing Treaty changes. Second, even where their membership is full of exceptions, full members remain nested in the Union's overall authority relations: its adjudication of disputes through the EU's shared law and the CJEU; its administration of multiple, complex, policy regimes; its day-to-day decision-making; and all that is required for Member States to get on with one another if they are to solve collective action problems and implement them on the ground.

Third, there are limits to how far the Union can coherently give decision rights to outsiders. When the EU insists on limits to how far outsiders can participate in those of its policies that involve shared law-making without accepting that the full members of the Union should have a monopoly on the making of Union laws, it is not trying to dominate, exclude, or even drive a hard bargain. Rather, it is simply stating a truism that making laws with others within a shared legal and political order, and bargaining together with others in the absence of such an order, are two different relationships. The first requires agreement on what rights and responsibilities should go with co-authorship of laws. Under the Treaty of Lisbon, of course, EU members have agreed that the fair and right way of co-authoring their own laws through the Union is ordinarily to give the Commission a right of initiative; to allow majorities of 55 per cent of Member States, representing 65 per cent of the Union's population, to co-decide legislation with the majorities of the European Parliament; and to accept the CJEU's monopoly of interpretation. There are limits to how far Union members can maintain that this is a free and fair way of making laws between themselves whilst legally obliging one another to recognise laws of non-Member States made in other ways. Yet only through some fair and effective mutual obligation to automaticity (Gstöhl, 2015) in up-dating laws can the UK enjoy similar access to the policy segment that it has valued most as a member: the single market.

VI Conclusion

I have argued that, as a member of the EU, the UK contributed to what many expected it to oppose: the development of the EU as an original form of political authority for managing relations between democratic states. By pressing for the single market programme, the UK was the single most enthusiastic supporter of the single most important step that the EU has taken towards political centre formation. The UK likewise contributed to the development of EU members into states of a distinctive kind (Bickerton, 2012), namely, states that have adapted their own law, executives, and representative institutions to their shared membership of the Union. For sure, complex solutions were needed to reconcile UK membership with continued European integration. But UK support for the differentiation of the Union's decision rules into the Community and Union methods allowed co-operation to expand so that even the core powers (Genschel and Jachtenfuchs, 2014) of the Member States are now co-ordinated through the Union. Even UK opt-outs turned out to be largely constructive forms of abstention that did not obstruct further integration. But differentiation, I have also argued, is easier inside, rather than outside, the EU. It is easier to abstain selectively as a member than to participate selectively as a non-member.

Notes

1 PRO CAB 134/295, "Constitutional problems involved in a supranational authority as proposed by M. Schuman 16 June 1950." PRO ZP 18/20, Memorandum by Permanent Under-Secretary's Committee of the Foreign Office 9 June 1950.
2 PRO C(51) 32, "United Europe," Memorandum by the Prime Minister to the Cabinet, 29 November 1951.
3 House of Commons Debates, 22 July 1971, Column 1906.
4 I thank David S. Bell for this wisecrack.
5 Makins to Strang, 28 June 1950, *PRO [CE 3353/2141/181]*.
6 Memorandum by the Minister of Defence, 1 July 1950, *PRO [CE 3452/2141/181]*.
7 *HP Bulmer and another* vs *J Bollinger SA and others* [1974] 2 All ER 1226 AT 1232_3.
8 PRO CAB 128 17, Conclusions of a Meeting of the Cabinet held at 10 Downing Street on Friday, 2 June 1950.
9 PRO F.G. (W.P.) (51) 43, Report of a Working Party Constituting the European Coal and Steel Community, 31 December 1951.

References

Armstrong (2016), "EU Membership, Financial Services and Stability", *National Institute Economic Review*, 236, London: National Institute of Economic and Social Research.
Attali, Jacques (1995), *Verbatim III: Chronique des années 1988–1991. Deuxième Partie*, Paris: Fayard.

Barnett, Anthony (2017), "Brexit is an Old People's Home – And It's English, not British", Open Democracy UK, available at: www.opendemocracy.net/anthony. barnett/brexit-is-old-people-s-home, last accessed 30 March 2017.

Bickerton, Christopher J. (2012), *European Integration: From Nation-States to Member States*. Oxford: Oxford University Press.

Bickerton, Christopher J., Dermot Hodson, and Uwe Puetter (eds) (2015), *The New Intergovernmentalism: States and Supranational Actors in the Post-Maastricht Era*, Oxford: Oxford University Press.

Blair, Tony (2010), *Mémoires*. Paris: Albin Michel.

Brouard, Sylvain, Olivier Costa, and Thomas König (2012), "Delors' Myth: The Scope and Impact of the Europeanization of European Law Production", in: Sylvain Brouard, Olivier Costa, and Thomas König (eds), *The Europeanization of Domestic Legislatures: The Empirical Implications of the Delors' Myth in Nine Countries*, New York: Springer, pp. 1–20.

Colley, Linda (1992), *Britons: Forging the Nation 1707–1837*, Yale CT: Yale University Press.

De Wilde, Pieter, Asimina Michailidou, and Hans-Jörg Trenz (2013), *Contesting Europe: Exploring Euroscepticism in Online Media Coverage*. Lanham MD: Rowman & Littlefield International.

Dyson, Kenneth (2000), *The Politics of the Euro-Zone: Stability or Breakdown?*, Oxford: Oxford University Press.

Eriksen, Erik Oddvar, and John Erik Fossum (2015), *The European Union's Non-Members: Independence under Hegemony*. London: Routledge.

European Commission (2017), White Paper on the Future of European, Brussels: European Commission, available at: https://ec.europa.eu/commission/sites/beta-political/files/white_paper_on_the_future_of_europe_en.pdf, last accessed 31 December 2018.

European Parliament (1998), "Resolution on Democratic Accountability in the Third Phase of EMU", (The Randzio-Plath report), Brussels: European Parliament.

Fabbrini, Sergio (2015), *Which European Union? Europe After the Euro Crisis*. Cambridge: Cambridge University Press.

Genschel, Philipp, and Markus Jachtenfuchs (eds) (2014), *Beyond the Regulatory Polity? The European Integration of Core State Powers*. Oxford: Oxford University Press.

Goodwin, Matthew, and Oliver Heath. (2016), "Brexit Vote Explained: Poverty, Low Skills and Absence of Opportunities", available at: www.jrf.org.uk/report/brexit-vote-explained, last accessed 20 November 2016.

Gstöhl, Sieglinde (2015), "Models of External Differentiation in the EU's Neighbourhood: An Expanding Economic Community?", *Journal of European Public Policy*, 22 (6): 854–870.

Heath, Edward (1970), *Old World, New Horizons: Britain, the Common Market and the Atlantic Alliance. The Godkin Lectures 1967*. Oxford: Oxford University Press.

Hobsbawm, Eric (1994), *The Age of Extremes: The Short Twentieth Century, 1914–1991*. London: Abacus Books.

Horne, Alistair (1988), *Macmillan, 1894–1986*. London: Macmillan.

Howorth, Jolyon (2018), "EU-NATO Cooperation and Strategic Autonomy: Logical Contradiction or Ariadne's Thread?" Berlin: KFG Working Paper Series, No.: 90.

Jervis, Robert (1976), *Perception and Misperception in International Politics*, Princeton NJ: Princeton University Press.

Jones, Erik (2015), "Forgotten Financial Union. How you can Have a Euro Crisis without the Euro", in: Matthias Matthijs and Mark Blyth (eds), *The Future of the Euro*, Oxford: Oxford University Press, pp. 44–69.

Leruth, Benjamin, and Christopher Lord (2015), "Differentiated Integration in the European Union: A Concept, a Process, a System or a Theory?" *Journal of European Public Policy*, 22 (6): 754–763.

Liddle, Roger (2014), *The Europe Dilemma: Britain and the Drama of EU Integration*, London: I.B. Tauris/Policy Network.

Lindseth, Peter (2010), *Power and Legitimacy: Reconciling Europe and the Nation-State*, Oxford: Oxford University Press.

Lord, Christopher (1993), *British Entry to the European Community under the Heath Government of 1970–1974*, Aldershot: Ashgate Dartmouth Publishing.

Lord, Christopher (1996), *Absent at the Creation: Britain and the Formation of the European Community*, 1950–1952, Aldershot: Ashgate Dartmouth Publishing.

Lord, Christopher (2008), "Polity Empowering or Polity Constraining? A Comparison of British and French Attempts to Legitimise the Constitutional Treaty", *Journal of European Public Policy*, 15 (7): 1001–1018.

Lord, Christopher (2017), "How can Parliaments Contribute to the Legitimacy of the European Semester?" *Parliamentary Affairs*, 70 (4): 673–690.

Majone, Giandomenico (1994), "The Rise of the Regulatory State in Europe", *West European Politics*, 17 (3): 77–101.

Mattila, Mikko, and Jan-Erik Lane (2001), "Why Unanimity in the Council? A Roll-Call Analysis of Council Voting", *European Union Politics*, 2 (1): 31–52.

Norman, Peter (2003), *The Accidental Constitution: The Story of the European Convention*, Brussels: EuroComment.

Patten, Chris (2017), "John Major was Probably the Cleverest Leader I Worked for", Prospect Magazine, 18 November 2017.

Rogers, Ivan (2018), "Brexit as Revolution", Lecture at Trinity College Cambridge, 10 October 2018, available at: https://share.trin.cam.ac.uk/sites/public/Comms/Rogers_brexit_as_revolution.pdf, last accessed 31 December 2018.

Sabel, Charles F., and Jonathan Zeitlin (2008), "Learning from Difference. The New Architecture of Experimentalist Governance", *European Law Journal*, 14 (3): 271–327.

Scharpf, Fritz W. (2009), "Legitimacy in the Multilevel European Polity", *European Political Science Review*, 1 (2): 173–204.

Schmitter, Philippe C. (2000), *How to Democratise the European Union and Why Bother?*, Lanham MD: Rowman and Littlefield.

Simonian, Haig (1985), *The Privileged Partnership: Franco-German Relations in the European Community*, 1969–1984, Oxford: Oxford University Press.

Thatcher, Margaret (1993), *The Downing Street Years*, New York: Harper Collins.

Töller, Annette Elisabeth (2010), "Measuring and Comparing the Europeanisation of National Legislation. A Research Note", *Journal of Common Market Studies*, 48 (2): 417–444.

UK Government (1971), "The United Kingdom and the European Communities Cmnd 4715 of 1971", London: UK Government.

UK Government (2017), "The Government's Negotiating Objectives for Exiting the EU: PM Speech", www.gov.uk/government/speeches/the-governments-negotiating-objectives-for-exiting-the-eu-pm, last accessed 30 March 2017.

Weale, Albert (2017), "The Democratic Duty to Oppose Brexit", *Political Quarterly* 88 (2): 170–181.

Weiler, Joseph H.H. (1997), "The Reformation of European Constitutionalism", *Journal of Common Market Studies*, 35 (1): 97–131.

Whitman, Richard G. (2016), "The UK and EU Foreign, Security and Defence Policy after Brexit: Integrated, Associated or Detached?", *National Institute Economic Review*, No. 238, November 2016: 81–88.

YouGov (2017), "Brexit and Leaving the EU", available at: www.yougov.co.uk/news/categories/politics.

13

CONCLUSION

A segmented political order and future options

Jozef Bátora and John Erik Fossum

I Introduction

The purpose of this book has been to understand and type-cast the European Union (EU) that has emerged from the crises and challenges that rocked it during the last decade or so. The point of departure was that the EU that emerged from the crises has been transformed; precisely how is less clear. Some analysts have argued that the EU's intergovernmental components have been strengthened; others argue that its supranational components have been reinforced. Our position combines elements of both, albeit in a distinctive manner. The contributions to the book have thus provided an alternative account of the political order that has emerged from the pluri-crises.

There appears to be a general consensus among analysts that the EU that has emerged from the crises has become increasingly differentiated. This is beyond differentiated integration, which assumes that all movements are in the same integrationist direction. Brexit was but the starkest of reminders to the effect that the EU post-crises is facing disintegrative pressures. Hence, it was necessary to shift the focus from differentiated integration to differentiation.

In this connection, as we noted in Chapter 1, a closer reading of the EU's crises reactions has left us with something of a puzzle. Given that differentiated integration in the EU context has been analysed and understood as Member States being granted exemptions, special status, opt-outs, and opt-ins from EU arrangements, it follows that an EU that is becoming more differentiated is one that is open to deviations in all possible directions, not only along an integrationist track but also along a dis-integrationist track. The upshot is that such an entity – given the highly diverse European setting – should reflect this and, as such, be open to various ideas, ideologies, rationalities, organisational and procedural arrangements, *etc.*

The contributions to this book have shown that this is only part of the story. As is shown in a number of the chapters herein, the EU's crisis response, especially in relation to the externally generated financial crisis, was one of a stubborn insistence on deficit and debt reduction, even amidst increasing Eurozone divergence, whose effects were proving to be the exact opposite to the sought-after convergence (the chapters by Tranøy and Schwartz, Holst and Molander, and Gould and Malová all present different aspects of this). The implication is that increased structural openness and diversity have been combined with cognitive and ideological closure. This observation is indicative of the need for a different term to designate the post-crises EU. The contributions to the volume have accordingly helped to substantiate the claim that the post-crises EU can best be understood as a fledgling segmented political order.

II The EU as a segmented order: Summary of findings

Several of the chapters in the volume have observed that there is a comprehensive literature on segments that spans a wide range of academic fields. From a political science perspective, a segment has been understood as a functionally de-limited network-type arrangement wherein persons located in different institutions hold common perceptions of what the relevant problems are, how these problems are to be solved, and what the relevant choice-set is. A key marker for a segment is a selection-bias. Each segment systematically selects certain world views, problem conceptions, and solutions, and, at the same time, excludes alternatives.

Segments have been identified in various sectors of modern democratic states. These were typically sector-specific and sector-confined; there was little meaning in thinking about segments as defining features of the polity, which is what is implied in the notion of *segmented political order*. The question that this book has grappled with is, therefore, one of *what* sets the post-crises EU apart, so that it makes sense to talk about the EU as a segmented political order. One important point that this book has underlined is that a segmented political order is a political arrangement which *structurally and functionally entrenches the biases* that we associate with segments. It follows that, when compared to a modern democratic state, a segmented political order is structurally imbalanced.

We obtain a clearer sense of this once we recognise that pre-modern political systems were quite often segmented, with significant built-in biases. A segmented political order is one in which bias becomes a structural imbalance. Thus, a segmented political order deviates from the political orders that we associate with modern democratic states. Modern democratic states are not only based upon the norm of territorial-functional contiguity; they also contain constitutional-democratic arrangements that either prevent segments from emerging or can undo biases when the latter have generated negative policy or political effects.

When discussing the EU as a segmented political order, the book has shown that such an arrangement is consistent neither with a supranational nor with an intergovernmental arrangement. In effect, the contributions to the book show that the EU as a segmented political order combines these two sets of institutional arrangements. In addition, a segmented political order typically reaches across levels, and as Fossum's chapter shows, combines vertical and horizontal dimensions in a distinctive manner with considerable variation across segments. The EU has one segment anchored in supranational arrangements in the internal market sphere and another anchored in the intergovernmental arrangements that mark the area of security (internal and external) and border controls.

In Chapter 1, we provided an analytical framework composed of six dimensions to help spell out the defining features of a segmented political order. These dimensions cover the following aspects, which are distinctly configured when they form part of a segmented political order: a) ideas, ideologies, and cognitions that make up distinct segmental logics; b) a biased range of policy instruments and a distinct policy style; c) institutions and procedures that lock-in biases; d) constraints on material and immaterial resources that reinforce lock-ins; e) patterns of dependence and vulnerability that also entrench biases; and f) particularly weak or under-developed de-segmenting arrangements and institutions. We noted that these vary in terms of whether they are constitutive of segments; some are, while others are more auxiliary, in that their main role is to lock-in bias. A segmented political order is typically imbalanced in that it is marked by particularly under-developed de-segmenting factors and forces.

In the following, we sum up the main findings of the book with reference to these six dimensions.

Six dimensions summed up

The first dimension refers to a "segmental logic," which can take the form of a cognitive and/or ideological *bias*. Such a segmental logic represents a form of "closing of the mind" to segment-external ideas and influences. The chapters by Tranøy and Schwartz, Holst and Molander, Olsen, and Gould and Malová all focus on the types of segmental logics that have emerged in connection with the Eurozone crisis and the refugee crisis, the two main recent segmenting thrusts. Tranøy and Schwartz identify an "epistocracy," which they define as an élite epistemic or knowledge community with its centre of gravity close to the European Central Bank. This knowledge community, the authors note,

> expected European Monetary Union (EMU) to spur economic growth and reverse "eurosclerosis" through convergence in pricing, production, and financing. Cognitive bias led that epistocracy to perceive the flow of economic data from the European periphery as a re-assuring pattern of stability and convergence. But even when this epistocracy was confronted with reasonably clear evidence that the data actually showed crisis-inducing divergence, these authorities doggedly continued to pursue solutions to the Eurozone crisis based upon austerity and "one size fits all" policies that conformed to their prior beliefs about appropriate economic policy.

The chapter by Gould and Malová shows that the austerity-sentiment found resonance across different parts of Europe. The authors point to Slovakia's strong commitment to fiscal restraint, not only in Slovakia but also abroad (they were slow in accepting the Greek assistance package of 2010 at the peak of the Eurozone crisis). The authors note that

> (w)ith the exception of the Great Recession of 2009–2010, Slovakia's governments have made it a policy to adhere to the fiscal expectations of the Eurozone and they have also supported International Financial Institutions' (IFI) initiatives to impose fiscal restraints at home and elsewhere.

The chapter by Holst and Molander lifts the sight to the broader question of the possible contribution to segmentation of the expertisation of politics – paying particular attention to the question of whether there are traits in the economics discipline that help to support such a development. One aspect is the increased role of economists in economic policy-making, while another pertains to a range of epistemic concerns that the authors present. They point out that making cognitive errors and narrow judgements is an inherent feature of epistocracy and of epistemic communities. Coupled with a systematic lack of democratic accountability, this form of segmentation is a major problem for the EU's political order. The authors underline that the problems are exacerbated under certain institutional conditions, and the EU's development post-crises is reflective of such conditions.

The chapters by Olsen, Bátora, and Fossum point to the presence of a second EU segment that they attribute to the manner in which certain core features associated with sovereignty and security have been embedded in the EU construct mainly because of the central role that Member States play in many of the EU's institutional arrangements, especially within the intergovernmental components. Such "statespeople," the chapters underline, share certain frames of reference that, in turn, shape and condition how they understand the world, how they depict the world, and how they understand themselves as state officials. Especially in connection with the so-called refugee crisis, which Olsen's chapter outlines in detail, the sovereignty logic was wedded to a securitisation logic, with a bearing on how the refugee issue was framed and the policy instruments and arrangements that were activated to deal with it. From an initial conception of the refugee crisis as a humanitarian crisis in which the *onus* was on the plight of the refugees, segmentation was fostered as the focus shifted and narrowed to securitisation, in other words, the concerns of states, which highlighted state security and border control.

All of these chapters – whether specifically focused on outlining segmental logics or not – testify to the need to consider the institutional and structural conditions that are important for cognitive closure to become a system-defining trait at the polity level. In other words, the book underlines that we cannot understand or analyse the EU as a segmented political order without paying explicit attention to the institutional conditions that lock-in and sustain certain ways of understanding and analysing the world.

The second dimension of segmentation refers to distinct policy attitudes/orientations embedded in a specific range of policy instruments. There is a distinct policy style at EU level, which is centred on regulation, especially in the realm of internal market. The book has confirmed the assumption that we set out in Chapter 1, namely, that a segment's framing of problems and solutions is affected by the *repertoire* of policy instruments and the *types* of policy instruments that are available. The two key features referred to a *narrow and imbalanced range* of policy instruments. Both features are associated with lock-in and segmental closure. How significant this is depends on the broader nature and shape of the polity's institutional-structural configuration, not least the resources that it can muster. The constraints on the EU's resources (Dimension Five further outlined here) significantly narrow the range of EU policy instruments and are key determinants in the EU's distinct regulatory policy style.

The third dimension of segmentation posits that there are certain institutions that help to entrench and lock-in segmental logics. One aspect that the contributions to the book have brought out is that segmentation occurs when there is a structural imbalance in the polity between experts and executives, on the one hand; and parliamentary-representative bodies, on the other. Many polities have, however, such imbalances without necessarily being segmented political orders. There are additional institutional features of the post-crises EU that help to lock-in segmental logics. One such set of factors, as Fossum's chapter shows, relates to the distinctive manner in which the EU combines the horizontal separation of functional spheres with the vertical fusion of levels. This helps to entrench two segments not least because the key pattern of functional separation at EU level is based in and operated by different institutional arrangements, one with its centre of gravity in supranational arrangements (the internal market), the other with its centre of gravity in intergovernmental arrangements in foreign and security and fiscal and tax policy. There are also overlaps between the two, since some of the institutions are involved in both. The Council is a case in point, serving mainly as a legislative body in the realm of the internal market, whilst serving executive functions in the foreign and security field. The EU's horizontal functional separation combines with a strong vertical fusion of levels, in the sense that the EU institutions are embedded in and interwoven with the Member States. This fusion underscores the point that a segmented political order cuts across levels of governing; hence, neither can be understood as a fully-fledged supranational nor as a fully-fledged intergovernmental political order.

The EU's institutional constellation ensures segmental lock-in through, on the one hand, the prevention or constraint of horizontal co-ordination, market correction, and fiscal stabilisation at EU level; and, on the other, by the fact that national officials are directly involved in EU-level decision-making, and hence they are co-responsible for what is going on. This is no less the case in the Eurozone, where

> (t)he institutionalisation of the Eurozone is a further instigator of EU segmentation. The Eurozone occupies a distinct space inside the two structural features of horizontal separation and vertical fusion, and is very difficult for parliaments to control. Broadly speaking, monetary policy, which is an exclusive EU competence, is situated in the one supranational track, whereas fiscal policy is situated in the intergovernmental track. The supranational Monetary Union is thus backed up by a system of fiscal coordination that is organised along intergovernmental lines.
>
> *(Fossum, Chapter 2 in this volume, p. 35)*

This distinct combination of horizontal and vertical institutional arrangements is conducive to locking-in segmental logics. This is amplified by a broader, more encompassing structural imbalance when compared to democratic states with fully developed executive, judicial, administrative, and legislative institutions that pry open segments and ensure an open contestation of different world views, forms of expertise, and different values and ideologies.

A key point that the contributions to this book have underlined is that the imbalances that we can observe are not just attributable to what the EU *can* do, given its distinctive policy style and institutional make-up; equally important is what the EU *cannot* do, in other words, the many constraints that are built into this system.

The fourth dimension of a segmented political order that we presented in Chapter 1 is precisely about the various built-in *constraints*. There are both important material and immaterial constraints. It is well-known and widely commented upon that the EU has very limited fiscal resources because of the many constraints built into the EU's ability to obtain its own resources. The EU has very limited slack, which greatly affected how it could deal with the financial and the refugee crises. Compared to all its Member States, the EU's resource constraints foreclose options that are available to the Member States in dealing with crises and contingencies.

An important aspect of the EU's historical development which the chapter by Lord highlights is the particular combination of quite rapid and dynamic integration within a context marked by significant constraints. This condition we may label "integration under constraints" and is closely associated with a segmented political order. Lord underlines that the UK was a strong supporter of market-based integration, because the UK sought a European internal market and not a European polity. Other Member States had more ambitious objectives and so did the EU institutions. Thus, the EU-based story of "integration under constraints" reflects the manner in which different conceptions of integration and what type of polity the EU is and should have been blended together over time.

The constraints on the EU's institutional make-up and resource-base shape the mechanisms that it has at its disposal to deal with crises and contingencies.

Bátora's chapter brings this out very clearly, with reference to the emergence of "interstitial organisations" set up to co-ordinate the delivery of policies across formally diverse policy domains and/or across legal jurisdictions. These include the European External Action Service (EEAS), the European Stability Mechanism (ESM), and the European Border and Coast Guard (EBCG). Interstitial organisations emerge in situations in which there is a need for problem-solving under strong institutional, legal, political, and resource constraints, and interstitial organisations were a frequently resorted-to EU crisis-handling measure. As the chapter shows, they tap into the resources of other organisations and help to bridge policy domains, but they also serve as vehicles for entrenching various segmental logics across EU Member States. This includes the neoliberal bias in the case of the ESM and the securitisation logic in the case of the EBCG. It is no coincidence that the EU's recourse to interstitial organisations increased during the crisis handling period. In this sense, interstitial organisations are the markers of a segmented political order, and they ironically help to carry or sustain this insofar as they contribute to problem-solving (showing how resource constraints can generate creative solutions).

The EU is thus imbued with significant material constraints. Equally important are the non-material ones pertaining to the values and principles that it can readily draw on to justify its role, status, and actions/outputs. A case in point, as the abstract to the chapter by Michailidou and Trenz notes, is how solidarity has been re-defined over the last decade or so. As the authors note, solidarity has historically been considered an important founding value and "a motor for social cohesion." Caught in the throes of crisis,

> a new politics of *differentiated solidarity* in the EU can be distinguished, which is different from the old politics of European identity. In line with – and as a consequence of – the intensified argument in favour of differentiated integration, differentiated solidarity entails a shift of emphasis from the promotion of European integration, which aims to establish a reciprocal relationship among equals, to the promotion of flexible arrangements among EU members, discretionary re-distributive mechanisms and hegemony. More specifically, during the Eurocrisis years, the following three mutations in the concept of EU solidarity can be observed: a) the exceptionality of charity: solidarity as acts of benevolence towards third parties; b) the exclusivity of egalitarian solidarity: national solidarity communities becoming more exclusive; and c) solidarity among non-equals: constant re-negotiation of the costs and benefits of solidarity as a rescuing mechanism, which binds donating and receiving countries together in a situation of emergency.

This mutated form is indicative of the constraints and contestations that the EU has faced through its efforts to grapple with the pluri-crises that have affected it.

Significant constraints on the nature and realm of EU action are now also increasingly emerging from the rise of Eurosceptic and Europhobe parties and social movements. They demand clear constraints on the EU's access to resources (taxing ability). In addition, their confrontational style and dismissal of experts gives impetus to experts and professionals to "hide" and seek out ways of working out problems with as little publicity as possible, thus indirectly helping to foster forms of segmental closure.

Media and their representations of problems and crises play an important role in conditioning and constraining action. Steuer, in his chapter, provides one of the first available insights into the public portrayal of the EU in three of the "Visegrád Four" Member States. Steuer's analysis shows that the selected quality newspapers reproduced some common patterns of the portrayal of the crises in the period from 2008 to June 2016, using tropes similar to those of right-wing populists between the domestic and European and the oppositional "European élite." These media representations help manifest perceptions of "natural opposi-tions"; as such, they reinforce constraints, and, hence, indirectly support segmen-tation in the EU setting.

The Polish and Hungarian cases yet again show how constraints are giv-ing impetus to EU segmentation, not necessarily EU dismantling, because the governments are happy to receive EU money and to have full access to the EU's internal market but, at the same time, seek to undermine domestic constitu-tional democracy with obvious ripple-effects. These developments represent awkward instances of "integration under constraints." In his chapter on Poland, Riedel outlines the illiberal tendencies in evidence and shows how these kinds of developments in Member States can support segmentation traits in the EU. There are, in particular, two aspects of importance here. First, governments with illiberal tendencies such as the one led by the *PiS* party in Poland, are prone to support various kinds of meso-level structures, which exclude pub-lic participation in democratic scrutiny of policy-making. Second, the *PiS* government has systematically been working to decrease the influence of the European Parliament (EP), thereby weakening one of the key de-segmenting institutions in the EU. The effect is to undercut democracy at both the EU and national levels.

The fifth dimension is closely related to the previous ones, in the sense that a political system with low levels of slack and which has very limited access to resources is not only quite dependent externally, but highly vulnerable to exter-nal forces and developments, as was borne out very clearly when the EU was hit by the financial crisis and the refugee crisis. Onderco, in his chapter, analyses a particular form of external dependence, namely, the EU's strong transatlan-tic links and dependence on legally regulated co-operation, both of which are challenged by the Trump administration. Onderco focuses more specifically on foreign policy preferences as a legitimacy constraint on the exercise of foreign policy by national actors; he finds that those that experienced the economic crisis are far less likely to hold positive views about the EU, and, in addition, that those in Central and Eastern Europe that felt their identity was threatened exhibited more negative views of the United States and more positive views of Russia.

These findings have bearings on the sixth dimension, which refers to the EU's generally less developed and, to some extent, sidelined *de-segmenting* arrangements. The analyses presented above are all testimony to a systemic imbalance in which those institutions relying on public participation, representation, openness, and transparency are all weakened in the post-crises EU. In this connection, it is important to underline that we see a weakening of democratic institutions and those legal procedural arrangements that enable representative bodies, the public, and the media to understand, question, and challenge what is going on; although such institutions remain in place, they have seen their role much reduced in the post-crises EU.

III Possible developmental trajectories

The final part of this concluding chapter will consider two possible EU developmental trajectories. As we noted in Chapter 1, such assessments must be undertaken with a view to keeping the EU's present situation in sight. In other words, the issue is not whether an option is interesting and plausible in the abstract; the issue is to establish how the EU can get out of its present predicament and what it takes to move in a given direction. Further, since the book has shown the EU's fragility, dependence, and vulnerability, we need to pay explicit attention to further fragmentation.

Trajectory I: Core consolidation around the Eurozone

Many practitioners and analysts alike have underlined the need for further integration in order to deal with the many problems facing the EU. For practical political reasons, the most obvious route would seem to be to foster further deepening of integration within the Eurozone in order to render the Monetary Union sustainable and in order to give the EU the action capability of dealing with such pressing issues as refugees, unemployment, social dislocation, increased Russian assertiveness, and the possible fallout of Brexit. Institutionally speaking, this could entail a fiscal union, a common treasury, an integrated defence, a common tax system, a common welfare system, *etc.* Some initial practical steps – long in the making – have already been taken, possibly laying the institutional groundwork for deeper integration among the countries of the Eurozone. That includes the December 2018 agreement among EU Member States to create a separate budget for the Eurozone.[1] In addition, the French–German Agreement on Bilateral Relations signed in Aachen on 22 January 2019 also paves the way for closer integration between the governments and economies of Germany and France – two key Eurozone partners.[2]

In the strongest, most explicit version, and for it to comply with democratic requirements, decision-making in the Eurozone would have to be popularly authorised and accountable, most probably through a Eurozone parliament and a Eurozone government capable of taking on the standard functions that we associate with federal governments. In practice, we would be talking about the building of a federation around the Eurozone.

This, in turn, brings up several important issues which resonate with the findings of this book. One is how the relations among the EU-level institutions are to be structured; another is how they will relate to the Member States. With regard to the former, the key issue is whether there will be some sort of parliamentary fusion or some sort of division of powers and competencies. With regard to the latter, it is a matter of what variant of federalism to opt for. We may distinguish between two main versions: bipolar and unipolar, which differ in terms of how the competences are divided between the two main levels (Scharpf, 1988). The most standard bipolar version of federalism is based upon a clearly delineated division of competences between the federal and the state level. The most important cases of bipolar federalism are the United States, Canada, Australia, and India. In contrast, the unipolar model of federalism understands the federal compact as embedded in a set of central institutions that have binding force on the parties to the federal compact, which entails that each sub-unit is directly represented in the central institutions; here the most obvious case is the German version of federalism (Jeffery and Savigear, 1991).

As has been shown here, the EU has clear traits of the German version, especially in the Community system. But the EU is not a fully-fledged copy, because the Intergovernmental track is not communitarised in the same way. If core consolidation entails full adoption of the German model at the EU's core, we will end up with a highly centralised system with Member States basically implementing the decisions that they have agreed to through their representatives at the central EU level. A critical issue then will be the EU's realm of competence. It is obvious that the type of market-driven fusion that we see in the EU's Community system will leave the scope for Member State independence or self-rule very limited indeed. For such a process of core consolidation to be acceptable to the Member States, it would therefore either seem necessary to scale down the EU's functional reach or to move towards a clearer bipolar federal arrangement which requires a competence catalogue and a delineation of tasks between the EU level and the Member States, in which the scope of shared competence is pruned down. Each option comes with its own challenges: a unipolar arrangement raises questions as to whether this is sufficient to undo the segmentation currently in place; a bipolar arrangement entails giving the institutions at EU level a freer rein in relation to the Member States. Member States and EU institutions must work out a new balance of what they entrust to the EU institutions (which they no longer control to the same degree) and what they seek to do on their own, and this has to be accepted by all.

The other issue is the nature and scope of the differentiation involved. The general assumption would be that the main lines of differentiation would go between those in the core, on the one hand, and those outside the core, on the other. Nevertheless, even this type of distinction needs to be clarified. A critical issue would be whether core consolidation would be a matter of differentiated *integration* or differentiation. The former would mean an extension of the current system of "enhanced co-operation," which means that while Member States travel at different speeds, the assumption remains that they will nevertheless reach the same destination. The latter can be, but need not be, based upon the assumption of getting to the same place, and envisages different dynamics. It is also possible to cast differentiation more narrowly by confining it to the following:

> first, cases where some states integrate more closely whilst, at the same time and for connected reasons, others disintegrate from their previous levels of involvement with the Union; and second, cases where even notionally full members come to be regarded as having different membership status.
>
> *(Fossum, 2015: 800)*

An interesting issue in the core consolidation scenario is the role of the European Council. On the one hand, we may assume that it will be re-fashioned along the lines of what Wolfgang Wessels (2016) has termed "the Council Model," to serve as the key executive at the top of the Council configuration. But if so, who should be represented in the European Council? If the decision is to include the representatives of all the Member States, as is the case at present, it would appear to be likely that the European Council would be composed of members with differentiated status along the lines of Eurozone "ins" and "outs."

This brief assessment of core consolidation shows that the "devil is in the detail" of the actual proposal, and especially that there is a range of different institutional solutions under the broad heading of core consolidation.

How to get there?

Clearly, whichever version of core consolidation is chosen, we are nevertheless talking about a major institutional and constitutional overhaul or reform of the present system, which raises a number of questions regarding feasibility. One major requirement is made up of the need for political vision, political leadership, and political ability. There is no doubt that this trajectory pre-supposes treaty change, whichever option of core consolidation is pursued.

With regard to political visions, and especially now that the UK's innate and generally misconstrued opposition to federalism no longer much affects EU internal affairs, there is more scope for federalisation, which is far from being equivalent with integration through centre formation (Fossum, 2017). As has been indicated here, even a consolidation of the Eurozone would probably involve rolling back some elements of European integration, as well as the safeguarding of important powers and prerogatives of the Member States, depending on the version of federalism that was adopted. Some of this would require a re-examination of the role of mutual recognition and the four freedoms, including the EU's current status of "over constitutionalisation" (Grimm, 2015). In this context, it should be noted that the hardline stances that both the UK government and the EU officials involved take on freedom of movement in the ongoing Brexit negotiations may make such a process of adjusting the four freedoms within the EU quite difficult. This is just one illustration of how the Brexit dynamics will impinge on the EU reform process.

On political leadership, the story appears to be ambiguous. The elections in 2017 that led to the election of President Emmanuel Macron in France and a new grand coalition (albeit with far weaker parliamentary support) in Germany do not bode for more than a sputtering integration engine that may well shy away from large-scale reforms.

And even if reforms were initiated, there remains the question of who can give them sustained impetus. If there is a decision to initiate a treaty change, there will have to be a Convention, and the relationship between that and the European Council and individual Member State leaders will be important determinants, as will be the procedures for ratification. This brings up the issue of whether a two-tiered Union will be accepted by all the Member States involved. An important determinant would be whether such a decision would require unanimity.

A further issue is whether this strategy will actually be a means of dealing with Brexit. The general view of the UK government expressed thus far is that the institutions needed to sustain the inclusive single market are so comprehensive and so intrusive (especially the Court of Justice of the European Union [CJEU]) as to dissuade the UK from entering it. The Conservatives remain deeply divided, whereas Labour underlines the need for a "soft" Brexit. Insofar as there is an agreement with the UK, the risk for the EU under this trajectory is that these developments will focus on the single market and detract attention from undoing the EU's segmental aspects.

Finally, we need to consider the nature and range of possible obstacles or countervailing forces. Some analysts have underlined that Brexit is likely to reduce the UK's ability to serve as a countervailing force, even if it retains access to the internal market. This hinges on the ability to disconnect Brexit from other possible countervailing factors, such as Euroscepticism and populist EU rejection, and opposition from the Visegrád states. Unfavourable election or referenda outcomes in Member States and/or a confluence of crises could undermine this option. Various developments may trigger a surge of populism and a further entrenching of immigration as a major political dividing line, especially since it can merge with nationalism and welfare chauvinism. A continued commitment to (some version of) neoliberalism will serve as a significant obstacle to fiscal union. Whether serious international economic constraints will transpire on such a course of action hinges on how the financial markets consider the option (whether fiscal union will stabilise the Eurozone).

This trajectory is not likely to materialise as a natural outgrowth of present trends; active course change is required. The strategy pre-supposes active political leadership and that those in charge will be willing to own up to the risks involved. It remains questionable how much leadership will emanate through a European-internal process. There may, however, be an important impetus from outside Europe these days. Trump and Putin may spur such a process insofar as their words and actions impress on Europeans that the EU is facing a real threat to its very existence. If so, Riker's (1964) main thesis that federalisation occurs through threats and crises may yet be borne out.

What would be the implications for Europe of such a trajectory?

A proper consolidation would render the EU more sustainable and democratically legitimate, especially the core. A competence catalogue would have the benefit of clarifying the lines of accountability by reducing the space for manipulation which is a major feature of today's EU. Federalisation in today's situation can also be construed in substantive and symbolic terms as a matter of taking back control, because it would become clearer who does what and who answers to whom for what. In addition, federalisation could produce a clearer delineation of the tasks that the EU undertakes as well as the tasks that are assigned to the Member States.

This might deal with the present EU structural problem of the fusion of levels of governing; this contains a structurally embedded temptation for the deeply interwoven Member States to expand the EU's remit of action, because they see the potential and think they can control the expansion. Federalisation can rein in some of the integrationist impetus that we find in the Court of Justice of the European Union (CJEU) and the Commission, and perhaps even in the EP. At present, these institutions appear far more prone to promoting integration than serving any federal balancing function. A clearer delineation of tasks should render this much more natural and easy. The system would be structurally differentiated. The problems and tensions within the EU would probably be shifted from the present strong North-South (and East-West) divide to the new divide between Eurozone "ins" and "outs." The democratic problems would be particularly pronounced for the latter.

Trajectory II: Fragmentation

Fragmentation refers to a process wherein the EU system's ability to ensure binding collaboration, forge common policies, and fashion joint visions and projects is increasingly limited, and *fully fledged fragmentation* entails that the system is no longer capable of holding together and gets disbanded. In discussing this trajectory, it is therefore important to distinguish between a process of fragmentation and fragmentation as the result of the process.

With regard to the institutions at EU level, a process of fragmentation can manifest itself in the withering or in the sidelining of the EU-level supranational institutions, through shifts in decision *locus* to informal arrangements that undercut the EU-system of legally and procedurally based decision-making, or through acts of recalcitrant Member States either rejecting EU provisions in their territory or blocking EU-wide action.

Fragmentation is marked by the undermining of hierarchical control, standardisation and harmonisation; there is a shift from rule of law to informality, hard-nosed bargaining, and/or the removal of co-operation. Rule-bound hierarchical control is gradually replaced so that the system of governing is no longer able to produce coherent decisions. Some of these elements have occurred during the crises and given impetus to EU segmentation. Fragmentation represents a further significant development along those lines.

There is an affinity between fragmentation and disintegration. Fragmentation can be a step along the road to EU disintegration, perhaps especially in an EU context, because the EU is so dependent on the Member States for effectuating policies.[3] Analytically, we may distinguish between the disintegration of the EU-level and fragmentation, which is a more open-ended process. A process of fragmentation at EU level can extend deep into the Member States, and offers no assurance of a return to a Europe of nation-states. What is also important to underline is that EU disintegration is also highly unlikely to stop at the Member States' borders. As this book has shown, the EU is so imbricated in the nation-states that it is difficult to think that EU disintegration will not also engender various forms of Member-State fragmentation.

How to get there?

Fragmentation may be driven by EU-internal factors, EU-external developments, or a combination of both. The process may focus mainly on the EU level, but it can also entail the fragmentation of Member States. Or Member States may form regional sub-groups within the EU, which would operate according to their own precepts (Kriesi, 2016). We can identify three main dimensions, all of which would greatly exacerbate the negative features that we have associated with segmentation as discussed above: a) a weakening or undermining of the internal mechanisms that keep the Union together, such as leadership, competence, and resources; b) a declining governing or problem-solving ability; and c) legitimacy problems and/or challenges. With regard to a), it pertains to a weakened normative and practical commitment to common European action, leaders and states actively orientating themselves to other parts of the world, states denying the EU the resources that it needs to forge common actions, a competence drain or a disassociation of competence and decision-making through decision-makers focusing on the caprice of opinion polls, and other contingencies of the moment. With regard to b), the shift to the new informality and a bargaining approach may exacerbate – rather than ameliorate – conflict and contestation because there is a higher premium for politicising decisions, especially for national leaders bent on profiling themselves as Euro-sceptics, and less likelihood of finding technically and scientifically based agreement. With regard to c), there will be actors actively seeking to undermine the European ethos and to replace it with a national ethos.

Brexit could have a bearing on points a) through to c), in the sense that a drawn-out and contentious process could expose weakness of will and leadership on the part of EU leaders, exhibit EU-internal tensions and weaken EU co-ordination, and give grist to the mill of Euro-sceptic arguments.

The case of Nigel Farage (UKIP) shows that Euro-sceptic populism is not simply a reaction to EU problems; it is a matter of political operators or entrepreneurs who see opportunity in political estrangement, disenfranchisement, and fear of loss of privilege. Somewhat ironically, in a number of cases, the EU has furnished them with a platform or launching pad for pursuing their political programmes, which they were unable to obtain in their home country (with a different electoral system such as, for instance, in the UK). This, in turn, offers up the paradoxical situation that the resurgence of narrow ethnic nationalism across Europe has a transnational aspect to it.

Nationalist resurgence naturally gravitates towards issues of immigration and welfare chauvinism; both right- and left-wing populist agendas converge on the *onus* of restoring the nation to former glory. The fact that such projects are, in many instances, mere fictions matters less (the pluri-national UK is a case in point: When was it ever a coherent nation?); what matters to fragmentation is that they are able to mobilise parts of the populace and direct them towards their anti-European agendas. The deeper structural issue is the decline in representative party government. European integration – and globalisation in general – serves to constrain the realm of action of established parties through emphasising the notion of responsibility (the carrying out of decisions made at other levels),[4] whereas populists have been left much more free to focus on responsiveness to the populace. The populists' construction of "us against them" enables them to label national governing élites as alien figures that are no longer responsive to "their" people.

There is a toxic mixture of technocracy and populism in today's Europe. Technocrats seek to avoid populist pressure in order to define thorny issues as technical and thus to de-politicise decisions; populists, in contrast, seek to politicise them and actively identify technocrats as the "unfaithful servants" of democracy. Representative party government is the loser because it is squeezed from both sides.

What is at stake is the control of the national socialising apparatuses of the state and of the mechanisms that foster social solidarity: the welfare states. The catch is that states are still hardwired in favour of the national account; if the populists of left and right obtain direct access to these mechanisms, the EU has very little with which to counter it.

The refugee problem can also spur fragmentation. If numbers increase and we see further terrorist onslaughts, it will reinforce the focus on securitisation and demands for further national border controls, which again will aid the populist rhetoric.

A possible dismantling of the Monetary Union could lead to fragmentation.

What would be the implications for Europe of such a trajectory?

Fragmentation may not only undermine European-level co-operation but can also have spill-over effects on the Member States. The nationalists' pipe dream of restoring nation-states to the illusion of their former glory is precisely that – a simple pipe dream. There are two main reasons for this. One is that, as the saga of Brexit has already shown, in today's interdependent world, beyond simple slogans, there is no clear conception of what it would mean to restore national sovereignty. The other is that the process of EU unravelling will engender conflict and bad feelings, and thus increase tensions and unleash patterns of domination. Unravelling will yield neither stability nor legitimacy.

To sum up, this book has shown that the multilevel political order that is anchored in the EU has – post-crises – undergone a significant mutation that requires a new designation, namely, that of segmented political order. This volume has provided a set of criteria for what constitutes such a political order and how it differs from other known entities and principles.

There is, at present, an important discussion on Europe's future: What Europe should be and who should do what where? This is a vital, existential discussion. It requires a clear sense of where we are now, and it is our hope that this book has provided some insights into that.

Notes

1 See "EU Agrees to Create Budget for Eurozone", *Financial Times*, 18 December 2018, available at: https://www.ft.com/content/2efa2276-ffbd-11e8-aebf-99e208d3e521, accessed on 25 February 2019.
2 See"Vertrag zwischender Bundesrepublik Deutschland und der Französischen Republik über die deutsch-französische Zusammenarbeit und Integration", available at: https://www.bundesregierung.de/resource/blob/997532/1570126/c720a7f2e1a0 128050baaa6a16b760f7/2019-01-19-vertrag-von-aachen-data.pdf?download=1, last accessed on 25 February 2019.
3 Webber (2014:2) defines disintegration as "a decline in: (1) the range of common or joint policies adopted and implemented in the EU; (2) the number of EU member states; and/or (3) the formal (i.e., treaty-rooted) and actual capacity of EU organs to make and implement decisions if necessary against the will of individual members."
4 *With responsibility* means "to act prudently and consistently and to follow accepted procedural norms and practices … responsibility involves an acceptance that, in certain areas and in certain procedures, the leaders' hands will be tied." (Mair, 2009:12)

References

Fossum, John Erik (2015), "Democracy and Differentiation in Europe", *Journal of European Public Policy*, 22 (6): 799–815.

Fossum, John Erik (2017), "European Federalism: Pitfalls and Possibilities", *European Law Journal*, 23 (5): 361–379.

Grimm, Dieter (2015), "The Democratic Costs of Constitutionalisation: The European Case", *European Law Journal*, 21 (4): 460–473.

Jeffery, Charlie, and Peter Savigear (eds) (1991), *German Federalism Today*, New York: St. Martin's Press.

Kriesi, Hanspeter (2016), "The Politicization of European Integration", *Journal of Common Market Studies*, 54 (1): 32–47, special issue.

Mair, Peter (2009), "Representative versus Responsible Government", MPIfG 09/8.

Riker, William H. (1964), *Federalism: Origin, Operation, Significance*, Boston MA: Little, Brown.

Scharpf, Fritz W. (1988), "The Joint-decision Trap: Lessons from German Federalism and European Integration", *Public Administration*, 66 (3): 239–278.

Webber, Douglas (2014), "How Likely Is It That the European Union Will *Dis*integrate? A Critical Analysis of Competing Theoretical Perspectives", *European Journal of International Relations*, 20 (2): 341–365.

Wessels, Wolfgang (2016), *The European Council*, London: Palgrave.

INDEX

For Product Safety Concerns and Information please contact our EU
representative GPSR@taylorandfrancis.com
Taylor & Francis Verlag GmbH, Kaufingerstraße 24, 80331 München, Germany